The New Electric Vehicles

A Clean & Quiet Revolution

Michael Hackleman

A
Home Power
Publication

The New Electric Vehicles:
A Clean & Quiet Revolution

Michael Hackleman
Copyright © 1996 Michael A. Hackleman

Publisher's Cataloging in Publication
(Prepared by Quality Books Inc.)

Hackleman, Michael A.
    The new electric vehicles : a clean & quiet revolution / Michael Hackleman.
    p. cm.
    Includes bibliographical references and index.
    ISBN 0-9629588-7-5

    1. Electric vehicles. I. Title.

TL220.H33 1996   629.25'02
                    QBI96-20268

Printed in the USA by
St. Croix Press Inc.
New Richmond, Wisconsin

Cover paper is a 10 pt. 50% recycled (10% postconsumer and 40% preconsumer) Recovery Gloss from S. D. Warren Paper Company.
Interior paper is 50% recycled (30% postconsumer) Pentair PC30 Gloss Chlorine Free from Niagara of Wisconsin Paper Corp.
Printed using low VOC vegetable based inks.

A
Home Power
Publication

Other Books by Michael Hackleman

Wind and Windspinners: A Nuts & Bolts Approach to Wind-Electric Systems
The Homebuilt, Wind-Generated Electricity Handbook
Electric Vehicles: Design and Build Your Own
At Home with Alternative Energy
Better Use Of: Lights, Motors, Appliances, Tools—in the Home and Shop
Waterworks: An Owner-Builder Guide to Rural Water Systems

Any inquiries to the author should be accompanied by a SASE (self-addressed, stamped envelope).
Michael Hackleman, P.O.Box 327, Willits, CA 95490
Internet email: michael.hackleman@homepower.org

About this Book

Richard Perez

The masters for this book were made electronically at a location (Agate Flat, Oregon) six miles from utility power. All the energy powering the computers was made using photovoltaic (solar-electric) and wind power with an occasional backup by a gasoline-fueled generator.

Three Macintosh computer systems were used to make this book.

• **Station 1.** Mac IIcx with 20 MB of RAM and a total hard disk storage of 880 MB on three drives. This computer system (with a 19 inch NEC 5FG monitor) consumes 283 watts of power.

This system was used by Michael Hackleman to produce the text and page layouts in Quark Xpress version 3.2. It was operated a total of 1120 hours and consumed 318 kWh of energy.

• **Station 2.** Mac IIci with 80 MB of RAM, a total hard disk storage of 10.8 GB on four drives and two magneto optical drives (1.3 GB and 230 MB). This computer system (with its 21 inch NEC 6FG monitor) consumes 405 watts of power.

This system was used by Richard Perez to digitize all photos using Adobe Photoshop version 3.1. A UMAX PowerLook scanned prints and oversize transparencies and a Polaroid SprintScan handled all 35 mm slides.It was operated a total of 200 hours and consumed 81 kWh of energy.

• **Station 3.** Mac IIci with 20 MB of RAM and a total hard disk storage of 1.4 GB on two drives. This computer system (with a 17 inch Apple monitor) consumes 270 watts of power.

This system was used by Ben Root to draw the art in Adobe Freehand version 5.1. It was operated a total of 96 hours and consumed 26 kWh of energy.

These three computers operated a total time of 1416 hours (over a nine month period) and consumed 424 kWh of energy. This is enough energy to drive an electric vehicle from San Francisco, California to Denver, Colorado, or roughly 1230 miles. It is also enough power to run the average American home for about 20 days.

All this power was made on site and over 97% came from renewable energy sources. The photovoltaic arrays produce a peak power of 2,025 Watts. The wind generator produces 1000 Watts. Energy was stored in a nickel—cadmium battery with a capacity of 1500 Ampere-hours at 12 VDC. All the electric power consumed by the computer systems was inverted—converted from 12 VDC to 120 vac, 60 Hz—using a 1000 Watt Exeltech sine wave inverter and a 2500 Watt Trace sine wave inverter.

Funky Mountain Institute, Agate Flat, Oregon

——Table of Contents——

1 WHY THE ELECTRIC VEHICLE? 10

Kinds of Electric Vehicles. Zero-Emission or Emission-Elsewhere? Efficiency of Electricity vs Gasoline. Energy Sources for the EV. The Politics of Oil.

Test-Drive an Electric: 14. Will the EV Change Your Lifestyle? The Limitations of EVs: 15. How Far Do You Drive? Operating Costs. Replacing the Battery Pack. The State of Battery Technology. Performance. Range. Building the Unlimited-Range EV. Infrastructure. The 1998 2% ZEV Mandate. Will the Automakers Do It? The Supercars are Coming. Are EVs Crashworthy?

EV Companies:.22. Solectria. Solar Car Corporation. Electric Vehicles of America. AC Propulsion. Green Motor Works. Electro-Automotive. MendoMotive. Eyeball Engineering. KTA Services.

2 THE EV CONVERSION .24

The Conversion as a System. A Reality Check. **Attributes of a Good Conversion:** 26. Style. Weight. Aero-dynamics. Compatibility. Automatic Transmissions. Power Steering. Air Conditioning. Power Brakes. Vehicle Condition. Availability. Space. Cost. Buy or Convert? Getting Help. Vehicle-Specific Plans. Basic vs Complete Kits.

A Sample Conversion: 32. Stripping Out the ICE. Initial Decisions. Sizing the Battery Pack. Installing the Motor. Other Under-Hood Components. Meters and Gauges. Charging Circuit. Odds and Ends.

Other Conversions: 37. The Honda EVX. Racing the EVX. Back on the Street. The Geometric. An Electric Porsche. Is This a Conversion? The Go-4. An Electric Mule. An Electric OX. **Conversion as a Business:** 49. Making Gliders a Reality.

3 THE SCRATCHBUILT EV 52

Easy, Fast, and Inexpensive? Build a Model. Are You Qualified? Getting Help. EV Subassemblies. Street or Work EV? Think Legal. Aesthetics. **Design Elements:** 57. Weight. Aerodynamics. Rolling Resistance. Hillclimbing. Efficiency. Ergonometry. Crashworthiness. Horsepower. **FrameWorks:** 64. Frame. Brakes. Body/Shell. Propulsion Package. The Mockup. The Test Mule. The Road Test.

Other Scratchbuilts: 70. Plan Cars: 70. Doran. Vortex. Production Prototypes: 72. Citicar. Tropica. Sunray. City-El. Impact. Proof of Concept: 76. Calstart. European Tour de Sol. Flash and SunRise. Horlacher Electrics. Viking Series. Sylph. Formula E. Final Thoughts.

4 HUMAN & ELECTRIC VEHICLES 90

The Solar Cup. The Bicycle.

The Two-Wheeled HPV 92. The Electric-Assist Bicycle. A Basic EAB. The EAB Drivetrain. EAB Design Considerations. Quick-Release Components. Electric Weight. Registration. Controller Options. Cost.

The Three-Wheeled HPV: 103. A Minimalist HPV.

The Pure Electric Bike: 105. The NoPed Series.

Three-Wheeled Electric Bikes: 107. An Electric Leaner. Electrathon USA. Electrathon as Education.

The Electric Motorcycle: 120. Bikers. Skeptics. A Motorcycle Conversion. The PowerBike. Restoring an Auranthetic.

The Three-Wheeled Electric Motorcycle: 126. The Windcar. Tackling Tradition. Trike or Motorbike? An Electric Speedster. Speedster Two. Beyond the Speedster.

License and Register: 132. **Insurance:** 133. Minimum Safety Equipment.

5 SOLAR-POWERED VEHICLES 134

Solar Cars: How Does a Solar-Powered Car Work? Let's Race! Designing Your Own Panel. Getting Started in Solar Energy. SunCoaster.

Air and Water: 144.**Electric Watercraft:** 145. Solar and Electric Boat Races. Electric Launches. Restoring an ELCO Boat. A Solar-Electric Catamaran.**Electric Aircraft:** 152. The Sunseeker. The Return of the Airship.

A World of Solar Cars: 157

6 INFRASTRUCTURE, ENERGY, & FUELS 158

POWERING THE EV: Home Charging. Worksite Charging. Opportunity Charging. EV Service Stations. The Fast-Charge System. The Limits of Fast-Charge Systems.

BATTERY EXCHANGE TECHNOLOGY: 164. Battery-Exchange in a Car. Battery-Exchange Technology. The Implications of Battery-Exchange.

ENERGY SOURCES: 166. **Sustainable Energy Sources:** 166. **Solar Electricity**. Solar PV Stations. **Wind-Power Systems:**

A Guide to Sidebars

Editorials, and design and technical information on EVs in this book is primarily contained within sidebars. There are three types of sidebar: Editorial, Application, and Techtalk.

E*ditorial*

Editorial sidebars contain comment by individuals on topics related to transportation generally or electric vehicles specifically.
Guest editorials include Richard King, Paul MacCready, Joe Stephenson, Bruce Severance, and James Worden.

For Access to guest writers, see People, Sources & References (pgs. 265-266)

A*pplication*

Application sidebars contain design and construction detail on specific vehicles, concepts or companies that offer electric vehicles, or supply components, kits, or other information on EV technology.
Guest writers for Applications include Gail Lucas, Dr. Michael Seal, Ben Swets, Marti Daily, Jan Olof Hellsund, Daniel Pliskin, Alan Kearney, Dann Parks, Brett Hackleman, Michael Leeds, Tom Bennett, Andrew Muntz, Michael Bittman, Richard Orawiec, Pete Stephenson, Eric Raymond, Kevin Cousineau, and Luis Vega, Richard and Phil Jergenson.

T*echtalk*

Techtalk sidebars contain design and construction details of a technical nature. These will assist the engineer or hobbyist without affecting the overall readability of the material as it might if it were located in the running text.
Guest writers for TechTalk include Olof Sundin, Dr. Michael Seal, Rick Doran, Paul MacCready, Chester Kyle, Jan Olof Hellsund, Daniel Pliskin, Tom Bennett, Joe Fleming, William Swanson, and Kevin Cousineau.

Each sidebar type—Editorial, Application, and Techtalk—is numbered sequentially through the book (Example: Application A1-A67). With the exception of Chapter 1, sidebars are called out from the running text or from another sidebar.

Photos and graphics (including tables and charts) are numbered within a chapter and have a prefix of the chapter number. (Example: Fig. 6-11 is the 11th piece of artwork in Chapter 6.)

List of Sidebars

E=Editorial   T=TechTalk   A=Applications
(If sidebar is without credit, work is by the author)

Contributors

The imagery in this book helps convey the reality of electric vehicles. Many people contributed to the making of this book. Or, as Jim Schley (Chelsea Green Publishing) expressed on seeing the initial manuscript,

"This book is a chorus of voices." The artists pictured here—through photographs, drawings, or proofreading—have made an extraordinary contribution to the book, and I thank them for their efforts.

C. Michael Lewis is a familiar face at events nationwide that demonstrate sustainable energy systems and zero-emission transportation. Easily 20% of the color photos in this book are from his extensive library of photo images of both human power and electric propulsion topics.

Donna Worden assists as detail maven, team player and spirtual touchstone. She has worked with TreePeople, Planet Eureka Productions, EarthSave LA, Hackleman-Schless race team, Speed of Light Solar Education, International Electric Grand Prix Association, Renewable Energy Development Institute, Dance Planet, Freedom Singers and Flight.

Mary Van De Ven is a Hawaii-based photographer and video producer. Science and nature are favorite subjects, especially underwater life. Mary and her husband, digitial artist Rob Campbell, have an alternative-powered house on the big island of Hawaii.

Ben Root rendered most of the technical drawings in this book. He is a recent addition to the *Home Power* magazine staff. Ben studied graphic design at Western Washington University in Bellingham, Washington, and renewable energy at Solar Energy International in Carbondale, Colorado

Many of the photos in Chapters 7 and 8 are courtesy of Shari Prange and Michael Brown of ElectroAutomotive.

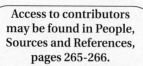

Stevi Johnson has been a photographer most of her life, with numerous years of professional training in photography and film. Her work is published in books and magazines internationally. She teaches B&W photography and lives in Hawaii. She handles advertising and public relations for Suntera.

Additional Thanks:

Farrington Daniels, C.G. Abbott, Vanessa Johnson, Sharman Rabe, Richard Jergenson, Phil Jergenson, Paul Shipps, Ed Rannberg, Ely Schless, Fred Daniels, Gunnar Lindstrom, Gerald Benson, Richard and Karen Perez, Brett Hackleman, Glenn Hackleman, Steve McCrea, Julia May, Kelly McGehee, Bruce Clayton, Bob and Doi DeWitt, Bruce Severance, Jon Frey, Clare Bell, Marilyn McCabe, Lorna Moffat, Mary Kay Finn, Melanie Livingston, Anne Chipley, Mira Crowe, Tim Considine, Otmar Ebenhoech, Ruth MacDougall, Wendy Raebeck, Bob Schneeveis, Jonathan Tennyson, Michael Brown, Shari Prange, Yugi, Ellen Holmes, Brad Westervelt, Bob-O Schultze, and Kathleen Jarschke-Schultze.

Access to contributors may be found in People, Sources and References, pages 265-266.

Introduction

The electric vehicle is revolutionary. Who would have thought it possible that we could develop a car that had *every* advantage of one using an internal combustion engine (running on gasoline) *without* all the disadvantages—pollution, noise, war, resource depletion, and general environmental degradation.

The electric vehicle (EV) is not just another way to make a car go. It does the same mile as a car with an engine, with only **one-third** the resource depletion and **one-twentieth** the air pollution (all in the power plant itself).

By itself, that's impressive. But—what if the power plant is a windmachine? Or a solar collector? Then, the EV is not only zero-*emission* at the point of use, it is indeed zero-*pollution!*

The electric vehicle is efficient. This explains its silent operation. Since there are no fuels or oils used, it is also extremely clean.

Sound like a fantasy? It's not. In this book is the proof.

Electric vehicles are not new. The technology actually preceded gas cars—it's more than a century old. Out of the eye of the general public, it has flourished. It has come back. It has grown up.

Electric vehicles offer us a better way to power vehicles of *all* types. Transportation is responsible for 50% of the pollution on the planet. The electric vheicle could make a *big* dent in this statistic.

My own awakening to the benefits of electric vehicles began in the mid-1970s. I was building a research center and wanted it *and* my home to be self-reliant. I began the search for an alternative to my gasoline-powered car and truck. At first, I investigated alternative fuels. Methane (biogas). CNG (compressed natural gas). Alcohol. Hydrogen.It was then that I discovered an ugly truth about internal combustion engine (ICE) technology. The engine itself was a bottleneck, wasting an average of 70% of the energy of *any* fuel it consumed as it did its work. And always will. It's basic physics.

My research also revealed that at the turn of the century, steam cars and electric cars had

dominated the roads. My list dwindled to one item—the electric-powered vehicle.

Could this work? I daydreamed about plugging a vehicle into one of my wind-electric machines. A few months later, this dream came true. I was driving a vehicle on wind-watts! I had found an alternative to the gas car and gasoline.

Over the years, I've discovered that thousands of EVs are in use on roadways across the nation. Most were built by individuals and small groups, largely unfunded. This book is really their story.

The ramifications of global warming suggest that, as a species, we must stop pumping carbon into the atmosphere. This is not about saving the planet. (What arrogance!) It's about saving ourselves. And sharing the planet with other lifeforms. And showing responsibility to our children.

Let's do it while we still have choices!

Michael Hackleman, Earth, Spring 1996

Chapter 1
Why the Electric Vehicle?

"Fifty percent of the problems in transportation today
may be traced to the use of the internal combustion engine ..."

An electric vehicle is one that uses an electric motor instead of an engine, and a battery pack instead of a fuel tank and gasoline. The electric motor is the size of a five-gallon water bottle, and it bolts right to a standard transmission. Each battery in the pack is similar in size and shape to the one that starts your car's engine, but there are many more of them. The vehicle's accelerator pedal is connected through linkage to an electronic controller. Pressing the accelerator smoothly delivers power to the electric motor in proportion to the amount of pedal you give it.

Fig. 1-1: Thousands of EVs are on the road today.

Photo:David Chung (M. Hackleman Collection)

Kinds of Electric Vehicles

The electric car is only one example of an electric vehicle (EV). An electric-assist bicycle is also an EV. An electric motorcycle is an EV. A trolley and a San Francisco BART train are EVs. A solar-powered car or a Formula electric racer is an EV. These vehicles have two things in common: electric propulsion and wheels!

The world is more than ready for electric vehicle (see Techtalk T1). Electric motors are in use everywhere.Wherever silent, efficient, reliable service is needed, you will find an electric motor at work. Electric motors power elevators, industrial assembly lines, ventilation and air conditioning units, refrigerators, blow dryers, washers and dryers, computers and printers, CD players and tape decks, and pumps. Ironically, an electric motor is also needed to start an automobile's engine.

Electric propulsion is a commonplace technology. The modern locomotive is diesel-electric. That is, a diesel engine is coupled directly to a generator which supplies the electricity to power the electric motor connected to the steel wheels.

Zero-Emission or Emission-Elsewhere?

It is a major step for an automobile to no longer emit exhaust gases. In fact, it is nearly inconceivable. Yet, this is a reason consumers will love zero-emission vehicles. No more smog. Not everyone can drive a solar-powered car, but driving an EV will help the sun to once more shine through clear skies.

In the literal sense, of course, the EV is the "emission-elsewhere" car. That is, the electricity to power the car has to be generated *somewhere*. Some of this energy is currently available from sustainable, clean energy sources like wind, solar, and water power. However, the bulk of electricity in the USA comes from coal- and oil-fueled power plants.

Doesn't the EV just transplant the pollution problem somewhere else?

No. This matter has been scrutinized extensively by the U.S. Department of Energy and several California agencies charged with air quality management. Their studies clearly indicate a dramatic reduction in emissions and resource depletion, mile for mile, for the EV over the gas car. This is at the

Wherever silent, efficient, reliable service is needed, you will find an electric motor at work.

heart of the hotly-debated 2% ZEV (zero-emission vehicle) mandate that California is imposing on the automotive industry in 1998.

Efficiency, Gas Cars, and EVs

EVs are very efficient. They have to be. A pound of lead-acid battery has 1/100 of the energy of a pound of gasoline.

The range of efficiency of the propulsion system in a gas car that gets 30 mpg is 15-30% of the energy of its fuel. The average range of efficiency of an EV's propulsion system is 40-60% of the energy stored in its battery pack.

Fig. 1-2: The solar (PV) roof provides charging electricity and shade for these electric vehicles.

Energy Sources for the EV

It has been estimated that 30 million EVs could be added (at night) to the grid nationwide without the construction of a single new power plant. This represents a lot of surplus energy that is currently available during off-peak periods.

In addition, energy from sustainable resources, such as wind and solar energy, is gaining ground. For example, California alone has 1.5 gigaWatts (one gigaWatt equals 1000 megaWatts) of generating capacity from wind machines scattered throughout the state. These produce enough electricity to power a city the size of San Francisco all year long.

Solar power plants have proved their worth, too. Southern California Edison's (LUZ-built) solar-thermal plants supply electricity to 500,000 people. These are 24-hour power plants, using CNG (compressed natural gas) to complement solar energy during stormy weather and at night.

Today, PV (photovoltaic, or solar-electric) technology is cost competitive with even modern coal power plants for applications further than one-eighth mile from the utility grid.

The Politics of Oil

Electric propulsion offers significant advantages over gas car technology through a

E_1 ditorial
Transportation & Environment
Richard King

In the United States, transportation sources are responsible for 69% of lead, 70% of carbon monoxide, 45% of nitrous oxides, and 35% of the reactive hydrocarbons released into the air. Furthermore, cars and light trucks are the largest single contributing sector of carbon dioxide buildup (33% of all emissions) by burning approximately eight million barrels of oil daily.

The statistics describing automobile use are staggering. The three hundred million cars in the world consume billions of barrels of oil, cost billions of dollars, and travel trillions of miles each year. More alarming is the fact that vehicle miles driven in the United States is constantly on the rise. This is a trend seen throughout the world as well.

Whatever form of transportation is used in the future, we hope it will consume less energy and produce less pollution. Electric vehicles are pollution-free during operation and, if used for urban commuting, will significantly reduce city smog.

T_1 echtalk
What's So Good About Electric Vehicles (EVs)?

Electric propulsion easily wins out over Internal Combustion Engine (ICE) technology for automobiles on a level playing field.

What advantages do EVs offer?
- EVs produce ZERO emissions at the point of use.
- Electric propulsion is 200 to 400% the efficiency of an engine.
- An EV, per mile, uses 30-50% the fossil-fuel resources (BTUs) an engine consumes.
- EVs can use electricity from anywhere. Most importantly, they can use energy generated from sustainable and clean energy resources—like wind, sun, and water.
- EVs are simple and silent. They are more affordable to own and operate than a vehicle that uses an ICE (internal combustion engine) machine.
- An EV produces only 5% to 10% of the emissions of an engine, per mile traveled. All of the EV's emissions occur at the power plant. Even if the power plant burns coal or oil in its turbine-generators, their average efficiency is easily 400% to 500% that of a car engine and the power plants scrub their own exhaust.

broad spectrum of criteria. Can such a simple technology address so many problems and be environmentally friendly, too? Why, you may ask, aren't EVs in widespread use?

The answer is: politics and the balance of power. Oil-based technology is entrenched worldwide. The oil business developed rapidly as a result of two world wars. Oil is, however, a finite resource. The planet's supply will run out. Yet it is being gobbled up as if there was no tomorrow. In the minds of the people who work in oil, there is only today.

The reality is: there's money to be made in oil. Gasoline is made from oil. It is priced low enough to ensure that sustainable alternatives cannot compete with it. Think about it. In many places, a gallon of bottled water costs more than a gallon of gasoline. In turn, cheap gasoline helps to sell cars. Cars are big business. Car sales. Car parts. Service and repair.

*E*ditorial
Evolution of the Species
Paul MacCready, Ph.D.

We are reaching the end of the era of unfettered growth, and plunging headlong into the era of limits. There are more people all the time. The population has tripled since I was born. That creates more demands and expectations — and less earth. One challenge is to change the transportation habits of the world. There are technological advances that can let transportation put much reduced demands on the resources and environment of the earth. We should make full use of these advances.

Space is not a safety valve. The great value in space exploration is the perspective it gives us. It gets us to think deeper thoughts. It challenges us to solve complex problems. Besides, our earth-related problems are rapidly getting so great that we may not be able to afford massive space ventures.

Technology helps with the challenge, but changing attitudes also helps. Open-minded thinking — what I call thinking skills — underlies both technological innovation and attitude changes. Thinking skills encompass creativity, but also include seeing many sides to an issue, having healthy skepticism, asking key questions, considering consequences, and understanding how our minds work. These skills are not taught in school.

One form of creativity is day dreaming, mining the subconscious. The origin of the Gossamer Condor came from just such a bit of daydreaming. Following our success in human-powered flight with it, we built the Gossamer Albatross. There are one hundred reasons why it shouldn't have succeeded the first time in crossing the English Channel, a distance of 22 miles, but it did. Subsequently, we built a solar-powered airplane. The Solar Challenger flew 165 miles, from Paris to England on solar-power only (no batteries or human-assist and reached an altitude of 11,000 feet.

Getting into the lecture circuit afterwards prompted me to marshall my thoughts on the process itself of accomplishing seemingly impossible tasks. The way I see it, there are three ingredients to success: knowing the goal, a clean sheet of paper, and unrestricted use of technology.

The greatest investment in creativity would be in 10-year-olds. Really! They have the vitality without the peer pressure and hormones. Kids in the right circumstances are very inventive. They just need tools, materials, and space — away from television.

We can help them retain their open-mindedness. Encourage them to ask questions and not to believe blindly in authority. What are we going to do about the greenhouse effect? Pollution? Topsoil erosion? Shrinking rain forests? Nuclear proliferation? Ozone depletion? Whole species disappearing? I don't have answers to these questions. It's time to liberate the minds that will.

I am pessimistic that humankind will reach a comfortable accommodation with the planet's flora, fauna, and resources. An accommodation will be achieved — but will it be a comfortable one?

Unfortunately, civilization is winning the war against nature. Humans, representing just one, recently-arrived species, are wiping out the others, paying reverence only to those with an obvious, direct, and practical importance to humankind. We should respect the other species sharing our cosmic journey, whether "useful" or not. Our descendants may find in the future the "expendable" species were more important than we realized!

More change happens in one year now than previously happened in a century. We have only the next couple of decades to turn the situation around. After that, it's probably going to get bad, with various unpleasant, irreversible effects in action.

We must get industry to produce efficient, low-pollution transportation. Gasoline costs the country many dollars a gallon, but we only pay a little more than one dollar at the pumps. The difference is the cost of some military preparedness, pollution cleanup, balance of payment troubles, and the future cost of replacing the energy consumed. A large gasoline tax would encourage the use of alternatives. Industry is capable of doing this.

We're in an exciting time. A culture shift. Keep it up. Contribute where you can. Above all, keep your eye on the big picture — and a desirable, sustainable future.

Fig. 1-3: Dr. Paul MacCready

Collision damage. Insurance. Highway construction. Parking lots. Parking meters. Traffic tickets. Health services. The lack of mass transit forces everyone to own a car. Or two. And the "more cars" policy, in turn, sells more gasoline.

What are some of the side effects of our oil-based energy policy? Pollution. Wars (to control the supply). Health problems. Humans killed and maimed in accidents. In the USA alone, 45,000 deaths per year, with another 1 million maimed, crippled or injured. None of these are included in the gas pump price.

A Greenpeace poster with a picture of the Exxon Valdez's captain summed up the current situation in one brief statement: "It wasn't his driving that caused the Alaskan oil spill. It was yours." The demand drives the economics of supply.

Oil and cars, together and individually, have proven hazardous to the planet. It's time to usher in the alternatives.

Fortunately, EVs aren't something we *have* to drive. They are something we will *want* to adopt! And not just for the planet, its species, or even our own species. People often begin driving an EV to make a statement. However, they continue to drive one regularly because they like it.

Test-Drive an Electric!

See for yourself what the rave is all about! Test-drive an EV. There are hundreds of EV clubs nationwide. The members of these clubs are common folk, who are usually happy to demonstrate their pride and joy.

Imagine that I've just offered to let you drive my EV. Your brain may be pumping questions through your mouth, but driving an EV for the first time will hit you on a gut level. It feels right. Turn the key. No whirrrr of the starter motor, no plume of exhaust, no roar of the engine, no vibration. Just a reassuring little thunk. That's the main contactor powering up the control system.

Then, silence. This car is waiting for you to do something, just like a computer. Take your time. No power is being consumed.

At this point, I'll be reassuring you that driving an EV is identical to driving an ICE car — with earplugs.

Of course there are other differences. For instance, you do *not* have to "warm up the

People who are afraid of getting caught out in the boonies with a dead battery pack don't drive EVs. The frequent EV user knows how quickly this "fear" dissipates.

motor" in an EV. Unlike IC engines, electric motors work great when they are cold. So, are you ready to go?

After all these years, it still delights me that this silent vehicle actually moves when I press down on the accelerator. Spectators are always awestruck by this feature. You'll feel it, too.

Quickly, we're up to speed.

If the EV has gauges, the next surprise awaits the moment you lift your foot off the pedal. Suddenly, no power is flowing, but you're still zipping along. "Gliding" is a better word for it, though. Every time you lift your foot off of the accelerator, it is as though the vehicle's transmission has slipped into neutral. On a level surface, you'll be surprised at how gradual the slowing is and at how far you can "coast,",too. Perfecting this art by anticipating traffic flow will even increase the overall range of the EV dramatically.

More delights lie ahead. Bring the vehicle to a stop, at a signal light, stop sign, or parking place. Silence. No vibration whatsoever!

At first, you'll worry that you've stalled the motor. But you haven't. It's just not *running*.

What does this mean? No more fuel wasted when a vehicle is stopped. No "idling emissions." No power consumed. Silence is the proof of efficiency.

Do you prefer an automatic transmission? Cars with automatic transmissions don't make good conversions (lousy efficiency). However, the beauty of the standard EV is that it lets you *drive* a vehicle with a manual transmission as though it *is* an automatic. Just stick the lever in second gear and forget the clutch. That's right. Push the accelerator and away you go. This will likely work all the way up to 45 mph in just the one gear, perfect for driving around town. Again, leaving the clutch alone, bring the EV to a stop. It will do it silky-smooth. It feels strange, but it's true.

An electric motor won't stall like an engine!

There's more fun yet. See that service station? Pass it by! And keep on doing it (if only to bug the owner). A few years back, my sponsor arranged a rented car for me in another city. I promptly ran it out of gas. I had completely gotten out of the habit of stopping at service stations! When I added the can of gasoline and, later, when I refilled the tank at the station, I realized that I had forgotten that refueling a "gas-hole" has a smell to it, too. (That's a term that came from 9-year old Sonya Rahders. On opening the gaslid and seeing an electric plug, she asked, "Where's the gas hole?") I was surprisingly happy to get back to my EV and just plug it in. Felt a lot more simple.

A frequent question is: "How long does the car take to recharge?" If I completely discharge the pack, it will take six hours to put 85% of the energy back in.

In reality, I always plug the EV into the socket when I get home. It's an automatic gesture. That way, when I'm ready to drive next, I'm usually starting out with a fully charged pack.

People who are afraid of getting caught out in the boonies with a dead battery pack don't drive EVs. The frequent EV user knows how quickly this "fear" dissipates. There are three reasons why.

First, the EV has a distinctive range. It varies, of course, with speed. But it's there. Measurable, repeatable.

Second, the slower the speed, the greater the range of an EV. If I need to "full range" my car in order to take care of business, I go into "conserve" mode. This means I'm careful on acceleration, I anticipate traffic more, and I take advantage of coasting.

And, third, if I've been my usual absent-minded self and the gauges say I'm low on juice, I go into my "ultra-conserve" mode. If I do run out of juice, though, I simply pull over and read a book for five minutes. The batteries will then "recover" and allow me a few extra miles. The bottom line: I've never been stuck out in an EV.

Currently, there is no infrastructure in place where I can charge up or exchange battery packs. What works instead are friends and businesses I frequent. They do not begrudge me the pennies per hour of electricity I might need if I'm a little low and need to plug in. An hour of charging gives me ten more miles for only 15 cents.

Will the EV Change Your Lifestyle?

Yes! Driving an electric car has taught me some humility. I don't mindlessly power myself around anymore. I always think about what I need to do, and how I will do it. Consequently, my trips are more productive. Somehow, everything gets done.

For two of the years I drove an EV, I had a backup vehicle. Each time I wanted to go

---

*E*ditorial
E₃ Will EVs Bring Back Nuclear Power?

I join others in their concern about EVs being an excuse to bring back nuclear power. I believe this to be unlikely for two reasons—both financial.

First, the electric utilities bore the brunt of the financial disaster of nuclear power plants. Witness safety and waste disposal issues, and the hundreds of accidents, including ones like Three Mile Island incident that were harder to suppress. Certainly, the utilities are unlikely to repeat the mistake.

Second, solar-electric and solar-thermal power plants have proven to be more cost-competitive than nuclear power even as start-up facilities.

There are simply too many hidden costs with nuclear power.

---

somewhere, I could choose between my electric Honda and my VW van. Alas, the van sat forlornly at the curbside the whole time! I always found a way to make the EV work!

Each day, then, the EV survived a reality check!

The Limitations of EVs

People who don't drive EVs like to talk about all of their limitations. It's time for my confession.

What do I miss by driving my EV?

I miss making appointments to have my gas-powered car serviced or repaired. I miss the oil and grunge in the "engine" compartment. Or on my clothes and hands after I work around one. I miss the oil spots on the driveway. I miss periodically replacing oil filters, air filters, fuel filters, fan belts, plugs, points, and plug wires. Or checking, adding, or changing the oil. Or adding coolant. Or adjusting the plugs, points, timing, and carburetor. I miss the tangle of pollution-abatement equipment. I miss smog checks. I miss waiting in gas lines. I miss pumping gas.

How Far Do You Drive?

The daily trip length for over 80% of the population in the urban sprawl of Los Angeles is less than 20 miles. At freeway speeds, the average converted EV will go three *times* that distance. The better conversions have a strong 80-90 mile range.

Want more range? Would 60-140 miles work for you in a day's time? The onboard battery charger permits worksite recharging

E *ditorial*
4

Silence & Technology

Joe Stephenson

As we move towards an orderly and sane world, we also move towards silence. It is not coincidental that the technologies of the future also reflect this movement to order and silence.

Our minds are captivated by the seeming effortlessness of photo-voltaic cells, electric cars, and many other promising creations. This obvious elegance in technology is, in part, expressed in its silence.

The history of human technology is deeply grounded in the laws of brute-force. "Clanging and banging" are the assumed expressions of the completing of "real work". The winding out of a five-speed transmission can almost bring a "teenage mind" to orgasm. We have come to identify with brute-force much like a hostage grows to love its abductor. We now feel at home in constant noise.

We read with the TV or CD on. Shop by Musak. Live in neighborhoods where every 10 minutes the sound of a lawn mower or leaf blower, chain saw or car alarm invades the silence. There is clearly a price for this noise and we all know it but can't comfortably admit it.

The nervous system of the human body needs silence. People live tense lives in tense environments and find themselves needing drugs for relaxation. We seek a peace or personal ease even while immersed in our noisy lives.

Safe silence is what we seek: silence which does not remind us of emptiness and death. We seek an institutional silence, the silence of the church, the bathroom, or the drug. Unfortunately, we must always resume our lives in the "grating and grinding" world.

The new silent technologies offer us not just a "safe silence," but also a total environmental silence. They allow us a choice in our union with noise. The photovoltaic panel not only lowers the background noise in our home but can also power the VCR and CD player. The electric car can transport us silently to the rock concert. We can witness that, overall, our world will become more quiet and less scary. It is a process of breaking an addiction to agitation and repetition.

We often create the technologies or make selections of tools based on our openness to ourselves and inner silence. With noisy minds, we have built jackhammers and internal combustion engines. We are gradually reflecting an increased collective sensitivity as we awaken from our dinosaur-like practices.

Perhaps as we grow less afraid of silence and ourselves, we can open to the possibilities now manifesting using sound and light waves, magnetics, etc. There are already many examples being used now. Lumber mills cut lumber with light beams. Refrigerators function silently. Stoves heat through induction.

We are on the verge of an intelligent technological age. As "Bucky" Fuller said it, "do more with less." Yes, it is a more complex world, but so is life, and complexity is only a perspective, not a static fact. This time around we all need to understand our world and ourselves. Technology must flow through us like song or speech — we *are* technology.

Whatever it is that is happening to us shows the promise for a clean and quiet future. A world conscious of its noise and respectful of its quiet space will be a reverent one. It is a world we unconsciously now grope toward anxiously. Let's just allow it to become fully conscious.

---

from a standard wall socket. Overnight charging, then, gets you to work. Recharging during the 8-hour workday will get you back home or wherever else you need to go.

Longtime EV users have discovered the economy of *renting* a car for the occasional long-distance driving they need to do. The avoided costs of registration, insurance, parking, and maintenance of a privately-owned vehicle easily offsets the occasional expenditure.

A new "superhighway" is coming, too. Telecommuting. You work at home, or at a nearby workstation (center) that connects you with your place of employment—minimizing the effort of transporting yourself around needlessly. An electric vehicle will complement this lifestyle nicely.

Operating Costs

The annual operating costs of an EV are quite low. Even high rates for electricity still produce a fuel bill that is 30-50% that of gasoline for the same mileage. Other than maintenance requirements for the battery pack at the current state of the technology— watering it (like flowers!) four to six times per year— there is no other component connected with propulsion that is likely to need adjustment, repair, or replacement. If your EV does not have regenerative braking (an electrical circuit that reclaims momentum as electricity, recharging the batteries instead of throwing it away in the brakes as heat), brake jobs will still be needed. An electric vehicle *with* regenerative braking will generally require less brake work than its gas car counterpart. The reclaimed energy will add to the vehicle's range, too.

Replacing the Battery Pack

Today's battery pack will need replacement every two to three years, depending on your driving habits. Heavy acceleration, extensive daily use, high speeds, and full-ranging the EV—these practices take a heavier toll on a battery pack's service life than conservative driving.

Battery pack replacement costs $1,200 to $1,800, depending on the size of the pack. Despite this large expenditure, careful record-keeping by many EV owners clearly shows that the operating cost of an EV is less than for a gas-powered car. Why? IC-engine cars accumulate repair and maintenance bills with more frequent visits to the shop over the same number of years.

The State of Battery Technology

The deep-cycle lead-acid battery is considered by automakers to be primitive and low-performing. Most are betting on exotic types now under development or undergoing testing.

This casual rejection ignores that a whole industry exists right now to recycle lead-acid batteries at a fraction of the cost and toxicity of other battery technologies. What's more, lead-acid battery technology has yet to reach its full potential. Improvements will come quickly when there is incentive to do so! The EV provides that incentive.

The Advanced Battery Consortium, formed by US automakers for purposes of obtaining funding from the government, has generally ignored lead-acid battery technology. Consequently, a Lead-Acid Battery Consortium has been formed to continue this research.

In this midst of this rivalry, it is important to remember, in the greater view, that a "better battery" is *not* the priority. Clean air *is*.

Performance

Electrics have something that engines don't until they're screaming: peak torque at takeoff. With utmost elegance, most EVs can beat almost any ICE car off the line at the traffic light. Whether you indulge yourself or not, it's nice to know that you can do it.

The average person is always surprised to find out that my EVX (a 1992 Honda Civic VX converted to electric power) has reached speeds just under 100 mph! After all these years

> *... a whole industry exists right now to recycle lead-acid batteries at a fraction of the cost and toxicity of other battery technologies.*

E*ditorial*
₅ Children & Challenges
Bruce Severance

When addressing a classroom, I routinely ask kids to tell me what some of the BIG problems are. They know. They hear it on the news everyday. I am no longer surprised when ten year olds matter-of-factly explain the greenhouse effect.

However, when asked how they feel about it, the faces change. The despair emerges. There is a general feeling that the problems are too big for any action to be effective.

When solar thermal electricity is already two cents a kiloWatt cheaper than nuclear power, the most basic issues to our global environmental problems are motivational and psychological.

Cultural norms and infrastructures resist change, leaving the younger generations with problems of overwhelming proportions and gravity. The resulting helplessness is debilitating, discouraging both a change in consumer behavior and inhibiting creative solutions. Despite their global proportions, environmental problems are the consequence of collective human behavior which can be changed. It is most important to educate and empower our youth to contribute and create clean solutions. If we counter the helplessness and isolation children feel, we will be able to cultivate a team spirit and the courage to pioneer solutions, regardless of how many have already climbed on the bandwagon.

What we do as individuals can make all the difference in the world. The race to save our earth begins with you and me. Unfortunately, so many individuals despair over the magnitude of our global problems and deny their own ability to have a "significant" impact. After speaking to many children, I have found almost universally, a reluctance to admit to a deep despair regarding our current environmental crisis.

My classroom experiences convinced me of the need to produce *The Race to Save Our Earth* — just for kids. I want to shake them out of their helplessness and into action by reinforcing the fact that *we* can do anything if we work as a team. At the annual solar and electric races in Phoenix, Arizona, there is great fervor among the teams as they work on their vehicles in the pits — a feeling that win or lose, what they are doing is important. Even as they compete against each other to win a race, they are working toward the same ultimate goal of helping the planet.

I am more than pleased by how kids and adults alike respond to the video. When the lights come on, questions and ideas fly around the room like sparrows, and many comment on how much more hopeful they feel. They are visibly excited about working to build the solutions. They dream about possibilities. How can anything be so unreachable if one solar thermal plant 80 miles wide and 80 miles long can produce enough power for the entire United States.

Children need an invitation to participate in assessing these issues. They are often disqualified simply because — they are children. This discrimination blocks their vision and discourages them from joining specific environmental efforts.

There are battles we must fight without any assurances of victory. We owe it to our children and to all generations, past and future.

of hearing that question ("How fast does it go"?), my best guess of the source of the misperception that EVs are slow is the golf cart! It's about the *only* kind of electric vehicle that most people have ever seen in their lifetime!

If an EV is observed accelerating slowly or going slower than the traffic around it, it doesn't mean it can't go fast. Joggers don't sprint through their morning routine. Like the EV driver, they are simply conserving energy for the long haul.

Range

EV owners know that range is not the major issue that automakers insist it is. EV owners *know* about range. Most EV owners drove gas cars before they discovered EVs. Before, they just *thought* they knew how far they had driven. Or how far away certain places were.

Like everyone else, they used to describe distances in terms of time. "L.A. airport is half an hour away," they might tell an inquiring driver. Rarely did they know the number of miles. Driving an EV changes that habit. Suddenly, you know exactly how many miles away everything is. Or can make a good guess.

"What if you need to go to cross country?" is a predictable response when I tell a group of people the range of my EV. "I fly!" I answer. Locally, I walk, ride a bicycle, or drive my EV up to 35 miles away (leaving a strong 35-mile reserve to come home). For distances beyond these values, I ride the bus or train, or fly.

Near-future battery technologies, even the most exotic, are not likely to improve range significantly (or economically) over lead-acid types. But—I can drive my EV probably twice as far as a novice who might drive it. I don't drive slow. I drive *smart*. An EV with a lead-acid battery pack driven with experience will outperform a more exotic battery technology (costing 3-5 times as much) driven like a car with an engine. At the Phoenix races *two* years running, my EVX beat the favored cars (using high-dollar motors *and* batteries) with my driver (Tim Considine) using these skills.

Fast-charge stations are also a questionable solution to the EV range issue. The benefits of such a fast-service utility would likely be outweighed by the decrease in service life of the battery itself. This practice would also add to electrical peak loads of the local utility, a

---

Editorial

E6 Ushering In the EV

James Worden

Without an infrastructure, I believe that EVs must have a 100-mile range before the public will take them seriously. With high-rate charging, it starts locally, using limited-range EVs. Gasoline cars started that way, with more and more pump stations. Daytime charging of EVs at worksites and parking meters is needed. It's not good if it adds to the peak electricity load, though.

I think right away most people in auto-making companies have their minds made up that electric cars are not practical. The general public is also skeptical at first, but they listen and ask questions. I always speak frankly about time, costs, and limitations. Very quickly, they discover that they like the idea. I feel like my experience helps me make pretty quick guesses about how much something will cost, and how well it will work for them.

I think the public is ready to embrace this technology. Their pocketbooks are a big priority,

though. The low price of gas, as artificial as it is, makes it hard for them to make a change. When we start paying at the pump what it's really costing us to use gasoline, we'll be on the right track. It will be hard at first, but we will flourish.

Right now, everything is secondary to economics. We can build cheap electric cars that are expensive to maintain, requiring a more frequent battery replacement. Or we can build an expensive EV that costs very little to operate. Either way, it's more expensive than a gas car — because of the price of gas. At $2 a gallon for gas, an EV would be competitive with a gas car. At $4 a gallon, like Europe and most countries in the world, there would be no way that a gas car could compete with an EV. (Europeans are way ahead of us on these things.) And—the price of oil will go up.

This is a free country, but if you're going to drive around in a car that weighs 2-3 tons, the least you can do is to keep it tuned! It maximizes the range and minimizes the pollution. There isn't much reason not to own a vehicle that gets 50 mpg. They're getting cheaper to buy.

The most difficult part is getting gas to be more expensive. That's got to happen. The big three [U.S. automotive manufacturers] see EVs as impractical. So, they do what they want. Air quality groups have set standards, so it's got to happen. Unfortunately, most EVs will have to come from entrepreneurs or some other country. The bottleneck is that gas is too cheap here. That's a simple fact. Look what they've done in Europe and Brazil, where fuels are not subsidized at the pump. I'd like to see it double or triple in price here. Alternatives *are* cost-effective.

All of this is going to impact the economy in a major way. But it's nothing like what it will be if we wait! In the transition, poor people will be hit hardest. I don't know all the answers, but I know that something has to be done. Contrary to what I hear from the car makers, an EV, even with a range limit, is still one half to one quarter the cost to buy and operate, when you factor in what it means to use fossil fuels.

The electric car is on its way in. It's definitely here. It works. It's only a matter of time now.

major no-no if we want to prevent the "emission elsewhere" scenario. Fast-charge technology would likely increase the need for more power plants, too.

Building the Unlimited-Range EV

Will service stations remain? Is an EV of unlimited range possible? The answer to both questions is yes.

If you're afraid of running out of battery power in a video camcorder, what do you do? You arrange to swap the depleted battery pack with a fresh one.

The same idea works with EVs. Where the battery pack is a module which fits into a receptacle in a car, a vehicle can zip into a "BatStation" and exchange a depleted pack for a fully-charged one in less than 30 seconds.

Sound like a pipedream? The concept was initially proved in the Formula E (Chapter 3) and duplicated in a full-size vehicle in the Geometric (Chapter 2).

The implications of cars equipped with fast-exchange batteries are profound. EVs, then, would not be range-limited. As well, by leasing a battery pack, an EV owner puts the responsibility of good battery technology, maintenance, and repair on the supplier, where it should be. Leased batteries lower the upfront cost of buying an EV, spreading the cost of using batteries over a long period of time. Owners can charge at home inexpensively, or opt to long-range the vehicle by exchanging battery packs and paying a service charge.

There are other benefits, too. Since there's no user access to the battery pack, there are no liability issues around exposure to battery acid or fumes, short-circuits, or shock hazard.

New battery technology becomes "transparent" to the consumer with the battery exchange scenario. The supplier can detect and amend problems when the packs come in for exchange or the mandatory maintenance swap every few months. At any time, only trained personnel handle the packs.

Finally, exchanged packs can be recharged at night, when utility rates are low and energy is abundant, avoiding the impact on daytime peak utility loads.

Infrastructure

In truth, one-half of the infrastructure is already in place to make EVs work.

Think about it! Virtually every home, office, and business uses electricity. Twenty-amp household circuits are adequate for most EVs. A little bit of "opportunity charging" helps batteries in a big way. An hour at a 15-amp recharge rate rarely costs 20 cents, an amount most restaurants and businesses can easily afford to provide for their customers. Or, they could charge 50 cents and make a profit! EV owners will gladly pay this and more.

Two years ago, a nationwide contest (*The Electric Vehicle and the American Community*) was sponsored in the USA to solicit specific ideas on ways to integrate alternative fuels and EVs into existing cities and communities. The results were remarkable, indicating there is great enthusiasm and solid potential for integrating EVs into mainstream cities, communities, and society.

The 1998 ZEV Mandate

A milestone is looming three years off. By 1998, 2% of all new cars sold in California must be zero emission vehicles, or ZEVs. Only electric vehicles (or vehicles using flywheels or hydrogen) qualify.

The 2% mandate means that an auto manufacturer must sell two EVs out of every hundred vehicles it sells. There will be a $5,000 penalty for each non-ZEV car sold beyond this ratio. This ratio will be based upon actual consumer *sales*. The tactic of cramming a big, heavy, boxy van full of batteries won't get the manufacturer off the hook with a "nobody wanted or could afford it" argument. Other states have also adopted this mandate and others are lining up. It makes sense. Even Canada is joining the ZEV club.

All of the large automakers are balking. The 1998 mandate, they claim, isn't a milestone. It's a wall. Influence-peddling is in high gear to kill, delay, or weaken the mandate. Much of the heat is unofficially aimed at CARB (California Air Resources Board), the agency charged with enforcing the 1998 ZEV mandate. At first, one of the giants in the auto industry suggested that they were "counting on the flexibility of CARB in this matter." At the time, CARB chairperson Jananne Sharpless' response was a suggestion that they "step outside in the real world and take a look around." Will CARB back off? "Any car company that can't deliver ZEVs in 1998," replied Sharpless, "won't be selling cars in California!" This is a big slice of pie. The 2% ZEV mandate for 1998 in California represents 40,000 EVs.

General Motors, owner of the prototype Impact, a stunning EV designed specifically to

> *"When we start paying at the pump what it's really costing us to use gasoline, we'll be on the right track."*
> James Worden

run on electricity, is one of the protesters. While GM is building fifty Impacts for customer testing, large-scale production was killed as "part of general downsizing." In its unveiling, the Impact was an immediate hit, surprising GM marketing personnel, who promoted the vehicle in an uncharacteristically apologetic manner. With sports car acceleration, good range, and a cruising efficiency that tops an equivalent 90 miles per gallon, the Impact validates thinking "light and aerodynamic." From a comparable size of car, the Impact has chopped aerodynamic drag by 50 percent and weight by 50 percent with no sacrifice of crashworthiness or safety.

How does CARB know that an affordable ZEV is possible? Jerry Martin says, "ZEVs are already being produced in California by smaller companies that meet our expectations and are comparably priced." CARB already certifies conversions (cars converted from engines to electric drive) and kits from Electro Automotive, Solectria, Solar Car Corporation, and others. This includes conversions of Geo Metros, VW Rabbits, Chevrolet S-10 pickups, and imports like the Kewet and City-El. CARB realizes that if small companies can make a profit on custom conversions, an automaker can do it in mass production.

Will the Automakers Do It?

It is the perception of most EV advocates that automakers have been dragging their feet on the issue of EVs for many decades. In the USA, much of this foot-dragging has occurred at the taxpayer's expense. Prototypes have ranged from embarrassingly awful to good. Despite favorable reviews in magazines and newspapers, though, there has been little follow-up. Automakers have all too quickly dropped R&D (research and development) work with EVs when gas prices dropped.

Comments like "We can't do it!" or "We need more time!" are especially revealing when you consider that the 1998 mandate for 2% ZEVs was actually announced in 1990. A joke circulating in the EV community is that a certain U.S. automaker hired a thousand lawyers to fight the mandate while a certain Japanese automaker hired a thousand engineers to figure out how to meet it.

*E*ditorial *7* What Do the Automakers Say?

The big automakers claim that electric vehicles are low-performing and limited in range. They claim that, since the battery pack must be replaced every two to three years, electric vehicles are too expensive to be competitive with gasoline-powered cars. They claim that technological breakthroughs in batteries and motors are required before the EV will meet performance standards that the driving public has come to expect from automobiles.

What nonsense! Every sixth commercial on the major TV networks is about cars. That's a lot of hammering about the freedom, success, sex, power, and prestige a new car will bring us. After 50 years, the message is still seductive. But it's also wearing thin. What most of us want is reliable, affordable, safe transportation in our daily lives. Something that doesn't mess up the planet, foul the air we breathe, and make us want to retire to the mountains to "get away from it all."

Clearly, the auto industry's anti-EV claims stem from a desire to continue selling the old technology. Lurking in the background is the oil industry, which stands to get downsized by 50% or more with EV technology in widespread use.

*E*ditorial *8* A Poor Track Record with EVs?

Automakers seem to feel disdain for anything that doesn't have an engine. What evidence supports this?

• The Vehma-built GVan and Chrysler TEVan—at 8000 and 6000 pounds respectively and sold at $75-125K (each) to utilities—represent conversions that no self-respecting EV designer would ever build. Every official I have talked to (from a utility owning a GVan) considers it a bad joke. It's like putting wings on a brick. You can do it—but don't expect it to fly!

• GM, Chrysler, and Ford recently accepted a commitment of several billion dollars from the Clinton administration, promising a 90 mpg car in ten years' time. The GM Impact, with half the weight and half the aerodynamic drag of an equivalent car, could probably meet that goal today with a fuel-efficient engine installed. (The Impact was largely designed and built by AeroVironment.) Still, there is definite resistance to building an electric version of the same model.

• Are four years really needed to produce a viable ZEV? Stock conversions by Solectria and Solar Car Corporation of a variety of late-model, four-passenger cars and trucks sold by GM, Chrysler, Ford, and Honda have already paved the way. A variety of automobile models are represented in conversions done by individuals throughout the USA.

It is important to realize that the big three automakers in the USA have not manufactured economy automobiles for many decades. Faced with mandated CAFE (Corporate Average Fuel Economy) standards, they opted to buy foreign-made vehicles, importing them or assembling them stateside, and renaming them. For example, the Geo Metro is really a Suzuki Swift.

There is a direct connection between good fuel economy and low vehicle weight.

The truth is, EV prototypes and production cars have already been built and tested worldwide—anywhere that gasoline prices are high. The U.S. market, with the cheapest gasoline in the world, is merely the last market for these EVs to penetrate.

Do automakers have a poor opinion of the US driving public? Or is it fear? In other countries, the wisdom of rail and electric bus dominates, minimizing the need for cars. When the American public awakens to the problems associated with engines *and* cars, will they follow suit?

The Supercars Are Coming

A magnificent paper with this title and written by Amory Lovins and the staff at RMI (Rocky Mountain Institute) was recently presented at conferences and in magazine articles worldwide. At last, someone has *quantified* the research findings from projects all over the world into an enlightening vision of what *is* possible in transportation. While it is not specifically written for the layperson, the paper's message is clear: the old way of building cars won't work anymore. Lovins is a master at both cranking out the numbers and providing the analogies that will help executives, engineers, designers, and entrepreneurs see the handwriting on the wall.

Anyone who has ever designed and built a safe, practical, affordable, lightweight, aerodynamic vehicle will appreciate this paper. (I strongly advise getting and reading the full text of the paper.) Here, the physics of energy, mass, velocity, acceleration and staid thinking are clearly revealed! Most of us know that square functions get big fast, but here's the proof that square functions get small even faster! The power of "less is best" is formidable. (For example, in a formula, if x is one-fourth, and y is one-third, and z is one-half, what's the value of xyz? One-twenty fourth!) This basic math is the secret of the GM Impact's success. Paul MacCready (and team) used the same principle to make the age-old dream of human-powered flight came true in the Gossamer aircraft series.

Supercars, like the ones Lovins envisions, combined with electric propulsion, would drive the BTU per mile consumption of our resources to very low values compared with today's use (or abuse) of these resources.

> *In other countries, the wisdom of rail and electric bus dominates, minimizing the need for cars. When the American public awakens ... will they follow suit?*

Are EVs Crashworthy?

Electric propulsion is an elegant technology that is nicely complemented by a lightweight chassis and aerodynamic body. Predictably, consumers are wary of small, light cars because of the issue of crashworthiness.

The ultralight aircraft industry was one of the first to demonstrate superior strength for a fraction of the weight, using lightweight composites as structural materials. Today's race cars also demonstrate the crashworthiness of lightweight vehicles. Again and again, drivers spin their Indy cars into the wall at speeds approaching 200 mph — and frequently walk away or sustain only minor injuries. Not so widely publicized is the fact that today's small car is no longer the easy loser when it tangles with a big car.

Lovins touts the advantages of carbon fiber and fiberglass construction, but there are relatively non-toxic alternatives, too. In the 1930s, Henry Ford actually built a car body out of (a form of) soybeans that was easy to shape, paint, and repair. Imagine a car body that you could shred and toss onto the compost heap! There is also a growing movement in the USA to legalize hemp, another source for the cloth-and-resin material needed to build composite bodies. While the Hemp Initiative is hampered by the ancient plant's association with marijuana, the USA may someday again have an organic, environmentally friendly alternative to oil and plastics, drugs and timber.

What Next?

When you turn the page, you will see some examples of companies that design and build electric vehicles for sale or lease. Others manufacture components and assemble kits so that anyone might make their own EV (you or your favorite mechanic).

At any time, if you want more technical information about EV systems—motors, batteries, chargers, etc.—leap ahead to Chapter 7 and Chapter 8.

Application A₁ Solectria Corporation

Solectria Corporation was founded with the goal of bringing efficient, more environmentally-benign electric vehicles to the U.S. commuter car market. Solectria's first production was the Force, a modified Geo Metro, which has repeatedly won the endurance (2-hour or 120-mile) stock EV races at Phoenix since 1991. Solectria has led the nation in EV design in lightweight, aerodynamic prototypes. More recently, Solectria unveiled a four-passenger EV sedan, Sunrise. With a curb weight under 1700 lbs and a drag coefficient of 0.17, the Sunrise features a monocoque composite structure (this EV has passed crash tests!), AC induction drive system, and advanced lead-acid batteries. A high-efficiency heatpump offers summer air conditioning or winter heat. A thermal management system for the batteries is offered for operation in colder climes.

Solectria Corporation
James Worden
68 Industrial Way
Wilmington, MA 01887
(508) 658-2231
Fax: (508) 658-3224

Application A₂ Solar Car Corporation

Solar Car Corporation (SCC) was started in 1989 in Melbourne, Florida. It is a licensed and bonded independent auto dealer which is certified to convert vehicles to propane or natural gas. SCC builds EVs for major utility companies in the USA, as well as universities, municipalities, fleet operators, corporations, and individuals, notably the conversion of Chevy S-10 pickup trucks. SCC has a reputation for finding and adapting off-the-shelf components from other technical applications for use with EVs. SCC is currently developing and testing an ultra-efficient heatpump capable of air conditioning or cab heating, and is involved in testing motors from Fisher, Hughes, Westinghouse, and other manufacturers.

Solar Car Corporation
Doug Cobb
1300 Lake Washington Rd
Melbourne, FL 32935
(407) 254-2997,Fax (407) 254-4773

Application A₃ Electric Vehicles of America

Electric Vehicles of America, Inc. (EVA) was founded in 1988 to serve the commercial and personal EV markets. An authorized distributor for Advanced DC, Curtis PMC, and Trojan Battery, EVA sells components and does conversions and consulting.

EVA is attempting to set an industry standard for safety, maintainability, and reliability in its truck conversions.

EVA was part of the Odyssey Team, grand prize winner of *The Electric Vehicle and the American Community* planning and design competition.

EVA originated the Mighty Red Button, the E/plug symbol, and a ZEV coloring book for children. EVA is opening an EV retail center.

EVA, Inc.
Bob Batson
48 Acton St., P.O. Box 59
Maynard, MA 01754
(508) 897-9393, Fax (508) 897-6740

Application A₄ AC Propulsion

AC Propulsion (ACP) was founded by Alan Cocconi after he left the Impact design team. Now, ACP offers the highest performance (200HP) electric drivetrain on the market, along with the most advanced battery management systems yet designed. Also including inverter, battery charger, and regenerative braking, ACP's ac system propels a converted Honda from 0-60 in 6.2 seconds.

AC Propulsion, Inc.
Alan Cocconi
462 Borrego Court, Unit B
San Dimas, CA 91773
(909) 592-5399, (909) 394-4598

*A*pplication

A5 Green Motorworks

Green Motorworks (GMW) was started in North Hollywood in early 1992. It was the first Southern California dealership to sell and service only electric cars.

GMW offers a variety of vehicles for sale, including Pontiac Fieros, Ford Escorts, Dodge Omnis, and S10 pickups. Even a battery-powered scooter is available. GMW also offers custom conversions, building cars to a customer's preference for body style and performance. GMW leases EVs of many types, is working with BART (Bay Area Rapid Transit) on station cars, and is bringing a Norwegian-designed EV into limited production in California.

Green Motorworks, Inc.
William Meurer
5228 Vineland Ave
North Hollywood, CA 91601
(818) 766-3800, (818) 766-3969

*A*pplication

A6 ElectroAutomotive

ElectroAutomotive (EA) was founded in 1979 to provide a complete line of quality EV components.

EA offers kits ranging from basic (major components) to deluxe (complete), which were the first to be certified as eligible for California tax incentives (sales tax exemption and credit up to $1,000 on CA income tax).

A subsidiary, EA Information Services (EAIS), offers training and education products and services, including the 3-day Pro-Mech Program, to train gas car technicians for the growing EV market.

EAIS also offers *Convert It*, a step-by-step manual on the conversion process, and provides instructional and documentary videos produced by Richard Rahders.

EA has also evolved the "E" Sports Racer, an electric-powered machine built for 25-minute closed-course racing.

Electro Automotive
Michael Brown & Shari Prange
POB 113, Felton, CA 95018
Phone/Fax: (408) 429-1989.

*A*pplication

A7 MendoMotive

MendoMotive (MM) was started in 1991 and is devoted to ZEVs (zero emission vehicles) and custom conversions, including Fieros, VW vans, and the Spyder replica. MM operates a design and service garage to make electric farm and garden equipment.

MendoMotive
Stephen Heckeroth
110 West Elm St.
Ft Bragg, CA 95437
(707) 964-1331
Fax (707) 964-6500

*A*pplication

A8 Eyeball Engineering

Eyeball Engineering (EE) was started in the 1970s to advance electric vehicle technology. In addition to conversions and custom prototypes, EE has produced electric drag motorcycles, and two- and three-wheel street and highway EVs. Recently, EE has focused on building the Lightning Rod, a streamliner that will challenge the world speed record for EVs.

Eyeball Engineering
Ed Rannberg
5420 Via Ricardo, Riverside, CA 92509-2415
(909) 682-4535, Fax (909) 682-6275

*A*pplication

A9 KTA Services

KTA Services (founded 1980) supplies EV converters, hobbyists, and Electrathon race teams with components, system design, and consultation.

KTA Services
Ken Koch
944 West 21st St, Upland, CA 91784
(909) 949-7914, Fax (909) 949-7916

Chapter 2
The EV Conversion

A vehicle converted from engine power to electric drive is the dominant form of EV today. Just find an appropriate vehicle, rip out engine-related components, and mate the electric stuff to the drivetrain. Stick in the batteries, add the controls, and drive away.

Well, almost!

The attractiveness of the conversion is that the vehicle is already built for the road. In essence, the vehicle is 95% done even before you start converting!

Fig. 2-1:
Electric drive
complements elegant style.

Photo courtesy Solectria Corporation

If you do the conversion yourself, you may find that statement hard to believe. You may look back on the hundreds of hours of work, reflecting on the sweat, toil, uncertainties, difficulties, errors, and other challenges you overcame in the process. How can I claim you contributed only 5% to the working vehicle?

Thousands of design hours go into *each* part of a manufactured vehicle. For example, the precise positioning of console and instrumentation, and seat angle and range of adjustment are just two of the thousands of engineering tasks required for *each* model of car. Each year's model is different. Millions of people-hours of work stretch back through time to form this body of knowledge, from which thousands of little "rules" may be inferred. These act like tiny parts in a massive machineworks, each acting as a tool a designer will use to refine, integrate, express, and finish. The "fit of the human" to the machine (ergonometry) is built into every car. Thus, when you do a conversion, 95% of this work has been done for you.

The conversion is chock full of amenities, or "creature comforts." Windshield wipers. Windows that roll down. A heater that defogs

the windows. Comfortable seats. A nice feel. A sound system. Brakes that work. A steering wheel. A keyswitch in the right place. Parts that you can order from a store near you. A service technician that doesn't ask, "What is it?"

These are attributes of a conversion. If you're starting from scratch, building a prototype, *all* of these and much more are added to your design list. In the conversion, they are done, done well, and off the list.

The Conversion as a System

The components of a good EV conversion comprise a system. Like all good systems, it integrates with the rest of the car. There's much to think about. Most of it is not obvious the first time you do it.

Buying the parts does not *make* the thing. The "Wow, I can have an electric car for only $5000 worth of components" fades quickly when the pile of hardware doesn't magically integrate itself into your vehicle. Assembly is required. Batteries may not be included!

This book (and others like it) works like a checklist. You will walk through many parts of the process. Rules of thumb come from this process, summarizing both knowledge and experience. After more than a dozen conversions, I'm still learning.

There is a limit to what I can teach you. Do not follow this path blindly. Your situation is unique. It will demand a unique solution. You must selectively apply what you see here.

A Reality Check

What do you want? The more clear you are on the "mission" you expect of your EV, the happier you will feel about the investment you have made.

What task will you ask the EV to perform? Personal transportation? Commuting? Hauling kids around? Hauling freight? Having fun? Sport?

Avoid the all-purpose vehicle. This is not the time to get wishy-washy. Station wagons do not make good EVs, literally *or* figuratively. Attempting to fulfill many missions will hamper the EV's ability to perform any one of them well. If you are unclear about the EV's mission, you will not be happy with the result of your conversion efforts.

The second-toughest question is: Convert or scratchbuild? Most people elect to do a "conversion." It makes sense. Choosing this path lends a realistic air to what can be achieved and how long it will take to do even that!

The "convert or scratchbuild" dilemma has another side: "How loose can the vehicle fit you?" If your needs are basic, it's a conversion. If you are picky, you may only know what you do *not* want. But—will you know when you *do* see it?"

Here's another question: Is driving an electric vehicle a goal for you—or is it a project? There's a difference. When it is a goal, *arriving* there is everything. If it's a project, *how* you get there is important. Assess skills, time, talent, knowledge, and budget. Do you have the tools and materials? Do you have experience in *working* the tools and materials? What is the ETC (estimated time of completion)? Is there a space that you can dedicate to the project—for the duration of the project?

Avoid the all-purpose vehicle. This is no time to get wishy-washy. Station wagons do not make good EVs!

Fig. 2-2: An Izetta makes a good EV.

Photo: C. Michael Lewis

Fig.2-3: EVs are ideal for the commute.

There are many ways to acquire an EV. Buy a new EV or a vehicle converted to electric. Do it yourself. Contract to have it done. Follow a plan or start with a kit. Before these options are explored, let's look at basic ingredients.

Attributes of a Good Conversion

Cars that top the list of ones that make good conversions are called *candidate* cars. I've also heard them called *donor* cars. Cars that come factory-fresh without engines and related components are called *gliders*. (Just some lingo to help you wind your way through the tech-talk of EV enthusiasts.)

Successful conversions are not built by chance. Beyond being mission-specific, the prospective EV builder considers factors such as style, weight, aerodynamics, compatibility, condition, availability, space, and cost.

Style

If owning and driving an EV is the most important thing to you, you can push the "style" factor toward the end of your list. It is at the top of my list because some vehicle body styles appeal to me, others do not. I am willing to slide only a little bit on style. Seeing myself in a particular vehicle is an important part of driving that vehicle. It matters to me what's under the hood, but I won't drive a piece of junk just because it's electric powered. I'd rather walk. What about you?

Many people I meet are in love with specific styles or models of cars. They'll ask me, "Can I convert it to electric power?" My answer is always the same. "Yes, but will you like it?" Alas, the list of cars that would make a *poor* choice for a conversion is longer than the list of cars that would make a *good* conversion.

Subject a vehicle you like to the gauntlet of this list. Be honest about your evaluation, and you will be happier with your decision.

Weight

After being involved with dozens of conversions and scratchbuilts, I cannot emphasize strongly enough the importance of low weight in the electric vehicle. The engine and related components you remove (fuel, exhaust, and cooling systems) may seem heavy to you, but they cannot compete with the weight of a battery pack. The typical electric conversion adds 1,000 pounds (net) to the vehicle's original weight.

There is very little that you can safely do to strip weight from the original body and chassis. In a sense, all manufactured (gas-powered) vehicles are compromised in this respect. Thus, the *only* way that you can assure yourself of the best performance from your EV is to be *selective* about the vehicle you choose to convert. There are many benefits to thinking "light."

At some point, weigh the candidate vehicle. The weight listed by the manufacturer (if available) may vary, depending on a multitude of options, by hundreds of pounds from the one you're looking at.

Aerodynamics

If you expect to take your EV out on the freeway, pay attention to the vehicle's aerodynamics. This defines its sleekness, its streamlining, its ability to move through the air cleanly. As much as fifty percent of the power needed to push a passenger sedan down a highway at 60 mph is used to move air aside.

Good aerodynamic design minimizes the frontal area (the number of square inches the vehicle displays when viewed head-on), and pays attention to the contour of component sections (i.e., sloped vs. vertical windshield), the closure angle (the taper of the car's rear), and the number of protrusions (i.e., sideview mirrors and windshield wipers).

For the most part, aerodynamics is built-in (or not) by the manufacturer. There are tricks of the trade you can perform to get more "aero." The best trick is to know what matters and cross off your list any vehicle that violates basic principles. There's little you can do to streamline a box.

And don't be fooled by the soft, rounded corners of certain late model cars. This "pillow"

Photo: Stephen Heckeroth

Fig. 2-4: A Spyder kit body/chassis is a way to stay light and elegant.

Photo: C. Michael Lewis

Fig. 2-5: The Hilltopper was built by students.

contouring is mostly styling. Alas, most of these slippery-*looking* cars would have less aerodynamic drag going down the road *backward*!

Compatibility

Avoid cars with automatic transmissions and power steering. As well, vehicles originally equipped with air conditioning and power brakes require special adaptation. In more detail:

• *Automatic Transmissions.* Even if you have learned to drive only a car with an automatic transmission, do *not* convert a car that has one. Automatic transmissions are *extremely* wasteful of energy. They require special effort to work with electric propulsion, too, since there's no engine vacuum to tell the transmission when to shift. Even so, the shift points fit engines, not electric motors.

There's some good news, though. EVs with manual transmissions can be driven as though they *have* an automatic transmission! Really! Just stick it in second gear and push the accelerator. The EV will stop and start without using the clutch. *You can't stall an electric motor!* With the wide powerband of electric propulsion, you should be able to drive in the speed range of 0-45 mph without any shifting of gears.

• *Power Steering.* Power steering can be accomplished in an EV but it adds complexity and cost. The pump must work even when you've stopped the vehicle, so there goes the silence. Just the presence of power steering in a car is suggestive of its heaviness. Pass it up. Keep things simple.

If the vehicle undergoes a 1,000-lb weight gain to become electric, you may wish that the car had power steering. Adding low-rolling resistance tires to my 3,000-lb electric Honda made it feel like I had *added* power steering.

Air Conditioning. Standard automotive air conditioners (AC) are energy consumptive and add a high degree of complexity and cost to the EV conversion. The presence of air conditioning in the car is not a reason to scratch the vehicle off your candidacy list. You can just dispose of the AC hardware along with

the rest of the engine-related components. However, getting the original AC to work in the EV is a *big* job.

Generally, EV owners make do without air conditioning. They compensate. They're more careful about parking in the shade. Some install small fans that turn on (with a thermoswitch) to keep the interior of a parked vehicle as cool as possible. More resourceful owners use holdover plates (like those used in sailboats for refrigeration) to provide some "cool." Like heating, this extracts a 5% toll on range if powered by the battery pack directly. Innovative designs use the recharging source to pump the heat away (while the EV is plugged in), building a reserve of "cool" for the short time the vehicle is driven.

Already, there are several working heat-pump prototypes in the emerging EV industry. These assemblies are dual-function, acting as air conditioners in the summer and heaters in the winter. They are powered directly from the battery pack, or utility power when the EV is plugged in. This eliminates the more clumsy

Fig. 2-6: Many owners show pride in their EV by lettering it.

Photo: ElectroAutomotive

arrangement of powering a compressor from the propulsion drivetrain, as is done with an engine.

In a few years' time, air conditioning will be available as an after-market item.

Power Brakes. Later model cars, even relatively lightweight ones, have power brakes as standard equipment. Power brakes work from vacuum. Engines have *lots* of vacuum, generated in the cylinders during the intake cycle. Electric motors have *no* vacuum. To get the power brakes to work, many EV conversions add vacuum-generating equipment or replace the power brakes with a stock brake cylinder (Techtalk T2).

Several good electric-assist brakes have been designed and built (Fig. 2-7). These are likely to appear in new, production EVs and may be available as after-market hardware in a few years' time.

Regenerative braking is *not* a replacement for mechanical brakes, but it will help minimize the workload imposed on the mechanical braking system of whatever type.

Vehicle Condition

A candidate car for an EV conversion should be subjected to an extensive vehicle inspection. A late-model car with a blown engine is a good score. A "clapped out" car (or "beater") with a clapped out engine is not. The older the car, the more suspect its condition.

The vehicle's condition, then, is not a matter of whether it needs a paint job, or has good upholstery. These are cosmetic details. Here, condition refers to operational attributes. Structural soundness. Safety and integrity.

Part of the conversion process itself is the restoration of a vehicle to its original operating condition (sans engine and related components). At a minimum, this involves brakes, springs and shocks. A brake inspection is essential. An overhaul of the brakes is likely.

Fig. 2-7: An electric-assist brake assembly designed and built by Ely Schless

The vehicle will need a different suspension (*beefier* springs, *larger* shocks) to compensate for the increase in vehicle weight. If the EV conversion shifts the vehicle's original CG (center of gravity, measured as a ratio of front-to-rear distribution), beefier springs will only *somewhat* compensate for this weight shift.

When the vehicle displays multiple rust spots or salt corrosion, the structural integrity of the vehicle may be compromised. If side panels are affected, how could the underside of the vehicle not be?

The addition of battery weight to the vehicle in making it electric will likely cause it to exceed the GVWR (gross vehicle weight rating). The battery pack must be supported by the car. If the car is tin, it's thin. And if it's rusted, it will have the strength of paper. Err on the side of conservative.

Availability

To be a candidate for an EV conversion, a vehicle must be available to you. I mean, it's got to be *real*. Something you can touch, inspect, consider, purchase, and convert.

Techtalk

T₂ EV Braking Methods

Does your electric vehicle *need* power brakes? The phrase "power brake" is somewhat of a misnomer. *Power brakes don't give a vehicle more powerful brakes. Instead, they function to assist the driver in applying the brakes.* That way, the driver doesn't have to push very hard to make the brakes work. Pushing harder on the power brakes, then, doesn't yield more braking power.

Standard Practice

Many converters add a vacuum-generating system to make the original power brakes work. This system consists of a small 12V vacuum pump, a vacuum cylinder, and a vacuum switch.

In an EV, a vacuum system complicates things at four levels.

Expense. The vacuum-generating hardware costs $350-450.

Noise. The vacuum-cylinder "stores" vacuum for the brakes to work, but it is depleted when you step on the brakes. Once the pedal is released, the vacuum pump will start up, refilling the cylinder. This occurs every time you stop. I find this very annoying. I like silence. EVs make silence a virtue. Vacuum pumps violate this silence. And they work when the vehicle is at rest, when their noise cannot be disguised by road noise.

Room. Space is often at a premium in a conversion.

Ratings. Today's pumps are generally inadequate for the job. They are industrial-rated (a #2 rating), *not* automotive-rated (a #5 rating). They are low-volume, high-vacuum units. What is required is the opposite: high-volume, low-vacuum. These exist, but cost more and are even *more* noisy.

The Alternative

Exchange the power brake unit with a stock hydraulic cylinder. Does this mean less braking power? No!

So, an alternative to installing vacuum-generating hardware is to remove the power brake assembly from the car and install a stock master cylinder in its place. This is a straightforward affair. Stock brakes require fewer components but require more pedal effort.

This work should be performed only by a mechanic licensed and trained in brake systems.

Fig. 2-8: Make certain there is room for the battery pack you will install.

Fig. 2-9: Electric motors will usually fit anywhere an engine was removed.

Fig. 2-10: The kit has arrived for this pickup truck.

Space

Batteries in an EV take up a lot of room. Make certain that the candidate vehicle has enough room to fit the propulsion system you want. Vehicles with 96V or 108V systems are often forced into these lower voltages for the lack of space to contain the few extra batteries needed to reach a higher voltage. If a smaller candidate is available but you'd like an EV of a higher voltage, make certain there is room for enough batteries.

Eyeball the vehicle for space. Have on hand a battery of the right size. Positioning a battery is the most accurate way to tell, but this is the least practical. The space may be already filled up, particularly under the hood. A tape measure is very helpful here. Have the measurements for the length, width, and height of the battery handy. Include extra for the battery posts (or terminals) you'll install.

Battery manufacturers are usually willing to loan you a battery case. This is a blessing, letting you examine battery positioning without having to heft any weight. At 50-70 pounds each, a finished battery is just too heavy for such positioning. If required, put down a deposit and get 4-5 cases.

Cost

Last but not least is, "Can you afford it?" Only you can answer this question. But — if a candidate vehicle passes muster on all of the aforementioned criteria, how can you afford not to use it? A fit is a *fit*.

A conversion requires an investment on your part. If you are buying a car already converted to electric power, most of this investment is money. If you will do the conversion yourself, money is only a fraction of the investment you will make. What about time? What about your energy?

Understand that you may be putting as much money into converting an earlier model

Too often, a prospective EV owner considers only one candidate, usually a vehicle they own. Or something that's sitting abandoned in a lot across the way. Or something a friend, a relative, or an acquaintance is getting rid of, is storing, or will trade for something they want. Avoid this scenario. It's likely to end in grief.

Shelling out a thousand bucks might *seem* too wasteful if something much less suitable is available for free. Generate a *real* list, and then evaluate all entries on the basis of *all* factors.

Another kind of availability is best represented by an example. The VW Rabbit is a popular EV conversion primarily for one reason. Rabbits with diesel engines blew up early in their service life. Unwilling to repeat the mistake, their owners exercised other options. One was getting rid of the car. If you like the look, the VW Rabbit is an ideal choice while ones in good condition last.

of car as you would into a brand new vehicle. So, it should at least *feel* brand new when you're done. Don't forget to include body work and a paint job in your project's budget.

Finally, do it right! A low-ball EV looks or acts low-ball. There's a saying that fits here. The bitterness of low quality is remembered long after the sweetness of low cost is forgotten!

Buy or Convert?

For many decades, there were only two ways to get an EV conversion. The first was to buy someone else's conversion. A ready-made conversion was neat but it also meant that you were getting someone else's "first effort" and, perhaps, very dated components. A second possibility was to do your own conversion. Now you could drive around your own "first effort!" If you were not mechanically-inclined, this option would never bear fruit.

Today's prospective EV owner has many more avenues to explore. There are a growing number of companies offering conversions for sale. Many companies also offer custom conversions. That is, you specify (or supply) the vehicle and they convert it. More often, these shops will offer several models of vehicles that they are willing to convert. Indeed, some companies have a small stock of conversions ready to "drive away" as soon as you complete the paperwork and write the check. Their choice of model may be based on availability or style, i.e., a Fiero or Porsche. Or they may go with conventional fleet models, i.e., a Ford Escort or Saturn. Some shops work to make the overall transaction affordable by using something like a Volkswagen Rabbit. Shop around!

Getting Help

When the EV conversion of your dreams isn't available on a showroom floor and you are hesitant to tackle doing it yourself, consider doing a project with qualified help. Automotive mechanics, machinists, metalworkers, engineers, and designers abound. While a successful EV conversion will need skills beyond those of any *one* of these occupations, more and more people are building EVs.

You are looking for someone who understands the challenges of any kind of project and possesses the range of skills that must be applied to reach success. Experience is very important. Where do I find people like these? Fabrication shops. Machine shops. Mechanics who race their own vehicles.

Another source of help is an EV club. The number of EV clubs has grown as the interest in EVs increases. Long-time EV clubs have seen their memberships double and triple in the last five years. One or more members of these clubs possess the necessary skills to make your project a success. Keep your eyes and ears open. Sort through the "wanna bees" and find the person who is really building stuff. Verify the quality of workmanship. After all, when you drive your EV, you will be trusting your life to this person's integrity.

Vehicle-Specific Plans

Vehicle-specific conversion plans exist for a wide variety of vehicles. There are three major advantages to vehicles with plans. One is that it's a good way to avoid many of the pitfalls awaiting any first-time converter. Two, critical information, like the vehicle's CG, may be included, giving you a reference. It may help you understand what particular effect some modification you make will have on the overall design. And, three, where you lack an idea, plans give you one. Don't worry. It won't prevent you from substitutions or variances. Conversion plans are like trail maps. They tell you the easiest ways to go up the mountain.

Many EV clubs have lists of cars that make decent conversions. These are not necessarily lightweight cars. More often, they are vehicles someone has converted and has documented. VW Bug. VW Rabbit. Honda Civic. Chevy Chevette. Datsun B210. Fiat X19. Geo Metro. Miata. Do plans exist for the vehicle(s) you are considering? Ask around!

Basic vs Complete Kits

A couple of decades ago, collecting the parts to do a conversion was a formidable job. On reflection, it wasn't as though there were that many choices for parts, but many good EVs were built and operated during these times. Instead, what was lacking was real networking. *Access* to the sources, then, was the challenge.

Today, many EV-related publications include complete lists of the many sources of components that have sprung up to serve the growing interest in EVs. Now, it is more a matter of sorting through the choices and making your selection.

A conversion project will get off to a good start with a kit. A kit is a collection of parts from one source. Kits come in three flavors: barebones, complete, and vehicle-specific.

Kits come in three flavors: barebones, complete, and vehicle-specific.

A *barebones* EV conversion kit includes motor, controller, and charger. A *complete* kit includes everything you'll need to convert almost any vehicle. A *vehicle-specific* kit is designed for a specific vehicle, i.e., a VW Rabbit, and includes a critical component: the adaptor plate.

Shop around for parts. Expect to pay more, at least 10-25%, for a complete kit. Two things justify this expenditure. One-stop shopping saves time, study, and the frustration of working with suppliers. The second justification is integration. Complete kits have evolved from experience on the part of the supplier. A good EV conversion is a system. To be more than the sum of its parts, then, everything must fit together.

A Sample Conversion

It's time for a walk-through of a conversion. The project I've selected to review is a 1991 Honda CRX conversion (Fig. 2-11).

This was a custom conversion for several reasons. First, I had no knowledge of this vehicle model having been converted before. So, no plans or guidelines were available. Two,

Fig. 2-11: A 1991 Honda CRX awaits conversion to electric propulsion.

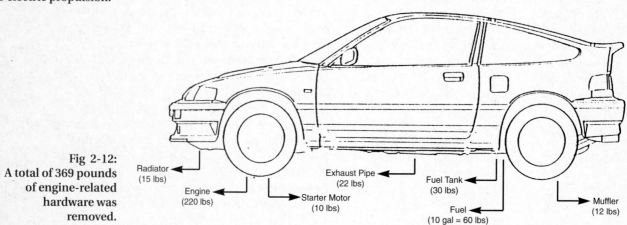

Fig 2-12: A total of 369 pounds of engine-related hardware was removed.

Radiator (15 lbs)
Engine (220 lbs)
Starter Motor (10 lbs)
Exhaust Pipe (22 lbs)
Fuel Tank (30 lbs)
Fuel (10 gal = 60 lbs)
Muffler (12 lbs)

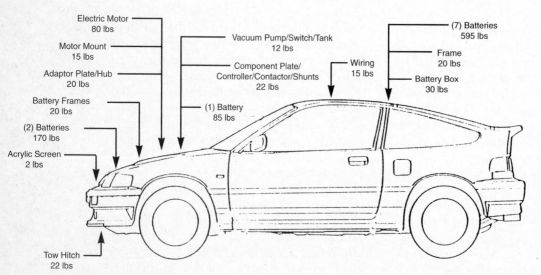

Electric Motor 80 lbs
Motor Mount 15 lbs
Adaptor Plate/Hub 20 lbs
Battery Frames 20 lbs
(2) Batteries 170 lbs
Acrylic Screen 2 lbs
Tow Hitch 22 lbs
Vacuum Pump/Switch/Tank 12 lbs
Component Plate/Controller/Contactor/Shunts 22 lbs
(1) Battery 85 lbs
Wiring 15 lbs
(7) Batteries 595 lbs
Frame 20 lbs
Battery Box 30 lbs

Fig. 2-13: A total of 1,106 pounds of electric propulsion hardware was added.

the conversion was performed in a carport (in Venice, California) without the support of even a modest machine shop. And, three, it had a tight timetable of eight (8) weeks.

I managed the project, dealing with the client and helping to design this custom conversion. I photo-documented it, too. Otmar Ebenhoech performed 95% of the actual conversion and incorporated many design innovations as the project progressed.

Stripping out the ICE

While Otmar and I discussed many aspects of the design itself, the first job was clearly to remove the ICE and related subsystems. The three existing shop manuals (general, electrical, and body repair) for the car were obtained to assist us in the dissection. These proved invaluable in determining what to remove and what to leave, and identified relays and wiring for later use.

I decided from the beginning to weigh all parts as they were removed. As much as possible, we wanted to preserve the front-rear weight ratio. I copied a side-view drawing of the car from one of the manuals and enlarged it. On it, I noted a component's weight and its relative distance from a reference point (Fig. 2-12). Later, as we added components, this would help us know which way to shift weight if we had a choice (Fig. 2-13).

This was the most modern car I had helped convert to date. I was amazed at the complexity of components, wiring, relays, and controls, including those related to the onboard computer. Out came the engine (Fig. 2-14), fuel tank and lines. Radiator and hoses, and muffler and exhaust systems followed. We were able to sell these components for $1,000 to a person interested in using them in a boat project.

Initial Decisions

From the start, we had decided to use off-the-shelf DC propulsion components: a 10HP series motor (Advanced DC Motors), a MOSFET controller (Curtis PMC, Model 1221), lead-acid batteries (Trojan), and an offboard charger (Lester). I was aiming for a 120V system, a low cg (center of gravity) for the battery pack, and a front-rear weight ratio similar to the original.

Sizing the Battery Pack

The CRX is a small (two-seater) car. The 1991 model we were converting had a tightly sloped hood that limited the available space

Fig. 2-14: Removing the engine is the first big job.

All photos of this conversion: Otmar Ebenhoech and Michael Hackleman

Fig. 2-15: Structural support will be needed to handle battery weight.

Fig. 2-16: Structural components are welded to the vehicle chassis.

Fig. 2-17: The battery box is plastic-welded together.

Fig. 2-18: The rear battery box is ready to install.

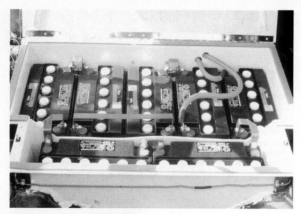

Fig. 2-19: The batteries in the rear pack are interconnected with copper strap.

Fig. 2-20: The hub is attached to the motor shaft.

Fig. 2-21: After the adaptor plate is bolted to the motor housing, the flywheel is attached to the hub.

Fig. 2-22: The motor assembly is bolted to the original transmission. Note the two forward battery frames.

under the hood. Once the ICE/components were out, it was obvious that there was very little room for batteries. Using 6V (220Ah) batteries was out. We clearly couldn't fit sixteen (96V), eighteen (108V), or twenty (120V) of them in the car. Even stacked behind the driver/passenger seats, this would shift too much weight to the rear *and* raise the cg.

On the other hand, ten 12V (110Ah) batteries would represent a relatively small size of battery pack for the acceleration, range, and speed that I wanted to achieve. Curtis technicians confirmed that the controller was at risk with a pack voltage of 144V, so we were limited to 120V. (Four years later, a 144V controller has become available from Curtis.)

In the midst of our investigations, Fred Daniel at Trojan Battery Company recommended the 5SH battery, a new deep-cycle battery with a higher capacity (145Ah). Installed in new polypropylene cases, nearly 10 pounds of weight was shaved from each battery over the original rubber cases.

Using empty cases, we were disappointed that we still could get only three of the 5SH batteries under the hood in the engine compartment. Rearward, structural components imposed their own limits. We settled on an irregular shape of battery box for the seven batteries located there, positioned flush with the bottom of the car.

Steel angle-iron frames were built to support the front and rear batteries (Fig. 2-15). A high-speed cutting wheel made a hole through the rear sheet-metal floor. The steelwork was welded to the car (Fig. 2-16) and reinforced with sheer plates to anything structural in close proximity.

A battery case and lid, constructed of polypropylene sheet, was cut and plastic-welded by Otmar (Fig. 2-17) to contain and seal the batteries. The completed assembly (Fig. 2-18) slipped into the metal framework.

Copper straps connected the batteries together in the rear portion of the pack (Fig. 2-19). Steel crossbars (not shown in photo) secured the batteries inside the rear battery box. Holes were drilled in the bottom of the plastic case. When the pack was hosed down, the water drained out.

A vent fan was added to the rear battery box. It was powered by the 12V auxiliary (aux) charger circuit in the Lester unit when it was plugged into the vehicle.

Installing the Motor

A Honda engine rotates in a direction opposite to most other engines. So, the 10HP motor was factory-modified for reverse rotation. Otherwise, it was a stock, off-the-shelf component.

The vehicle's adaptor plate, motor hub, and motor support were built in separate shops. The hub (Fig. 2-20) and adaptor plate (Fig. 2-21) had to be re-worked, but worked beautifully once installed. The stock motor mount was also extensively modified to work. The electric motor was an easy fit (Fig. 2-22).

Heavier spring-shock assemblies were installed on all four wheels from a heavier Honda model of the same year.

Other Under-Hood Components

The controller and potbox, meter shunts, and contactor were installed on a plastic plate, centered over the motor and forward of the rearmost battery under the hood (Fig. 2-23). The front batteries, motor, controller, and front-to-rear circuitry were connected with super-flex welding cable (Fig. 2-24). Standard battery tie-downs were used for the batteries under the hood.

Otmar blocked off airflow through the CRX's front grate with a black plastic plate to help improve overall aerodynamics. A 12V cooling fan was added to the controller to prevent thermal overload (a self-protection feature) when the vehicle climbed hills in hot weather.

The battery pack was wired with a 400-Amp fuse. A circuit breaker was installed between (and behind) the front seats within the driver's reach. The keyswitch operated the main contactor.

The CRX's power brakes were retained. Vacuum was supplied via a 12V pump and switch (Fig. 2-25). A PVC (vacuum) reservoir and gauge were mounted under the component plate.

The vehicle's original auxiliary battery was replaced with a deep-cycle one. A Todd charger was adapted to supply 12V directly from the 120V pack.

The under-hood area quickly filled with all these components and looked busy (Fig. 2-26).

Meters and Gauges

An ammeter (0-500A) and an expanded-scale voltmeter (105-135V) were mounted on a plate and wired into a 3-position rotary switch (center off), so the 12V (aux) battery could be

Fig. 2-23: Most of the control circuitry is located on a central plate.

Fig. 2-24: Motor and control circuits are wired together with cables.

Fig. 2-25: The vacuum pump and switch are needed if the power brakes are retained.

Fig. 2-26: The addition of batteries completes the under-the-hood installation.

Fig. 2-27: Wire the meter assembly for easy removal.

Fig. 2-28: The meters blend in with the center console.

monitored, too (Fig. 2-27). This unit was positioned in the radio slot of the CRX console (Fig. 2-28).

A sender unit was fabricated to operate the vehicle's stock tachometer. An aluminum hub, with two magnets fitted on opposite sides, was

T3 *echtalk*
CRX Project Challenges

Even in 1991, it was difficult to find, order, and receive parts in a timely fashion from the EV industry. Here's a short list of problem, result, and remedy in this project to convert a CRX.

• The polypropylene cases for the 5SH batteries had not been flame treated. As a result, the glue between top and case did not take, and electrolyte leaked out. The vent caps also spewed electrolyte during gassing. Consequently, the specific gravity of the cells went whacko, and they were replaced (by Trojan, gratis) within four months of installation. Aluminum and steel parts under the hood were corroded by the battery acid and had to be extensively steel brushed and re-painted.

• The vacuum switch (designed to detect low vacuum and start the vacuum pump) malfunctioned on numerous occasions, suddenly disabling the brake system. Dangerous and scary. A strong handbrake proved invaluable.

• The meters did not function initially. The manufacturer was certain we had wired them wrong. They were sent back and found to have had components installed incorrectly. Fixed and returned, they appeared to work okay. Subsequently, against a standard, the ammeter was found to be in error by 15%.

• The adaptor plate, hub, and motor mount did not fit first time around. A new hub was re-manufactured. A machine shop worked out a clearance problem with the adaptor plate by machining down the flywheel's diameter. Otmar significantly re-fashioned and welded together a motor mount. The final pricetag was three times the original quote.

• The onboard, experimental charger was problematic. Its GFI (ground fault interrupt) device repeatedly tripped. Sprayed electrolyte (discussed earlier) provided a path for electricity to the battery tie-downs (rubberized metal bars). The charger was removed. In a subsequent trial with another EV, it destroyed itself after three hours of use.

• I seriously under-estimated the time and money involved in this project. The self-imposed 8-week deadline was absurd. Without adequate tools, an enclosed workspace, and basic shop equipment, the job was grueling. Otmar and I both lost power and hand tools (and Otmar's camera) to a thief in the carport.

• The CRX did not achieve the range goal (45 miles) at freeway speed. Nominal ratings for batteries do not apply to EV operation, and performance was difficult to predict on the basis of the available technical information.

secured to the motor's shaft where it came out of the rear plate. This provided the signal to work the tachometer's electronics.

Charging Circuit

The space behind the gas lid was modified to hold two receptacles. One was a 30-Amp DC receptacle (Fig. 2-29) that received the output of an offboard Lester charger (Fig. 2-30) set up at the base station. The other was a male receptacle for a standard extension cord (from 115VAC) to power an experimental, 15-lb charger obtained from KTA Services. The receptacles were positioned for an interference fit, so that both could not be plugged in simultaneously.

Odds and Ends

An immersible heater element mounted in pipestock (Fig. 2-31) was built to supply heat directly to the original heater/defroster radiator via a small 12V pump. Rated at 120V, the unit would take its power directly from the 120V battery pack. This was not installed. The client opted to wait for a PTC heater coil.

Fig. 2-29: Match a NEMA receptacle and plug to the ampacity of the charger.

Fig. 2-30: Plugging the EV into the charger is a welcome alternative to the gas station.

Fig. 2-31: A homebuilt heater, with a small 12V pump, will mate to the existing system.

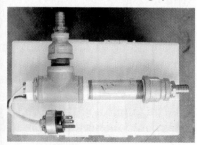

Fig. 2-32: A tow hitch helps transport the EV to shows and makes EVs work with RVs.

A stock tow hitch was modified to fit the vehicle. Studs were welded to the vehicle's frame to accommodate this hitch (Fig. 2-32). The client wanted to be able to tow the vehicle long distances.

Otmar performed a minor miracle in disguising the presence of the rear battery pack. The meters fit the console so nicely that there was little to give away the fact that the vehicle was now electrified.

The client seemed very happy. The CRX, from start to finish, took just eight weeks to convert and test.

Every project has its challenges. I have taken the time to identify the problems encountered and the remedies enacted in the CRX project (Techtalk T3) in the hopes of providing some perspective for the novice.

OTHER CONVERSIONS

A multitude of conversions exist as examples of what can be done with almost any type of vehicle and application.

I will review six EVs: The EVX. The Geometric. John Sprinkle's Porsche. A workhorse Go-4. A Mule. The Ox.

The Honda EVX

In early 1992, I was given a project car from American Honda by Ann Palmer. It was a sleek 1992 Honda Civic VX. From the moment I first saw it, I knew it would make a great conversion. It was light and aerodynamic. Best of all, there was ample space under the hood for batteries to balance the ones that would be placed behind the seats.

With the 1992 Phoenix race only a few months away, I recruited a team to get the Honda ready to run in the "stock" class. I wanted to perform a rapid recharge, as with the Lead Sled (a vehicle I ran in the previous year's race). While I had the option of using exotic batteries, I wanted to be competitive with *off-the-shelf* technology. Trojan Battery supplied batteries and enough support to make the effort a worthwhile attempt.

Fig. 2-33: With only a thousand miles on the odometer, a Honda Civic VX awaits conversion.

Photo: Daniel Pliskin

Fig. 2-34: Every detail is important in a race.

Photo: Daniel Pliskin

Fig. 2-35: Driver Tim Considine brings the Hackleman-Schless stock car entry in the Phoenix races across the finish line first.

Following the conversion (Application A10), I tested "EVX" by commuting between home and shop on Los Angeles freeways. At times, these are natural speedways. My commute included Sepulveda Pass, a stretch of road that had tested the mettle of many an EV.

Fig. 2-36: The heat sink was retained for street use of the EVX.

Over time, these tests suggested a mounting of the controller *through* the hood. In this location, the controller did not go into "thermal cutback" while going up the pass at 75mph!

Racing the EVX

In 1992, I predicted the EVX's design would be highly competitive and was rewarded with a 1st place trophy in the 25-mile heat race. The EVX placed 2nd in the two-hour endurance event when the race was red-flagged (stopped) after the 1st place car spilled battery fluid.

In 1993, I returned with the same vehicle, unmodified. EVX won another 1st place trophy, snatching the 25-mile heat away from the favored car. Problems with the offboard battery pack forced us to settle for a 4th place in the two-hour endurance event.

A_{10} pplication — An Electric Honda VX ("EVX")

Anne Palmer of American Honda came through with a car for the "stock" category of the Phoenix races in 1992. It was a sleek 1992 Honda Civic VX. It was given to me as a project car for anything I'd like to do with it. It was ideal for Phoenix, but

Fig. 2-37: Four batteries fit next to the modified bumper behind the nosecone. This area also contains the tow bar attachment points.

we had rolled into February before it was ready to pick up. This seemed too late! Trojan Battery's willingness to supply batteries encouraged me not to give up.

It was Ely Schless (Schless Engineering) who performed the Honda VX conversion at his shop in North Hollywood. Next door, he was building the Formula E (see Application A28) racer for the Hackleman-Schless team to run in the "open" category.

For the most part, this was a standard conversion process. Out came the fuel, engine cooling, and exhaust systems. The 20HP Advanced DC motor was bolted through a Schless-designed adaptor plate to the stock transmission. A Curtis PMC controller was mounted through the hood to a multi-fin heat sink positioned in the airflow for maximum cooling.

Special Projects personnel at American Honda, including Charlie Curnutt, assisted with suspension changes for the 1,000-lb gain in the vehicle's curb weight. They adjusted the ride height with Honda Prelude springs and installed Coni shocks set to maximum stiffness for the race.

Instead of using twenty 6V batteries, I installed twenty 12V, Trojan 27TMH deep-cycle batteries in the EVX. These were wired into two, parallel packs of 120 Volts each. This choice was dictated by the fast-recharge scheme I intended to use in the races at Phoenix.

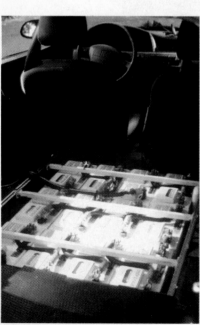

Fig. 2-38: The rear battery pack is recessed through the floor, secured by cross-bars, and fitted with a Lexan cover.

Back on the Street

When it wasn't racing at Phoenix, the EVX was used on the street, highway, and freeway. It was my everyday car. For two years, my 1965 VW bus sat at the curb to back up the EVX. However, I *always* found a way to get where I was going with the EVX. I understand, then, the desire for new EV owners to keep another car until they're certain their EV will do the job!

What I have liked most about the EVX is that it flies in the face of people's perceptions about EVs. It clearly validates the idea of putting electric propulsion in late model cars. Older cars converted to electric drive appear to give the impression that EV technology itself is somehow "dated" or "antiquated." After going for a test drive in the EVX, people felt reassured that, indeed, I had not ruined a perfectly good car by converting it to electric power!

The EVX had so much underhood space that the installation avoids the crammed and cluttered look experienced with so many other EVs. I was always happy to open the hood, knowing that the first thing people would notice was the simplicity. Electric propulsion *is* simple technology. I believe that it is important to *demonstrate* that simplicity whenever it is integrated into vehicles. Burying the motor under batteries, a common practice to make things fit, gives the wrong impression. Virtually every EV is under scrutiny today.

After going for a test drive in the EVX, people felt reassured that, indeed, I had not ruined a perfectly good car by converting it to electric power!

Evenly distributed through the EVX (eight under the hood, twelve directly behind the driver and passenger seats), the batteries shifted the vehicle's front-to-rear weight ratio less than 2% to the rear.

The viability of twin, paralleled packs of 12V batteries in an EV for everyday use is questionable. With twice the number of cells as a 120V pack of 6V batteries, there *is* more overall resistance to current flow. Fortunately, there are other virtues to the paralleled packs of batteries (see Techtalk T90, Chapter 8).

Fig. 2-39: Even with eight batteries, the motor compartment feels spacious.

Proof of Concept

To date, the EVX's best mileage on a charge is 72 miles at a steady 60 mph with a passenger and 200 pounds of baggage. This was logged during its 520-mile round trip (with recharge stops, of course!) for SEER in 1992.

In the spacious EVX, the batteries, motor, and controller are easy to point out. Standard black welding cable was substituted for the dayglow orange superflex cable commonly used in propulsion wiring, avoiding the "busy" look. For the same reason, peripheral hardware (contactors, shunts, potbox, and relays) were mounted on the sidewall, keeping things simple and tidy.

The original power (vacuum-assisted) brakes were replaced with a stock hydraulic cylinder to eliminate the clutter and noise of the vacuum pump, switch, and reservoir tank.

The onboard battery charger and DC-to-DC converter were mounted in a body side panel (behind the driver) so a hose can be used to wash the engine compartment free of dust without harm to exposed components.

Fig. 2-40: Control components are located on the sidewall. The controller is mounted under (and through) the hood.

Photo: Mary Ann Chapman

The Geometric

Fig. 2-41: A Geo Metro convertible weighs 1,700 lbs with an engine.

All photos of this conversion: Schless Engineering, Inc.

The Geometric was a conversion that represented an intersection of many ideas, each one of which had been proved in a prior application. As with the CRX, there was little room for batteries under the hood, or in the back seat or trunk. Like the EVX, the candidate vehicle—a 1992 Geo Metro—was lightweight (1,700 lbs). Like the Hackleman-Schless Formula E (review Application A28), the Geometric's battery pack was designed to be exchanged.

Fig. 2-44: EV designer and builder, Ely Schless.

Fig. 2-42: The Geometric's batteries are arranged in one large module.

A Application A11

The Geometric

The Geometric was born out of the experience of exchanging battery packs in the Phoenix races. Following the 1992 successes by the Hackleman-Schless team with its Formula E (electric) racer, it was time to implement a battery swap scheme in a standard car.

Ely Schless converted a new '92 Geo Metro to electric propulsion. A receptacle was installed so that a battery pack could be inserted from underneath the car. A steel case was built to contain the batteries and interconnects, forming a module. A trunk-mounted winch could lower, raise, and hold the battery module in place.

Applied commercially, battery exchange technology (BET), would look different. Here, the machinery to perform

Fig. 2-43: A winch in the trunk lowers the battery pack in a few seconds' time.

The Geometric was designed to prove that an EV need not be limited in range. Everything about the conversion of the Geo Metro to electric propulsion was standard—except the battery-swapping scheme that was implemented (Application A11).

How did it work? In the prototype, when the GeoMetric's driver wanted a fresh battery pack, he (or she) drove up behind a fresh (fully-charged) battery module, parked, opened the trunk, and operated a winch, dropping the depleted pack (3 sec). A quick walk around the car unhooked the anchors (10 sec). The car was then pushed (or "motored" using the onboard auxiliary battery) to a position directly over the fresh pack (15 sec). The anchors were then re-affixed to the module (10 sec). The winch was operated, pulling the module up into the receptacle flush with the bottom of the car (4 sec).

By this method, then, a 1,200-lb pack is exchanged in 42 seconds' time.

Applied commercially, an EV owner could drive into any battery-exchange station and follow a similar process (review Techtalk T47, Chapter 6). The exchange could be initiated with a credit card (a "BatCard"). The car's type and size of battery pack would be identified, and the driver would be queried on possible options, i.e., size and type of battery pack desired. The BatCard would debit the owner's account for the exchange service and credit the account for any energy remaining in the old pack. The battery pack would then be exchanged automatically in 30-60 seconds.

Fig. 2-45: The battery module is disconnected from the vehicle.

the exchange would typically be built into a stationary structure and operate like a cross between a service station and a car wash.

The Geometric clearly proved that a depleted 1,200-lb battery module could be quickly and easily exchanged for a freshly charged one. The low, centralized battery pack yields good stability and handling, increases side-impact protection in the car, and gives this EV "unlimited range" with existing battery technology.

A duplicate of the Geometric that Ely built for a client currently holds the world record for miles traveled in a 24-hour period (1,348 miles) by an electric vehicle. (See Application A58 for more detail on the Geometric battery exchange system.

Fig. 2-46: The Geometric moves over the fresh battery pack.

Fig. 2-47: Once removed, the depleted battery pack is ready for servicing and recharge.

An Electric Porsche

Car lovers know that something is amiss when they pull up alongside John Sprinkle's 1949 Glockler Porsche at a stoplight. The attractive styling and metallic pewter color naturally attract any meandering eye. But the curiosity is soon replaced with puzzlement. Even tuned engines produce some noise at idle—this one is dead silent. A Porsche owner that stops his engine to save on gas? No way!

The mystery deepens when John gets the green light and pulls away from a stop. Instead of a throaty whisper, this one smoothly accelerates to speed with a slight whine. What's it got under there? A turbine? Nope. It's an electric motor!

Fig. 2-48: Electric propulsion complements the quiet of a morning drive in the foothills.

All photos of this conversion: David Chung (M. Hackleman Collection)

Fig. 2-49: Opening the "trunk" exposes the electric drivetrain.

Fig. 2-50: The electric motor, controller, cooling blower, and other controls take up little room in this EV.

Application

A 12

An Electric Porsche

John Sprinkle started his project of building an EV in 1985, purchasing a fiberglass replica of a 1949 Glockler Porsche—the predecessor of the popular 1950s Speedster—from Mroz Coachbuilding. The kit was designed to fit a VW Bug chassis.

Initially, John was enchanted with the idea of a hybrid. (The fear of getting "stuck out" was strong.) Like many early EV builders, his first design used an aircraft generator for a motor, and used an 8HP Kubota diesel engine-generator as an additional source of electricity. Six 12-Volt Diehard batteries, wired as two paralleled 36V sets, formed the battery pack.

The first test drive was a bad experience. The engine produced mostly vibration and noise. Overall performance was poor. But, with 2 years of hard work and thousands of dollars invested in the vehicle, John wasn't ready to give up just yet.

An Improved Design

After completing vehicle registration with the DMV, John took a hard look at the overall design and components — engine, motor, battery type, and voltage.

John decided to get rid of the hybrid setup. He also swapped the inefficient aircraft generator "motor" for a G.E. 21HP series motor. The battery pack underwent two changes: type and number. Deep-cycle batteries (Alco 2200) were installed and the overall pack voltage was increased to 96V. Perseverance paid off. The new propulsion system more than doubled the previous performance.

What does John like most about his vehicle? He's got a list. "It's quiet! It

Opening the engine compartment proves it once and for all. There's no engine block, belts, wires, pumps, or generators. Inside, there's a cylinder the size of a water cooler bottle stuck onto the bell housing — the electric motor. A blower assembly, complete with air hoses, is there, ready to help cool the motor at high speeds. That rectangular black box is the electronic controller. Cables as thick as your thumb connect all the pieces together.

Is This a Conversion?

Many early EV enthusiasts discovered the viability of electrifying a VW chassis. John Sprinkle's Porsche takes this one step further (Application A12). By perusing the wide assortment of fiberglass body styles that are custom-built to fit the VW chassis, John got the body style he wanted without the weight or expense of the original vehicle. This conversion, then, is a mix of two major subassemblies—a common chassis and a lightweight body.

The most serious challenge John faced was battery placement. John took advantage of the lack of doors, mounting a singular file of batteries in each of the thwarts, the side panels of the car body. Each thwart contains 5 deep-cycle 6-Volt batteries. Another six batteries cluster directly behind the two bucket seats in the passenger compartment, completing the battery pack. Wired in series, the 16 batteries make up the car's 96V battery pack.

The overall weight of Sprinkle's Porsche is a relatively low 2,500 pounds. Top speed is 65 mph. Acceleration from 0 to 50 mph is a respectable 9 seconds. At a 60-mile street range, a 40-mile freeway range (at 55 mph), and a 90-mile maximum range, this is serious transportation.

doesn't produce any emissions. There's virtually no maintenance. And — I don't have to buy gasoline for it!" Charging by a Lestermatic dual charger takes 8-10 hours at the slow charge rate.

John had some words for the fledgling EV enthusiast who's thinking about doing a conversion. "After taking a ride in an EV, find a system you like and duplicate it." Homework is John's next suggestion. "Read everything you can on electric vehicles and conversions — by people who have experience," John says. This saves hard dollars and lots of frustration. "For a while there," John recalls, "I dreaded the midweek thought of working on the EV the upcoming weekend."

A common mistake of EV enthusiasts is the early purchase of the battery pack. "I was optimistic about the amount of time it would take me to do my project," John admits. "By the time it was finished, so were the batteries! They had sulfated from disuse."

Fig. 2-51: Some of the propulsion batteries are situated forward of the motor compartment.

Does he use the Porsche for other than commuting? "You bet!" John exclaims. "If it's still light when I get home and the weather is nice, I like to take it out for a spin. I have to be careful in shopping malls," he warns, "Nobody hears me coming! But it's a pretty nice feeling to pass all the gas stations right by!"

Fig. 2-52: The remainder of the batteries are mounted in the thwarts (where the doors would normally be).

The Go-4

An ideal niche for EVs is the utility service vehicle. Both industry and municipal fleets have fixed routes and fixed mileages. This takes the guesswork out of fitting EVs into the daily routine. Assign the EV to any route that fits its demonstrated range. The benefit is more than lower operating costs. They can help a municipal fleet meet the CAFE (average fuel efficiency) standards and pollution-abatement mandates.

Fig. 2-53: The Go-4 is designed for utility service on the streets.

An ideal niche for EVs is the utility service vehicle. Both industry and municipal fleets have fixed routes and fixed mileages.

Fig. 2-54: The Go-4 uses a series motor and a drivetrain adapted from the automotive industry.

Application A 13   The Go-4

The Go-4 was designed around a Ford Festiva engine and drivetrain. Ely Schless (Schless Engineering) opted to use the stock drivetrain for the convenience of the mounting points. Except for 1st and 2nd gear, all gears (including reverse) were removed from the transmission. An 8-inch (17HP) Advanced DC motor was adapted to the transmission. A Model 1221 Curtis PMC controller links up with the accelerator pedal for motor speed control.

A 12V vacuum system handles power brakes and pneumatically shifts vehicle speeds between the two gears. In low (1st gear), the overall drive ratio is 13.3:1. In high (2nd gear), the drive ratio drops to 7.3:1. The driver selects low for a 0-30 mph range, useful for marking vehicles or

One example is the Go-4, a two-person utility vehicle designed exclusively for service in meter citations. Originally manufactured with a gas engine by Westward Industries in Manitoba, Canada, a half-dozen of them have been converted by Schless Engineering to electric propulsion (Application A13). A re-engineered Go-4 frame is on the drawing board. It will better accommodate the battery pack.

In the conversion, the low-mounted battery pack increases the vehicle's weight and stability. With a BVWR (battery-to-vehicle weight ratio) of 41%, most of the Go-4's weight is assisting propulsion, supplying a dependable 45-mile range, most of it stop-and-go.

Fig. 2-55: The Go-4 has doors that slide easily and lock solidly.

climbing extreme grades. High gives a broader, 0-50 mph range, helping move the Go-4 to and from a work area. A DPDT contactor provides electric reverse.

The battery pack consists of eighteen (18) 6V sealed, glass-matte lead-acid batteries wired in series for 108V. The original 1,400-lb vehicle weight increased to 2,400 pounds after conversion.

Fig. 2-56: The batteries are serviced by opening the rear cover.

Fig. 2-57: The exo-skeleton framework gives that warm-tummy feeling to a small vehicle.

Fig. 2-58: Tom Carpenter finds the electrified Mule a perfect vehicle for the many microclimates on the big island of Hawaii.

An Electric Mule

Harry MacDonald manages the production of awapuhi (Hawaiian ginger) on a 67-acre organic farm outside of Hilo, on the big island of Hawaii. He wanted a work vehicle that would haul compost, deliver machinery for maintenance *without* breaking up the fragile turf, and emit no exhaust. To this end, Harry called in Tom Carpenter to convert a 2WD Kawasaki 500 Mule to electric propulsion (Application A14).

The Mule's steady work is hauling compost around the farm. The four-foot-square flatbed is designed for dumping, tilting to drop its load.

All photos of this conversion: Tom Carpenter and Michael Hackleman

*A*pplication
*A*14

An Electric Mule

In the first step of converting a Kawasaki 2WD Mule to electric propulsion, Tom Carpenter removed the engine, transmission, and engine-related components. A 3/8-inch aluminum motor mount was welded together and bolted to the original engine mounting holes. A 6HP Advanced DC series motor was coupled to the locking differential (internal 6:1 ratio) with a 1:1 ratio of timing belt pulleys.

The potbox for the Curtis 1205-201 controller (36-48V, 350A) was connected through the existing throttle cable to the footpedal. Forward and reverse are handled through the stock (mechanical) linkage. A DC contactor was selected for keyswitch operation, and a DC-DC converter handles 12VDC (aux) loads. A dual main circuit breaker was added to isolate the battery pack from the vehicle for servicing. With a wet climate in mind, Tom installed the controller, contactor, pot box, meter shunts, and a 12VDC fuse strip inside a plastic Carlon box. An outdoor timer box, mounted under the front seat, houses the circuit breaker near the driver.

There was room for six batteries in the Mule, five in the rear and one under the single front seat. Would the batteries be 6V or 12V? Since the vehicle was intended for farm work, rather than recreational or street use, Tom opted for 6V batteries, for a pack voltage of 36V.

Sealed, absorbed-glass matte, deep-cycle batteries were selected for the Mule. Used in wheelchairs and other motive power applications, the Concorde 6V batteries weigh 68 lbs each, are rated at 180Ah (20-hour rate), and use lug terminals. To support the five batteries, Tom fashioned an aluminum frame from 1-1/4 inch aluminum angle and popriveted it together. The sixth battery of the pack is mounted on the metal floor just under the front seat.

Fig. 2-59: The controller and other system components are enclosed in water-tight boxes.

Fig. 2-60: The DC series motor ensures good torque at low RPM.

A drop-pin hitch secures a trailer that adds an additional 0.5 cubic yard of capacity. Sometimes the Mule is on roads of dirt and loose gravel. Other times, it's on slick turf. It routinely transports mowers and weedwackers to work areas.

The Mule is solar-charged. Originally, it was designed to recharge from one of the three solar energy stations located on the awapuhi farm. Also, Tom re-rigged the Mule's system to power tools at remote sites directly (with an inverter), avoiding the use of an engine-generator. The silent ac power was an instant success. Remarkably, the 6-Amp charge rate from solar panels installed on the Mule's roll bar kept the battery pack topped off despite the constant drain of power tools through the workday. Drivers got into the habit of always parking the Mule in the sun. After four months of continuous operation, Tom realized that the Mule had never been plugged into even one of the solar stations!

How about performance? In a trial run, Tom went 35 miles at an average speed of 13.8 mph, with the top speed (downhill) reaching 27 mph. Adding two more batteries (bringing the pack up to 48VDC) brought the Mule's average speed up to 17 mph for the same distance of 35 miles.

Fig. 2-61: The electric Mule's quietness is a blessing for field work in wildlife areas.

Far from utility lines, the Mule is charged by solar power. Initially, it was designed to recharge from several solar "stations" sited throughout the land. Each station is composed of a dual-axis solar array (15 Solec S100s), a battery pack (24VDC, 1,400Ah capacity), and an inverter (Trace 4024 sine-wave 4kW, 120vac). A K&W charger (120vac input, 24VDC output) was purchased to recharge the Mule's batteries.

A subsequent expansion of the Mule's role revealed an alternate charging system. A new building was planned. Normally, the Mule would lug a 5000 Watt generator to a worksite when power tools were needed. Instead, Tom tried out an idea, rigging the Mule as the power source. He attached a quick-release plug to a Trace inverter (36VDC input, 120vac output) to tie into the battery pack. Since the Mule would be sitting all day at the building site, Tom also installed three 100-Watt Solec panels on the Mule's roll bar assembly. A Heliotrope CC20 charge controller was added to protect the batteries from overcharge.

The silent ac power was an instant success, with the meager solar input keeping pace with the intermittent high-power consumption from tools.

At any time, the Mule's driver can scan the dashboard-mounted ammeter and voltmeter to check battery condition. Tom plans to replace them with something simple, like an Ananda Smart Light. The Smart Light is a 3-color display that, through steady or flashing lights at various setpoints, tells the operator the battery's SOC (state of charge).

A cycle computer (VELO) was added to watch vehicle speed, distance, and time. It also recorded the maximum speed and accumulated distance. The magnetic sensor was glued to the left rear wheel, the magnetic pickup was secured to a brake line, and the computer was calibrated to the tire's circumference.

What did it all cost? The basic conversion kit ($2,160), battery pack ($600), DC-DC converter ($190), and miscellaneous hardware and aluminum angle ($250) totaled $3,200. Add to this 30 hours of Tom's time. And this was a prototype!

Fig. 2-62: A gearbelt delivers motor power to the stock transmission, eliminating the less efficient infinite-ratio drive unit.

An Electric Ox

I am not surprised at Tom's success in using the Mule as a silent and mobile power source. My first EV was a revived industrial electric vehicle that I transformed into a farm vehicle. Its 36V battery pack was a close match for use with my farm's 32-Volt, wind-generated electricity.

For seven years, Ox was our farm's workhorse vehicle (Application A15). It traversed every kind of terrain. Its series motor would kick in the torque to tackle the steepest grade or the softest ground. The heavy duty FNR (forward-neutral-reverse) switch and the accelerator pedal were the only operator controls. No meters or other instrumentation were ever installed. The original six-position series-resistance controller proved adequate for our needs.

The greatest discovery with Ox was that an EV is a *portable power station*. I rigged up a receptacle box on Ox's side. Wherever we went, we could plug in a variety of 32V tools — a drill, cutoff saw, welder, etc. Eventually, an inverter added 110vac capability to the mix. I spent whole afternoons typing away out in a meadow with Ox parked silently nearby, supplying the power for the electric typewriter. I wrote big pieces of several of my books out there! When I sold my farm, Ox stayed to give the same service to the new owner.

My fondest memory of my 10-year adventure in farm living outside of Mariposa, California is the way that Ox and my windmachines complemented the silence of the land that surrounded our home.

Fig. 2-63: Wind-generated electricity was used to recharge Ox.

Fig. 2-64: Ox was our favorite way to give a tour of the alternative energy projects on the farm.

A pplication
15
An Electric OX

My career in electric vehicles began with a humble conversion. I found the original chassis for Ox, an industrial vehicle, abandoned in a Goodwill resale yard in Orange County in 1973. It looked awful. A closer inspection revealed good tires, a motor and gearbox free of smoke or oil deposits, and a solid frame. It had six 6V deep cycle batteries below the flatbed. We bought it, coaxed it up into a flatbed truck, and drove it home.

I tried for a month to revitalize the batteries (understanding very little about sulfation at that point). They gassed so badly during charge that eventually a spark blew one of them up and I traded them in for a new set.

Modifications

While I was undecided about what I wanted to do with this vehicle, its ungainly front end wasn't part of *any*

Conversion as a Business

The fantasy of every EV enthusiast is the ability to purchase a "glider." A glider is a commercially-manufactured car that does not have an engine or related components (fuel, cooling, and exhaust hardware).

In theory, if it were possible to snatch a car off the assembly line before these components were added, the work of adapting a car to electric propulsion would be reduced by 30-40%. Furthermore, if the absence of these parts (and the labor to install them) were reflected in the list price of the glider, it should sell for only 50-60% of the pricetag for the complete car!

Imagine the implications! You could choose a car of any color from a dozen different makes and have it delivered directly to the shop that would do your conversion.

The smart automaker could take this process further still. It could make the glider available with oversize suspension components. This is not as difficult as it seems. The range of models (and options) available each year from a major automaker often includes the ability to interchange components among models to handle different loads and applications. For example, my '92 Honda VX uses springs from a Honda Prelude, a car that normally weighs 1,000 lbs more than the stock VX. As an electric, the VX weighs the same as the Prelude. There's no modification involved in the installation of the springs. They are a straight bolt-up.

Making Gliders A Reality

At this time, automakers are unwilling to supply gliders. Why? Liability issues and attributes of the assembly line head the list (Techtalk T4).

Manufacturing cars is a business. Berating an automaker for the lack of gliders or appealing to them to produce gliders is unlikely to get much further than the corporate communications office.

Presenting a business plan is something else altogether. Automakers understand proposals and business plans. Approach them with one. Address *their* issues. Show that you've done your homework. Crunch the numbers. Give 'em tables, graphs, or charts they can read. They're busy people. Keep it brief. How is what you want to do going to benefit them?

> *A glider is a commercially-manufactured car that does not have an engine or related components.*

---

scheme. I set about with a torch to cut it off. Once done, I was surprised at how much it had weighed. Suddenly, I had a very spry electric!

I had fantasized great things for this EV. In the end, the reality of what I *did* have soaked in. Instead of adapting it to be a street machine, I worked within its constraints to build something for use around the farm. I bolted in a new front seat and rigged up a tiller for steering. I welded together a front assembly to protect the passenger and driver, and the steering, brake and accelerator linkages. I named it Ox.

Ox plugged directly into our windmachine(s) whenever it was not in use. This helped it maintain a high state-of-charge. A monthly water and hydrometer check, equalizing charge, and battery washdown was the only care it got. It was a happy feeling to drive around the farm on wind-watts.

Eventually, I restored an old 220-Watt vibrator-type inverter for use in Ox. It supplied 110vac (60-cycle) directly from Ox's 36V battery bank for soldering irons, power tools, and even my typewriter.

Fig. 2-65: On the farm, Ox helped move stuff from one place to another.

Automakers and Gliders

Generally, automakers are unwilling to supply gliders. Why? Liability issues and practical limitations of the assembly line are two reasons.

Liability. To supply a glider, in a legal sense, supports and condones the notion of the BYO (build your own) car. In truth, the automaker has no idea (or control of) what an individual will do with the glider. Judging from the quality of workmanship I've seen in most owner-converted cars, I can appreciate their concern.

So what, you say? In the USA, if an injury or accident occurs with a conversion based on a glider, a lawsuit is certain to notice the "deep pockets" of the automakers. Whether or not they are in any way responsible is not an issue. In a jury trial, responsibility is often the victim of sympathy. It's impossible for a large company to keep a low profile in these matters. A big company is a big target.

The Assembly Line. The assembly line is another stumbling block in acquiring a glider. An assembly line, after all, is the more visible part of the process that aims to mass produce a product. At what point do you pull the car off and make it available as a glider? For example, some wiring is necessary for functions present in either an ICE or electric car, i.e., headlights, turn signals, rear window defogger, etc. In the same bundle are wires directly related to controlling, monitoring, or adjusting engine functions. How is one separated from the other?

Upon closer inspection, the main assembly line is merely the final stage of production. It is, in turn, supported by many hundreds of assembly lines that produce components, subassemblies, and wiring harnesses. Backing up further, we find many layers of design work and schedules so that everything is available at the right time and place. At a minimum, a glider would have to "leapfrog" through the main assembly line to ensure its completeness even if ICE propulsion hardware is absent.

For an automaker to build a glider, then, ripples all the way back to the drawing board itself.

What makes it worth their while to listen to what you say? Address the relevant issues (Techtalk T5).

An automaker that supplies you with gliders is going to want the electric components warranted and to feel assured that replacements can be obtained quickly. Components with SAE ratings help a lot.

The volume of your order will be important. Smaller automakers will more easily handle a small volume, but even this may feel like a large number to you.

Don't worry too much about a vehicle being an import. General Motors (GM), Ford, and Chrysler corporations do not manufacture lightweight, fuel efficient cars. To meet CAFE standards for fuel efficiencies in fleets in the USA, they make deals with smaller automakers overseas for parts, components, and subassemblies. These are imported, assembled with other components, and sold under a new name. The distinction between foreign and domestic cars is blurred by this process.

Fig. 2-67: Traffic enforcement has gotten the word that EVs can go fast.

Fig. 2-68: Suzuki manufactures the parts that make up this Geo Metro.

It may be possible to re-design some components to make the conversion process even simpler. For example, I cut a hole in the midsection of my '92 Honda Civic VX to accommodate batteries. The primary battery box, then, is positioned low and in the center of the car. The piece I cut into is actually one large piece of shaped (stamped) metal that is welded to other similarly stamped metal pieces and structural members.

This one piece of shaped metal, then, could be redesigned to BE the battery box, and be installed in place of the other one on the assembly line. Of course, because of the greater weight (once the batteries are installed), the structural members might also require re-design. The point is: an electrified Honda is more *similar* to a Honda of the same model with an engine than it is *different*.

One tough cookie is meeting vehicle safety standards. A small manufacturer, producing and selling only several dozen vehicles a year, will be exempt from many standards that apply to companies mass producing thousands. Still, make certain that the vehicle you select will meet import standards.

Finally, be realistic about your own market. The attrition rate of small, well-intended vehicle manufacturers is high. Seeing a need and filling it are two different things. Without a solid marketing plan, good machines sit idle and gather dust.

*T*echtalk

T₅ Bargaining for Gliders

Generate a plan to be eligible for gliders. Address key issues. How would your plan work? How much trouble will it be? Can it be done? How much will it cost? If you still want to proceed after you've generated it, good. Learn the automobile manufacturing trade. Speak their language.

Some suggestions:

• Take a sample assembly procedure for a car that would make a good EV candidate. List the thousands of steps, in the series and parallel lines, used to make it. Identify what is the same and different between car and glider.

• Use warranted components. Automakers warrant their cars and the components in them. They deal with thousands of vendors called OEMs (original equipment manufacturers). Prices, delivery volumes and dates, schedules, what will happen if there are failures — these are all agreed to beforehand. If something doesn't work, the automaker needs to know the OEM will replace or fix it. If it is shown to be a high-failure item, will it be redesigned? Recalls are *very* expensive.

• Obtain supplier lists. Know your suppliers. Will they be there tomorrow? Service centers and parts houses will want to order and stock the parts used.

• Use SAE ratings. Automotive standards are 2-3 times better than most industry hardware. Why? If a compressor fails in a supermarket, the two phone calls made are to a technician (to fix the problem) and a wholesaler (to replace the food that goes bad). When a component fails in a car, the two phone calls may be to the coroner and a lawyer. There's a big difference in the consequences of a failure. Little wonder that SAE ratings on components are similar to those used in aviation and space flight.

• Establish a volume. Automakers rarely do any custom work. That's left to after-market houses. How big an order are you going to make? You might shudder at the idea of delivering a thousand cars. To the major automakers, this is peanuts. For them, modifications to the manufacturing process are only cost-effective when they number in the tens (or hundreds) of thousands of units.

• Approach smaller automakers. The Geo Metro is a popular, lightweight car sold by General Motors in the USA. GM does not make it. They import the components and *assemble* it here. Where does it come from? Look for a Suzuki Swift. Look familiar? That's right—same car. The difference is that the Swift is produced and assembled overseas and imported into the USA.

• Meet import standards. There are hundreds of good vehicle designs circulating in the world market. Do they *qualify* for US import? Will they meet DOT (and other) standards. Crashworthiness is a *big* issue.

• Tailpipe emissions are another issue. The fact that you don't plan to use anything that would need to be smog-checked will not magically open any doors. A formidable bureaucratic wall stands between the manufacturer and the consumer. The US is one of the tougher ones. "Likes paperwork" is an important skill on your bio sheet for this undertaking.

• Nothing short of the momentum of a sizeable corporation is likely to penetrate the paperwork to pursue vehicle qualification on a number of fronts. There are volumes of specifications from each of many agencies you must deal with in this process. Crash testing for *one* design can cost a million dollars a pop!

• Establish your market. There are a large number of hobbyists and auto enthusiasts who would love to talk about the possibility of buying a glider. Can you gather them together? Or reach all of them? Will they commit? Are they willing to give you a sizeable, non-refundable deposit? Can they agree on the color? On one car, one year? Will they wait while you go through the process?

The fact is: not that many people want to *build* their own car. And when they buy it, they expect it to come with a *warranty*.

Chapter 3
The Scratchbuilt EV

A scratchbuilt electric vehicle is one built from the ground up to be electric. It is the alternative to the conversion of a stock, commercially-manufactured vehicle. A scratchbuilt goes by many names. Prototype. One-of-a-kind. Proof of concept. Testbed. Rolling your own. Custom-built. The scratchbuilt electric vehicle is all of these things.

The primary attribute of a scratchbuilt vehicle is that it may be the only way to get exactly what you want in an EV.

Fig. 3-1: A lightweight, aerodynamic electric vehicle.

Photo: Solectria Corporation

When it's done right, the scratchbuilt vehicle usually demonstrates the best that electric propulsion has to offer. Here, the creator is truly originating the design rather than modifying an existing one.

The attraction a scratchbuilt holds for the designer is that no design factor has been compromised. It's a clean slate. Weight, aerodynamic drag, and drivetrain efficiency are just so much clay in the hand. What do you want it to look like? What do you want it to do?

Easy, Fast, or Inexpensive?

Contrary to popular thought, the scratchbuilt EV is *not* the fastest, easiest, or least expensive way to own an EV. Building a vehicle from the ground up is a big, big job. It will take a long time to do, and it will probably cost as much as a conversion would. Maybe more. There *is* a pricetag for the freedom of having exactly what you want.

Automakers, in many ways, make it all look so easy to do.

Build a Model

Do you have a "better" idea? Make a scale model that perfectly describes your idea.

"What?" you say. "Make a model? I don't know how to do that!" If you can't make a model of the car you want (and like how it looks), you're already in trouble. Unless you can buy your way out of this situation, you have *very* little chance of building a prototype that will satisfy you for very long. More likely, you'll give up before you get very far.

Successful scratchbuilt vehicles are likely to begin with a model (Techtalk T6). Make it to scale or the fantasy will never become a reality. An advantage of the scale test model is that its aerodynamics can be checked in a windtunnel.

Are You Qualified?

I love to pipedream all kinds of prototypes. In reality, many of them stay in that place. That is, I would never try to flesh them out. I may have the dream, but dreams are whimsical. What if the dream disappears in the middle of the project?

If you think you'd like to scratchbuild an EV, you must first pass a test. Ask yourself these questions and await honest answers. Do you have the necessary skills? Time? Money? Talent?

The Test Model

T6 *Techtalk*

What is a model good for? A model is a good way to check component positions and driver ergonometry, and vehicle aerodynamics in a windtunnel.

Build a model of what you want in a vehicle. Use wood dowels, modeling balsa, or straws for the spaceframe. Once completed, analyze the relative position of components and the structural support needed for the driver, subassemblies, powertrain, electronic/electrical components and shell. CAD analysis is great, if available. Just perform this analysis.

Don't overrate components in the full-size version. For example, tubing sizes should vary in the design. If they don't, the frame is either too heavy or too weak.

Windtunnel Testing

The aerodynamic testing of scale models of various designs remains the best option for selecting the shape and layout of a scratchbuilt EV. Small windtunnel test facilities are available in the engineering departments of many colleges and universities. A good presentation before an open-minded staff can get a model into one of these tunnels, usually with some student help. The test usually takes just a few minutes. It supplies critical information on the drag coefficient and components of pitch, roll, and yaw.

Here are some thoughts on a successful test in a windtunnel.

Scale. Each model tested should be to scale, i.e., 1/6th or 1/4th, for calibration reasons.

Size. Select the largest scale that will fit, including the ability to rotate the model 20-30 degrees to the left or right to check for the effect of sideforces (i.e., wind, or gusts from passing trucks). The larger the scale, the better the accuracy.

Finish. A 1/6th scale model will be subjected to very high wind velocities to simulate the airflow of a full-scale vehicle at normal road speeds. The scale model should be precisely made and finished to a smooth, high-gloss finish. Build it strong, too.

Conclusions. The test of a model is—a test of a model. It gives you a reasonable idea of what power is required to move that shape through the air at normal vehicle speeds. Actual horsepower requirements will be greater in the full-scale version. Estimate a bit high on losses and a bit low on efficiency and you'll be satisfied with the vehicle's performance.

Perspective. Texts on aerodynamic design suggest the construction of a vehicle with a low frontal area. However, it's important to remember that you want a vehicle layout and profile that encloses and helps support the subsystem components and driver. Sleek designs that ignore driver comfort and safety or the serviceability of the vehicle are only short-term winners.

Patience? Knowledge? Experience? Ability to budget? What's your ETC (estimated time of completion)? Shop space? Do you have the tools? Tool-working skills?

Do you have a goal or is this just a project? Make certain that you have all the prerequisites (Techtalk T7).

Ultimately, a scratch-built EV requires an evaluation of competence and ability. Few people *can* build an EV. Fewer still *will* build one. That's just as well. Thousands of pounds of human and machine hurtling along at 55 mph is horribly unforgiving of design or construction error.

Getting Help

The next best thing to doing it yourself is finding someone who is qualified *and* will work under your direction (Techtalk T8). Automotive mechanics, machinists, metalworkers, engineers, and designers abound. A successful EV prototype will require *all* of these skills. You may find one person who possesses these skills. In the end, you want someone who understands the challenges of any kind of project and the range of skills that must be brought to bear to complete it.

This chapter reveals the successful efforts of many individuals and groups that have transformed ideas into reality. As you browse through the pictures and descriptions, try to see behind the scenes. Look for the focus, the energy, and the resolve behind the shape and substance of the machine.

Many of these projects required teamwork. Some people don't like to design by "committee." However, a good team will often

Fig. 3-2: Students at CSLA test a model in the college windtunnel.

Photo: Stan Carstensen (CSLA)

carry a project faster and further than an individual effort (Techtalk T9). Even if you wouldn't do it for yourself, how about one for your community? A project makes it possible to solicit funding, and that means local jobs (Techtalk T10). Successive projects make sponsorship progressively easier to find.

EV Subassemblies

The wise scratchbuilder does not re-invent the wheel. Instead, this person uses subsystems, like steering subassemblies, and brakes and suspension systems from other vehicles or applications. The right combination of these subassemblies can result in a lightweight, efficient, aerodynamic vehicle.

Hardware stores are *not* a good place to shop for parts for a scratchbuilt EV. The car is a low-tech, low-speed ballistic missile. If commercial hardware has an engineering and safety value of one (1), industrial hardware is three (3) and automotive hardware is five (5). The normal wear and tear of driving demands a tough, reliable, well-engineered, and sensibly-constructed vehicle.

Are you experimenting or are you trying to build a solid piece of transportation? Vehicle layout, the proper location of vehicle cg (center of gravity), and other factors demand evolved

Thousands of pounds of human and machine hurtling along at 55 mph is horribly unforgiving of design or construction error.

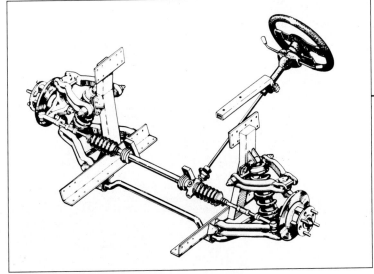

T_7 echtalk
Prototyping Prerequisites

Prototyping your own vehicle is a devilish temptation. The propulsive requirements of a high-performance, lightweight, aerodynamic EV are absurdly simple.

Of course, for your project to succeed, you must possess:

- **Savvy.** The ability to define the relationship between any two of the following factors: performance, safety, acceleration, speed, hill climbing ability, range, environmentally-benign technologies, recycling, maneuverability, crashworthiness, aerodynamics, lightweight construction, cost/benefit ratios, and prototype development standards.
- **Knowledge.** A smattering of knowledge about batteries, motors, control systems, steering, suspension, brake systems, fiberglass construction, electricity, and electronics.
- **Experience.** What sub-assemblies are lightweight or otherwise useful to your vehicle, i.e., Pinto or Baha Buggy steering, brake, and suspension systems.
- **Demonstrated skills** in drafting, design, fiberglassing, survival, diaper-changing, massage, and singing before hostile crowds.
- **Attitude.** It helps to feel okay about being a half-bubble shy of level, and to have lots of friends that fit that description. If you don't have disposable income and a dedicated space, you get creative. What's creative? A strong ability to mesmerize curious skeptics and convert them into workers willing to perform menial, dirty tasks for long hours at no pay while retaining the feeling of how lucky they are to be working with you. The *Huckleberry Finn* touch.

Okay, do you still feel teased into building your own EV? Great! Give it *lots* of thought, glean every bit of info you can from anyone who is doing anything that looks interesting, and go at it. Please — be careful. Too little knowledge is *so* dangerous. None of what is written here is gospel truth. The final arrangement of this stuff—into something you'll drive down the road—evolves from a process. Winnow through the factors and see what fits.

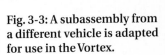

Fig. 3-3: A subassembly from a different vehicle is adapted for use in the Vortex.

Drawing: Dolphin Vehicles

Building Your Own EV

Olof Sundin

I have become convinced that our society largely defines reality on the basis of our short-term conveniences. Despite evidence that our rate of depletion and pollution is "unsustainable, many believe that consumerism is a path to happiness. That's a nice way of saying they commit robbery and violence against future generations.

Cars such as the Impact are still built with the "life-of-the-planet-threatening" mind-set of excessive weight, power, and equipment. Home-built conversions, the Peugeot 205, and the Fiat Panda Electra are too heavy. The very talent and energy of the build-it-yourself'ers ("Anyone can build their own car!") prevents the spread of EVs. The overwhelming majority of people simply cannot or will not build their own. Body styles range from simply unstylish to the totally absurd and largely do not express the essence of a "no-noise, limited power/range, minimal depletion/pollution" approach.

All the technology, equipment, and know-how is available for a car that could do the following on hydropower (grid source) and PVs alone.

• Carry 2 persons maximum daily 10 miles freeway, 5 miles city, 10 miles freeway (return), plus 10 miles suburbia.

• Be reliable and mechanically sound and safe.

I look at "safe" within the perspective of being a bicycler and a motorbiker. I drove CV-2's and even a 3-wheel Messerschmitt car in my youth. The current 1-2 ton car is *not* "safe" for future generations because of depletion and pollution, and the larger cars are unsafe vis-a-vis the smaller, and ought to be restricted.

Not having realized the full implications of the above, our family cannot "afford" to have an expert build the car above for its true development and labor cost. We would never spend $20-40K for cars, anyway.

With some luck and persistence, we have found people with the engineering and mechanical skills who are helping to build various elements of the car above, as they share our outlook on the environment and transportation. We are providing some capital, support, promotion, and some help with related/unrelated work.

I am adding 200-400 Watts of solar panels to our car. Only ultralight, expensive race cars with huge panels can run on solar alone. So, the panels add weight and cost and risk (of damage) but will extend the range. Besides, it shows PV technology wherever we drive and reminds us how costly and involved it really is to generate power, and how it is only too easy to squander it.

The car is frugal but it will be weatherproof and have a modest heater. I will be happy to be out of the destructive and addictive ICE (internal combustion engine) loop.

technology. If you don't know what I mean, you shouldn't be building a vehicle for the road. Sponsor a project if you must, but stay out of the design side. Such ignorance is not habit-forming. You may only kill yourself, but you may take others with you.

Dann Parks has a word for what's needed. Invest. Actually, in *VEST (*Vision, Energy, Structure, and Time.

Street or Work EV?

Building an EV from the ground up will quickly bog down in compromises if you just walk out to the shop and start cutting metal. A more sensible plan is to write and sketch everything that you can about what you want. Is the vehicle intended to transport people (street) or have utility (work)? There's a big difference (Techtalk T11).

Think Legal

An EV that will spend any time on the roads must be certified, registered, and licensed. Purchase a copy of the Vehicular Code (current year) for your state (TechTalk T12). Look it over for anything that might apply to an EV. Don't let your idea get snagged by a technicality!

Three-wheeled scratchbuilt EVs hold a bureaucratic edge over most 4-wheeled vehicles—they're treated as motorcycles! See Chapter 4 for licensing, registering, and insuring larger three-wheelers.

Fig. 3-4:
Small EVs are a
big hit
in the annual
Tour de Sol
in Switzerland.

Photo: C. Michael Lewis

The local Highway Patrol office is a place to ask questions. For registering and licensing the vehicle, DMV inspectors will make certain the Vehicular Code is upheld. If you are planning something unusual, find out what's needed for registration. You may be referred elsewhere. Wherever you have to go, get the information *before* you proceed. Hopefully, none of the requirements will be anything that you didn't already have on your list.

Aesthetics

Aesthetics is a matter of personal preference. Should it be a design factor? Buckminster Fuller was once asked the same question by a member of an audience. He replied (something to the effect), "No. Aesthetics is not a design factor. However, when we are finished, if the design does not *look* beautiful, then we know that something is wrong."

DESIGN ELEMENTS

It took building a solar car for me to get a handle on the relative importance of the many design elements in building a car. Power input, efficiency, weight, aerodynamics, and rolling resistance dominate in the solar car arena. Riding shotgun on these factors is reliability. To win a race, you must first *cross* the finish line.

Techtalk 9 — Starting a Project

The attributes of a successful project include a good proposal, talent, reliability, communication, and timing.

• *Proposal.* A good proposal is important. It solidifies dreams, defines goals, and promises ability and capacity. It is as essential to the team as it is for getting sponsorship.

Beyond an outline defining the five W's (what, why, who, where, and when), expect to do some research. Review articles, papers, books, and videotapes of similar projects. Demonstrate an awareness of *other* projects. Clarify how this one is unique.

• *Project Talent.* Many projects are funded on the basis of the people involved, not on the specific machinery that will be built. The team must be credible. Sponsors must feel assured that the project will be handled competently and finished. Bringing an expert in for some consulting may add a strong element to the project proposal. The project must be administered and managed. Who will do this? A range of skills and experience in the team will make it more solid. Skillful coordination and scheduling will avoid wasting donated time.

• *Reliability.* The project must work as a system. The reliability of the system is no greater than its weakest part.

• *Communication.* Communication is essential. It builds the proposal, gets it to receptive sponsors, and starts and sustains the interest of participants involved in the project. Completing the project is *not* as important as communication.

The format of team meetings makes or breaks the project. Everyone must be given the opportunity to speak. Design meetings will tend to stay on track when constraints are imposed. A common one is to set the "quit time." A more interesting technique is a style adopted by Paul MacCready and team during the Gossamer series meetings. Everyone stood in a circle holding hands for the duration of the meeting!

On days when brainstorming is required, all egos should be checked at the door. Ideas should be solicited and noted—without critique, on a blackboard of flipchart—until everyone has spoken. Only then should evaluation begin. Consensus is preferred and should be sought. When a task is decided on, figure who will do it and when, too. Establish realistic milestones. Build task lists, where items can be scratched off and added.

• *Pacing the Design.* The desire to "get going" can be strong. Be careful. You can spend a long time building the wrong machine. Don't be afraid to back up, scrap an idea, and start over. Re-evaluate any new direction relative to all other issues affected by these factors.

Photo: Vehicle Research Institute (WWU)

Fig. 3-5: Lab technician Russ Moye and student Bill Greene work on Viking V at WWU.

Designing a roadworthy vehicle shuffles these factors into a slightly different order. Briefly:

Weight

Power in an EV is consumed in accelerating the vehicle, climbing grades, and running at speed. The most power is typically consumed in the stop-and-go operation and hillclimbing (particularly at high rates of speed), and the least consumed at steady highway speeds.

Fundamental laws are at work here. A body at rest tends to stay at rest. Acceleration of anything consumes more power than a steady-speed state. A low rate of acceleration, then, uses less energy than jackrabbit starts. Accelerating a smaller weight uses a *lot* less energy.

Even many so-called lightweight vehicles have excessive weight. It's okay! It isn't easy to offset a lifetime of working around high-density fuels (like gasoline). Expect to fight every step of the way to avoid the accumulation of weight. It is a non-stop battle. It is one that you may not win, but you must fight it anyway. Can you merge two functions? Can you find a lighter version of something you need? Can you do without it? Stay lean and clean. Clutter adds weight. Don't spend a fortune and bushels of time on carbon fiber

---

Techtalk
Viking Vehicle Series
10
Michael Seal, Ph.D.

Since 1972 more than twenty vehicles have been designed and built by undergraduate students and faculty at the Vehicle Research Institute at Western Washington University in Bellingham, Washington.

I believe that innovative vehicle design starts with a specific goal or need to meet a design criteria. A free-wheeling brainstorming session is used to look at as many possibilities as can be dreamed up, regardless of whether that idea has ever been used before or how outlandish it might seem. Each idea must be examined to see how closely it meets the goals. Only after the very best solution has been found do you begin to eliminate, change or make compromises to utilize the resources available. Things such as time, budget, material availability, etc. now begin to influence the final design.

Briefly, here are some examples in the Viking series of designs that impact EV design.

The Viking II was our first venture in aerodynamic design for automobiles. A series of 1/10 scale windtunnel models were built. The design chosen had low frontal area with a well-rounded front and tapered back to a minimum area on the rear. The Cd was .34 which was considered very good for the time, especially as most automotive designers were of the opinion that drag aero below 200 mph was insignificant with regard to fuel economy. Viking II won the SEED rally with a fuel economy of 58 mpg on LPG.

Viking IV is an aluminum monocoque streamlined coupe originally built to win its class at the Bonneville National Speed Trials. Fitted with a 1500 cc turbocharged diesel engine, it was entered in the Sea to Sea Econorally, winning awards for lowest emissions and best economy as well as 1st overall. We began our investigation of low rolling drag radial tires with this car, and achieved highway fuel economy of more than 100 mpg at 50 mph in cross-country rallies.

Viking V is a lightweight version of Viking IV, using a fiberglass aerodynamic shell in place of the aluminum one on Viking IV.

Viking VI was developed under a contract with NHTSA to show that a fuel efficient, low emission vehicle could meet or exceed federal crash-worthiness standards. Two of these vehicles were built. The first unit was fitted with anthropomorphic dummies and crashed at 43 mph into a concrete barrier. The dummies survived with HIC numbers of 552 and 286 with no injuries. The second Viking VI achieved 118 mpg at 50 mph. The exhaust emissions are: CO-.89, HC-.09, NOx-.86 when running on unleaded gasoline.

Viking VII was a high performance sports car built to determine if high fuel economy and clean exhaust could be maintained while offering "Supercar" levels of performance. Although fuel economy on the highway is only 50 mpg and less on the L.A. 4 cycle, the car accelerates to 60 mph in 5.3 seconds and can generate over 1 G in cornering power.

Viking VIII was an effort to capitalize on the success of Viking VII and introduce a limited production sports car to be built in Costa Rica and sold in the USA. A single experimental prototype was built along with plastic tooling suitable for an initial production run. Unfortunately, the client ran into financial difficulties and the initial production run never materialized.

Viking X—XIX were built in the summer of 1989 on student-built tooling in nine weeks.

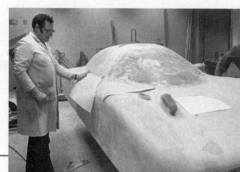

Fig. 3-6: Dr. Michael Seal and a student work on Viking VI.

Fig. 3-7:
Viking II, IV,
and V at
Western
Washington
University
in 1979.

*Low vehicle
weight is the
major goal in the
scratchbuilt EV.
If you can't build
a vehicle that
weighs half
of what a
conversion will
give you,
why bother?*

T11 Techtalk — Street or Work EV?

Will the scratchbuilt EV be a street or work machine?

•**Street Machine.** The street machine is the result of breeding a sedan to a bicycle. Lightweight but tough. A big chunk of the vehicle's running weight is that of the people in it. In today's cars, you're a dust mote on the steering wheel, for all the engine knows. The street machine can obtain good speeds and good range, but each at the appropriate moment. It's important to be zippy. At times, it's nice to be as nimble as a cat.

The street machine has a framework designed primarily for driver/passenger protection. In an emergency, its low center of gravity gives it a level of certainty in matters of control, snappy maneuvering, and responsive steering.

•**Work Vehicle.** The work machine is the broken-mirror image of the street machine. It does not have to be light, only tough. The work machine is designed for work, work, work. Surprisingly, you don't need to worry so much about the batteries' energy. You won't go far in the work machine and you won't go fast. You'll get a hefty amount of work done for relatively small battery capacity. Add as many fringes as your work ethic dictates. A spotlight at the most for darkness work. Ugly, ungainly, unsightly maybe—but real practical. Pure function.

T12 Techtalk — Vehicle Codes

Obtain a copy of the Vehicle Codes for the state in which you intend to register the EV you are building. Use a highlighter to mark EV-related topics. Don't worry; you can tell what's important and applicable. Better yet, tear the sheets out of there and staple them together. Re-cycle the rest of the book.

There are at least four different categories of equipment: functional, legal, safety, and luxury.

• *Functional* equipment includes hardware like the motor, batteries, controllers, brakes, steering and suspension system, etc.

• *Legal* defines the equipment, i.e., horn, headlights, brake lights, emergency brake, windshield, etc. that the Vehicle Code requires for the state in which the vehicle is licensed and registered. There can be *big* differences between states. When in doubt, check your own state's codes for its rulings, laws, and wording. Check with the DMV or Highway Patrol on anything you suspect may represent a problem. These are the folks that will check out your vehicle, and it is *their* interpretation of Vehicle Codes

that is important, not *yours!*

• *Safety* equipment is there to help you "see and be seen." To be legal is to be safe, since safety equipment is often a mandatory part of the vehicle codes. However, add anything that will help in the safe operation of the vehicle and provide some measure of protection in case of an emergency

• *Luxury* equipment is anything that doesn't contribute to the function, safety, or legality of the EV. It includes air conditioners, CB radios, stereos, cigarette lighters, a fax machine and the cellular phone.

Aerodynamics

A standard car—speeding down the highway at 55 mph—requires fully 50% of its propulsive effort to move air aside. As more attention is given to the ways a vehicle can more easily slip through the air, this power consumption is reduced, as is the need for the size of propulsive machinery. There is no mystery to this—we wouldn't have aircraft that could do 2,000 mph if there were—but, for a long time, solid aerodynamics has been lacking in most cars.

The main culprit is "style"—truly aerodynamic vehicles are thin and taper at the rear. Since we are quickly reaching the point where conspicuous consumption of fuel is no longer possible, the "style" is getting cleaner—softer edges, lean lines, recessed fixtures, and more attention to detail. However, there is still a lot more "trend" than "slick" in most manufactured bodywork.

What are the important aerodynamic considerations in landborne vehicles? A brief but accurate list includes five factors: shape, frontal area, skin effect, closure, and ground effect.

The ideal *shape* of vehicles in the 0-60 mph range is a teardrop, rounded at the front and slowly tapering to a point in the rear.

Frontal area is the number of square feet of silhouette when the vehicle is viewed "head on." You want this as low as possible, suggesting that the vehicle be a thin teardrop.

Skin effect describes the effect of air moving over a surface that is very large in area. A solar panel may have a very thin frontal area but incur large aerodynamic losses because there is simply so much area to the panel (top and underside). Air must interact with the surface area in passing over it.

Exhaustive tests have concluded that a good *closure* (the way the vehicle tapers in the rear) occurs at less than 14 degrees total. That's only seven degrees each size of a centerline through the vehicle!

Ground effect, in this context, defines a natural relationship between a road surface (or any surface) and the sky. A vehicle interacts with, and generally messes up, this intimate relationship in a way that defies easy description or remedy. It gets progressively worse with speed. Vehicles minimize the resultant drag in three general ways:

• *skirts*—shrouding that dips down to the surface to keep air from getting under the vehicle);

• *underpans*—smooth bottoms that minimize the yo-yo'ing of air between vehicle and ground), and;

• *isolation*—maintaining an elevation above the road surface that fools the road surface into thinking your vehicle is a low-flying airplane.

Careful attention to the five factors above—a clean shape, low frontal area, minimal skin effect, good closure, and minimal ground effect—will minimize the amount of energy needed to move the vehicle at speed.

A measure of a vehicle's aerodynamics is its *drag coefficient* (Cd). This is unaffected by the vehicle's propulsive power or weight. Streamlining is the art of achieving a low drag coefficient. Airflow that moves smoothly over a surface is called laminar flow. When it "separates," the air is turbulated at the parting, rolling and swirling. This produces a thing called a vortex, and it is a real drag to the vehicle that experiences it.

and install heavy gauges. Here, it helps to be a serious backpacker. Think essentials. Less weight really means "no more weight than necessary." The dividends are performance and range.

I believe that low vehicle weight is *the* major goal in the scratchbuilt EV. If you can't build a vehicle that weighs half of what a conversion will give you, why bother?

Aerodynamics

Aerodynamically speaking, most cars are a real drag. Most people drive boxes. All those flat fronts and backs and sharp edges catch and turbulate the air through which the vehicle moves. It takes energy to do that, and it's part of the tax the propulsion system must pay.

At freeway speeds, good streamlining conserves energy. At street speeds, up to 35 mph, it's no big thing. What speeds will your EV see?

There are a few good texts on what does and does not constitute *good* aerodynamics. In some areas, the relevant factors may surprise you. Check it out.

A slippery EV is no surprise. At every stage of the design and construction, you must think "aero" (Techtalk T13). I've seen slick designs marred by windshield wipers and side mirrors.

For a street machine, there are a number of basic ways to minimize drag in the overall design (Techtalk T14).

Fig. 3-8: Smooth surfaces without projections are at the root of this design.

Fig. 3-9: Keep the designwork clean all the way to the end of the vehicle.

Rolling Resistance

An EV's weight affects another factor: rolling resistance. The tires in a vehicle must make good contact with the road for traction during braking, acceleration, and maneuvering. There is a penalty for traction: rolling resistance. Rolling resistance is a function of contact area, tire type, and the weight and speed of the vehicle.

When the overall power consumption of a vehicle is scrutinized, the losses due to rolling resistance become significant. Avoid small tire diameters, wide profiles, and knobby tires. Maintain correct inflation pressures, too!

The expanding EV market has brought about the design of new tires which have low rolling resistance. When I added a set to my EV, I felt like I now had power steering! The new tires work at 55 psi. For a standard tire, this inflation pressure would be dangerous. However, the new tires are specially strengthened to survive this pressure throughout their service life.

Hill Climbing

A vehicle on a level road surface uses power at a specific rate. At the same energy rate, the vehicle will go fast downhill. At the

Photo: C. Michael Lewis

Fig. 3-10: The SUNGO tapers the width of the vehicle to stay "aero."

Photo: C. Michael Lewis

*T*echtalk

T₁₄ Reducing Drag

A lower drag coefficient is possible in a vehicle when all protuberances—mirrors, windshield wipers, and door handles—are streamlined or removed. Aerodynamic drag can be further reduced by offset tandem seating, natural air flow, and alternate heat-exchange techniques.

•**Offset tandem seating.** The frontal area of a passenger vehicle can be cut 35-45% by offset tandem seating. Simple tandem seating positions a passenger behind a driver, instead of side-by-side, and offers the greatest reduction in frontal area. This is unpopular in cars because it affords the passenger a "view of a head" rather than a direct view ahead. A better idea is offset tandem seating. Here, the passenger sits slightly to the rear of the driver, minimizing the interference of shoulder and elbow interaction. Moving the passenger back only 9-10 inches from the driver allows the distance between them to decrease easily by 12 inches or more. The decrease in width immediately translates into less frontal area for the vehicle, as demonstrated in the Sylph (review Application A27).

• **Natural air flow.** For passenger air, identify the high-pressure and low-pressure points on the vehicle's body. Then, design the air cooling system, positioning inlets in the high pressure points and outlets at the low pressure points. The Viking XX used this technique to keep its drivers cool in transcontinental races (review Application 47).

• **Alternate heat-exchange techniques.** One draggy device is the air scoop. Typically, a scoop is any device that forces air to enter and move through some portion of the vehicle. With far fewer cooling needs than an engine, the EV is able to eliminate air scoops except for passenger comfort. In fact, the front grill of a car, normally used to pass air through the radiator, is blocked off in most EV conversions.

Smart use of heat-exchange techniques and technology can transfer waste heat from the electric motor and controller without scoops or electric blowers. Modern electronic controllers protect themselves when overheated by automatic cut-back and shut-off. When mounted flush with the exterior body, effective cooling is assured at high vehicle speeds. Although the porcupine-looking heatsink used on the EVX (see Application A11) is not a shining example of this technique, it was perfect for the hot Phoenix racetrack when drafting another vehicle at speed. The same technique may not prevent overheating when the EV is climbing hills at slower speeds, since the airflow is low. For heat-exchange at low vehicle speeds, use a larger heat sink or add a blower (or fan). Wired to a thermoswitch, a blower will add airflow when things get hot.

Fig. 3-11: Solectria's Flash was an easy winner at PIR in the lightweight class.

same rate, the vehicle will slow down going uphill. Why? In one instance, gravity assists propulsion and, in the other, resists it.

If you are accustomed to driving or riding around in a big car, you may have never really noticed the effect of gravity on a vehicle. One simply depresses the gas pedal when the car starts to climb a hill. My experience in climbing hills initially came from the front seat of an old VW bus. Needless to say, in the first vehicle, there's a conspicuous *excess* of horsepower available and, with the latter, a damnable *absence* of it.

Gravity is an acceleration. Therefore, a vehicle climbing a hill is accelerating the whole time. Acceleration on level ground gobbles power at a rate that is 3-5 times faster than that used at "cruise." Uphill, the motor will gobble even more power without a noticeable increase in vehicle speed.

The higher the percentage of grade, the greater the acceleration and the higher the power consumption. The percentage of grade equals the number of feet of rise in 100 level feet. A 6% grade rises 6 feet in a 100-foot span.

Efficiency

Efficiency is one of those factors that gets talked about a lot but is as elusive as smoke when it comes time to wrestle with it.

Efficiencies don't add. They multiply. Suppose that you have three things working in a chain that are, respectively, 40%, 85%, and 65% efficient. What's the system efficiency? (No, you do not add them together and divide by three; that's the *average*!) In this case, the answer is 22.1%, and it's found by multiplying these three values together.

Don't like calculations? A more general way to express this relationship is: The efficiency of a system cannot surpass the efficiency of any one part. Indeed, the value of 22% is less than the value of 40%.

> *The efficiency of a system cannot surpass the efficiency of any one part.*

In design work, to ignore one factor and take painstaking effort with another is counterproductive.

You do *not* need to know the efficiency of your EV. Here, a guestimate (an exquisite blend of guess and estimate) will work. Err on the side of liberal in losses and conservative in gains, and things will generally work better than expected.

Ergonometry

The driver is *the* most important part of the machine. An uncomfortable driver is preoccupied, and the machine's performance suffers. Too hot or cold, too restricted in movement, odd positioning of controls, etc.— these factors take their toll on the brainbox.

Ensure that all operator controls and instruments are easy to reach and manipulate,

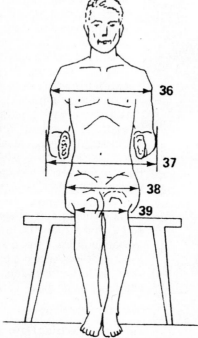

Fig. 3-12: Mil-Std-1472C (May 1981) contains useful dimensions for ranges of sizes of men and women.

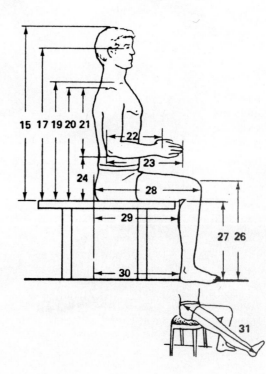

Fig 3-13: Obtain a book on criteria and values for fitting a machine to a human.

and intuitive in function and operation. A maze of boxes, wires, switches, indicators, and meters may began to form around the driver's position. Be willing to backtrack to make things cleaner and simpler.

Crashworthiness

A major design effort must be expended in the design of the scratchbuilt vehicle in the area of crashworthiness. Each year, our current transportation system kills hundreds of thousands of people worldwide, and injures or maims millions. The effect of collision from the front, side, or rear of the vehicle is most likely to be the result of a two-vehicle interaction. Of course, a collision involving a stationary object (i.e., a tree or wall) can be just as deadly.

Although this subject is important in the design of *any* type of vehicle, it is especially important in lightweight vehicles. It is a basic *law* of physics that more of the energy of a collision is transferred to the lighter of two vehicles. While both weight and speed are involved, above 45 mph, speed is the killer.

Why? Weight is a *linear* function. At double the weight, a vehicle has twice the energy at the same relative speed. Speed is a *square* function. So, at twice the relative speed of collision, the energy and effect of the collision is four times as great.

In view of this, if you're neurotic, you don't drive. If you're sane, you drive as little as

Fig. 3-14:
The Amick Windmobile
combines a fixed "sail"
with excellent side collapse distance.

Photo: Douglas Amick

*T*echtalk
T15   Crashworthiness

Crashworthiness is about retaining compartment integrity, avoiding the penetration of lethal objects, and dissipating collision energies. Coupled with restraint systems and air bags, these factors help a vehicle's occupants withstand the deceleration forces of the collision, escaping serious injury or death.

Fuel-efficient cars are usually lightweight. They're also amazingly crashworthy except when they mix with heavy, "hard-nose" vehicles. Physics says the "soft-nose" car bears the brunt of a collision and the consequential deformation and penetration.

While the day of the big car is gone, they linger on, conspicuously gobbling up dwindling resources and dealing out death to people and wildlife. Siding with motorcycles, bicycles, and pedestrians in the design of a scratchbuilt vehicle makes you fair game for the hard-nosed stuff. It's not a sure thing. In many instances, that extra little bit of steel probably wouldn't have helped anyway. Look how many people die in the hard-nosed machines!

Crashworthiness is not a matter of luck. If you're building your own, stay aware of four things that help: strength, collapse distance, design, and mass.

• *Strength* is often confused with weight, massiveness, and metals. Carbon fiber and fiberglass materials, and composite construction (fiberglass sandwiching) techniques make a lightweight vehicle tough. Stronger, in fact, than a vehicle several times heavier.

• *Collapse distance* recognizes the importance of spreading the impact of a collision over the greatest amount of time possible, decreasing the *rate* of energy transfer. All that sculpting of metal that occurs in vehicle crashes actually helps the occupants by dissipating energy. It slows things down, converting energy into noise, heat, and motion. The idea is to absorb energy that a softer body, like a human being, dissipates in a more messy and irreversible fashion.

• *Design* confronts the possibility of a collision from any direction. It figures out how to be tough. Tough means hard but malleable, helping dissipate energy more slowly. You do *not* worry about what happens to the vehicle. Every reasonable effort is made to keep a careening car or a telephone pole from penetrating the space occupied by driver and passenger(s).

•*Mass* does not always work in favor of the occupants in a collision. Sufficient steel may prevent penetration in a collision. However, everywhere else in the vehicle, that steel "plants" the vehicle, resisting the forces that would, for a lighter vehicle, cause it to start sliding. Careening off into a second collision is not a pleasant thought, but surviving the initial collision should be the first priority!

In the same situation, a lightweight vehicle will more quickly start sliding. Provided that the occupants are restrained and padding or air bags are present, the end result is a greater degree of survivability, since the collision energy is spread out over both distance and time. This has been demonstrated in a test crash between the small, lightweight Horlacher and an Audi (review Techtalk 24).

possible. If you're cautious, you drive something slow and heavy. If you concede that life is all about risks, you drive small and lightweight and stay very, very alert.

Watching the driver of a racecar walk away from a 200 mph impact with a concrete wall is revealing. With exotic materials (lightweight alloys) and computer study, it isn't difficult to make a vehicle that will weigh less and take more punishment than today's cars (Techtalk T15). The cost is no longer out of reach for the little guy. Advances in homebuilt aircraft make the technology available off-the-shelf. Anyone who has built a composite aircraft possesses the necessary skills to shape a lightweight EV.

Lightweight EVs with long aerodynamic bodies, are typically a designer's nightmare when it comes to crashworthiness. Front and rear impact zones are relatively easy directions to fortify. Side impact protection is the tough guy. How can you be narrow and still withstand side impact?

There are several solutions to this dilemma. One is demonstrated in the Amick Windcar (review Application A43). Note the position of the driver relative to the wing that comes out to join the arch. A collision from the side will first contact the vehicle some 18-24 inches away from the driver. This may not

A battery pack that extends the full width of the vehicle at bumper height is another way to fortify a vehicle against side-impact. This was an unexpected side-benefit of the Geometric project. Battery module and receptacle alike can be designed to help absorb impact. The lead in lead-acid batteries is soft, helping by the way it will absorb energy.

Horsepower

Horsepower is an old-time term. When horses were the prime energy source, it was very functional. Today, it is more precisely defined (TechTalk T16).

Horsepower defines the rate at which work is done. It defines a relationship between three things—mass, distance, and time. Horsepower is needed to make the vehicle move—to overcome inertia and rolling resistance and to accelerate the vehicle's mass (weight).

Do not confuse the horsepower ratings for internal-combustion engines with those for electric motors. Engine horsepower is rated as a *maximum*, or peak. Electric motor horsepower is rated as *continuous*. Any electric motor will exceed its HP rating by 3-4 times for brief periods.

In a vehicle, horsepower is translated into either torque or speed (Techtalk T17).

A battery pack that extends the full width of the vehicle at bumper height is another way to fortify a vehicle against side-impact.

Fig. 3-15: The Tropica's chassis is light and strong.

Photo: Renaissance Vehicles

sound like much, but sit in your car and measure the distance from your body to the outside of the car. Due to the Windcar's unique wing-like structure and the rear wheel housings, this would be a tough distance to collapse. At least, it will dissipate much of the collision energy and help prevent penetration.

Frameworks

The expression 'frameworks' means a lot more than merely a framework. Frameworks includes steering, suspension, wheels and tires, and brakes. It mounts and secures batteries, motor, and drivetrain. Good planning leaves

*One horsepower
(1 HP) is
equivalent to 746
Watts of electrical
energy*

When 550 pounds of weight is lifted straight up for a distance of one foot in just one second, one horsepower has just been demonstrated. (Don't actually try this at home, please!)

If it takes two seconds (twice as long) to lift the same weight the same distance, one-half a horsepower has been demonstrated. Or, if the same weight is lifted two feet in two seconds, you're back to one horsepower. The same goes for half the weight lifted two feet in one second. Still *one* horsepower.

It is possible for a human being (an athlete) to demonstrate a horsepower — for a few seconds. However, most of us would find it difficult to exert 1/10th of a horsepower for a sustained period of time.

Electric Horsepower. One horsepower (1 HP) is equivalent to 746 Watts of electrical energy. This equation is very useful to the EV enthusiast for several reasons. One is that motors are rated in horsepower and battery packs have voltage and current ratings. The product of these two ratings, voltage and current, equals Watts, or wattage. If you know either the wattage or the horsepower, this formula will help you calculate the other rating.

It may surprise you to learn just where all the horsepower is going. Much of it goes into moving air aside. Some of it is spent in fighting gravity during hillclimbing. It is also dissipated as heat in tires and bearings. At every stage, it is lost when energy is converted from one form to another. We hear it, feel it as vibration and heat, and see it in the brush arcs of a motor.

A rule of thumb for these losses says that one horsepower (746 Watts) gets to the wheels for every kiloWatt (1000 Watts) of electricity.

Horsepower, then, is an expression of how much work is needed to perform a task. Be certain to include the losses of conversion and transport functions. The work rate varies with the duration and frequency of the tasks we ask of the vehicle.

*T*echtalk

T 17   Torque and Speed

Torque and speed are two terms of the dozens you'll hear when talking about vehicles and propulsion systems. It helps to understand a bit about how they interrelate in the design of the EV.

Torque. Torque is both a physics word and an automotive word. If you've ever handled a torque wrench, you'll know it's calibrated in foot-pounds. Torque means force through a distance. Leverage. Or a lower gear. Or a higher ratio. The capacity to climb walls. It's what Sampson got from his hair. Or Popeye from his spinach. Mechanical advantage.

To learn more about torque, pull out that dusty copy of Physics I. Study gear ratios. Whether a farm or street machine is on the drafting table, it will need torque. In a street machine, torque is the essential ingredient for coming off the line fast ("chirping" the tires) and climbing hills at speed. In a farm EV, torque is what totes that barge and lifts that bale.

Speed. Speed is the rate of distance covered in a given time span. It's the reading on the speedometer. Speed is a ratio of gears in the drivetrain where the speed of the wheels gets closer to the speed of the motor. It means the difference between sticking to the side streets or safely holding your own out on a highway or freeway. Speed is what you need if you want to go a distance in a reasonable period of time.

Torque vs Speed. Electric motors have a wide powerband. Unlike engines, electric motors develop a lot of torque from a standstill. An EV needs a 2-speed transmission where a car with an engine will require a 5-speed gearbox.

Under 1,500 lbs of running weight, many EVs will get by with a single-ratio drivetrain. Acceleration from a stop will seem brisk and a top end of 45-60 mph will be possible without exceeding the motor's rated rpm. In hillclimbing, the speed will probably drop to a comfortable 45-55 mph.

Above 1,500 lbs of running weight, an EV will often need a 2-speed box. Low gear will handle the torque of high acceleration and hillclimbing. High gear will handle speed and cruise.

EV weights above 2,500 lbs will make the 3-speed gearbox more and more attractive.

The Frame

The frame can be made of a number of materials. Steel, aluminum, and plastic are the basic choices. In steel, what's used depends on what part of the EV we're concerned with. The front axle, the main frame members, or bumpers may use heavy angle iron, or I-beams. General support structures, braces, and ribs will be made of lighter materials—angle iron or even metal tubes. Whether you use low-cost steel or more expensive aluminum, the difference will not be discernable once a coat of paint is applied. If plastic is used, the frame will look more like a molded body.

For most situations, there will be an individualistic blend of the three—steel, aluminum, and plastic—determined by fate more than design. Wood won't be of much use as a frame material. Without special workmanship, it doesn't have the high strength per pound that the other materials offer.

Considerable thought must be given to what material is going to work best with the tools, skills, and experience you possess. Are things to be bolted together, or welded? Where are things located?

Look at somebody's homebuilt vehicle. Like it? Does everything seem to be in its proper space, evenly proportioned, no waste, clean lines, etc. Now, turn your back and sketch it out as you saw it. Or go home and make a model.

Not too easy, is it? It's a shame that all of us don't possess that very unique ability of forming the picture in the mind's eye, and then forming it from the clay of materials about us. That comes from talent or skills painstakingly-acquired. The rest of us must labor at the drawings and curse as we bungle and end up with two things trying to occupy the same space. The problem is not *what to do* so often as it is *how to do it* without inadvertently messing everything up, all the way down the line.

Several things will help the frame plan. First, don't try to do it all at once. The first part calls for putting down the number of wheels that you plan to use and where they go. Experiment!

Use graph paper to do the initial layout. Everything must be to scale, or you're just drawing and crayons will do. If you know the approximate tire diameters, sketch those in to scale. Once you start the process, you will be amazed at how much you can do with what little you may know about such things. Components must be positioned and space allowed for the way they work. Wheels are usually the tough one to work out in the mockup. Will they clear framework and fenders as they swing? etc. etc. etc.

I've found that there may be a thousand ways to arrange something, but there's something special in a natural fit.

space for a yourself and, perhaps, a passenger. Don't forget to leave some room for groceries!

When everything is there, the frameworks is finished with fiberglass, wood, plastic, or metal (or combinations of these) to make it streamlined and weatherproof. Give it an affectionate name. After all, automakers name their models of cars!

Let's look a little closer at elements of the frame, brakes, suspension, body and shell.

Frame

The frame is the structural component of the frameworks. It may be a metal or aluminum chassis to which a body is attached. If it is integral with (and indistinguishable from) the body, it's probably a monocoque design. Monocoque is *very* cool stuff.

The frame holds things together and determines the shape of the beast. It's a skeleton onto which you'll hang the various assemblies—powertrain, battery bank, steering, suspension, axles, and wheels. It won't do to have our assemblies separating from one another as we take corners or bounce along a rough road. Rigidity and strength are two prerequisites of the frame (Techtalk T18).

Brakes

EVs rate good brakes. EV conversions need them because these vehicles are normally heavier than their gas-powered counterparts. Lightweight scratchbuilts will probably be driven fast. Irrespective of type or purpose, then, ensure good brakes.

Disc brakes are preferred to drum brakes.

LEFT ➡ ➡ RIGHT

Fig. 3-16: The frame of Suntera's Sunray.

Fig. 3-17: The floor part and shell part.

Fig. 3-18: Sunray's rear wheel assembly.

Fig. 3-19: Suspension, steering, and brakes.

Fig. 3-20: Earlier Suntera prototypes.

Designed for larger and faster vehicles, they offer better overall braking performance than drum-type brakes. This is due primarily to their greater cooling capacity under heavy use. In the same situation, drum-type brakes "fade." The drums and shoes get so hot that effective braking is reduced.

When a vehicle is braked, most of its weight shifts to the front wheels. This explains why many cars have disc brakes on the front only and drum brakes on the rear. The scratchbuilt EV will want to have supergood, heavy-duty brakes.

Oversize drum brakes are available as replacements on many vehicles. Check for this possibility if you want to upgrade a subassembly you've already purchased.

> *...continuously remind yourself of the final vehicle's job, weight, and aerodynamics ... ideas will compete with each other ... it's your job to keep order.*

Body/Shell

Constructing the body or shell of a prototype is usually the most challenging part of any project.

Ultimately, the body of the EV (also called a shell or skin) involves the construction of "parts" that, when assembled with components, will form a vehicle.

The traditional method of fabricating the EV body involves building plugs and molds to build the "parts" (TechTalk T19). At least two parts (and, more often, many more) are needed. If all goes well, the part will require little or no sanding. It is ready to be mated to the other parts that will form the body shell.

Thin and low describes both a sleek, fast EV and a speed bump. The ability to see and be

All photos:
Stevi Johnson
(Suntera)

Techtalk

T19   Body and Shell

Fabricating a body or shell is a 3-part process: plug, mold, and part.

• *Plug*. The plug is a fake vehicle. It has the shape, volume, and solidness of the final vehicle. A plug is usually constructed with ribs, foam, and glue. Shaping tools will speed making the rough outline. This is followed by several cycles of sanding, body putty, sanding, filler, sanding, etc.

Read several books on this process and search out the "tricks" that will speed the process and get the best result possible. Attend a class at a college to acquire the skills. Or work as an apprentice to a boatbuilder or surfboard manufacturer.

• *Mold*. The mold is the mirror-image of the plug and it is used to make a part of the shell. The advantage of a mold is its ability to make many parts, each an exact replica of the original part. The mass production of a product often requires the construction of many molds.

The mold transfers the smooth shape of the plug to the part. A part is only as good as its mold, and a mold is only as good as the plug it's made from. In this three-part process, then, the plug deserves the lion's share of attention.

Once the plug is mirror-like, you must make decisions about how the mold will be split. Several molds are taken from a plug, each representing a specific portion of the plug. A mold, then, is a manageable piece, like a bottom and top, nose and tail, and left side and right side.

The mold is made in a three-step process. First, apply a release compound to the plug. Then, add fiberglass cloth and resin. Next, add a framework to the mold for structural reinforcement. When the mold is separated from the plug, this will help retain the correct shape.

• *Part*. The "part" is made from the mold. When combined with parts from the other molds and plugs, the shell will form the complete body of the vehicle and look identical to the plug.

The shell is made in much the same fashion as the mold. A release compound is applied. If color is to be added to the part, it is added at this time. Next are resin and cloth. If the part requires structural reinforcement, nomex, foam, or ribs may be added.

Where the weight of the part is an issue, the technique of vacuum-bagging may be applied. A thin, porous plastic is added over the layered work, then an absorbing material, followed by a plastic bag. Once sealed, a vacuum is applied. Atmospheric pressure on the layers of materials will force any excess resin into the absorbent sheet. Once cured, this will strip clear of the inside of the mold and leave a strong, lightweight part.

T_{20} Techtalk

The Mockup

To build a prototype mockup, you need space, components (or facsimilies of components), and scale.

•*Space*. Clear a section of floor in the garage or wherever. Give your idea space.

•*Components*. Arrange your components as you see them connected together. It's helpful at this point to have a lot of blocks of wood—2x4s and 4x4s and 1x6s, of varying lengths—to actually place the items relative to each other in three dimensions, not just two. Boy, is this an eye-opener!

•*Scale*. Make up a sizing graph. Locate the vehicle mockup close to a wall or prop up a 4x8 sheet of plywood alongside the mockup. Pin up construction paper with ruled lines of 6 or 12 inches.

An important part of any vehicle is the room left for the driver and passenger(s). The mockup will allow you to fit them in accurately. Be certain to account for people of different sizes. The sizing graph makes it clearer how much leg room and head room you'll *really* need for people in the vehicle's construction.

Use a mirror to see yourself doing this. I've used a light mounted at a distance to cast a shadow onto the graph. The best shadow is the one cast using the sunlight of early morning or late afternoon. It's sharp, to scale, and moves slowly enough to be useful if you have prepared properly.

If there's just you doing all of this and nobody will pose for you, use the timer of your camera to catch yourself sitting in the appropriate place(s). When the film is developed, you'll be ready for the next stage. And have documentation of what you've done, too.

T_{21} Techtalk

Coastdown Testing

How aerodynamic is the vehicle you're building? How much drag is there in the drivetrain, brakes, and bearings? Answers to these questions can be found in a coastdown test. A coastdown test involves getting the vehicle up to speed (unpowered) and measuring the time it takes for the vehicle to coast to a stop on a level road surface.

Five factors will slow a vehicle: gravity, headwind, brake and bearing drag, rolling resistance of the tires, and aerodynamic drag. Coastdown over a level surface eliminates the effect of gravity, still air means no headwind, and brake adjustment can avoid the effect of brake drag.

Of course, steering, suspension, and brakes must be installed and working in the vehicle. A working speedometer or tachometer (calibrated) is required. A camcorder (video) is a wonderful piece of test equipment since it usually includes a clock (turn on the display!), shoots 30 frames per second, and can record instrument readings. See if you can borrow one. A stopwatch, a pencil, and a piece of paper works, too.

Since coastdown testing is often performed *before* the drivetrain is installed (the vehicle is not self-propelled at this point), the test vehicle must be allowed to roll down a hill to gain the needed speed.

Gravity testing uses any downhill grade that is adequate to get the vehicle up to the desired speed.

At the point where the speedometer or tachometer needle reverses its direction and the vehicle has started to slow, begin the test. Start your timepiece, and record the speed (or rpm). Record the total time it takes to a come to a complete stop. Also note the speedometer readings at 5 mph increments. Repeat the test to verify these readings.

Aerodynamic drag is a square function. Rolling resistance is a linear one. Plot the results. The area under the curve contains both rolling and aerodynamic resistances. However, the effect of each can be "separated" by extending the line formed in the 0-20 mph range. Below the line is the effect of rolling resistance. Above is the aerodynamic drag.

These tests will not easily supply you with numbers. However, they will provide you with a benchmark or reference. Experiment with changes, then retest, noting the relative gain or loss of aerodynamic efficiency.

Fig. 3-21: Ely Schless takes the Formula E out on the race track for the first time.

seen is vital to the safe operation of a vehicle on a street and highway. Drivers of other vehicles that have difficulty seeing a scratchbuilt EV from the side, rear, or front are likely to steamroll it.

Propulsion Package

The propulsion package includes the motor, drivetrain, controller, battery pack, and all peripheral power and operator controls. What will your vehicle use? Review the Applications in this book and select designs of the approximate size and type you want to build (review Fig 3-76). Now, scrutinize the propulsion packages of these designs. This should approximate the propulsion package *your* EV will need.

The Mockup

At some point, you'll be ready for the mockup (Techtalk T20). This allows you to see your vehicle in a way you can't on paper or in your head. Here's how you find out what's right and wrong with the vehicle you've been envisioning.

It's important to continuously remind yourself of the final vehicle's job, weight, and aerodynamics. Many ideas will compete with each other. You are the chairman. It's your job to keep order. Give each idea its full measure, then make the decision. Don't hurry but don't stall, either. Get as much information as you need. Sort through the facts, possibilities, and various arrangements. Your final mockup may look very different from the first. At any moment, for any reason, you can decide to use or reject any idea.

The Test Mule

A smart process is to build a test "mule." A mule is a foundation on which you can mount components and test their functioning, relative positioning, or otherwise evaluate things. The test mule is a good alternative to, or the next step after, building and testing a scale model in a windtunnel. The mule is where you make the mistakes. It will teach you what you know and what you don't know. A good mule rarely looks pretty. Its job is make sure your beautiful machine doesn't get progressively uglier! Boxbeam, the material used in the Panther Electric project (review Application A39)is ideal for a test mule.

If you are deeply concerned about aerodynamics and rolling resistance, the mule may give you the numbers through a "coastdown" test (Techtalk T21).

Once you've made all the decisions, it's time to cut, lay out, and weld the frame/chassis, add steering, suspension, and brakes, and mount components.

The Road Test

Perform a road test before finalizing the body, shell, and paint. This road test can help fix things before they make additional work for you (Techtalk T22).

Everything checks okay? Smile! Call the nearest DMV for an appointment for registration and licensing!

---

*T*echtalk

T_{22} The First Road Test

Before you finalize the body and other vehicle component systems, complete the powertrain, steering, suspension, braking, and battery assemblies and add the essential ingredients of a control system. Then, "road-test" the critter.

The road test consists of three phases: checkout, gravity run, and power.

Checkout. Check *everything* over to make sure that, in your haste and excitement over this event, you didn't connect something wrong or forget to do something. Put together a list of everything that must be checked. Establish a proper sequencing of these checks.

Gravity run. Find a long downhill section of road with limited access (i.e., a driveway). Start near the bottom (but still on the grade) and allow the vehicle to roll unpowered. Check the brakes, including a panic stop. Move the vehicle further up the grade with each successful braking and maneuvering run. Steer a snakey line once in a while to work the steering and suspension. Achieve higher and higher speeds. If there are *any* bugs, go back to the shop, remedy the problem and start over.

Power. This phase is powered flight (just a manner of expression). It is started on a level surface. Again, follow your list (and heart) and give the machine a thorough checkout. First the visual check, then the drive. *Gradually.* The major objective here is to illuminate and isolate major and minor problems without doing damage to the vehicle—not to find out how well it corners at maximum speed. There are always bugs in newly built systems. Find them here. Major ones spell torch and chop, refit and reform. (Yay boxbeam!) An inconvenience here? Yes—but it's a mistake *compounded if* that formfitting body no longer fits!

Here's a question, problems or not: Did you have fun? Good!

Once the system is proved, fit the other vehicle systems and the body. Allow easy access to all subsystems. Design the body for easy removal. Prototypes evolve. They'll tell you things to adjust, tweak, and modify. And—new ideas will blossom as you enjoy your creation. Add what you wish!

Remember. Some bugs stay hidden for a long time.

OTHER SCRATCHBUILTS

Scratchbuilt vehicles built by individuals and small companies defy easy classification. Some are natural extensions of an existing idea. Others demonstrate innovative thought. Some make use of off-the-shelf hardware. Others utilize custom-built parts.

For these reasons, I have loosely separated various designs into three classifications: plan cars, production prototypes, and proof-of-concept vehicles.

• *Plan cars* are prototypes that may be duplicated by anyone who purchases a set of plans from the designer/owner.

• *Production prototypes* are vehicles intended for production. This includes vehicles that are (or were) in limited production, or are awaiting capitalization or licensing for higher production volume.

• *Proof of concept* (POCs) are prototypes that aim to demonstrate what is possible when the technology is put in its best light.

PLAN CARS

Two examples of plan cars are the Doran and the Vortex prototypes. Three-wheelers are safe when done correctly (Techtalk T23)

Doran

The Doran, designed by Rick Doran, is a simple, snappy three-wheeler (Application A16). The fiberglass body fits onto a metal chassis. The front two wheels are powered.

Vortex

The Vortex uses composite technology to merge body and chassis (Application A17). Major subassemblies are attached to the composite structure at hardened points. Designed and built by Dolphin Vehicles, the Vortex powers the single rear wheel. The vehicle is built directly from engineering plans, CAD-drawn plan sheets, and a 64-page booklet.

Techtalk
T23 — Three Wheel Design
Rick Doran

Is a three-wheeler stable? A common fear held by the general public is that a 3-wheeler is more susceptible to a rollover than a 4-wheeler. However, a properly designed 3-wheeler can have an overturn resistance as good as or better than many 4-wheel cars. To be safe at speed, two of the three wheels *must* be in the front of the vehicle (Fig. 3-22). The front track of the motorbike should be as wide as practical, with the center of gravity low and close to the front axle. The vehicle will handle very similar to a front wheel drive car. In tight turns, the tires will lose adhesion long before enough side force can be developed to roll the vehicle.

A three-wheeler with one wheel in front (the trike) gets into trouble fairly easily (Fig. 3-23). Note that the resultant of the braking and cornering forces goes outside of a line connecting the three tires. Bad. The vehicle will roll with little provocation.

In sharp contrast, the motorbike layout requires a higher magnitude of acceleration to flip the vehicle than the vehicle is genuinely capable of doing. Very few vehicles can accelerate as fast as they brake. Zero to 60 mph in 8 seconds is only 0.3G (, whereas braking of 0.8G is common for today's tires and brakes. In a vehicle such as the Doran, the cg is located far forward (about 0.33 of the wheelbase from that axle) but it would still require a braking force of 2.14G to flip over the front axle. The Doran design, then, has a safety factor of two.

There is a practical limit to the width of the front track. Both steering angles and the turning radius are adversely affected if the vehicle track is too wide.

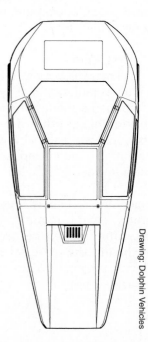

Fig. 3-24: The raindrop shape complements Vortex's motorbike layout.

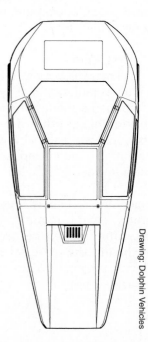 *Drawing: Dolphin Vehicles*

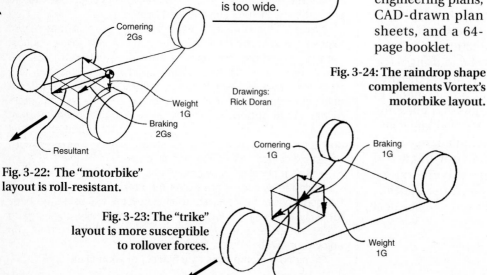

Drawings: Rick Doran

Fig. 3-22: The "motorbike" layout is roll-resistant.

Fig. 3-23: The "trike" layout is more susceptible to rollover forces.

$\mathcal{A}$pplication A 16   Doran Electric

The Doran is a two-seat, 3-wheel vehicle. Three wheels were chosen to minimize weight, lower the rolling resistance, and ease licensing. The motorbike arrangement of wheels is stable, minimizing the frontal area and allowing a low-drag teardrop shape. The drivetrain is built around a 1980-89 Subaru Hatchback transmission/transaxle.

After several years and several thousand miles of road tests with a gas engine, the Doran was modified to run on electric propulsion. Shortly thereafter, Rick Doran decided to offer plans so others could duplicate his efforts. He put together a 94-page book on design and construction (including fiberglass notes) of EVs generally and the Doran specifically.

Photo: Rick Doran

Fig. 3-25: Rick Doran with the Doran prototype at Phoenix International Raceway.

$\mathcal{A}$pplication A 17   Vortex Electric

The Vortex is an innovative, three-wheeled sports vehicle designed to be home-built from plans (with average tools and craftsman skills). The three-wheeled layout and simplified drive train allow the body to be shaped in one of the best aerodynamic profiles known: the raindrop.

Butterfly-wing doors lift up and forward for greater clearance on entrance and egress from the spacious side-by-side cockpit.

The Vortex body is hand-shaped and built of urethane foam and fiberglass. The chassis is a plywood monocoque structure. Suspension components are attached to metal sub-frames which are connected to the chassis through wide-based mounting plates to spread stress loads.

The engine, rear swing-arm, axle and tire are mounted to a cradle which slides into the rear of the vehicle. The entire "power train" can be removed in one piece for major repair. The front suspension is a sophisticated double A-arm unit from the Triumph Spitfire, including rack and pinion steering, anti-roll bar, and oversized disk brakes. Race-car systle coil-over shocks and low profile Pirelli P-7 tires complete the package.

Fig. 3-26: Good design allows complete access to the propulsion package.

Photo: Dolphin Vehicles

Photo: Dolphin Vehicles

Fig. 3-27: The Vortex runs the raceway at PIR.

PRODUCTION PROTOTYPES

Five production prototypes of interest are the Citicar, Tropica, Sunray, City-El, and Impact.

Citicar

In 1960, veteran EV builder Bob Beaumont brought the Citicar into limited production. The Citicar was a modest, two-person, purpose-built EV designed for use on the streets. Approximately 5000 of them were sold before an overzealous US Transportation Department shut down their production. The issues of safety that were raised about the Citicar related more to its general *size* than its specific *design*. Hundreds of these vehicles are still in use today, and their owners swear by them (Application A18).

> *"If I need to drive across country, it will be much more convenient and cost effective to rent a car for the trip."*
>
> *Gail Lucas*

Tropica

The Tropica is Beaumont's latest revival of a private-venture EV (Application A19). Body stylist Jim Muir is responsible for the Tropica's vibrant look. Whether or not the Tropica will go into production is unknown at this point. With an aftermarket rooftop, it would make a fine all-weather commuter EV.

The eight 6-Volt batteries—plus one 12V battery I added to the Citicar for the lights—are easy to access for maintenance. When it's time for replacement, the set will cost half as much as the 16-24 batteries needed in most EV conversions.

A friend and I take the Citicar grocery shopping. I often purchase a 50-lb sack of bird seed and there's room behind the seat for it *and* groceries for a week. I can tell at a glance before I open the door that no one is lurking in my car, an important consideration for a woman in Las Vegas. I doubt that anyone could hijack my Citicar.

I have passed gas-powered cars stalled in the flooded streets on rainy days. I was rear-ended by a mid-sized American sedan and, although noisy, absolutely no damage was done. I can move the car around the driveway without looking for the keys. Or push it out of the way in the event of a problem on the road. I have upgraded the control system to a PMC controller and have no problems along this line.

The EV community seems to feel that the Citicar should not be presented as a real electric vehicle, that it will tarnish the image they wish to project to the public. This is a totally unfair assessment of these adorable, wonderfully maneuverable little cars, many of which are on the road seventeen (17) years after they were built. I hope the auto manufacturers will realize that the electric vehicle advantages—no pollution, little maintenance, and convenient, economical refueling—are more important to many people than high speed and cross country travel.

Photo courtesy Gail Lucas

Fig. 3-28: Gail heads up the local EAA chapter in Las Vegas, and readily shows off her EV at community events.

Photo: Renaissance Vehicles

Fig. 3-29: The smiles say it all.

capable of being 1,800 lbs. The ABS body avoids fiberglass usage. The classy sports car body is a Jim Muir design.

The classification of "sports car" frees the design from needing a roof, bypassing many regulations (windshield glass, strong roof structure, etc.) that would involve more bureaucracy. (The same tactic is used by some automakers with various types of minivans and sports vehicles.) Rooftops would certainly appear as an aftermarket item, to lend all-weather utility to the vehicle.

The Tropica is a savvy design worthy of further study by anyone interested in the growing EV market.

Photo: Renaissance Vehicles

Fig. 3-30: A test drive.

Photo: Bob Abraham

Fig. 3-31: The Sunray is designed for use in the islands.

Sunray

The Sunray is a product of the islands. It is a production prototype designed and built by Jonathan Tennyson, who lives on the big island of Hawaii (Application A20).

Tennyson is an EV pioneer. Although his vehicle, Mana La, was no match for GM's Sunraycer, it was a little guy/big guy matchup in the Australian Solar Challenge, the first transcontinental race of solar cars in 1987. The fifty-fold difference in project funds set the tone of the race.

Tennyson's dream has been to bring EVs to the mainstream, and what better place than the islands! It's a natural niche. No range issue. Tourists year-round wanting to enjoy paradise. Too much imported noise and pollution in the

Fig. 3-32: Jonathan Tennyson and team designed and built the Sunray and Pickette at Suntera.

All photos:
Stevi Johnson
(Suntera)

Fig. 3-33: This Pickette was delivered to the Hawaiian Power Company.

Application A20 — Sunray & Pickette

Detroit and the big island of Hawaii don't have much in common — or do they? If Jonathan Tennyson and his crew have their way, Hawaii may become the newest state to churn out automobiles — using electric drive.

Jonathan has been designing and building EVs for a couple of decades. His newest prototype is the Sunray, a compact two-seater that may help the islands regain their former clean and sunny look.

"Hawaii is ideal for electrics," says Jonathan. "There's no destination further than 80 miles away! Remember, people come here for the sunshine and breezes!" Jonathan adds.

The modular, 3-wheeled design is clever and cute. With only eight feet of length and a bit more than five feet in width, it requires less than half the space needed to park other vehicles. Its 6-foot height ensures a profile that will be visible to the drivers of other cars.

The most noticeable aspect of the body style is the "happy face" when viewed head-on. The composite/epoxy body won't rust in the tropical air. It is designed to tilt away to expose the mechanical and electronic components for easy servicing. The 12 HP series motor, 120V lead-acid battery pack, and solid-state MOSFET controller will move the 1500-lb curb weight along briskly on the street or highway. The belt drive will preserve the revered island ambiance.

Fig. 3-34: One chassis is common to both the Sunray and Pickette.

form of cars and gasoline. A need for personal transportation. Best of all, there's year-round sunshine to power the dream. Lightweight, quiet, open-air, zippy little machines taking you to magic places!

The Sunray is designed for the task. Short length for curbside parking. Two-person plus baggage. A sturdy 3-wheeler that speeds licensing issues. The 120V battery pack gives the Sunray zip, while its centralized weight gives low-down stability for that warm-tummy feeling. The two-stage, fixed-ratio drivetrain uses gear belts for silent, low-maintenance operation.

Viewed straight on, it's hard to miss the vehicle's happy-face.

City-El

The USA has the lowest price of gasoline in the world. Other countries, including those in Europe, pay as much as $3-5 (or more!) for a gallon of gasoline. While this does not stop the use of automobiles, the playing field is more even for alternatives to compete. Thus, not only are EVs more prevalent in these countries, they are smaller and designed to be less wasteful. Downsizing the transportation machine, then, should focus more on its utility than its power, speed, and ability to "go anywhere."

The City-El is a good example of a neighborhood EV (Application A21). Licensing of the City-El is eased because it is a three-wheeler and is most certainly not designed for significant speed.

Downsizing the transportation machine should focus more on its utility than its power, speed, and ability to "go anywhere."

Application A21 — City-El

The City-El is one of many EVs manufactured in Europe that is also available in the USA. It is a beautifully-designed vehicle that glides noiselessly and easily through traffic.

The City-El has an adjustable driver's seat that is comfortable. Visibility is excellent in all directions. The controls are easy to operate. The single-ratio drive means no shifting. The instrument panel has a trip recorder (re-settable odometer) and the battery gauge is simple and accurate.

Although lightweight, the City-El is built strong. With monocoque sandwich construction and a rollover bar, both driver and passenger are protected. The entire upper half of the vehicle lifts for entrance and egress.

The Sacramento Municipal Utility District has purchased 100 City-Els. It will make them available for use by customers for short periods of time for consumer evaluation purposes.

Fig. 3-35: The City-El's upper body shell opens to admit the driver

Photos: Tom Whitney (SMUD)

Fig. 3-36: The City-El has a good profile, is all-weather, and is easy to park.

Impact

In 1990, General Motors unveiled its bold new prototype, Impact. It was the first prototype of its type that leaped beyond "proof of concept" and went directly to being a production prototype (Application A22). That is, the molds were specifically engineered and fabricated to stamp out aluminum body parts —in place of the fiberglass ones used in the initial prototype. With one-half the aerodynamic drag and one-half the weight of a similar size of vehicle, the Impact requires only one-fourth the energy to go the same mile.

The Impact's powertrain was, at the time of its release, the most advanced in the world. Merging the best of the electronic and motor technologies, it demonstrated that an EV need not be limited in its performance. The Impact's sophisticated electronic control system is getting a good workout. A test program is putting Impacts in the driveway of average citizens for two-week trials. Their reaction? They don't want toOn the surface, GM still questions the existence of a market for electric-powered cars. Fortunately, its subsidiary, GM Hughes, is producing the Impact drivetrain system (motor/controller) for sale to other OEMs (original equipment manufacturers).

PROOF OF CONCEPT

Here are seven other vehicle types that span the range of Proof of Concept vehicles: Calstart, Flash and Sunrise, Horlacher, Viking, Sylph, and Formula E.

CalStart

CalStart is one of many companies that has started up to serve the growing interest in EVs. Based in Burbank, California, it intends to move aerospace engineers into designing lightweight, aerodynamic space ships for use on the ground (Application A23).

With some capable designwork by individuals such as Bruce Severance, CalStart has produced several prototypes as showcases for their diversified efforts. (Note the similarities in the top profile of the CalStart and the Doran prototypes.)

Hoping to make plowshares out of swords, CalStart is one of many consortiums that hopes to attract ARPA money. No doubt, if money is pushed at the transportation industry like it's been available for defense contractors, a sizeable industry will emerge.

It was a good sign for the '90s that General Motors unveiled its bold new prototype, Impact. This is a car that most environmentalists would enjoy — it's pollution-free, quiet, uses 1/5th the energy from fossil fuels as regular cars, and has a recyclable battery pack.

The Impact demonstrated a respectable 90 miles of range — whether cruising along at freeway speed or in the stop-and-go "urban driving cycle." Finally— the aerodynamicists and stylists have gotten their act together. The Impact has a competitive look, yet boasts one of the lowest drag coefficient in the history of commuter vehicles.

The battery pack is mainly off-the-shelf technology — lead-acid batteries that pack a lot of energy, are low in weight, and recharge quickly. Since the batteries are sealed (recombinant), no watering maintenance is required.

The Impact prototype is a concept advanced and built primarily by Paul MacCready and the team at AeroVironment. (Some of this crew is responsible for the Gossamer series of human-powered aircraft!)

The Impact is a high-performance electric vehicle. The footage shown during its introduction proves that. From a standstill, the Impact "blew away" a Miata and a Mazda 300ZX in the quarter mile. Obviously, the design was intended to blow holes through the perception that electric vehicles are golf carts with pretty bodies over them.

The big question on GM's mind seems to be: is there a market for electric-powered cars? That GM is unsure about this is revealed in the way they announced it—underselling both the vehicle and technology. GM claims that operating expenses for the Impact are double that of a standard ICE (internal-combustion engine) car, that the Impact is handicapped with periodic battery replacement, and that it is not a get-in-and-drive-anywhere car. The Impact also needs an infrastructure to recharge and service this new type of car. GM appeared genuinely surprised at the excitement and warm reception given it by industry, government, and the general public. They probably thought that everyone was going to laugh. Nobody did!

Still, GM faces an interesting dilemma: its marketing effort must tiptoe through any comparisons that could hurt its greater investment in ICE-based technology.

Will GM hold out for market share and delay aggressive tactics until other car companies have tested the waters?

With a thorough aerodynamic facelift, a GM Impact set a new land speed record for EVs in its class. It broke a two-decades-old record by reaching over 183 mph!

Photo: General Motors Company

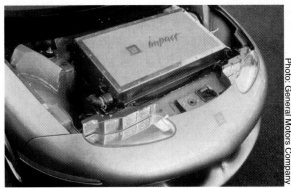

Fig. 3-37: Impact's electronics are located in one large box.

Photo: General Motors Company

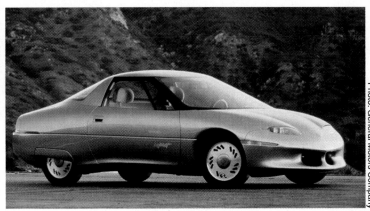

Fig. 3-38: The Impact is a high -performance electric vehicle.

Application 23

CalStart SEV

CalStart focuses on many different aspects of design for EVs, understanding that integration is the key to their commercialization. With participation by many industry leaders, CalStart aims to develop the components that respond to specific challenges EVs face in fitting into the real world.

For example, air conditioning represents a large load for the EV battery pack. At 1/100th of the energy density (per pound) of gasoline, batteries have no power to waste in heating and cooling the driver (and passengers) in the EV. Since the goal of air conditioning is driver and passenger comfort, CalStart engineers have focused on installing cooling systems *inside* the car seats, reducing the overall energy load.

CalStart has built a number of prototypes. It has declared a goal of building cars *in* California *for* Californians *by* Californians. Whether this happens or not, the goal of putting people to work building some of the pieces of the EV puzzle is an idea worthy of investment.

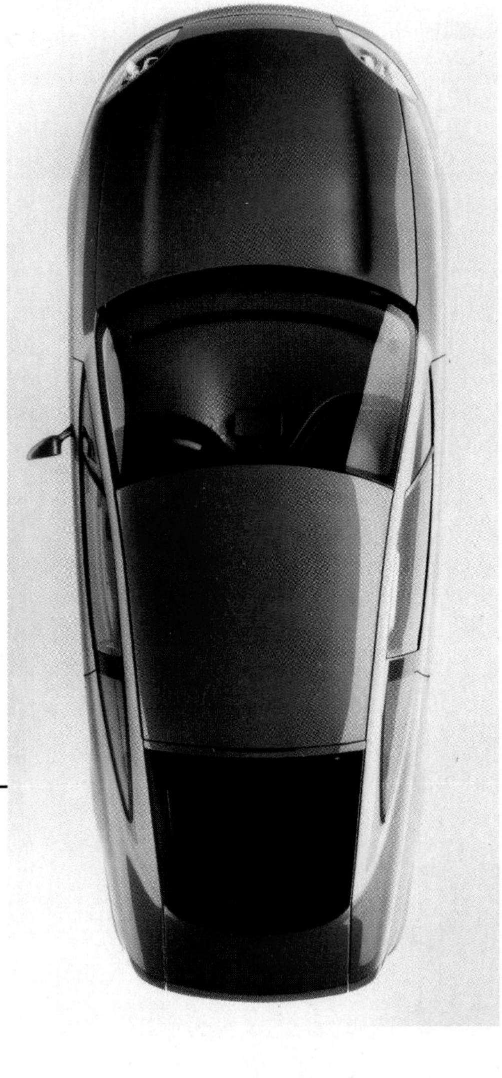

Fig. 3-39: The showcase vehicle from CALSTART, body by Bruce Severance.

CalStart engineers have focused on installing cooling systems inside the car seats, reducing the overall energy load of air conditioning.

Vehicles of the Tour de Sol in Europe

Fig. 3-40: This vehicle design has a strong European flavor.

Fig. 3-42: Entries must have a solar source equal to the amount of energy they use.

Fig. 3-41: Sponsors are an important part of this annual event.

All photos:
C. Michael Lewis

Fig. 3-43: The public gets an eyeful as entries in the Tour de Sol stop for a noonday recharge.

Fig. 3-44: The event is held in any kind of weather, but entrants like it when the sun is out!

Fig. 3-45: Some designs look like scaled-down versions of large cars.

Fig. 3-46: EVs like this one use every design tool available to them.

European Tour de Sol

Rather than re-inventing the EV, any company that declares an intention to design and build good EVs would do well to look at the European designs that have been running in the Tour de Sol races in Switzerland for almost a decade.

Flash and Sunrise

Many people believe that the EV of the future looks nothing like a standard car. The Flash and the Sunrise will not disappoint them.

The Flash, designed by James Worden at Solectria, is an example of a scratchbuilt EV that confronts the issues of weight and aerodynamics upfront (Application A24). Subsequently, the Sunrise was developed to seat four people, appeal to the driving public, meet ZEV standards mandated by CARB (California Air Resources Board), and pass crash tests. (It has!)

Application

A24   Flash & Sunrise

The Flash was the proof of concept vehicle that led to the development of the Sunrise from Solectria. In turn, the Flash was an outgrowth of Solectria's Lightspeed prototype.

Flash. The Flash is a softly-rounded. gull-wing two-seater made of composite materials. It uses twin 30 HP brushless motors in a dual-independent, single-ratio rear-wheel drive. Four-wheel independent suspension and rack and pinion steering complete the chassis setup.

The Flash uses an 8 kWh battery pack. It is recharged from an onboard unit that plugs into a standard wall socket. A 200-Watt PV array is built into the vehicle rooftop for utility-free charging.

With a curb weight of 1100 lbs, the Lightspeed accelerates 0-60 mph in an impressive 8.5 seconds. Top speed is 80 mph. Range on one charge is 120 miles.

Sunrise. Sunrise is an EV sedan with four seats It combines low weight (1700 lbs) with a low drag coefficient (0.17 in the scale model) with a monocoque composite body/shell that is nicely styled. The ac induction drive system and sealed lead-acid batteries yield a 120-mile range before recharging is needed

Sunrise has many amenities, including power brakes, AM/FM stereo, dual air bags and cruise control. The battery pack is automatically kept warm during winter driving. A heat pump supplies either AC (air conditioning) or heating. Battery monitoring and charging are provided onboard.

Sunrise was developed by Solectia as a Northeast Alternative Vehicle Consortium (NAVC) project, co-founded by the Advanced Research Projects Agency (ARPA) and by Boston Edison Company. (See Chapter 1 for more detail on Solectria.)

Sunrise successfully passed its crash tests in 1995.

Fig. 3-47: The Solectria Flash is efficient, sleek, and light.

Photo: C. Michael Lewis

Fig. 3-48: James Worden has been building EVs since his teens. He is the founder of Solectria Corporation.

Photo: C. Michael Lewis

Fig. 3-49: Sunrise is the latest vehicle from Solectria.

Photo: Solectria Corporation

Fig. 3-50: A "City" Horlacher is parked near the windmachines that will re-charge it.

Horlacher Electrics

Boris Horlacher's EVs are a familiar and welcome sight at the annual Tour de Sol events in Switzerland. They sprint up alpine grades with the best of them. Folks who have driven one of the early prototypes say that the Horlacher meets *all* of their expectations.

Propulsive power for the earliest Horlacher vehicle came from a 12 HP Brusa drive. It was the motor-controller combination used in all the winning Tour de Sol electrics. It pushes this peppy 3-wheel, twin-seater at speeds up to 45 mph for an hour or more.

Two more recent releases from the Horlacher design facility are the Sport Two and the City prototypes. The Sport Two is constructed from FRP using foam core parts, and includes an "impact belt" laminated into the body-chassis unit. The vehicle has a GVWR of 1,210 lbs, including 550 lbs of battery. It can reach 77 mph with its 12 kW ac drive, yet uses a frugal 100 W-h/mile in normal driving, i.e., stop-go, uphill-downhill, and cruising at speed.

A head-on, crash test of the "City" vehicle (Techtalk T24) proved the viability of the design concept used by Horlacher AG in their vehicles.

Fig. 3-51: The interior of an early Horlacher is simple and intuitive.

Fig. 3-52: The sliding door/roof on the Horlacher makes for easy access in this 2-seater.

Fig. 3-53: The Horlacher "Sport" (right) sits beside an early production model.

Horlacher Electrics

Three striking EV designs have been developed by Horlacher AG (a design company in the European community) over the past 15 years (Application A25). The first went into limited production. More recently, the Sport Two and City prototypes have been released.

DOT (Department of Transportation) regulations and Federal Vehicle Safety standards will play havoc when *any* small, lightweight vehicles are introduced into the USA. The real questions is: how do we get 2-3 ton monster vehicles off the road to make it safe for environmentally-sound cars like the Horlachers?

Horlacher AG has asked a different question: how can the occupants of a smaller car survive an encounter with a large, hard-nose vehicle? The Horlacher's "impact belt" and hard-shell, ultra-stiff design approach has done much to deflate the image of the little car always being the loser (Techtalk T24).

Viking Series

One way to eat a big watermelon is one bite at a time. Michael Seal of Western Washington University (WWU) is willing to let a good EV design evolve out of projects that focus on specific issues. The result is the Viking series of vehicle projects that combine grants, goals, and students at the Vehicle Research Institute at WWU (review Techtalk T10).

These experiences led to the design and construction of a solar racer, the Viking XX (#20), that challenged many concepts of what a competitive vehicle looks like. The Viking XX's success in both the US and Australian

Photos:
Horlacher AG

Fig. 3-54: A Horlacher "City" is crash tested against an Audi 100.

Fig. 3-55: The "City" vehicle had a static deflection of 150 mm.

Techtalk

T24

Horlacher Crash Tests

Crashworthiness is a *big* issue with small EVs. To demonstrate the viability of an integrated approach to crashworthiness in small EVs, the Horlacher "City" was crash-tested.

With the 600 kg City traveling at 32 mph and an Audi 100 at 16 mph, the test results of a head-on collision were revealing. The static deflection of the City: 150 mm. The Audi: 350 mm.

Of course, automakers utilize large "plastic" deformation of the steel vehicle structure for occupant protection. The Horlacher's design brings the body-chassis into compliance with the vehicle mass, producing light-stiff vehicles that would be compatible with big-soft cars on the road.

Air bags, pre-tensioned seat belts, and sufficient run-down distance (inside the vehicle) are also essential to safely decelerate the vehicle occupants in a crash.

Fig. 3-56: The Audi had a static deflection of 350 mm.

Fig. 3-57: Viking 21 is a hybrid designed to address street and freeway driving.

Photos courtesy
Vehicle Research Institute
(Western Washington University)

Fig. 3-58: The inner (chassis) and outer (body) components in Viking 21.

Fig. 3-59: Denet Lewis demonstrates the light weight of the Viking 21 chassis.

Application A 26

Viking 21
Michael Seal, Ph.D.

Following our success with Viking XX (review Application A47), we decided to see if it would be possible to put the lessons learned in the previous 20 years of Viking cars into a prototype for the 21st century.

Viking 21 has been designed, and it is now fully funded by the Washington State Ecology Department, the Bonneville Power Authority, and Puget Sound Power and Light Company.

If the greenhouse effect is real—and I have little reason to doubt its verity—then all the rules for low-emission vehicles have changed. The only viable automobiles will be electric cars, and the power to run them must come from non-fuel-burning sources. The solar/electric car is rapidly becoming a viable alternative as an urban commuter but has little hope—with the current battery and solar cell technology—of being acceptable for intercity use.

Viking 21, a parallel hybrid, is the Vehicle Research Institute's solution to the consumers' desire to do what they can to help the environment yet not give up the freedom to travel by personal transport over long distances. The Viking 21 does not, of course, eliminate carbon dioxide production but should go a long way toward reducing these emissions. It uses presently-available technology and requires a minimum of adjustment on the user's part.

In the urban environment, it has a 100-mile range on solar/electric power, while converting to a clean, fuel-efficient, internal combustion-powered vehicle with an additional 200-mile range on compressed natural gas.

The solar/electric hybrid is a two-seat coupe with occupants seated side by side. The front wheels are each powered by a 13 lb brushless DC motor. The rear wheels are powered by the IC engine through a 5-speed gearbox and differential. All four wheels can be driven during ice and snow to enhance traction.

transcontinental races in 1993 proved the benefit of a clean slate and an open mind (review Application A47).

More recently, the Viking XXI (#21) has merged solar and EV propulsion, hybrid technology, and a lightweight and aerodynamic monocoque shell to show what is really possible (Application A26).

Sylph

In 1975, Matt Van Leeuwen was inspired when he saw a student pedal an aerodynamic 3-wheeler to 41 mph at an HPV (Human Powered Vehicle) race in California. He rushed home and hired a design student to help with the sketches and the construction of a quarter scale model. The scale model produced a drag coefficient (Cd) reading of 0.097 in the 10-foot wind tunnel at Cal Tech, the lowest recorded there for a ground vehicle. Matt named his creation Sylph (Spirit of the Wind).

Solar cells are mounted on the upper body panels to collect solar energy to store in the fiber-NiCd batteries while the car is stopped at a stoplight or parked. The turbo-charged, intercooled, fuel-injected, natural gas engine powers the car at speeds above 50 mph. The chassis is composite materials with one of the two filament-wound, natural gas tanks down the center backbone providing additional torsional stiffness.

Viking 21 has wheels that mount two tires on a single rim, much like a dual truck tire assembly. The two tires will be very different, however: the inner tire has a hard compound rubber and round section giving a very small contact patch, and the outer tire has a wider tread patch and uses very soft, high-grip rubber.

During normal operation, the wheels run at negative camber so the outer tire does not quite touch the road. During cornering, normal chassis roll causes the outer wheel to become perpendicular to the road surface. The outer tire now grips the road securely, allowing higher cornering power. When the brakes are applied, a micro switch sends a signal to a solenoid valve which allows high pressure from the fuel tank to pressurize a central hydraulic system. Slave cylinders mounted at the outer end of each wishbone cause all four wheels to become perpendicular to the road, greatly increasing traction when stopping.

As the car is designed to demonstrate near-term viability, it has automatic safety belts, full road-lighting equipment, heater, defroster, and radio/tape deck. It also has air-conditioning.

Although Viking 21 does not have all the answers, I believe that it demonstrates to the public and to the world's automakers that an advanced concept car can be comfortable and easy to drive *and* significantly reduce CO, carbon dioxide, HC, and NOx emissions, as well as reduce fuel consumption to minimum levels.

Photo: C. Michael Lewis

Fig. 3-60: Solar cells are integrated into the body to eliminate aerodynamic drag.

Photo: C. Michael Lewis

Fig. 3-61: Viking 21's doors "seal" by inflating an O-ring around the full perimeter of each opening.

Fig. 3-62: Matt Van Leeuwen and Sylph.

All photos:
Bruce Severance

From the beginning, Matt wanted to use electric propulsion. Disappointed with the state of the art at the time, he finally selected a 1978 1000 cc Honda Goldwing engine and gearbox for the propulsion system.

The Sylph prototype graces this section because it represents the kind of packaging

Application A27 — Sylph

"Engineers will tell you it's important to design from the inside out," Matt Van Leeuwen admits, "but I wasn't going to compromise the aerodynamics. Sylph is designed outside in."

The shell is based on a NACA 66 series airfoil. Unlike most airfoils that are bulbous in front and taper quickly, this one is narrow in front, and grows gradually toward the midpoint. This gave me good space utilization." Even with a steel frame inside, there's ample room behind the rearmost seat for storage. The rear seatback folds forward to provide an ample sleeping platform or baggage area. The engine, transmission, rear wheel, and suspension assembly sit flat below this area. Up front, the suspension is also fully contained below the floorboard.

"Sylph far exceeds the spaciousness of many two-seat roadsters," Matt points out. "As an electric, Sylph would probably have a 100-mile range at 80 mph with lead-acid batteries."

Matt is a firm believer in design-as-you-go. An example? "The roll cage," Matt replied. "I sat inside and looked out. I wanted a big view. I didn't need two symmetrical fighter aircraft pillars." Instead, Matt built three big beams of high-tensile steel, brakeformed C-section channels running in an asymmetrical configuration inside the fiberglass shell. This complemented the staggered tandem seating. The passenger, then, had an excellent view ahead, instead of a view of the back of Matt's head. The offset seating permits a 22 percent airfoil and a comfortable 33 inch width at the driver's seat.

"Without the pressure of schedules, bosses, or money investments," Matt claims, "these in-process modifications let the design evolve to my heart's content."

Most people are enchanted by the look of three-wheelers but are phobic about their stability and safety. Matt's reaction puts the issue in the right light. "Think of a 3-legged stool," Matt

Fig. 3-63: Sylph easily handles Matt's 6'3" size.

Fig. 3-64: Low weight and clean lines make steep grades a cinch to climb.

suggests. "No matter how rough the surface, it's always firmly planted. The same can't be said of four "legs" — stool, table, or vehicle. Until you drive something on a dry lake bed, you don't realize how uneven *all* road surfaces are. A four-wheel vehicle (four corners on a rigid chassis) is always floating through road undulations.

With good weight distribution, the Sylph proves that a three-wheeler is stable and maintains strong adhesion with very little wheel travel. Driver and

Fig. 3-65: The low frontal profile of Sylph offers little resistance to its movement.

that would complement today's EV technology (Application A27). It maintains a high profile for street use, arranges the driver and passengers in a 3-seat, offset-tandem style that conserves space and maintains clean lines despite its payload.

Fig. 3-66: Sylph seems to stretch out as it moves away.

passenger are more centralized between the three wheels, too. There's less bump experience and better overall ride comfort. "Sylph doesn't have to accommodate the road," Matt assured me. "The stiff suspension ensures solid roll resistance and stable cornering."

Matt faced many challenges in the design of the two steered front wheels. To minimize aerodynamic drag, wheel pants enshroud the twin 155 x15 tires with minimal air gap. They turn in unison with the wheels. An airfoil fully encloses the suspension and steering rods. Clever design permits needed articulation without exposing drag-inducing edges.

How did he manage the fit? "The front suspension is very similar to a swing axle," Matt explained. "To minimize the negative swing axle effect of the A-arms, they're pivoted as low as possible, right inside the belly (and on the centerline) of the car. I factored in a little rear compliance, about 5 degrees declination toward the rear of the vehicle." Mercedes Benz utilized low center pivoting, swing axle suspensions on their cars, including racers, for many years with great success. "This gives it a nice ride over the bumps, keeps it simple and sturdy — and leaves a flat floor in the vehicle!"

"A transverse spring suspends the two A-arms," Matt continued. "This leaf spring doesn't have much travel but, then, it doesn't need it. Remember, this is a three-wheeler. Initially, I used a carbon fiber spring, but after several years, it started to de-laminate. I replaced it with steel, and I'm happy with it. The A-arms pivot in teflon-lined, spherical aircraft bearings. I've got a lifetime of zero play. It's solid."

Two short wings complete the Sylph profile rearward. Each is driven by its own linear actuator with large rocker switches mounted in the dash on the right, just above the shift lever. These were designed-in early. "I figured that my vertical airfoil shape would be all over the road when the wind started gusting, "Matt admitted. "The wings add stability, allowing me to add some downforce to the rear wheel. Initially, I figured to use dive brakes (fins that fold flat against the vehicle when not in use) to preserve the sleekness," Matt said, "but the wings are better.

As with any design option, one may be chosen over another because it helps in some other way. "The independent travel of the wings make turns possible at faster vehicle speeds," Matt explained. "I just pick up the inside wing about 30 degrees, just short of stall so I don't induce much drag, and the downforce counters roll in the turn. As well, the wings mount brake lights, running lights, and turn signals in their trailing edges. They also sport streamlined tip lights with running and turn signal functions. This helps traffic behind and to the side of me to *see* Sylph."

What's it like to drive the Sylph? Breathtaking! "The transmission is geared for a 700-lb motorcycle, and Sylph is twice that (1450 lbs). Everything gets better and better with speed — above 70 mph, it's a rocketship." What speed has Sylph seen? "I've had it up to 130 mph. That was uphill," Matt added, "and against a headwind." What will it do? "On paper, 150-160 mph with the stock motor and higher gears. Presently the gearing limits top speed." Matt laughed. "Maybe it's just as well!"

Matt drove Sylph for the first time in December of 1985. On a skid pad at Ford Aerospace in Orange Country, he pulled 0.82Gs. Subsequently, he added a hefty anti-roll bar and firmed up the springs further. There's no discernible roll now, and Matt is still looking for the cornering limits on mountain roads.

"Sylph is big fun to drive!" Matt noted. What's next? "I'd like to build a new vehicle. With a carbon fiber composite monocoque body, Sylph could weigh half of its current weight." Toward this end, Matt is taking a class in composites and plans to make both a plug and shell for the new vehicle as his class project. The list continued. "I'd look hard at electric propulsion again. I want a one-piece suspension/wheel foil up front to eliminate any aerodynamic forces in the steering and simplify construction. Also, this time I'd have a single, top-opening door. And use a lower body airfoil. Overall, I'd like to push the concept. And include improvements that would be too expensive or time-consuming to put into Sylph."

Fig. 3-67: What is the vehicle's speed?

Fig. 3-68: Good closure and a mirror-like finish keep the "aero" high.

Formula E Racer

The Formula E racer was built by Ely Schless and raced at Phoenix by the Hackleman-Schless team, sweeping the first-place trophies in its class in *both* events (1992 and 1993).

The Formula E proved many concepts (Application A28). One major innovation was its exchangeable battery modules. While a 500-lb battery pack would be weighty at any time—and especially so when quick exchange is desired—it was tamed by the natural split of the pack into two "modules" of 250 pounds each. Arranged saddlepack-style, the

Fig. 3-69: Ely Schless takes the electrified Formula 440 racer out for the first run.

twin modules represented the *only* way to adapt the original Formula 440 chassis to electric drive without major reconstruction.

To ease the manufacturing of the many modules that would be needed for the 90-mile race, the module design was standardized so *any* module could be used on *either* side. Essentially, then, each module was made in an E-cell (the EV equivalent of a D-size cell like that used in flashlights).

The Formula E ran at sustained speeds of 85 mph in the Phoenix races with a single-ratio belt drive. Its acceleration from a stop was strong. While the race was run with the large Advanced DC motor (20 HP), its early test runs demonstrated equivalent performance with a series motor rated at only 10 HP. The larger motor, then, was used as extra protection against heat accumulation and for its easy swapout, if needed.

These factors — single-ratio drive, 20 HP propulsion motor, saddlepack batteries, and a curb weight of 1,200 pounds—represent an

---

A28 Formula E Racer

The Formula E racer was one of two vehicles built by the Hackleman-Schless team to compete in the Solar & Electric 500 races at the Phoenix International Raceway in 1992 and 1993. Except for the body, it was entirely constructed by Ely Schless at his shop facility in North Hollywood, California.

Fig. 3-70: Formula E at Phoenix in 1992.

Trojan Battery was the primary sponsor of the Formula E, offering both product and monies to build the car. A used Formula 440 race car was purchased and its 65 HP, 2-cycle engine and transmission removed. Two saddle-packs were added to hold the 120V battery pack. A 10 HP Prestolite motor and a Curtis PMC controller were purchased from Eyeball Engineering for the initial trials.

Although this vehicle was never intended to be more than a "mule" for testing various motors, controllers, and batteries, it proved an adequate chassis. Following 100 miles of test driving at both the Willow Springs (CA) and Phoenix (AZ) tracks—at sustained speeds of 85 mph with several pack exchanges—the Prestolite motor was replaced with a 20 HP (9-inch) Advanced DC motor. The Prestolite performed fine. We simply wanted to use

a motor we could replace quickly at the race, and a spare for the bigger motor was easier to obtain.

A fast-swap battery scheme was designed, and it worked right the first time (review Application 57). With only six weeks to the race, Trojan Battery recognized a winning entry and sprung for the money to have a custom-built fiberglass body fabricated for the car. It was built by Pete and Mike Stephenson (Clean Air Machines). Ely fitted it to the chassis and designed flip-up cutout doors to ensure quick access to the battery saddlepacks. He then sanded, painted, and applied graphics to the finished car. It was ready to race.

The Formula E placed 1st in both the 25-mile heat race and 120-mile endurance races in 1992.

With slight modifications, the Formula E repeated these victories in the 1993 races.

exciting template for the designers of a four-wheel street machine. Shortening the drive ratio, positioning the driver and passenger above the battery pack for better visibility, and retaining the exchangeable module idea (saddlepack or transverse alignment) will make a strong, unlimited-range vehicle. This may be just the formula (no pun intended) for the NEV (neighborhood EV) or station car.

Fig. 3-71: Formula E at Phoenix in 1993.

Final Thoughts

A scratchbuilt EV is a challenging project. Feel encouraged by the many individuals who have accepted this challenge and succeeded. If it seems too formidable, take heart. The next chapter will cover EVs that are smaller in size and scope than the ones shown in this chapter.

Fig. 3-72: The Hackleman-Schless team swaps E-packs during a pit stop.

All photos:
Schless Engineering,
Daniel Pliskin, and
Michael Hackleman

Fig. 3-73: The Formula E's drivetrain. Note the rams used to secure the batteries and make electrical contact.

Fig. 3-74: The body could be quickly removed for access to chassis and components.

Fig. 3-75: The Formula E in victory circle.

Fig. 3-76 : Specifications

| Vehicle | | Weight | Funding | Battery Pack | | | |
Name	Type	in lbs.	Source	Type	Voltage	Ah	BVWR
NoPed II	STR	125	Schless Eng.	SLA	144	7	48%
PowerBike	STR	150	Schless Eng.	SLA	36	34	67%
Lightning Two	RCR	165	Dann Parks	SLA	24	70	39%
Sunseeker	ACR	204	Eric Raymond	NiCd	100	4	17%
Suncoaster	STR	220	Tom Bennett	GLA	60	12	20%
Shawk	STR	485	Schless Eng.	SLA	48	35	36%
Solar Eagle	RCR	485	CSLA	SZ	120	40	32%
SolExplorer	WCR	485	Stevenson Projects	SLA	24	55	33%
Speedster II	STR	760	Paul Lee	FLA	72	105	47%
Formula E	RCR	1,400	Schless Eng.	FLA	144	85	43%
Spyder	STR	2,700	Mendo-Motive	FLA	120	125	47%
Lightning Rod	RCR	2,700	Arivett Brothers	SLA	312	105	45%
EVX	STR	3,100	Michael Hackleman	FLA	120	210	36%
'92 Honda Civic CX	STR	3,200	AC Propulsion	SLA	336	50	38%

Vehicle Type: STR = street, RCR = racer, ACR = aircraft, WCR = watercraft
Vehicle Weight: Curb weight (no driver/passenger) of vehicle in pounds. *Table is sorted by vehicle weight.*
Battery type: FLA = flooded lead acid, SLA = sealed lead acid, SZ = silver zinc, NMH = nickel metal hydride, NiCd = Nickel-Cadmium
Battery A-h: Ampere-hour capacity of batteries in pack.
Battery Pack BVWR: Ratio of battery pack weight to vehicle curb weight, expressed as percentage (%).

for Electric Vehicles

Motor			Drivetrain	Top Speed	Brakes	
Type	Winding	HP		in mph	Type	Regen
DC	PM	1/4	DR/Chn/Blt 17.1:1	21	Bicycle	Yes
DC	PM	1	DR/Chn/Blt	32	Disc	Yes
DC	PM	1	SR/Chn 5:1	40	Drum	No
DC	Brushless	5	SR/5:1 Prop	100	NA	No
DC	PM	1	SR/Chn 5.8:1	19	Bicycle	No
DC	Series	6.5	SR/Grblt	40 4.5:1	Disc	No
DC	Brushless	20	DR/Grblt	85	Disc	Yes
DC	(2) PM	1.5	DD/11/4 Prop	6	Rev. Thrust	No
DC	Series	6.5	SR/Chn 4.5:1	50	Disc/ Drum	No
DC	Series	20	SR/Grblt 3:1	100	Disc	No
DC	Series	68	Stock	90	Disc/ Drum	Yes
DC	Series	100	SR/Grblt	200+	Disc	No
DC	Series	20	Stock	90	Disc	No
AC	Induction	200	Stock	85	Disc	Yes

Motor type: DC = direct current, AC = alternating current.
Motor Winding: PM = permanent magnet
HP: Horsepower, continuous rating
Drivetrain: Stock = original transmission, SR = single ratio,
   DR = dual ratio (jackshaft), Chn = chain, Blt = belt, DD =
   direct drive, Prop = Prop, i.e, 11/4 (11" diameter, 4 pitch)
Top speed: claimed mph
Brakes: Bicycle (rim), Disc, Drum, Reverse Thrust
Regen: Regenerative braking included

Chapter 4
Human & Electric Vehicles

The primary advantage of the scratchbuilt EV is the way in which it complements the elegance of electric propulsion. The lesson is clearly: keep it light. The less that is needed, the more simple everything becomes.

What if highway and freeway travel is not the transportation goal? What about something basic, practical, and reliable? Is there a road machine that honors genuine simplicity? What about something that fits pedestrians, bicyclists, and the planet?

Fig. 4-1: Peter Talbert races a human and electric powered vehicle at PIR.

Photo: Burkhardt Turbines

Downsizing from the machines described in Chapter 3 is like climbing down a cliff. It is much easier to do *if* you've already climbed up it. So, this chapter starts off at the simplest expression of self-propelled transportation for human beings–the bicycle—and works its way up toward the smaller machines described in Chapter 3.

The Solar Cup

My awakening to the merit of a fresh approach to electric propulsion began in 1988. I attended the Solar Cup in Visalia, California, the first solar car race in the USA. Rob Cotter pieced this event together, pitting James Worden's Solectria 5 and Jonathan Tennyson's Mana La against each other in a road race.

What I saw there surprised me. I had come to see solar cars, but it was the human-powered vehicles (HPVs) that captured much of my attention. I videotaped images of many two- and three-wheeled HPV designs zipping along. I saw lightweight, streamlined shells. With the addition of a small electric motor and

battery pack, I was certain the result would be serious, all-weather transportation.

The Bicycle

The evolution of transportation was forever changed with the invention of the wheel. From that intersection, human beings were provided with an alternative means of transporting heavy loads and themselves about. Consequently, the load shifted from a human's back to an axle and self-transport moved from the horse to the bicycle.

The modern bicycle is a highly evolved piece of machinery. There have been few changes in its overall design in the past 75 years (Techtalk T25). It is light, reliable, and affordable. Its owner can pick it up, move it over obstacles, or carry it up a flight of stairs into an apartment. It is found in every country in the world, and studies clearly reveal its leadership in efficient travel for human beings.

Still, the role of the bicycle in the overall transportation mix is missing. People who do *not* use them have a formidable list of "complaints" about its viability. The reasons I've heard? The bicycle is relatively slow. It is not all-weather. In a mix of cars and trucks, a bicycle and its rider are difficult to see. Hazards abound in road surfaces, drainage grates, and opening car doors. Despite its efficiency, it requires effort to operate. A substantial amount of drag is induced by the bicycle and rider, so more effort is needed for higher speeds. When used for commuting, the rider arrives in a sweat, so a shower and a change of clothes are required. (Progressive corporations are installing such amenities as onsite gyms.) A shift in weather brings its own problems, more than a shower and dry clothes can help to alleviate.

Still, the owners of automobiles must fantasize, as they're stalled in traffic, about slicing through such congestion with a bicycle. Ben Swets can tell you how to make it work (Application A29).

The Two-Wheeled HPV

Every bicyclist feels the "wind" their fervent pedaling brings. In downhill sections, this pressure of air will water the eyes and flap clothes. Indeed, the HPV movement came about when race officials forbade the use of streamlining devices in bicycle races.

*T*echtalk
*T*25 The Bicycle
Paul MacCready, Ph.D.

Almost a century ago, after several decades of design innovations, the conventional bicycle emerged with its two equal-size, tangent-tension spoke wheels, pneumatic tires, and chain-driven rear wheel. The modern bicycle differs from this ancestor only in detail. Except for the gear shift, the changes would scarcely be detectable to the casual observer.

One reason the 1986 and 1890 bicycles are similar is that the 1890 version was so good — efficient, safe, easy to ride, and simple and inexpensive to build. Another reason is that bicycle competitions, which tend to set technological standards, dictated that the vehicle not be improved to give a rider an unfair advantage. Like a species of animal, the multitude of these satisfactory bicycles fitted well their broadly based and economically driven "ecological niche," and the design evolved only very slowly and in minor ways as the decades went by.

A modern view of natural evolution has a new species sometimes evolving out of a stable, established species via a major, rapid, adaptive change. In 1975, the International Human-Powered-Vehicle Association (IHPVA) was formed to stimulate the development of fast human-powered vehicles without the inhibiting effects of rules. The sole criterion of success was "going fast," with no concern about the mechanism or configuration. The resulting evolution of new designs was rapid, as a small number of inventors (initially in Southern California) found what worked in this new isolated "ecological niche." Fantastic speeds are now being achieved.

After a few years of strictly speed competitions, IHPVA added competitions for "practical" vehicles, thus establishing a broader "ecological niche". The definition of "practical" is still in a state of flux, as are the criteria for judging the vehicles, but overall aim is clear: a human-powered vehicle which offers safety, speed, versatility, comfort, and economy, and which would be attractive both to commuters and long-distance riders. The designs evolving from the practical-vehicle competitions so far have fallen far short of achieving the overall aim, but the competition stimulates further refinement. It is an important subject inasmuch as human-powered vehicles, which help with health, recreation, and transportation, will play an increasing role as civilization edges toward accommodation with the ecology and resources of our limited globe.

Fig. 4-2: Ben Swets uses his bicycle for all-weather commuting.

Photo: Ben Swets

*A*pplication
*A*29 City Bicycling
Ben Swets

There is no time to exercise. That is why I pedal a bicycle instead of using a car for any of my Los Angeles errands up to 20 miles with less than 50 pounds of load. I have the choice of taking the car or a bicycle but find bicycling more efficient and rewarding than the four-wheel slavery that seems to dominate my fellow citizens.

Strangers at street corners often wonder what is in my pannier bags, where I am from, and whether I race. I tell them that I am no more interested in racing this vehicle than the average motorist is interested in stock car racing. This is just my mode of crossing town.

My bags contain nothing more mysterious than does the trunk of the average car: tools, clothes, books, and food for my tank. My tools happen to be photographic, since I shoot pictures for the newsletters of many corporations.

My crosstown speed is consistently predictable at any hour of the day regardless of whether it is light traffic or "rush" hour — when cars slow down. My cartful of gear parks free of charge directly at my destination's door, if not inside it. For corporate clients that may regard a bicycle as a mere toy and a sign of non-professionalism, I park my steed two blocks away.

The main attribute of the HPV is the aerodynamic shell, or fairing. It is this one component, missing in the standard bicycle, that immediately rewards the rider's propulsive effort with a higher speed. Or, above 10 mph, less effort for the same speed as an unfaired bicycle.

Fig. 4-3: This shell combines good streamlining with foul-weather protection.

When an acquaintance across town asks whether I "rode" today, the answer is yes—if a car brought me. The phrases "drive a car" and "ride a bike" should trade first words. The former denotes action, the latter passivity. It is obvious which pilot—that of a 2-ton internal combustion vehicle requiring gentle ankle bending for acceleration, or that of a human-powered bicycle—is more active.

It is pumping steadily toward a place to do a task that gives me the feeling of productivity I crave. The slow-witted, poison-coughing beasts are blocked by each other, or by curbs and fences which my two wheels can be lifted over. Sometimes I am alone, free from the proximity of nearby sag wagons. I am in almost a state of physical and mental meditation. I strive to perfect each stroke of the crankarm. I feel the air on my skin, and I hear the hushed rolling of rubber on asphalt.

If it is a cold night, I enjoy the chill in my nostrils and the ample warmth generated by my working metabolism under a windbreaking garment. In rainy weather—which fills the streets with more cars than ever—I expect to get wet. The human body is designed for complete contact with water. My pannier bags contain plenty of waterproof material to protect my cameras and extra clothes into which I change at my destination.

I refuse offers of a ride home for me and my bicycle, even from a long distance. Automobiles cost money to run, heat, park, insure, and they pollute the shared atmosphere. At the same time they promote the atrophied heart condition of the passive pilot. Time and again, the bicycle gives passage to a place, health to a body, and self-sufficiency to its pilot.

The fairing's job is to move the HPV and its rider through the air cleanly (Techtalk T26). Compared with water and rock, our atmosphere appears almost a vacuum. When you stick your hand outside the window of a moving car, the "apparent" wind you feel tells you something different! Palm forward, it feels strong. Put a karate edge forward and the pressure lessens. Air has substance and density. A shape that moves through it, as a knife through soft butter, will require less effort to move.

The best fairing for an HPV is unbroken, fully enclosing the rider and machine. This

*T*echtalk
T26 Human-Powered Vehicles
Chester Kyle

The Human-Powered Championships have spawned the most efficient vehicles ever built by man. They consume less energy per mile per pound carried than any other transportation means. The single passenger vehicle is capable of traveling on the level at about 30 mph with less than one-quarter horsepower input. With training, almost any younger person in good health can produce this much power continuously. How can such amazing efficiency be achieved? Almost entirely by aerodynamics.

As the availability of fossil fuels diminishes in the next century, inventors will no doubt look to other sources of energy to solve our transportation problems. Human-powered vehicles may come to play a role in answering our commuting and local transportation needs. Although the bicycle is an efficient means of transportation, it is an imperfect solution for commuting because it provides no protection against inclement weather. It also is not as efficient as it might be because of the drag created by an upright rider and machine. Using featherweight materials and streamlined designs, future innovators may create vehicles to revolutionize human-powered transportation.

Fig. 4-4: A composite shell adds greater structural integrity.

is the profile of the HPVs that set speed records (Application A30). Part of the reason it is done with teams is so that there are team members close by the HPV when it comes to a stop. Without their support, the vehicle and rider would topple.

HPVs are still a fledgling technology. Many ideas are sprouting from the original concept, spurred on by competitions and newsletters from the IHPVA and other groups. To support their activities, advocates work at improving the practical side of HPVs and serving a growing market. Efficiency, then, is merely one factor, among others like affordability, function, and practicality.

There are many possible manifestations when electric propulsion is mixed with

Fig. 4-5: Marti Daily powers the rear of this all-terrain HPV as Rob Cotter describes the course in the Solar Cup in Visalia, CA in 1988.

*A*pplication

*A*30

The IHPVA

Marti Daily

The knowledge that aerodynamics could dramatically affect a bicycle's performance has existed since the early 1900s. The International Human-Powered Vehicle Association (IHPVA) held the first International Human-Powered Speed Championships in April of 1975 at a drag strip in southern California. Vehicles of every size, shape and description gathered to compete against the clock for 200 meters, governed only by the rule that all power must come from human energy. The fastest of the fourteen vehicles was clocked at 44.87 mph.

By 1978, Northrup University's White Lightning had broke the 50 mph benchmark. In 1979, the tandem tricycle became the first HPV to break the national 55 mph speed limit for automobiles. Later the same day, the triple-rider prone tricycle VECTOR took the record, with a speed of 57.07 mph.

In 1983, the DuPont Corporation offered a prize of $15,000 to the first single rider vehicle to achieve a speed of 65 mph. This led to a series of record attempts throughout the country and around the world. Don Witte, owner/builder of ALLEGRO, from Boulder, Colorado, assembled his team in the mountains of Colorado to take advantage of the thinner air. Witte inched the top speed record upward from 58.89 mph (set in 1990) to 62.98 mph over a period of ten months. Among these runs was one that set a women's record: Rachel Hall of La Garita, CO

Fig. 4-6: Gold Rush set a new HPV record of 65.48 mph in May of 1985.

achieved 51.85 mph in August of 1985.

However, it was veteran competitor Gardner Martin, owner/builder of GOLD RUSH, who claimed the price. "Fast Freddy" Markham, on May 11, 1986, rode GOLD RUSH to a speed of 65.48 mph near Mono Lake, California, at an altitude of 7,000.

Not all human-powered vehicles compete on land. The Gossamer Condor (the human-powered aircraft that won the first Kremer prize in 1977 by completing a one-mile figure eight) was built by Dr. Paul MacCready, International President of the IHPVA. The prize-winning Gossamer Albatross and Bionic Bat, MIT's Monarch and the German Musculaire I and II all demonstrated new levels of flight using human power.

Fig. 4-7: Low-profile 3-wheel HPVs use a recumbent position for the rider.

bicycle and HPV technology. These vehicles may sport two, three, or four wheels. Both hybrids (human/EV) and pure EVs will result. The designs of larger, faster, or more powerful machines will shift to the use of motorcycle technology to add strength and ruggedness.

In no way do I wish to suggest that any of these vehicles are less roadworthy than those described in the previous chapter. These vehicles are distinguished from other EVs only in that their drive components, design weight, and applications allow the use of bicycle or motorcycle technology in their construction.

But not all accomplishments are motivated by prize money. A team of engineers and engineering students from MIT worked for five years to plan an HPA (human-powered aircraft) that would re-live the Greek myth of Daedalus. The dream was to fly from Crete to the Greek island of Santorini across the Aegean Sea, a distance of over 74 miles. In April, 1988, the myth was made reality as Greek cycling champion Kannellos Kannopoulos piloted the new plane with an old name, the DAEDALUS, into history.

A third arena for technological advances is exemplified by a variety of watercraft in recent years. Allan Abbott and Alec Brooks built the first human-powered hydrofoil, the FLYING FISH, in 1986. This vehicle claimed all the first-place prizes at the 1986 IHPSC in Vancouver and in 1987 in Washington, DC. However, in years since, the FLYING FISH II has had some stiff competition. Catamarans, a hovercraft and a plethora of hydrofoil designs have all taken a shot at the $25,000 DuPont Prize for human-powered Watercraft, which will be awarded to the first craft to achieve 20 knots over a 100-meter course. A record number of water vehicles competed in the 17th IHPSC held in August, 1991 in Milwaukee, Wisconsin. Mark Drela and the Decavitator, an MIT hydrofoil, made good use of a redesigned foil and waning days of autumn to soundly demolish existing records by achieving a speed well over 18 knots in October, 1991.

Yet another example of human power is exemplified by vehicles known as "all-terrain" — those that can traverse not only paved roads, but sand, mud, and bodies of water as well. First devised as kinetic sculptures, such vehicles have competed for years in a three-day, cross-country race in northern California. Those interested in the development of efficient transportation in developing countries, however, have begun to take a new look at these vehicles as perhaps being most practical for areas with few paved roads, little access to motor vehicle replacement parts, and increasing gasoline costs.

And what does the future hold for human-powered vehicles? A $20,000 prize has been waiting for more than ten years for the first successful human-powered helicopter. A revitalized interest in utilizing arm-power, especially among those who are physically challenged, is emerging. New vehicles combining pedal-power with small electric or even solar-powered motors have been designed and built. The possibilities arising from the efficient use of human power have only begun to be tapped.

Fig. 4-8: This HPV uses sideflaps to allow the rider to stay upright when stopped.

Fig. 4-9: Adding hydrofoils to watercraft increases the speeds achieved by human power.

Fig. 4-10: The Flying Fish was one of the first craft to achieve a significant leap in speed over water.

Photo: C. Michael Lewis

*T*echtalk

*T*₂₇ Electric-Assist Bicycle Design

What are the attributes of a good EAB (electric-assist bicycle)? My own research and a review of other designs leads me to generate these conclusions:

- a mountain bike or an older 1- or 3-speed bicycle is an ideal chassis.
- electric-assist adds the benefit of energy accumulation.
- human effort handles startup and all peak loads.
- the motor/battery pack will weigh 1-2 times the bicycle weight.
- electric-assist must not interfere or interact with the stock chain drive.
- regenerative braking recovers some of the energy of momentum and provides a strong braking function.
- electric-assist works best at or near the bicycle's cruise speed.
- installation must involve simple tools, and the motor and battery pack should be installed on mounts for easy removal for bicycle-only use.
- a low-cost electric-assist option for a bicycle is possible.

Fig. 4-11: A simple EAB uses a small motor and a battery.

Fig. 4-12: The ZAP system can drive front or rear wheels.

*A*pplication

*A*₃₁ ZAP Power System

Want a non-polluting commute? Something a bit more than the reliable, lightweight bicycle? Are you ready for 20 miles of electric-assist for your bicycle at 4 cents of electricity? Scramble up that hill, punch through that headwind or rush-hour traffic, pedal like a champion cyclist or just cruise? Increase your fitness level, gain in overall mobility, or simply enjoy the outdoors?

The ZAP Power System is the result of a three-year-long project to design and produce a practical, non-polluting power source for a bicycle that would help with hills and headwinds. ZAP (Zero Air Pollution) is a bolt-up electric propulsion system that installs in an hour. A ZAP-equipped bike is a true human/electric hybrid. It is clean, silent, and efficient.

The ZAP Power System uses a front-wheel or rear-wheel tire drive. It employs a unique torque-sensing mount for best traction and efficiency. To accommodate a variety of bicycles and trikes, ZAP is available in four

Fig. 4-13: Mike Saari uses electric-assist on a faired HPV recumbent.

The Electric-Assist Bicycle

I had been working with EVs for more than fifteen years before I witnessed an HPV competition. Still, it had not even occurred to me to build an electric-assist bicycle. I simply did not see the bicycle the way I do now.

In retrospect, I understand why. First, I had underestimated the bicycle's capacity. The Gossamer series of human-powered aircraft awaken me to the true power and potential of HPVs. Second, I had dismissed bicycle technology as being too light to carry much in the way of batteries. No one came up to me and said, "So what?"

In the electric-assist bicycle (EAB), the human effort still reigns supreme. The "electrics" are there to help. The EAB's operator, then, gets help with acceleration, cruising, hillclimbing, and braking.

In bike circles, a favorite discussion is the "accumulator." Bicyclists hate to stop at intersections because braking a bicycle throws away the energy of momentum (dissipated as heat in the brakes) expended with leg muscles. The accumulator, then, is a technique of storing the bicycle's momentum and using it for takeoff. Regenerative braking is electricity which is generated from momentum. In the EAB, then, a battery pack *is* an accumulator.

Another virtue of the EAB is its ability to handle "cruise." The energy required to accelerate *any* mass to some speed is several factors higher than the amount needed to sustain that speed. Since cruise requires only a fraction of the energy consumed by acceleration, the size of accumulator can also be reduced, making a tighter overall package.

My own experience suggests that many bicyclists will find a well-designed EAB a pleasure to operate. And, because it has a "powered" component, the operator becomes a "driver", no longer the lowly "rider" designation that bicyclists suffer at the hands of non-bicyclists.

The mating of a stock bicycle and electric propulsion feels like a natural marriage. Since the pedals are retained, this becomes a hybrid vehicle (Techtalk T27).

In the past, the term "moped" (a blend of the words motor and pedal) has been used in the same context. Typically, the "motor" was really a gas-fueled engine. The moped has a reputation of being a motorcycle with pedal-assist. Anyone who has tried to pedal one of these machines to the nearest gas station or garage will attest that it was never intended to be powered by human effort alone. More likely, the moped was originally created to circumvent the restrictions of motorcycle codes by pretending to be a motorized bicycle. Where a moped is clearly awkward and heavy, most EABs clearly favor human effort in their design *and* operation.

---

configurations: single and dual motors for bicycles and trikes.

The kits are meant to supplement leg power, not replace it. Still, without pedal input, a Single 500-Watt motor pushes the bicycle to 15 mph and a Dual to 20 mph. Trikes use a high-torque, 350-Watt motor, with a Single reaching 8 mph and a Dual 12 mph. Pedal input increases these ranges, while hillclimbing and higher speeds decrease them.

Sealed lead-acid, gel cell batteries make up the ZAP's battery pack, and two sizes are available. The smaller one (17 Ah) will take a bicycle 10 miles on battery alone (dual system, 1st speed range). The larger pack (33 Ah) will push this range to 20 miles. With pedal input, expect the small pack to give you an hour of transportation, while the larger pack will give you two hours. With proper care, the batteries deliver 400-1200 cycles. Charge from stationary or onboard units, or a solar panel.

Are you ready for 20 miles of electric-assist for your bicycle at 4 cents of electricity?

The Single-motor drive uses a simple one-speed controller. ON for go, OFF for coast. Downhill and ON gives regenerative braking.

The motor, controller, and mounting hardware weigh in at 5 lbs (without battery) and are adequate for flat terrain. The Dual-motor setup uses a simple 3-speed controller (non-pedal 11/16/20 mph), weighs 8 lbs, and is recommended for hillclimbing and higher power and speed operation.

What does it cost? For the bicycle, Single ($299) and Dual ($399). For the trike, Single ($315) and Dual ($425). Buy the 17 Ah ($62) and the 33 Ah ($71) batteries locally to save shipping costs. Options include: 55-Watt halogen headlight ($35), stationary 10-Amp charger ($68), onboard 4-Amp charger ($60), and solar panel (available on request).

A Basic EAB Design

The basic EAB is composed of a small PM (permanent magnet) motor, a 12-24V battery pack, a fixed-ratio drivetrain, and a control unit. It includes mounting brackets and hardware, a wiring harness, and a battery charger.

When installed, the electric-assist option could add 12-22 pounds to the bicycle's weight. The amount of battery capacity (short vs long range) accounts for the weight variance. Weights greater than 25 lbs seem to severely compromise pedal-only input and dictate the addition of better suspension. Circuits for regenerative and dynamic braking should be added to help brake the additional weight.

Note the similarity in the design details of the the commercially-produced ZAP (Application A31) and BEAT specifications (Techtalk T28.

Electronic motor control is not recommended for an EAB. Commercial units are expensive ($175-225). Also, regenerative or dynamic braking features are not included in the design of these units (mid-1990s) and defeat their use in the EAB. The ZAP uses a unique speed control technique that does not interfere with regenerative braking.

Since the drivetrain is a fixed ratio in the EAB, the motor must be "geared" for the desired operational speed. Ask yourself, "How fast do I want to go?" When geared for high-end work, the EAB will accelerate slowly and gobble power on startup if there is no significant pedal input.

The EAB Drivetrain

Many designs exist to transfer motor power to bicycle propulsion. Hub, tire drive, rim-pulley, and spoke-pulley are examples. None of these designs interact directly with the bicycle's stock chainworks (pedal, chain, sprocket, and idler system).

There are two reasons why it is not a good idea to mix electric propulsion with the existing chainworks. First, most bicycles use a "free-wheeling" rear wheel. This allows power to flow only one way: from the pedals to the wheel to the road. A ratchet inside the hub between the axle and the wheel performs this job, engaging in one direction, but slipping in the other. Hence, the clicking sound. When you stop pedaling, the pedals and chainworks stop, while the wheels keep on turning.

---

*T*echtalk *T28* — BEAT Specifications

The BEAT (bicycle electric-assist transporter) has these specifications.

- **Motor:** 12Vdc, PM (permanent magnet), 2700-3500 rpm, demag current max greater than 20-25 Amps, 3-4 lbs weight. Mounts to frame behind and below seat.
- **Controller:** High-current DPDT relay, slaved to a 2-position toggle switch, selects 12V (slow) or 24V (fast) to the motor by configuring the battery pack into paralleled (12V) or series (24V) wiring. Downhill regen braking in 12V position. A GO (push) button connects pack to motor, and is released during slow-fast selection. The addition of a switch, microswitch, and additional relays adds two dynamic braking rates (resistor and short).
- **Circuit breaker:** Rated to protect the motor from demag currents.
- **Thermoswitch:** Attached to the motor. Interrupts motor current when motor overheats.
- **LED panel :** 3-5 LEDs to indicate speed positions (lo-hi), dynamic braking positions (one and two), circuit breaker trip, and overheat conditions.
- **Battery Pack:** Two 12V batteries (lead-acid, NiCd, or nickel-metal hydride) make up the battery pack. At 10-15Ah each, a 10-20 lb pack is possible.
- **Drivetrain:** V-belt, cogbelt, or chain. At 25 mph, a 26-inch wheel is turning at 325 rpm. The stock spoke-pulley is 14 inches in diameter. With a 1.5-2 inch pulley on the motor, a 7-9 to one ratio will result. An 8-12 tooth cog on the motor and an 80-120 tooth gearbelt rim pulley will also complete the EAB drivetrain.
- **Wiring Harness:** Includes wires, fuses, and molex connectors to aid in motor and battery removal, and battery charger connection.
- **Dynamic Braking:** Engaged at speeds below the point where regenerative braking is effective, and dissipates motor power (current) as electric heat. In Resistor Mode, motor current is routed to a resistor up to 20-25 amps (demag limits) in downhill grades. In Short Mode, the motor is simply "shorted out" (again, not exceeding demag), providing a strong braking action to nearly zero bicycle speed.
- **Parking Brake:** Left in Short Mode, the BEAT will be very difficult to move from a standstill and is almost impossible to pedal away. A good anti-theft feature.

Fig. 4-14: There are many ways to configure electric-assist.

Fig. 4-15: Three sources of energy power this vehicle—human, electric, and solar.

Photo: C. Michael Lewis

Photo: C. Michael Lewis

Free-wheeling has the obvious benefit of maintaining efficiency. More importantly, it keeps the road and wheel from powering the chainworks. If the road and wheel could power the pedals through the chainworks, the pedals would never stop rotating while the bike was in motion. At high speeds, this could be nasty. Integrating the electric motor into the existing chainworks would partially defeat this feature, allowing both the wheel *and* the pedals to be powered by electric drive.

There's a second problem when the motor drive is interfaced with the existing chainworks—the finished system loses the ability to employ regenerative or dynamic braking. If a free-wheeling rear wheel will not "power the pedals," it also will not transfer momentum into the motor via the chain! Ergo, no regenerative or dynamic braking.

A hub motor would be an ideal solution here. When built into the hub, the motor is effectively on the road side of the drive system. So, it doesn't "motor" the chainworks and it allows regenerative braking to work.

Fig. 4-16: A wiring diagram for an electric-assist bicycle (below). Where both regenerative and dynamic braking functions are added, the positioning of control circuitry (right) is critical to the safe operation of the vehicle.

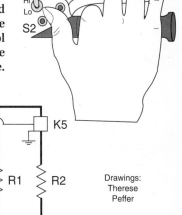

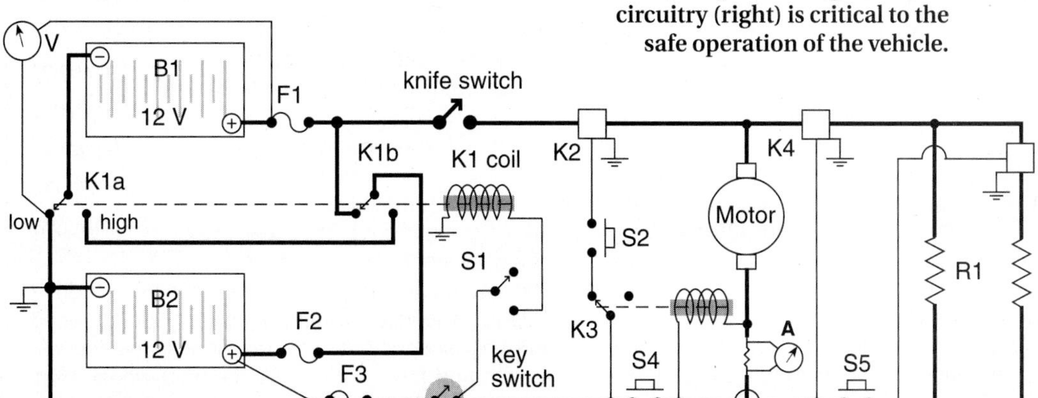

Drawings: Therese Peffer

F1, F2: max motor current x 2 = rating, F3: 5 A slo-blo
Wiring: Motor circuit: #10 stranded or larger. Control circuit, Metering: #18 stranded or larger
Digital meters: Radio Shack, Micronta model 22-171A. Shunt: 50 Amp 50 mV

For any other types of motors, the preferred methods of motor connection—tire drive (Techtalk T29) or a separate pulley drive (Techtalk T30)—operate independently of the bicycle's freewheeling hub. Each transfers power directly to the tire or the wheel on the "pavement side" of the wheel axle. Thus, they work in *parallel* with the stock chainworks, while powering the vehicle or recovering power during braking.

EAB Design Considerations

There are other design options in the EAB. Let's look at quick-release components, electric weight, licensing, controller options, and cost.

• *Quick-Release Components.* For the EAB class of operation, you may want to retain the option of quickly converting your electric runabout back into a standard bicycle. Motor mounts, battery holders, and all wiring are best installed permanently. Quick-release bolts or fasteners should ease the removal of motor, battery pack, and controller when non-electric operation is desired, or to prevent theft. If these fasteners are padlocks, you've now got a security system. Hardware designed to protect the illegal removal of solar panels from their mounts will fit well here.

•*Electric Weight.* There *is* an optimum weight for the electric-assist bicycle. Twenty-five (25) pounds seems to be the upper limit of hardware—motor, battery pack, controller, and wiring. Above this amount, pedal-only operation is difficult and additional suspension is required.

Techtalk T29

Tire Drive System

One method of connecting gas engines or electric motors to bicycles is the tire (or wheel) drive. Here, the drive wheel on the motor's output shaft is brought in direct contact with one of the bicycle's tires. Typically, the drive wheel is a hard rubber (or plastic) cylinder-shaped block attached to the motor shaft. The motor is positioned directly above the front or rear wheel and secured to the bicycle frame. To engage, the driver operates a mechanical lever that rotates the motor about a pivot, bringing the drive wheel in contact with the tire itself.

Tire drive has some attractive qualities. It is simple, eliminating the need for additional sprockets, belts, or pulleys, or drive ratios. The high peripheral speed of the wheel's tire is a close match with the high rpm a motor will generate. When not in use, the drive wheel may be rotated away, eliminating all drag.

One advantage of a rear drive setup is that clever design will ensure that the drive wheel is "pulled" into the rotating tire. In the front, there is usually no clearance to install the motor behind the front forks to get this same effect. Instead, mechanical design (and strong springs) may be needed to maintain a strong drive wheel-to-tire contact.

Front tire drive has a slight advantage over rear rim drive in uphill grades because the front wheel "pulls" the bicycle uphill. In downhill situations, however, the rear mounting is generally safer. A sudden initiation of strong regenerative or dynamic braking will severely brake the front wheel. A loss of steering or stability may result.

There are several challenges in using a tire drive system. One is slippage. To work at all, tire drive requires a steady, strong pressure of the drive wheel against the tire. Too little causes slippage. Too much causes heat and excessive tire wear. Adjusted for riding on a smooth roadway, this pressure may be wrong on wet or graveled roads. In these conditions, the heavy loads of acceleration, steep uphill grades, and regenerative or dynamic braking will cause the drive wheel to break contact and buck against the tire. At high speeds, this can lead to a dangerous vibration, like driving on a "washboard" road. Or result in a total loss of traction between drive wheel and tire. Downhill, electrical braking (regen or dynamic), for example, could suddenly disappear.

Another issue with tire drive is tire wear. Most of this is caused by slippage. Any time the speeds of the drive wheel and tire are different, a scrubbing or grinding effect occurs. Since rubber is the softer of the two materials, the tire can be quickly stripped of its tread depth. Conversely, gravel and sand that sticks to the tire acts like sandpaper, abrading and scoring the drive wheel itself.

Of course, tire wear was noticed in early attempts to use tire drive. At that time, drive wheels had knurled or ridged surfaces to maintain traction under moderate pressure. Eventually, designers went to drive wheels with smooth surfaces, relying instead on contact area and increased pressure. The increased toughness of tires and the increasing softness and resiliency of drive wheel materials (particularly with plastic and rubber polymers) has improved this overall situation.

Another safety issue also suggests a rear rim drive. A blowout of the front tire is hazardous with most bicycles at *any* time. If a front rim drive is in use when the blowout happens, the effect is nothing less than catastrophic. Under pressure, the drive wheel will depress toward the rim, squeezing the flattened tire and probably snagging it. The resultant shredding will snag on brakes and forks, locking up the front wheel. How many somersaults will ensue? What's the probability that *you* will be under the bicycle when you make contact again, at speed, with the roadway?

> *Tire drive ... is simple, eliminating the need for additional sprockets, belts and pulleys, or drive ratios.*

Allow 3 lbs of motor and 2 lbs of controller for the EAB. Limit the battery pack to 15-20 lbs. A 12-Volt, 25-Ah NiCd or NMH (Nickel-Metal-Hydride) battery pack will weigh approximately 18 lbs.

• *Registration.* In California, a motor-driven bicycle is easy to register (license) and requires no insurance. A helmet may not be required for an EAB, but its operator should wear one. Surely, the vehicle will not be driven like a bicycle. As such, it may be at greater risk when operated in traffic because of its greater speed and faster acceleration than a standard bicycle.

• *Controller Options.* An electronic controller boosts the price of an EAB by $200. Electronic control adds a nice touch but it is more sophisticated than the EA-bicycle warrants. And—no regen braking

(unless it's built into the controller). The question you must ask yourself is: what do I want my EAB to do? If precision control of speed is important, an electronic controller is the best control that money can buy. If you want to commute or just get from here to there, the simple controller is an option.

Here's something to consider when operating an EAB. First, when you accelerate from a stop, you may accelerate at the fastest rate possible. When you are at speed, you may opt for the highest speed. With an electric controller, this is full-throttle—the same as ON in a series-parallel controller. With a running weight of 200 lbs (driver and EAB), most EA-bicycles will coast a long way once you come off the power. So, intermittent operation of the series-parallel controller—ON, then OFF

Free-wheeling ...keeps the road and wheel from powering the chainworks

Fig. 4-18: Larger electric-assist applications may use two motors.

Photo: Joe Stephenson (Green Motorworks)

Photo: Dann Parks

Fig. 4-17: A simple EAB can use one motor.

Fig. 4-19: Wheel-pulley drive on the Lightning I allows the use of wheel skirts

Photo: ZAP Power Systems

Photo: Daniel Pliskin

Fig. 4-20: The Schneeveis "leaner" uses gearbelt drive on the front wheel.

T₃₀   Wheel Pulley Drive

An alternative to tire drive for electric motors on bicycles is wheel pulley drive. Here, a large-diameter pulley or sprocket is attached to the wheel at the hub, spokes, or rim. A small-diameter pulley or sprocket is mounted to the motor shaft and this assembly is bolted to the bicycle frame. A V-belt, cogbelt, or chain completes the installation. (For the remainder of this treatment, a V-belt and pulley combo will be described; gearbelt and chain/sprocket assemblies may be substituted.)

The wheel-pulley idea avoids the limits and dangers of tire drives, since the V-belt tends to wear rather than the tires. Too, a flat tire is just a flat tire. However, the drive motor is always engaged; when the wheel turns, *it* turns. If the motor is a PM type, this adds noticeable drag. Slipping the belt off for bicycle-only use will alleviate this somewhat, but it looks and feels a little awkward, at least.

Attaching the wheel-pulley to the rear wheel is a challenge. Stock rear bicycle hubs are asymmetrical (with respect to their rims) to compensate for the existence of the standard 3-5 rear sprocket assemblies and derailluers. This makes the addition of a large-diameter pulley on the *opposite* side of the wheel's chainworks a dilemma. If it attaches to the wheel at the hub (near the axle), even a medium-size (diameter) pulley will interfere with the rear trailing arms. A relatively large-diameter pulley will be needed here to match motor rpm with wheel speed. For this reason, the wheel pulley is traditionally secured to the rim or to the spokes themselves.

The wheel-pulley in an electric wheelchair is an example of a rim-mount. It is designed to receive power from its motor via a gearbelt. Here, the pulley ring is equipped with three or four L-shaped brackets that are bolted (or riveted) directly to the rim through its underside.

The spoke-mount wheel-pulley has different origins. Many years ago, in countries throughout the world, there was a need for a way to install small gas engines on bicycles, converting them into motorized transport. The criteria for the drivetrain were simple. It had to be cheap, fit a standard bicycle, install quickly without tools, and work ruggedly. Enter the spoke-mounted wheel pulley, or spoke pulley.

The device itself is a pulley ring with a series of slotted studs welded to its side. These are intended for a bicycle wheel of a specific size. At the time, the 26-inch bicycle was the standard. With the wheel removed from the bicycle, the pulley ring is attached by lining up and sliding the slots of the studs over the crossover points on the spokes. Then, a washer is fitted over each of the protruding studs and a screwdriver (or knife) is used to wedge the slots open further. This presses each washer against the spokes, firmly securing the pulley ring in place. Once installed, the spoke-pulley evenly distributes motor power through the 6-8 spoke studs, to the rim and to the road. Any crimping tool (pliers) will easily push these slot tangs together, freeing the washers and stubs, to remove the spoke-pulley for servicing.

The spokes of an EAB using a spoke-pulley will get some abuse. How much? A fractional horsepower series or PM electric motor can deliver higher torque peaks than the 3.5-5 HP gas engines that powered these bicycles years ago, particularly at startup. However, I've never experienced a bent or broken spoke with an electric drive using the spoke pulley, and have not heard of it happening to anyone else. The spoke-pulley seems to complement the toughness of a mountain bike, but it may be quite the oddity mounted on a racer or road bike.

Bicycle advocates, particularly those who true their own rims, will consider the spoke-pulley a rather crude device with little likelihood of finding its way onto their bike. Still, rim-mounted pulleys tend to be heavier than their spoke-pulley equivalents.

Either type of drivetrain—tire drive or wheel pulley drive—seems well-suited for adding electric power to a bicycle where the motor rating is close to one (1) horsepower.

Once installed, the spoke-pulley evenly distributes motor power through the 6-8 spoke studs to the rim and to the road.

Photo: Burkhardt Turbines

Fig. 4-21: Pulley-wheel drive works well on the rear wheel of this hybrid human-electric machine.

Photo: Burkhardt Turbines

Fig. 4-22: Peter Talbert sits in an early generation of the Electric Fish.

and coast, then back ON—rarely uses more Ah of energy than a steady (i.e., 70%) throttle input of an electronic controller.

• *Cost*. A barebones, owner-built EAB will cost about $100 (1994). That allows $20 for the motor, $35 for the battery, $25 for the components of a simple two-speed controller, and $20 for miscellaneous hardware and wiring.

The Three-Wheeled HPV

An HPV that will stay upright at rest is the three-wheeler. The addition of one extra wheel makes the HPV a whole new species of machine. Having three wheels gives the HPV width, increasing its visibility to cars and trucks, particularly from the front and rear. Pedestrians are more apt to see the swift machines, too.

A three-wheeled HPV makes it more practical to add a complete aerodynamic shell, adding the benefit of all-weather use. Whereas a simple fairing with a two-wheeler will improve aerodynamics, its rider may still get wet or cold. The stability of the three-wheeler allows a designer to add a draft-free, waterproof shell.

The fully-faired shell adds something to HPVs. Grace. Elegance. Style. Sleekness. Call it what you will, the bicycle is longer naked. It is no longer a chassis of tubing, running gear, cables. It is "fleshed out."

Above all, the faired HPV approaches commuting—the idea of moving human beings to and from their work—from an entirely different angle than that of the automobile. Is a 2,500-lb vehicle the best way to move one person from here to there? True, it's not likely that people will move out of their cars and into HPVs without a lot of crying and screaming. However, anyone who has attended a solar car race or HPV competition, or driven one of these small, clean, quiet machines, cannot help come but away with the feeling of merit in the idea of "less" and "more simple."

Almost any 3-wheeled HPV design is able to incorporate electric-assist in a manner similar to that of the BEAT and ZAP systems. There are some differences. Expect the ratings of motor and battery pack to increase by about fifty percent (50%). Remember that the addition of a third wheel, extra structural support, and the shell itself will add some weight. A streamlined shell, while more aerodynamic than an unprotected bicycle and rider, will likely have a higher frontal area. Anticipate the overall drag component to increase somewhat.

A Minimalist HPV

A good example of the evolution of a 3-wheeled EAB is the one started by Jan Olof Hellsund. He refers to it as his "minimalist" vehicle. When its construction began, Jan was not certain what the electric propulsion system would look like, or how it would mate with the existing chainworks (Application A32). Since he wanted it to work well as a stand-alone HPV, he was careful not to compromise the design in terms of weight, strength, and efficiency. Jan also used the chassis as a testbed, to prove the machine's strength (Techtalk T31).

A Minimalist Design

Jan Olof Hellsund

A 32

I was exploring the question of how small, simple, and inexpensive personal transport could be. I wanted a hybrid of human power and electric propulsion. I generated a wish list for the motive power source. A high yield per pound of weight. Easily replenishable. Quiet and efficient. Easy and inexpensive to service.

The design philosophy of this machine began with the simplest possible vehicle (like a skateboard or a luge)—vehicles that can significantly increase a person's speed and range, but are a fraction of the size and weight of the driver. Features were grudgingly added on only to bring the vehicle into compliance with the previously-stated basic requirements.

A thing's complexity seems to increase exponentially with the number of features added to it. During the design stage, for every hour spent on designing a new feature, I spent another three hours reducing it to its simplest form. The less there is, the less there is that can go wrong. Thus, many components and structures ended up performing multiple functions.

The length, width, height, and general shape in this minimalist design were dictated by the smallest frontal area a regular person could achieve without assuming an uncomfortable or undignified position. The smaller the frontal area, the less air the vehicle needs to displace while moving forward, and the less aerodynamic drag the vehicle has to overcome. Aerodynamic drag at higher speeds constitutes 90% of vehicular impedance.

The supine position was chosen because it results in a small frontal area, places the head high for visibility, does not interfere with breathing, and is an efficient pedaling position for human power input. Wouldn't it be nice to be able to pedal your car to the nearest gas station at a leisurely 30 mph after you've run out of juice? The final shape ended up looking a lot like a fish. Nature itself evolved the fish for fluidynamic efficiency.

Three-wheeled design was chosen over two-wheeled design. It's true that two-wheeled human-powered vehicles have demonstrated aerodynamic superiority in recent speed record successes. Still, an enclosed two-wheeled design would be terribly awkward in negotiating side-winds, and is difficult to maintain upright while waiting at a stoplight.

The arrangement of two steered wheels up front and a single drive wheel in the back complements a proper fish-like shape with large frontward cross sections, tapering rearward. This allows air that has been displaced enough time to reorganize itself into a smooth laminar flow before the vehicle leaves it behind. A large component of air drag is the air turbulence left behind by a vehicle. In an environment that is 800 times more dense than air, fish-like shapes leave behind very little turbulence.

The framework, built by Brian Beaudette, is my own design. It is a triangulated spaceframe of chromemoly tubing, virtually fitted around the driver. There is no discernable flex in this frame. Every conceivable stress was compensated for by an appropriate frame tube size.

Compared with other similar three-wheeled designs, the front, steered wheels were moved rearward in relation to the driver. This places the center of mass very closely behind the steering wheels, enhancing vehicle stability. I was afraid that hard braking would cause the vehicle to pitch forward. In testing, there was no discernable pitch, even under extremely hard braking. I suspect that the center of mass of the frame/driver unit is not much higher than the front wheel axles. Consequently, not enough force is produced even during extreme braking to leverage the center of mass upward and over the front wheel.

The rear wheel, normally supporting very little load, provided virtually no braking power. It tended to skid during deceleration. During high speed (60 mph) deceleration, the rear wheel brake was used exclusively for its stabilizing effect. The front- wheel brakes provide almost all the braking power.

This vehicle was originally conceived as a strictly human-powered vehicle, fitted tightly around the driver with as little unused space as possible. Aerodynamic and pedaling considerations dictated the shape of the canopy. The resulting open space will probably help prevent the driver from the feeling of being too claustrophobic.

An unavoidable open space resulted between the back of the driver and the rear wheel. At first, I was inclined to somehow eliminate it. Eventually, I found myself shifting the design philosophy to human-power with motor assist.

I wanted a shell and canopy. To this end, I made a foam core. The body was designed by making a silhouette of the actual frame and driver, and sketching an aerodynamic shape around the outline. Cross sections were calculated and cut out of plywood and then attached to a wooden representation of the frame. Chicken wire was stapled on and paper mache was smoothed over it. Polyurethane foam was sprayed on the resulting shape and sureformed smooth. (This was never completed.)

The interior consists of a fiberglass seat that extends up to cover the front wheels and results in a nice arm rest. The steering levers will also be moved up from their current position to the top of the arm rests. The interior and exterior of the vehicle will form a double-walled monocoque structure. This adds crashworthiness. Extremely light, double-walled, carbon-fiber monocoques have proven very effective in protecting auto racing drivers in 200+ mph accidents.

Fig. 4-23: Jan Olof Hellsund and his minimalist HPV.

Fig. 4-24: The minimalist drivetrain is designed for the addition of electric-assist.

Photos:
Jan Olof
Hellsund

Fig. 4-25: The shell is sized to enclose the framework and allow for crankarm revolution

*T*echtalk

*T*₃₁

A Baja Test Run
Jan Olof Hellsund

After completing the frame and running gear, I decided to test my vehicle out in the infamous 73-mile Tecate-to-Ensenada bicycle ride. This annual event pits over 10,000 bicyclists of varying degrees of skill and experience against bumpy Mexican roads and 100-degree-plus desert heat. As this procession zipped through the villages, locals were predictably surprised when I rolled by in what appeared to be a lawn chair on wheels!

One of the highlights of the ride was an eight-mile, curved and bumpy downhill section. It is extremely fast, but it's bumpiness prevents life-loving cyclists from exceeding 45 mph.

With my rolling lawn-chair, I was prevented from exceeding 60 mph by all the 45 mph cyclists that kept getting in my way! The tires maintained minimal contact with the road because of the bumpiness, but the vehicle's low center of gravity kept it from becoming unbalanced. The three drum-brakes slowed my vehicle down much faster than my two-wheeled companions were able to slow theirs. So—the frame design is good.

These are marks of a good designer. Novice builders would be wise to walk a similar path.

Building a shell is a formidable task. If inexperienced in working with foam and fiberglass, the novice builder is advised to attend a class. Or work on a project where the experience can be gained. Learning by doing one's own the first time is not recommended. The materials are expensive, the process is long and involved, and many pitfalls await the unwary.

Peter Talbert, of TranSport Studios in Fort Bragg, California, has taken an alternate approach. With only slight modifications, he adapted the Hellsund prototype to fit inside the Murphy Aerocoupe shell, a production formed-ABS body popular in the Electrathon circuit. The Aerocoupe's designers, Mark Murphy and Eric Raymond, designed their shell to allow for the swing of pedals. Talbert added electric propulsion to the design.

The result is the hybrid Electric Fish. Talbert boldly drove it (*sans* body) at the electric car races in Phoenix, Arizona in the ultralight class. The design is evolving through more road testing.

The Pure Electric Bike

Many EV enthusiasts are not interested in adding human-power to the propulsion package. Still, like all good scratchbuilders, they want lightweight, off-the-shelf components that are readily available and cheap. When they eye bicycle and moped technology, then, it's just the *parts* they are after. ("Parts is parts.")

In building a lightweight, pure-electric road machine, a designer couldn't do much better than to choose a mountain bike as a starting point. It has the strength and stiffness of a motorcycle, and a solid 100 years of engineering in two-wheel geometry behind it. It's also mass produced.

NoPed Series

A 33

In the first NoPed, the entire pedal assembly of a mountain bike was removed. In its place were installed a long rod that supported folding foot pegs, a side kick-stand, and the idler assembly for the drivetrain. A single, sealed Conrad-style bearing was mounted on this core rod to accept the idler (jackshaft) sprockets.

A series of motors (PM and series types, including gear motors) were tested for use in the NoPed. From these, a surplus 1/4 HP motor was selected. Its drive end was bolted to a plate that clamped to the bicycle chassis tubes. A two-stage drivetrain was designed to match the motor's 3,000 rpm to the rear wheel. A timing gearbelt handled the speed interface between motor and idler (on the pedal core), and a stock bicycle chain and sprockets completed the overall 17.7-to-one ratio.

Unlike most hobbyists, Ely Schless approaches new designs from the top down. This means he'll spare no expense to ensure a successful prototype that demonstrates the best that technology and integration can offer within the design envelope. For example, Ely selected a servo amplifier from Advanced Motion Controls for the bike's controller. This is industrial-standard equipment that is expensive but offers features like adjustable current limiting and regenerative braking. The unit's many feedback loops ease the designer's task of investigating design parameters. This wrings out all the variables, identifying the important ones and bypassing a lot of wasted effort at a drawing board or in making changes to the prototype itself.

Choosing this controller, with its efficient DC-DC conversion technology, permitted the use of a high-voltage battery pack. Twelve Powersonic, 12-Volt, 7 Ah, sealed lead-acid batteries neatly fit in an aluminum box slung under the top tube of the bicycle chassis. The 144-Volt pack, then, could deliver 300 Watts of motor power at a mere 2-Amp rate. Proof that most electric motors are rated conservatively is evident here. At three times its design voltage, the motor is only warm to the touch after a long hillclimb (i.e., 5 minutes).

The mountain bike's weight of 26 lbs jumped to 122 lbs in the NoPed prototype. Still, the NoPed leaps off the line, settling into a perky 20 mph after an impressive acceleration of only 4.5 seconds. A range test of 30 miles fully depleted the pack. So, the NoPed has a solid 15-mile range at full performance and only 50% DOD. Vehicle range and speed are monitored through a standard clamp-on bicycle-type sender-and-display unit.

The charger is a 12V unit that plugs into 110vac and is rated at 35 Amps. It may be carried onboard to take advantage of opportunity charging (it easily removes, too). It evenly distributes its current to the batteries in the pack through a unique parallel wiring scheme that involves Molex plugs. The service life of the first battery pack was shortened when rapid recharge was attempted. A subsequent pack, charged at design ratings, fared better.

The NoPed's performance may be attributed to the freewheeling rear wheel. As with any bicycle, if you stop powering the rear wheel, it spins free, allowing a long coastdown. The servo amplifier controller does have fully proportional, regenerative braking. To use it, however, means locking the rear sprocket to the wheel, defeating the freewheeling effect.

As much as a 3-Amp (400-Watt) regenerative braking effect was noted. This rate is adjustable from the same twist-throttle used for acceleration and speed. This feels a little weird when switching between acceleration and braking. Transferring this function to the rear braking lever would take care of this condition.

The loss of the freewheeling function is noticeable in normal coast mode. However, the Advanced Motion Controller can be used in its "voltage-to-voltage" mode for normal driving, and switched to its "torque" mode for maximum regeneration. This mode "electronically" decouples the motor from the battery circuit, and the motor freewheels. This will still spin the chain, but the drag will be minimal.

What does it all cost? Batteries: $400. Controller: $350. Motor: $50 (surplus). Battery charger: $150. Ely estimated that machining and hardware would cost another $200. Of course, add the cost of the mountain bike itself.

NoPed Two. With 100 lbs added to the curb weight of the mountain bike, Ely had found the ride a little rough on rough surface streets, even with a sprung seat. NoPed Two, then, got some highly modified Honda XR-75 motorcycle front shocks. Ely welded dropouts to retain the quick-change feature for the front tire and shortened the shocks by 12 inches. The effort was fruitful. NoPed Two has real road-quality dampening with only eight more pounds of weight.

NoPed Three. The last in the NoPed series was *not* a modification of NoPed Two. Instead, Ely started over. The midsection of a stock mountain bike was cut out and a monocoque-style aluminum housing fashioned to contain the batteries and controller, filling the space between front and rear wheel. The rear suspension employed a normal front fork that was converted into a swing arm, ensuring no chain slack when the suspension compressed. Hatchback-style gas shocks were added to dampen the springs.

The NoPed Series

I was privileged to witness the rapid evolution of a pure electric bicycle in the NoPed (No Pedals) series of prototypes, designed and built by Ely Schless (Application A33).

In building his first electric vehicle (an electric motorcycle, the Shawk), Ely isolated weight as *the* design factor that, when reduced, gave the best reward for the effort in trying to improve performance. After setting some goals, he realized that the mountain bike could handle the 100 pounds of EV propulsion hardware (mostly battery pack) he would add (Techtalk T32). In the first NoPed, the only major chassis modification was changing the trail of the rear swingarm to help the vehicle work better on a roadway.

I drove all the NoPed prototypes. They offered stunning performance (Techtalk T33).

Three-Wheeled Electric Bikes

The pure electric 3-wheeler is a popular configuration of scratchbuilt EV. As the propulsion effort is shifted away from human power input, the vehicle's curb weight increases, most of it due to the bigger battery pack.

The greater weight creates a problem with using bicycle spoke wheels. They are likely to collapse in tight turns! Unlike a

---

*T*echtalk
T32
NoPed Specifications

Motor. Motronics, rated 50VDC, 1/4 HP, 900 rpm PM (permanent magnet).

Controller. Advanced Motion Controls. Servo amplifier, adj current limiting, regen.

Battery Pack. Powersonic. Twelve 12-volt, 7Ah, sealed lead-acid.

Battery Charger. 12-Volt, 35-Amp, DC-to-DC (switching), 2.5 Amps per battery.

Chassis/Frame. Mountain Bike, 26-inch tires.

Drivetrain. Overall ratio is 17.7-to-1. Motor-to-idler, Gilmer timing belt, 20-tooth (motor), 96-tooth (idler). Idler-to-rear wheel drive, standard bicycle chain, with sprockets reversed, 13-tooth (idler), 48-tooth (rear wheel).

Fig. 4-26:
Ely Schless and Noped I.

Fig. 4-28: Front and rear, heavier suspension is used in Noped II to handle weight gain.

Fig. 4-27: The two-stage drivetrain uses the original pedal assembly hole for a jackshaft.

Fig. 4-29:
Interconnects for the batteries are terminated in Molex connectors to assist with charging.

*T*33

Driving the NoPeds

I enjoyed driving each of the NoPed prototypes. Each was fast, quiet, and fun.

Wherever I stopped, people didn't hesitate to walk up and ask where I got it, how fast it went, and how much it cost. Everybody seemed to grasp that it was electric. Comments from bystanders and test drivers alike were always positive. "Great acceleration." Or "Wow — that's quiet!"

Motorists were often surprised I could pull away from a light so quickly, or stay with them, or even turn left in front of them as a light changed. However, some drivers tended to treat "no pedaling" as the same as "no acceleration," and would pull out in front of me.

I had trouble with the NoPeds, too. Twice, I almost fell over. As with motorcycles, there's restricted turning you won't find in most bicycles. The battery pack (weight) is high because of its position. Lowering it would affect operational characteristics in a negative way. The effect of a motorcycle in turns may be st be described as a reverse pendulum. If the weight is shifted too low, it can be dangerous in operation. Still, the standing-still balance takes getting used to, as it does with most motorcycles.

The twist-grip throttle is second nature to motorcycle owners, but I found it awkward. I just didn't feel like I could plant my body weight through two arms on the handlebars. Instead, I wanted a thumb lever for acceleration speed control, like that found on many ATVs.

I nearly had a major accident, power ON, moving the bike while walking alongside it, through a gate. Because of the restricted radius of turning, I grabbed the handlebar for support, the throttle rotated — and the power came on. The bike launched, jamming my hand in that position against fence, wheels still spinning. Electric motors deliver incredible power and torque — but they give no warning that they are ready to be energized, like an engine will.

After 30 miles of experience on the NoPed, I felt that a battery pack of lower voltage would be better, supplying a flatter power curve over the vehicle range.

Although I had a variable throttle, I found myself either in full ON or full OFF modes. With a running weight of 300 lbs (130-lb Noped and 170-lb operator), you need the juice to get to speed, and then you'll want to take advantage of coasting. This argues for a series-parallel controller. It's hard to beat electronic controllers if strong acceleration is warranted.

As is, the retail parts cost for the NoPeds averaged about $1,200. This feels a little. However, the NoPeds are no-nonsense transportation and that can be worth a lot!

bicycle, which leans into turns, and keeps the load perpendicular to the axle, a 3-wheel layout induces loads *parallel* with the axle that the spokes cannot handle. It is a question of "when" rather than "if" a collapse will occur in a skid.

An Electric Leaner

What if a 3-wheeler could be designed to lean the wheels into a turn? It's a classic puzzle that intrigues the designer looking for something a bit complex to tackle.

Bob Schneeveis' "leaner" appears to be a successful solution to this puzzle (Application A34). The prototype was developed after a close examination of an earlier version built by EV pioneer, Ed Rannberg. Bob's leaner was so successful a wildcard in the Electrathon America circuit that there is now a specific rule that prohibits its use!

Wherever I stopped, people didn't hesitate to walk up and ask where I got it, how fast it went, and how much it cost.

*A*34

Schneeveis Leaner

Daniel Pliskin

It was a leaning three-wheeler, designed and built by Ed Rannberg, that inspired Bob Schneeveis to build his own version. Ed's Leaner had the back two wheels linked together in such a way that if one wheel went up, the other was forced down. In this way, Ed had a three-wheeler that would handle like a two-wheeler. I saw it myself for the first time at the next Electrathon race in Pacifica. By then, Ed had shortened the vehicle and was running four 12-Volt motorcycle batteries.

As it was configured, Ed's leaner wasn't all that competitive. Nevertheless, the concept of a leaning trike had awesome ramifications. Leaners put no lateral forces on the wheels (rims). This allows the use of bicycle wheels without having them go unstable in the corners. Also, the driver doesn't have to be close to the ground to keep the vehicle flat in the turns. For handling reasons, leaners actually have to be tall to be safely operated on the street.

Bob and I discussed the design of a competitive leaner on the drive to and from the third Electrathon race in Ukiah, California. Bob began construction of the new vehicle using a bicycle frame. Batteries were mounted behind the seat tube. Two trailing arms straddled the batteries, attached where the crank had been. A pivoting fiberglass spring arrangement became the rear suspension. The motor, mounted on one of the trailing arms, drove one of the back wheels. It looked primitive and ugly, but it handled like a dream.

Electrathon

One of the finest examples of a 3-wheeled electric vehicle that uses bicycle technology is the Electrathon racer. Electrathon racing is a popular, 15-year-old sport that is held quarterly in Great Britain and Australia.

The Electrathon format of competition is described in one question: how far can you go in one hour on a closed track with three wheels and 64 pounds of deep-cycle, lead-acid battery?

Unlike the transcontinental, solar-powered competitions held in the USA and Australia in recent years, Electrathon is a different breed of electric racer. The imposition of limits of battery capacity and type, the use of a time-distance endurance format, and a ballasting of all drivers to 180 pounds is a smart combination. It helps Electrathon-class racing avoid the high cost and sophistication that permeates the solar car racing circuit. (There is an unfortunate correlation between the expense of solar racers and their finishing order!)

Electrathon rewards strategy, skill, and common sense (TechTalk T34). Do you know the capabilities of your vehicle? Can you pace yourself? Can you drive smart and fast while using the least amount of energy per lap?

Clark Beasley built his Electrathon racer, Slingshot, in Australia. When he married and moved to the USA in the late 1980's, he brought the trophy-winning Slingshot *and* the Electrathon format of racing to the USA (Application A35).

Photo: Daniel Pliskin

Fig. 4-30: Bob Schneeveis takes the Leaner out for a test run.

If form followed function, how could a vehicle that worked so well look so bad? The next night I woke up with a start, scribbled "air cylinders" on a scrap of paper, and went back to sleep with a smile on my face. Bob and I discussed the idea next morning. I did some calculations to determine what size air cylinders would be needed.

With a race only a few days away, I assumed that the idea would have to wait. I was wrong. Bob's leaner was at the starting line with a custom aluminum motorcycle-type front fork and front wheel drive. The trailing arms were pieces of aluminum square tubing. And the rear suspension was reduced to a pair of interconnected and pressurized air cylinders! These functioned as leaning mechanism, springs and shocks.

I had the misfortune of racing again Bob's leaner at Sunnyvale. It was passing me like it had a spare battery or two. I mused, at first, thinking that Eleodoro (Bob's driver) would soon see the error of his ways, running out of juice well before the race was over. But it didn't happen. When the hour was over, Eleodoro had run 92 laps. The second, third, fourth and fifth place vehicle had run 84-85 laps each. The leaner ran over 8% better than the other racers!

Bob put a third battery in this leaner for use on the streets, so he can keep up with local traffic. He commutes to work on it regularly. It can legally go in bike lanes, on bike paths, and park in bicycle parking areas. A one-time fee of $7 registers it with the California DMV as an electrified bicycle.

Fig. 4-31: The Leaner is amazing to watch or drive.

Photo: Daniel Pliskin

In an official race event, competitive Electrathon entries ration the battery pack's capacity to a rate that lets them go the distance. It's the classic tortoise-and-hare race. Everybody has their own race strategy, so some designs may sprint away and lap vehicles that have set a more conservative pace. Smooth and steady reigns supreme, as does reliability. The novice drivers, even in strong designs, are easy to pick out. Battery power is easily wasted in braking, dodging traffic, and acceleration.

Monitoring gauges is critical. Experienced drivers have small tables pinned alongside the meters, showing current or voltage values at 5-minute intervals. Combined with a timer watch, these data readings inform the driver of the SOC (state of charge). So, for example, if the voltmeter reading is higher 15 minutes into

*T*echtalk
34
Electrathon Racing Format

A new breed of racer has found its way from Australia onto USA streets. Electrathon! Since its appearance in 1989, the sport of Electrathon racing is growing quickly.

Why the popularity? There are several reasons. One has to do with the challenge itself. The format for Electrathon racing—64 lbs of lead-acid, deep-cycle batteries, a one-hour race period, drivers ballasted to the same weight, three or four wheels—takes the emphasis off technology and unfair practices.

Cost and competitiveness are other factors. Unlike the prohibitive cost associated with racing solar cars and the fluctuating rules of the stock and open classes at the annual Phoenix EV races, the Electrathon format rewards strategy and reliability over cost and sophistication. More than a decade of evolution in Great Britain and Australia stands behind it, too. A competitive design need not exceed $1,200 in total cost.

Simplicity is a third factor. Tool and fabrication skills taught at the high school level are sufficient to build an Electrathon racer. I'm excited by the implications of this. What better arena in which to educate and train young people than a high school auto shop! As well, competition is not a good word for this sport. The races I've attended feel more like a good outing with friends and peers than the crazy win-lose weirdness I find with other sports. Sure, you'd like to come up with the trophy, but it all seems more like good sport, participation, and the refinement of skills.

The ability to compete *often* is another attractive quality of Electrathon racing. Currently, dozens of races are run each year in California, most of them in parking lots. Linking up with other events, like the Electric Grand Prix, Phoenix, and SEER, has been a smart move for Electrathon organizers. This provides additional incentive for a builder-owner to go the distance required for a competition. Like other sport racing, points accumulation through many races each year decides the overall champion.

Fig. 4-32: Slingshot, an Electrathon racer.

*A*pplication
35
The Electric Slingshot

Viewed head-on, the first thing I noticed was an elliptical image, complete with a human face, that seemed to float unsuspended as it approached. As the vehicle turned, the front wheels became obvious for the first time, spokes spinning in their own elliptical orbits. The shape was elegant. Then, it was past me. A subdued whine betrayed the presence of a drivetrain as it glided away.

How fast does it go? In the Electrathon circuit, the Slingshot can hold better than 35 mph for an hour. Sounds slow, doesn't it. Once around the circuit inside this vehicle will bury that perception. When your fanny is an inch off the ground, and 90% of your body is horizontal, driving flat out will challenge your reflexes in spotting and avoiding the next pothole.

A closer look at the Slingshot is a pleasure. Looking down on it, you'll spend the first few minutes just admiring the simplicity of it.

A 3-wheeler, it is configured as a motorbike, with two wheels up front to handle steering, while the rear wheel connects to the drivetrain.

Fig. 4-33: Clark Beasley brought Electrathon racing to the USA from Australia.

the race than the table's value, the pace is picked up. If it's lower, it's time to back off a bit. Later in the race event, this strategy pays off. As the hour ticks down through the last minutes, flashier vehicles often slow, some to a crawl or to a stop. Experienced drivers can lap these contenders, and regain the lead.

Photo: Daniel Pliskin

Fig. 4-34: The Blob is appropriately named and very, very fast!

Fig. 4-35: The Blob's controls and meters.

Photo: Daniel Pliskin

The joystick captures your eye. Shove it left or right, its linkage causes the front wheels to turn in unison.

The Slingshot is outfitted with an electronic controller. Your finger moves a trigger on the joystick to vary motor current and vehicle speed.

The Slingshot motor is *small*, a bit more than 1/2 horsepower in capacity. It is a 24V series motor, salvaged from it's original duty of lifting the tines of an electric forklift. A timing belt chain transfers its output to a sprocket on an intermediate shaft. Sturdy bicycle sprockets and chain complete the overall gear reduction, translating motor speed into torque at the rear wheel.

The Slingshot depends upon bicycle drum brakes mounted in each of the front wheels for braking. These are activated by a foot pedal in the nose of the vehicle. A standard grip lever on the joystick adds some braking effort to the rear wheel.

The simple elegance of the Slingshot's design is no accident—it's time-won. Actually, it's the 4th vehicle that Clark has built. This is another advantage of the Electrathon format. Build one, race it, discover what works and what doesn't, change it, and race again. It is an evolutionary process. Theoretically, each design is better than the one before it.

T echtalk ──────────

In the Workshop
Daniel Pliskin
T 35

Bob Schneeveis would rather be throwing together an electric vehicle than talking about it. During the gas crunch of the seventies, he had gone over to electrics. Not the conservative electrics that we so often read about, but hell raising fast ones.

"Electric vehicles have to be fun in order to sway the public," Bob says. "Get the kids involved and they'll have fond memories of fun electric gadgets so that, as adults, they won't be swayed by skeptics."

Bob's current project was an Electrathon racer prototype, a three-wheeler, using go-cart parts and aircraft aluminum. He didn't wait for the controller he'd asked me to build. Instead, he wired it up with just a contactor and push button, and test drove it. It was scary, fast, and unstable.

Engineers, all too often, seem to take on an assignment, come up with some specifications and start in on the arduous calculations. Bob takes a different approach. As a master machinist, he can try things out, see if they work, learn from his mistakes, and go on to the next design. For racing, he starts light and makes things heavier only if they fail. An axle he bent jumping off curbs at 30 MPH was replaced with a stronger one the next day. The three-wheeler became a four-wheeler to get more stability in tight turns. It took two or three designs to come up with strong-but-light brakes. It was still fast, but stable and fun.

The search for a good motor isn't about reading or believing manufacturer 's specifications. Bob would buy one, install it, and give it the "smoke test." Nearly a dozen of them lay broken and burned in a pile before he found one that could do the job. The same was true for batteries. Just because the manufacturer says that the battery weighs 31 lbs and has a reserve capacity of 25 Amps for 90 minutes doesn't mean that it's true. Bob laboriously tested each one. The results were astonishing. And, until the Electrathon America rules were changed to exclude a vehicle of this type, Bob's leaner was winning all of the races!

Fig. 4-36: Bob Schneeveis checks Wendy Raebeck out on controls.

Electrathon America

A few years back, Electrathon racing was challenged by a new breed of vehicles that included designs based on go-carts and "leaners" built by Clean Air Revival and Bob Schneeveis (Techtalk T35). These fast hounds began racking up trophies. The races looked different, too. Certainly wilder and maybe a little intimidating to slower vehicles, things heated up. A struggle ensued to define the qualifications of an Electrathon racer. A division occurred.

When the dust settled, Clark Beasley had formed Electrathon USA to further the sport in the traditional style. Ten bucks will buy the Rules book, which includes a healthy section on design and construction tips for the novice. The package includes an

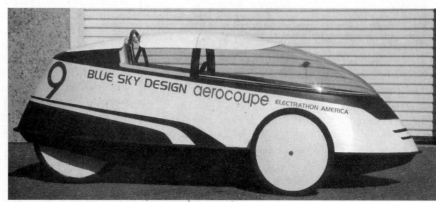

Fig. 4-37: Mark Murphy's Aerocoupe is made from blown ABS, designed for pedal swing, and available commercially.

Fig. 4-38: Where did the Aerocoupe go? Look for the kids.

Fig. 4-39: Race time!

Photos:
Mark Murphy

Fig. 4-41

Fig. 4-40

Photos:
Clark Beasley

Fig. 4-45

Fig. 4-46

Fig. 4-42

Fig. 4-43

Fig. 4-44

Fig. 4-47

Fig. 4-48

application to enter Electrathon races, and a newsletter with race results and the dates and locations of upcoming events.

Electrathon America rules contain three specifications that exclude the race-busting designs. One, the minimum wheel diameter is sixteen inches. Two, leaners must be automatically self-righting. Three, the driver must be fully enclosed in the vehicle. Sorry, no "bail-or-fly" designs (bail if you see the crash coming, fly if you don't).

Electrathon as Education

Electrathon vehicles are great educational tools. They're inexpensive. Build them in a garage or in auto shop class Application A36). Commercially-available shells, like the Murphy Aerocoupe, fast-track any project to completion.

Fig. 4-49: Willits High School students scribe a wheel hub for drilling.

Fig. 4-50: Jergenson BoxBeam is cut for the vehicle chassis.

All photos: Alan Kearney

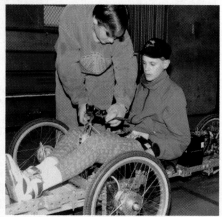

Fig. 4-51: Getting everything to work together helps people work together, too.

Fig. 4-53: Bob Schneeveis acts as an escort for a test run of the WHS vehicle

Fig. 4-52: In building an Electrathon vehicle, students learn how to handle both tools and materials.

Fig. 4-54: Members of the WHS Electric Car Club with instructor Alan Kearney (left).

A 36 High School Electrathon

Alan Kearney

The general response from my advanced auto students was "you've got to be kidding, this car doesn't make noise or burn rubber." I had just shown them a videotape of the Electrathon race at SEER '91 in Ukiah, California. At 25 mph, the vehicles driving the track circuit weren't impressive. Nevertheless, a few months later, some of these students formed a club, the Willits High School Electric Car Club (WHSECC), to build an Electrathon race vehicle.

Raising money was a difficult task in our town. Every school activity is under-funded and each group goes around town with their hand out every year. Tenacity helps here. We approached potential supporters in person, following it up with a brochure mailer, and a personal call. Once we had made some progress that we could show, contributions, in the form of money, materials, technical support, and contacts with different equipment manufacturers, came more easily.

We kept the cost of building the car to a minimum. Altogether, we spent $500 cash and used about $800 worth of materials. Local businesses donated materials, custom welding, batteries, etc.

Our goal was to race safely in as many different events as possible each school year. For this reason, we used a combination of the designs of Electrathon USA and some Northern California groups.

The WHSECC vehicle uses three wheels to avoid the rolling resistance of the four-wheeled design. The 20 inch "free style" wheel was chosen for its strength. Larger bicycle wheels and 3/8 inch axles will break down on the rougher race courses.

The main chassis and front axle are aluminum box tubing. Suntools, a local company, donated 50 feet of it to the project. Phil Jergenson showed us how to drill holes every 1.5 inches. This allowed us to easily vary the configurations during the design process. For example, our first vehicle had a TRIKE layout (one wheel up front and two in the rear). While this simplified steering and brakes, the vehicle would tip over on fast, tight turns. We quickly rejected this for the current MOTORBIKE layout.

We selected the Bosch electric motor for our drivetrain. Its high speed (3400 rpm) did present some problems when direct driving the rear wheel. A stock Curtis PMC unit is the controller. A Curtis battery fuel gauge, ammeter, and a digital voltmeter complete the instrumentation. Propulsion wiring is # 2 gauge wire. Our wheels are made from a utility hub which takes a 5/8 inch sealed bearing. These are custom spoked to 48-spoke Araya rims using the "4 cross" pattern. This design allowed us to use stock Go Kart 4.5 inch drum brakes.

The front-wheel spindles are 5/8 inch (grade 8) bolts welded to seamless, thick-walled (1/4 inch) steel tubing. The spindles pivot around a similar 5/8 inch bolt that acts as a king pin. Of course, the inside wheel must turn tighter in a turn than the outside wheel. We fabricated the steering arms from 1/4 inch steel plate. Bent in and back, these yield the Ackermann steering needed to reduce tire "scuffing" (and wear) in turns. The connection of the tie rod point at the steering post is adjustable so that we can change the steering radius of the vehicle. We use zero degree for camber, zero toe-in for low rolling resistance, and ten degrees positive caster for steering stability on bumps.

A double-coil, auto valve spring has been inserted into the front king pins to aid with suspension. More recently, we have been replacing the Japanese spokes (as they break) with "DT" brand (Swedish), 18-gauge stainless steel spokes.

Safety is very important to us. The battery is enclosed in plastic and we have the required seat belts, roll bar, main electrical disconnect switch, and rear view mirrors. Our brakes will stop the vehicle in 40 feet @ 25 m.p.h. In this area, the terrain is too hilly for the vehicle to travel far afield. I live in town and can easily commute to school (3/4 mile) in the vehicle.

We have competed in many races. The first race track was so rough and bumpy that we broke 25 spokes and blew a tire after 45 minutes. This prompted us to carry a spare wheel and tires. In the second race, we finished ahead of all other high schools at De Anza College Days. Our third race was at SEER '92.

Knowing how to read your instruments is as important as their quality. Teammembers keep track of the number of laps and the elapsed time in the races and report it to the driver every 15 minutes via a chalk board. Prior to each race, we make timed test laps on the track with a spare (second) set of batteries. We calculate the battery reserve and best gear ratio to use on the track and make the needed changes. Our racing batteries are maintained at a full charge by a solar panel right up to race time.

The importance of this project is difficult to limit to a few points. I like it that we are instilling an awareness of alternative energy sources in these students. It's a good place to apply practical math skills and problem solving. We have taken our vehicle to two other high schools in our area, hoping to spark interest in students and teachers alike. The students are easily interested. The teachers are more difficult to sway because it means donating time and energy. I estimate that we have 400 hours of construction time in building this vehicle.

Competition helps evolve hobbyist designs, like Dann Parks' Lightning series. The lessons learned with Lightning I (Application A37) were applied in Lightning II (Application A38).

Young people are often hassled about gas-powered hobbies, whether they are radio-controlled planes and cars, or ATVs (all terrain vehicles) and motorcycles. The

Fig. 4-55: Dann Parks and Lightning I.

Fig. 4-56: The body shape of Lightning I (#54) keeps the vehicle above the drag of ground effect.

Fig. 4-57: Using a wheel pulley does not interfere with aerodynamic wheel disks.

All photos: Dann Parks

Fig. 4-58: The motor is part of a one-piece, lightweight swing arm.

Fig. 4-59: This body design fits a human body like a glove.

A 37 Lightning One

Dann Parks

I have been designing and building vehicles for almost 20 years, including design and construction of the Vortex with Steve Pombo (Dolphin Vehicles). When I first heard of Electrathon, I thought it would be a fun way to learn about electric vehicles and experiment with lightweight construction.

For my first Electrathon vehicle, I wanted to investigate new construction materials and techniques. The Vortex had been constructed of urethane foam, fiberglass and polyester resin. I found the foam dust and resin very irritating to my skin. With its small size, I thought an Electrathon vehicle would be a good chance to try some of the new, less irritating epoxy resins and Styrofoam, as well as the more expensive Kevlar and carbon fiber fabrics.

One of the design criteria was to reduce rolling resistance to the minimum. To this end, I chose 27" bicycle tires. These tires cannot withstand high side loading, so I initially designed the vehicle to lean into corners. This employed a simple arrangement of air cylinders and required that the driver balance the vehicle. Electrathon rule changes (which I agreed with) later outlawed this type of vehicle. That was just as well, since the design suffered in operation from friction in the cylinders.

I was able to continue using this vehicle by adjusting the air cylinders to lock the vehicle in the upright position. I also modified the wheels to heavy-duty spokes. I figured the side loading problem would only happen on tight tracks. On the banked velodrome track, I expected the vehicle would do 30-34 mph. without problems. At the time, the one-hour record was only 28 miles.

Number 54 (Lightning I) is best described as a motorbike (two steered wheels in front) with a monocoque chassis and 3-wheel suspension. The teardrop shape of the body complemented the leaning concept, lifting it high in turns to clear the ground. Even as an upright vehicle, the body has low drag because it is aerodynamic and moves above the drag of "ground effect." Positioning the batteries in the space between the driver's legs helped the taper of the body. Besides helping keep the body narrow, battery positioning helped shift the vehicle's center of gravity forward.

The chassis is constructed entirely of Kevlar and fiberglass using a moldless composite construction technique pioneered by Burt Rutan of Voyager fame. This is an easy way to build strong, complex shapes.

The process is straightforward. First, I carved a male plug for the left and right side of the vehicle out of Styrofoam. This is an easy-to-shape and non-irritating foam used in building insulation. Next, the plugs were covered with the Kevlar and fiberglass, and wet out with epoxy resin. After the resin cured, most of the foam was removed from the inside, leaving a strong shell. Finally, where the shell needed to be stronger, the remaining foam inside was covered with glass cloth and resin. This "sandwich" of glass-foam-glass is extremely strong, especially in areas of compound curves. Altogether, three bulkheads were integrated into the chassis. I used an aerospace honeycomb material (available at aircraft surplus outlets), but high-grade marine plywood could also be used. The bulkheads provided mounting points for the suspension.

The front suspension is an A-arm design. Each arm shares a pivot point at the center line of the vehicle. The design allowed the foot (12") of suspension travel needed to lean the vehicle. The interconnected air cylinders allowed one wheel to move up and the other to travel down in equal amounts. After the rules changed, the interconnect between the cylinders was removed so the vehicle remained upright. Adjusting the air pressure in the cylinders adjusted the vehicle's "ride."

The heart of the #54 rear end is a single-sided swing arm that combines the rear wheel, motor and suspension in one assembly. This swing-arm was constructed of carbon fiber and Styrofoam with the same composite construction technique used for the chassis. It is very strong. The suspension is leveraged by a pull-rod forward to an air cylinder. The rigid, one-piece rear drivetrain seemed to simplify the overall design and eliminate alignment problems. I used a V-belt to drive a belt "ring" that attached to the spokes. This system is lightweight, quiet, and has minimal slip.

A joystick positioned between my knees handles steering and supports a brake lever. I steer with my right hand. My left hand manipulates the lever of a Curtis PMC potbox (and its controller) for speed control. The vehicle uses two 22NFD batteries and a Bosch motor. The vehicle weighs 80 pounds without batteries and 324 pounds in race-ready condition, with the driver ballasted to 180 pounds.

> *"The chassis is constructed entirely of Kevlar and fiberglass using a moldless composite construction technique pioneered by Burt Rutan of Voyager fame."*
> **Dann Parks**

Number 54 has been quite successful. The suspension is excellent and can be adjusted to provide a soft ride on any track. The vehicle reaches 38 mph at 40 Amps on a flat surface. High-speed cornering is a problem, even on the banked velodrome. It wears the tires quickly and stresses the spokes to their limit. The small drum brakes are just adequate. #54's best run is 32.7 miles at the San Jose velodrome.

Photo: Clark Beasley

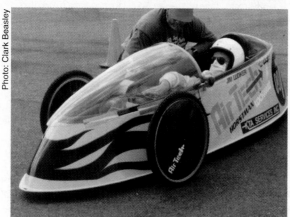

Fig. 4-62: Jim Ludiker's vehicle is a consistent winner in the Electrathon circuit.

Photo: Clark Beasley

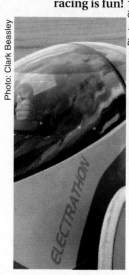

Fig. 4-63: Win or lose, Electrathon racing is fun!

Photo: Clark Beasley

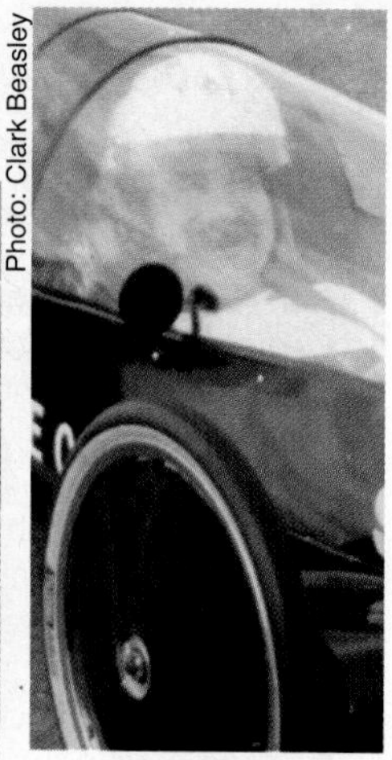

Fig. 4-64: Hey, when is this race going to start!

Application A38

Lightning Two

Dann Parks

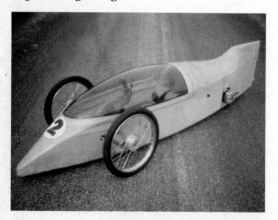

All photos of Lightning Two: Dann Parks

Fig. 4-60: Lightning Two.

I wanted my next vehicle (#2) to be more robust and capable of high-speed cornering. Where Lightning I was gossamer, Lightning II would be a tank. A lightweight tank. In it, I wanted a drivetrain and suspension design that I could eventually use in a lightweight street vehicle.

The wheels were the most difficult part. I felt bicycle wheels, even 20" plastic rims, were too light to handle the loads at the speeds these vehicles can achieve. Replacing tires due to wear, at $75 per race, was unreasonable. Then, I discovered and purchased a cache of moped tires from a local garage. These rims are robust, have a large alloy-drum brake, and mount a tire that looked like it could last the whole season at $39 per set. I was able to modify them for a 1/2" axle. They look perfect for a lightweight street vehicle tire, too.

I opted to use the Doran/Scott motor in the #2 Lightning. It seems more rugged than the Bosch motor. It uses a standard keyed shaft, while the Bosch has a weird, threaded shaft that requires the fabrication of a sprocket. I decided on chain drive this time, for two reasons. First, the moped rear wheel had a sprocket attached. And, second, I felt that #54's V-belt was slipping a bit. Other design goals included keeping the body shell small, minimizing parasitic drag (by enclosing mirrors, axles, etc.) and using the same air cylinder suspension.

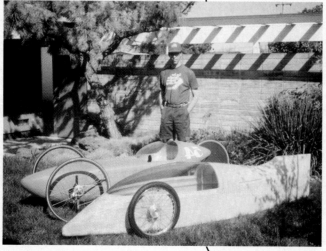

Fig. 4-61: Dann Parks with both Lightning-series vehicles.

Lightning #2 is an all-monocoque chassis/body made of Styrofoam and fiberglass and epoxy resin. I repeated the composite construction method, but eliminated the Kevlar due to the difficulty I experienced in working with it. The body design has a long, tapered tail to eliminate the drag of vehicles chopped short. I

Photo: Clark Beasley

Fig. 4-65: Vehicles line up for the start of the one-hour race.

silence of the Electrathon race makes it possible to hold an event around a neighborhood block, or back and forth on a wide street. Cheers and shouts of encouragement from the gathering crowds are the only evidence of the race itself!

Currently, Electrathon races in the USA require the pilot to have a valid driver's license. This is not true in Australia or Great Britain. While the issues of liability and driver experience are at the core of the US regulation, it's unfortunate that young people are not able to participate more directly in Electrathon races.

positioned the batteries behind me this time, out of the driver compartment, behind a bulkhead (for safety), and easily accessible. The rear end is a tubular metal swing arm which also mounts the motor. The swing arm is leveraged with a push-rod to an air cylinder.

The front end uses a solid front axle suspended from the chassis with two air cylinders. The axle pivots on two carbon fiber leading-links mounted to the sides of the chassis. A tiller arrangement is used to steer the vehicle. Pushing right causes a left turn (it sounds more confusing than it is). The brakes are activated by a lever pulled by the right hand. The throttle is a pistol-like trigger on the tiller. It turns the rheostat of a disassembled PMC controller potbox.

I deemed good access an important design factor in this vehicle. Consequently, the entire canopy (from an Aerocoupe) pivots upward for easy entrance and exit, and provides access to the front suspension. The tail section is a single layer of fiberglass that removes for access to the motor, batteries, chain and suspension cylinder. Gauges include an ammeter and a bicycle speedometer/timer.

Everything works exceptionally well. The tires have proven to be just what I wanted: bulletproof and long wearing. The suspension is just as subtle as the first vehicle, only more robust. I'm still dialing in the gearing. More races will determine how competitive the vehicle will be. Still, it looks to be a front runner. Most importantly, the chassis design has proven itself worthy for street applications. That's where I want to go next.

Fig. 4-66: Lightning Two is comprised of several pieces.

Fig. 4-67: Races afford the opportunity to look closely at a competitor's design.

Fig. 4-68: The entire rear assembly is bolted to the main body.

The Panther Electric project (Application A39) clearly demonstrated that students have the aptitude to build an EV. As well, I found every young driver respectful of the vehicle when operating it.

Fig. 4-69: Each student who worked on the Panther Electric project got to drive the vehicle around the school track.

Fig. 4-70: The project begins.

Fig. 4-71: Josh Shreffler and Glenn Hackleman check control circuitry prior to a test run.

Fig. 4-72: Stephen and Ian adjust the suspension.

The Electric Motorcycle

Need something stronger than bicycle technology but lighter than an automobile for your vehicle? Look at motorcycle technology.

First, however, look at the motorcycle itself. Without much effort, motorcycles get great gas mileage. The resons are simple: a high horsepower-to-weight ratio and minimal frontal area.

A 39 *pplication* — Panther Electric Project

The Panther Electric project came about when I engaged my younger son's GATEs class in building an Electrathon vehicle. This involved more than a dozen seventh and eight grade girls and boys enrolled in a Problem Solving class at San Lorenzo Valley Junior High. From the beginning, it was clear that most of the students lacked even basic material-working and tool-handling skills. In retrospect, I'm glad that we purchased the blown-ABS Murphy Aerocoupe shell for the body.

Our smartest move was using Jergenson aluminum BoxBeam for designing and fabricating the chassis. Like Leggo pieces, this permitted the constant shifting of components, support, and suspension elements throughout the project. The vehicle was reconfigured about fifty times! At the end, only one component was welded. I'm certain we could have found a non-welded alternative, but we chose expediency over purity to get it done.

Another innovative feature was building the front suspension with skis as springs. Two laminated (micarta, aluminum, and steel) skis had their tips and tails chopped off. These were spaced and stacked (see photo) to support Hime joints at the top and bottom of the kingpins, approximating the traditional twin A-arms setup. A castor (rake) angle was built in, and camber is adjustable.

Students scrounged an amazing array of bicycle parts, rims, and tires during the project year. After several trial setups, we finally settled on a full set of modified moped rims and tires from Dann Parks.

Using a motorbike layout of the wheels (two steered in front, a single powered wheel in the rear), we assembled a rough framework. Since one of our goals was to have the vehicle licensed for the street, the main inside frame rails were located at bumper level. The students were very concerned about safety. They thought it smart that the vehicle be able to bounce away from a collision instead of getting steamrolled. Several students measured the height of bumpers of cars in the school parking lot, and we settled on the main rails at an 18-inch ground clearance.

The rear suspension system is a maze of box-beam pieces. I am impressed with the students'

When it comes to motorcycles, people seem to fall into one of two classes: bikers and skeptics.

• *Bikers.* Bikers like the *ride.* They feel the advantages. The acceleration, the vibration, the speed, the feel of the wind in their face, and the openness around them. Rush-hour traffic isn't much of a bother, particularly on the freeway. You learn how to glide your motorcycle between the long rows of slow-moving (or halted) cars and trucks. Insurance is relatively inexpensive, and a gallon of gasoline goes a *long* way when it has to. Admittedly, it's hard to resist the rush of doing zero to seventy in under ten seconds.

• *Skeptics.* The skeptics are people who won't try a

Fig. 4-73: Children love to drive electric-powered vehicles.

tenacity and creativity in designing and building it. The motor shaft is at the center as the suspension pivot. Irrespective of suspension travel, then, the tension of the V-belt (soon to become a chaindrive) does not loosen or tighten.

Currently, the vehicle uses a simple series-parallel control circuit. This feeds 12V (low speed) or 24V (high speed) power to the motor. Another DPDT contactor performs the job of "reverse," simplifying the drivetrain.

The year-long project was completed just as school ended. Entering it in the hometown parade before we were finished revived the flagging interest of students. A few big afterschool and weekend sessions pounded out the detail stuff.

An hour of roadtime both days before the parade wrung out problem areas and adjustments were made. Karl Applegate drove the Panther Electric in the parade, doing little figure eights in the roadway to the delight of the crowd, then speeding off to catch up with the parade. Spectators were impressed with the little vehicle, and what the students accomplished. The project was part of a cover story for the local "hot" weekly Santa Cruz paper.

On the last day of school, every student that had put in serious time on the project got to drive the Panther twice around the school's athletic track.

Final Thoughts

This project was a lesson in patience for me. A car was built, primarily by students, and it worked! I found it interesting to see the students settle into natural areas of interest in the project. Some liked mechanical work, and others were more enchanted with the electric propulsion system. Several students showed real skill at drawings. Many students attempted videotaping, but the majority of the footage was pretty shaky and nauseous to watch! Fortunately, several students mastered the skills, and it's all been edited into a documentary piece!

Overall, I think the students obtained some insight into what it takes to accomplish a goal. There's so much more to managing a project than assembling something. And how everybody feels at the end, not the vehicle itself, is a reflection of how well the project was conducted.

Fig. 4-74: Instructor Carter Milhous, Karl Applegate, and Beau Axton check the fit.

Fig. 4-75: An old pair of skis helped out with the suspension.

Fig. 4-76: Control circuitry is mounted on one plate for easy access.

Fig. 4-77: The Panther Electric is finished in time for the town parade.

motorcycle. Or won't do it *twice*. They see all of the disadvantages. Motorcycles are intimidating. Roar, vibration, clutch, massiveness. They are definitely not all-weather vehicles. There is no real crashworthiness to them. They don't have a trunk or backseat in which to carry things. It's hard to straddle them in a dress. The helmet messes up your hair. Some people look askance at you. Cars will cut you off—their drivers either don't like you or don't see you.

Advocates of electric propulsion are not quite certain what to do about the motorcycle. There are some attractive qualities to it, namely low frontal area, low weight, and low power requirements. There are negative ones, too. Where is there room for enough batteries to get a decent range?

Lead-acid batteries add weight *fast*. This will affect the motorcycle's acceleration, that "muscle feeling" a rider likes.

A lightweight composite body, like those found on many HPVs, could supply streamlining and all-weather protection for the motorcycle. Still, adding a shell to a motorcycle is not as easy as it sounds. The rider must be able to keep the vehicle upright when stopped.

As efficient as the electric motor and controller are, these components' ratings are likely to be "pushed" if encased in a

Fig. 4-78: Ely Schless with his prototype, Shawk

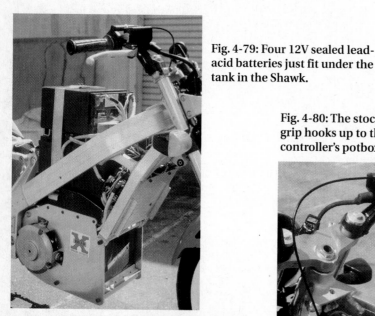

Fig. 4-79: Four 12V sealed lead-acid batteries just fit under the tank in the Shawk.

Fig. 4-80: The stock throttle grip hooks up to the controller's potbox.

Fig. 4-81: An electric refill uses 25 cents' worth of electricity.

Fig. 4-82: Fast acceleration and the absence of noise helps Shawk's operator.

Shawk

Ely Schless is used to designing and building things fast. That's his profession. His company, Brand X, builds mechanical effects for the movie and TV industry. There's rarely time to contemplate the various possibilities when someone calls. It's usually last minute, with people expecting to buy their way out of a jam. Sketch, design, build, test, and deliver—*now*.

Ely's first run-in with electrics was a vehicle to be used onstage with the music group, Berlin. This experience gave him the basics. The idea for his second one came in the middle of an engine rebuild for his primary racing bike, a 650 cc, 1988 Honda Hawk.

"Its engine needed $1,500 worth of work," Ely explained. "I had already lightened it for racing, stripping 100 pounds from the original 400 pound curb weight. Well, as soon as the engine was removed, I realized that I had had it. Racing had stopped being fun. What I wanted was a 'non-oil' entity. I wanted an electric."

Ely placed calls to locate the necessary components. Some of the folks he talked to were as excited about his project as he was. "I got a ton of information, " he says. "Brand X has taught me to stay basic with design — size, weight, handling, space, packaging. Not sure about something? Try it — now. Find out, and go on. I had a defined frame width and height. The Shawk is what I wanted it to be." (Ely affixed a matching 'S' in front of the HAWK to originate the catchy name.)

Ely went to work on the conversion, custom-fitting the series motor, sealed lead-acid batteries, and the electronic controller into the Hawk frame, drivetrain, and throttle controls (Techtalk T36).

The result is a user-friendly machine. "Everyone who has driven it, from bike people to someone off the street, loves it," Ely claims. People who have never driven a motorcycle seem willing to try the Shawk. Remember, there's no noise, no smell, no clutch and no possibility of "stalling" the engine. Everyone gets it right the first time.

What did the Shawk cost him? $140 each for 4 chargers, $120 each for 4 batteries, $450 for the motor, and $500 for the controller. Ely works his own well-equipped machine shop, so everything needed to make it all fit cost him only the materials. "I don't consider the Shawk to be a pragmatic approach to getting people to use electric vehicles," Ely admits. "Not at $3,500 for the bike, and $2,000 for the electrics."

What would he do differently? "Start from scratch," Ely responds. "The Shawk is compromised — in cost and weight. I like to build with something that's in my hand. The Hawk was there, so I used it. It's got the look, too. That takes good design. If something looks homebuilt, people often won't try it. It scares them. People nowadays are 50% visual about acceptance."

I asked Ely if he had any advice to lend to tinkerers. "Build it to be intuitive. If it requires an owner's manual to figure out how to work it, it's wrong!" Ely thinks the average modern car stereo, with its five miniature buttons in a tiny grid pattern with abbreviated terms in two millimeter-high letters, epitomizes the abuse of technology. "The older-style button radios were safer," he points out, "because your eyes didn't have to leave the road to find and select a station. A tactile control, not a microvisional one, is required here. High-tech should help us, not make us feel inadequate and stupid."

Is there any other value in the Shawk? "Yeah," Ely adds, "there's a lot of hot-rod people out there who want something new to chew on. They're serious and they're good, and they'll advance this technology really fast."

Techtalk T36 — Shawk Specifications

The Shawk uses a series (Advanced DC) motor rated at 4.3 HP (continuous) and 36-48 Volts DC. There was room for four batteries. Ely selected the 35-Ah Dynasty series battery. Its absorbed glass-matte, lead-acid design made it a sealed battery. A Curtis PMC mosfet (electronic) controller, rated at 350A and 48VDC, complemented the motor size. The controller's pot box was connected directly to the bike's throttle cable. At the rider's fingertips, then, was as much torque as available from popping the clutch on a 18 HP engine! Converting the lightened Hawk (it weighed 300 lbs with its engine and transmission) to electric power resulted in a net gain of 85 lbs to the original motorcycle (for a total of 485 lbs).

The Shawk's drivetrain, with its #40 chain, was a bit larger than necessary. Ely figured it wasn't worth the trouble to change. It definitely maintains that beefy look a street bike should have! Ely installed a 12-tooth chain gear on the electric motor and a 51-tooth on the rear wheel. The 4.25-to-1 ratio was just right. Acceleration is like a 250 cc motorcycle and the Shawk pushes itself all the way up to 40 mph at that rate.

The Shawk is a no-frills bike. Without a tachometer, speedometer, or battery current and voltage gauges, the values for range, speed, and acceleration are all guesswork. Ely's taken it out on a 10-mile round trip that used city streets—stop and go and strong accelerations—and still had battery power to go further at the end. From this info, he figures the Shawk's range at 20 miles.

When it's time to plug in, Ely hand-carries out his chargers—one for each battery—on a rig that supports them. These are Todd chargers, rated 12-Volt and 25-Amperes. The outputs of each are terminated in a tough 8-pin plug that fits into a flush-mounted receptacle on the bike. At about 70% DOD (depth of discharge), the Shawk is 80% recharged in an hour, and fully topped-off after 3-1/2 hours.

motorcycle's shell and, therefore, require extra cooling. The high aspect ratio (greater height to width) of a body shell is likely to make the vehicle "sail" in high crosswinds. For this degree of modification, it is often wiser to invest in the design of a three-wheeler than a two-wheeler.

Combining electric propulsion with motorcycle technology boils down to three choices: Convert it without embellishment, scratchbuild a smaller version, or add a third wheel.

A Motorcycle Conversion

A good example of a straight conversion of a motorcycle to electric propulsion is the Shawk (Application A40). Designed and built by Ely Schless, the Shawk started life as a Honda Hawk. Ely brought his experience as a racing motorcycle mechanic and competent machinist to the project. It was needed. In the space normally occupied by the engine, transmission, gas tank, and exhaust pipes, Ely cleverly adapted the small space to hold four (4) batteries, motor, and controller.

With virtually no background experience in EVs, Ely got it all right the first time (TechTalk T36). The novice EV designer might think the Shawk's system undersized. with 4-1/2 HP of motor and only 48 Volts of battery pack. However, the

---

Application A41 — Schless PowerBike

When I drive a vehicle, I like it when I run out of courage before I run out of performance. That's what it's like to test drive the PowerBike. Off the line like a startled cat. Momentum recharges the battery pack every time you use the brake, with a braking force that you can control. Maximum could pitch you over the handlebars.

I'm no stranger to the NoPed series of machines that Ely Schless has developed. Although I've never liked the idea of adding 100 pounds of machinery to a bicycle, I got over that notion just minutes into the test drive by adding, "...except when it can go this fast." Thirty-two miles per hour on level ground on a bicycle is *fast*. Any feeling of heaviness in the machine at rest evaporates at speed and is replaced by blissful momentum. It's nice to know there's some weight to help keep the PowerBike on the ground. This machine has a propensity to fly.

That brings up the issue of bringing the PowerBike to a stop. With so much acceleration, speed, and weight, the PowerBike is operating beyond the capacity of stock rim brakes. Front and rear, this machine has disc brakes. These, however, form the *backup* system. The primary system is regenerative braking, a feature that is built into the prototype of a new controller from Curtis PMC. Ely got a "beta" unit (he uses it and reports back to Curtis on how it's doing). This is a long-awaited unit for low voltage (12-48VDC) operation of one horsepower PM (permanent magnet) motors. (Sorry! The controller will not work with series motors.)

Right away, I realized there was no real protection in a bicycle helmet for the sting of wind in the eyes. (A motorcycle helmet is more appropriate for this machine, anyway.) Watering eyes make it hard to see the road surface. Believe me, at this speed and with tires this skinny, you need to spot, categorize, and plot your path for as far ahead as you can manage through the many undulations, cuts, drain guards, aberrations, flotsam, jetsam, and other unknowns that inhabit the "bike lanes." In, short, city streets can be unmerciful to such revolutionary machinery.

Amazingly enough, despite all the stupid things I attempted to do (or forgot I wasn't supposed to), I never dumped it or lost it. There were never any moments of sheer terror. In reflection, I realize I remember only the *joy* in cruising around town and through traffic.

In the tradition of the NoPed series, the PowerBike has simple controls. *Everything* is on the handgrip throttle. A separate switch disables the throttle, but it's there mostly to avoid accidental launches of the vehicle.

What happens at the throttle? Let's take a test drive. Hopping on, it's reassuring to feel the suspension "work," fore and aft. Footrests are mounted where the footpedals used to attach to the bike frame. This shaft doubles as part of the drivetrain. My knees are a comfortable fit against the battery saddlepacks. I ease the throttle on. With nary a whisper or whine, the PowerBike moves away from a stop. It seems like you can increase the rate of acceleration forever, it's got so much potential. It is possible to spin the tires and to jump teeth on the motor drivebelt. If you've an urge to impress someone, use just one-half throttle. To anyone watching you, you're on a bicycle with saddlepacks.

When you *back off* the throttle, the brakes come *on*. Regenerative brakes. The further you back off, the more braking effect. Let go of the throttle, and you get full regen. It's all intuitive to use. It is the way throttle and brakes should be—on *one* pedal. In this case, a handthrottle. Within a few blocks, I realized I had as much braking as I would ever need and more than I've ever had before—relative to the weight of the machine.

Exciting is the word that best fits the roadtest. I enjoyed the speed, talking with folks when I came to a stop, and the relaxing excursions through the countryside. The silence contributed greatly to my enjoyment.

The controller and charger reside inside a center module. Each saddlepack can be exchanged with a duplicate set (freshly recharged) in 30 seconds' time. Or the PowerBike plugs into the nearest receptacle.

motor is a series type, ensuring high torque at zero RPM. It's enough to move 550 pounds of bike and rider off the line with gusto. The PMC controller will channel 350 Amps to the motor if the batteries are able to deliver it. At 35Ah, the pack is light on energy density but easily delivers the high current (power density) to meet the motor demands. If you do the math, this combination of motor, controller, and drivetrain is able to deliver as much torque as an 18 HP engine.

Ely was test driving the Shawk when I first met him.. Several months later, I test drove the Shawk for myself. It felt perfectly natural to get on, turn on the key, and power it into the street. When fully charged, the batteries will let you chirp the tires. Acceleration is brisk—all the way up to its 40 mph cruise speed.

The direct-drive system of the Shawk strips the motorcycle of its intimidation to the novice. In addition to the lack of vibration and engine sound, there are no gears to shift and no clutch to operate. The motor cannot be stalled. Even at speed, sounds from the environment can be heard through the helmet. The Shawk leaves a silent wake.

The PowerBike

The experience of designing and building the Shawk prompted Ely to think even lighter, and the NoPed series of electric bicycles was the result (review Application A33).

These experiences led Ely to design the PowerBike (Application A41). I like this machine a lot—the way it looks, works, accelerates, brakes, and feels.

Restoring an Auranthetic

Several years ago I had an opportunity to trade some work with Ed Rannberg (Eyeball Engineering) for an old Auranthetic frame. Motor and batteries were absent. I thought this might be an interesting project for my older son, Brett, so it became his birthday present (Application A42).

In the late 1970s, a company in Los Angeles, California, manufactured this small, purpose-built, electric-powered motorcycle. The size of a scooter, the Auranthetic sported a 1/2 HP PM (permanent magnet) motor, a two-step controller, and a 24-Volt battery pack.

Fig. 4-83: Ely Schless on the PowerBike.

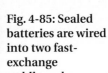

Fig. 4-84: A gearbelt connects motor to jackshaft. A chain completes the transfer to the rear wheel.

Fig. 4-85: Sealed batteries are wired into two fast-exchange saddlepacks.

Photo: Glenn Hackleman

Fig. 4-86: Brett checks out the Auranthetic with dad, Michael.

To the casual observer, the Auranthetic looked like a small motorcycle, complete with a teardrop-shaped gas tank. Up close, you could see that it was all fake. Instead of a fill spout, there was a keyswitch and a small (linear) voltmeter mounted in the top of the tank. A 3-prong receptacle, recessed in a hole in its side, was ready to receive a standard extension cord that would allow you to plug it into any standard wall receptacle for recharging. The battery charger (a transformer and two diodes) was carried onboard. The vehicle could recharge anywhere it went.

There were several major flaws in the Auranthetic's design, so I designed new control circuitry based on series-parallel operation. Brett and I yanked out the old contactors and wiring. We worked out safer hand controls, too. The battery frame was enlarged to hold two Trojan 27TMH batteries.

The Auranthetic is a fun runabout that will handle rough roads. However, after experiences with comparable EVs, I find it rather unwieldy. If you find a complete Auranthetic, great. Use it "as is." Otherwise, build something lighter.

The Three-Wheeled Electric Motorcycle

Want something with more capacity than a two-wheeled motorcycle? Take a long, hard look at the three-wheeled motorcycle.

Like the 3-wheeled HPV, there are many advantages to the 3-wheeled format of motorcycle. The result is *not* a motorcycle with an extra wheel. That would be better represented by a motorcycle with a sidecar.

An attractive quality of using motorcycle components in a small EV is that they seem to offer an easy way to obtain a lightweight, high-performance EV without the cost, bureaucracy, and complexity of a four-wheeler.

For example, motorcycle wheels can handle strong static (weight) and dynamic (corner, bump, brake) loads. The addition of an extra motorcycle wheel increases the static load capacity by 50%, nicely compensating for the weight of the battery pack. Typically, a 3-wheeled vehicle using motorcycle wheels more easily achieves (and surpasses) the 33 percent battery-to-curb weight than most 2W and 4W vehicles.

Application

A 42

Restoring an Auranthetic

Brett Hackleman

It all started when my dad, Michael Hackleman, said, " Let's go over to the Eyeball Engineering shop and pick up your birthday present."

I was very excited, even though he had already told me what it was. I had always wanted some sort of electric motorcycle or go-cart to zip around on, and my dad found someone who owned one. So we car-pooled to Ed Rannberg's shop to pick it up.

What I saw there was sort of a shock to me. His shop was crammed with electric scooters, motorcycles, cars, tools, and pretty much everything else you could imagine. Outside I saw another thing. A pile of gas engines heaped on the ground. I guess it was some sort of a burial ground!

Finally, we found what we were looking for. It was my very own electric motorcycle. It didn't look like much of anything, but I had plans to change that. The seat was shredded, rust was everywhere, a brake handle and the rear wheel sprocket were gone, and several other things were missing from years of people salvaging parts off of it. Still, we loaded it up into the back of the van and took it home.

I started working on it as soon as I could. I was armed with WD-40 and ready to face the challenge. I got a lot of the rust off and then I could see what I needed to do to fix it up. I needed to totally re-wire the controller and get a motor, batteries, and a key switch.

My dad knew somebody who had the same exact motorcycle so we called him up and got a wiring diagram. My dad then found out that he had the exact motor that we needed so we installed that. We then bypassed the old keyswitch by taking it out and installing a temporary switch. Then all we needed were some batteries.

I knew that we would be going to the U.S. Battery Manufacturing Company in a couple of days, but I wanted to just see if it worked. We borrowed the batteries out of our gas-powered cars. It worked great and I loved it. Unfortunately, I had to give the batteries back so we could use the cars.

When we went to the battery company, I got some deep-cycle batteries for the motorcycle. The cold L.A. air stung my face as I raced along at 25 mph.

I think I like this over a gas motorcycle (even though I've never tried one) because there is no hassle with gas or oil, and it's much quieter. Now the only problem I have is that I'll have to wait a few years to drive it legally on city streets!

Another attractive quality of the 3-wheeler using motorcycle components is that of a simplified drivetrain and a layout that lends itself to the natural application of aerodynamic principles.

In the 3-wheeled motorcycle, almost every distinctive characteristic of the motorcycle is gone. Sorry, no more squeezing between longs lines of cars stalled in traffic. No more "lean" in the corners. No more "rolling stops" at stop signs and traffic signals.

The Windcar

The first good 3-wheeler I came across in my EV career was the Windmobile, or Windcar (Application A43).

Designed and built by Jim Amick, the windcar was initially intended to be a wind-powered ice racer. For this role, the Windcar design was flawed. The "sails" would not work when vehicle speed fell below 14 mph. A tight turn or a fluctuation in the wind's speed could stall the windcar and leave it helpless on the ice.

Instead of scrapping the design, Jim substituted wheels for the skates, added electric propulsion, and made the windcar a road machine. Shortly thereafter, it made the cover of Popular Science (1976), and I saw it for the first time.

pplication
A 43   **Amick Windmobile**

Jim Amick's Windmobile, or windcar, is today still a novel road machine.

The windcar was originally designed to be a wind-powered ice sailer. The vertical component on each side of the arch is an airfoil acting as a sail. Empty except for driver and steering cables, Jim attempted to control the Windcar on the ice using two concentric steering wheels (one inside and smaller than the other). This would allow the machine to "tack." Once it got going, the machine was fast, amplifying the speed of the crosswind into a vehicle speed five times (5x) as high. A 15-mph crosswind, then, would take the windcar to 75 mph!

When the design failed to work on ice (or, more specifically, on wind power alone), Jim modified it to run on the road. An electric drive system was added. A 2 HP PM motor was added at each of the rear wheels (at the base of the arch on each side). In headwind or no-wind conditions, the electric drive supplied the needed power. Where wind was present and blew across the road, the wing lightened the propulsive effort, or altogether replaced it. The additional weight and the added resistance of tires on the road (compared with steel skates on ice) brought the wind-amplifying speed down to a threefold (3x) effect. A 15 mph crosswind would take the vehicle up to 45 mph once the windcar was brought up to speed (14 mph).

Jim Amick, with his sons, retired the original Windcar and developed several new vehicles. One of them, the Voltec, used an experimental aluminum-air battery. The wing is still there, but reduced in size. The only claim made for the wing of the Voltec is the stability it adds to the vehicle.

Fig. 4-87: Brett Hackleman with his restored Auranthetic.

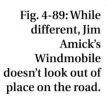

Fig. 4-88: Contactors arrange the batteries in series or in parallel for two motor speeds.

Fig. 4-89: While different, Jim Amick's Windmobile doesn't look out of place on the road.

Photo: Douglas Amick

The New Electric Vehicles   127

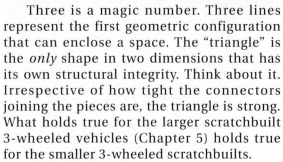

Fig. 4-90: The Windmobile is at home in a storm.

As a road machine, the Windcar had excellent potential. Of particular note is the inherent crash-worthiness of its layout, particularly from side-impact. Subsequently, Jonathan Tennyson adapted this design for the Mana La (review *A World of Solar Cars*, Chapter 5), sheathing the entire outer surface of the arch with solar cells in an unsuccessful bid to lead the pack in 1987 in the World Solar Challenge across Australia.

Tackling Tradition

To some people, four wheels on a vehicle is like one sun rising in the morning. The way it should be. If you have two wheels, you're a glorified bicycle or a motorcycle. Go to one, and you're a unicyclist. But why would anyone choose just three!

All Windmobile photos: Douglas Amick

Fig. 4-91: Pick a route that gives plenty of side-wind for energy-free operation.

Three is a magic number. Three lines represent the first geometric configuration that can enclose a space. The "triangle" is the *only* shape in two dimensions that has its own structural integrity. Think about it. Irrespective of how tight the connectors joining the pieces are, the triangle is strong. What holds true for the larger scratchbuilt 3-wheeled vehicles (Chapter 5) holds true for the smaller 3-wheeled scratchbuilts.

Trike or Motorbike?

There are two practical layouts of wheels: the trike and the motorbike.

• *Trike.* The Trike has a single, steerable wheel up front and twin drive wheels rearward. Traditionally, a child's first set of wheels is the tricycle. Later, the child graduates to the bicycle.

• *Motorbike.* The motorbike reverses the trike's layout, positioning two wheels up front for steering and a single wheel in the rear. In the simple designs, the rear wheel is powered. A stronger design powers the

Fig. 4-93: The wing was formed in a catenary curve.

Fig. 4-92: The body is shaped with foam strips and covered with fiberglass and resin.

steered front wheels. There are attributes to both single- and twin-wheel drive. Look over the many applications that use each and decide what appeals to you.

An Electric Speedster

Michael Leeds, with the help of Dick Rahders and Dr. Paul Lee, started the construction of a solar car in 1990. Wanting to use off-the-shelf and affordable components and lead-acid battery technology, Leeds built a test mule he dubbed the Speedster (Application A44). Subsequently, the solar car project was terminated. The test mule was transformed into a vehicle that could compete in the lightweight class at the Solar & Electric 500 races at Phoenix in 1992.

Photo: Richard Rahders

Fig. 4-94: Drive the testbed before you add the body.

Photo: Richard Rahders

Fig. 4-95: Michael Leeds designed and built the original Speedster.

Photo: Jesse James (R. Rahders)

Fig. 4-96: It was clear to the spectators at the Phoenix races that the Speedster was from California!

Application A44 — Speedster (One)
Michael Leeds

The Speedster is a kind of a hybrid mutation—go-cart, mini-bike, motorcycle, forklift, mountain bike, surfboard—with an aerobic spandex body.

We took it to the electric car races in Phoenix to compete in the ultralight class. Our first run on the 140 degree F. racetrack melted our high pressure, low-rolling resistance tires. The wheels collapsed under the strain, too. Fortunately, a local shop helped rebuild the front wheels overnight using heavy-duty rims, and the car was put into the race without further testing.

The race started. With each successive lap, I opened the throttle a little more. I built a five-lap lead on the field. The car was "singing."

I've built a lot of fast hot rods and I've drag-raced motorcycles but this was different! The car was practically silent. Only one moving part. There was a perceptible hum from the motor and whine from the high performance go-cart racing chain.

The rest was just the sound of the wind. It was a special moment for me.

With the pedal to the metal, the Speedster was clocked at 71 mph, a track record in the lightweight open class. I ran the car until the batteries were depleted. We went home happy.

Most recently, I have been distilling my experience into a next generation alternative, environmentally-correct, personal street machine. A safe, sexy, rubber-burning, electric road rocket. It will charge in 3-4 hours at my place, from grid power or a solar array on the roof. Or it will "do it" wherever I'm going. It will have a 60+ mile range. Easily 70-90% of my lifestyle needs — business, shopping, errands, and recreation — fit these performance parameters at a 13 cents per gallon gas equivalent.

I tend to think that solutions are not incremental improvements of existing technology that survive our "investments." Perhaps the real answer to the challenge of our times and the emerging "global tribe" are in the areas of "lifestyle pioneering." The art of energy efficiency is a critical element.

As we move through time and space, the trail of garbage we process through our bodies as lifestyles, chemicals, hydrocarbons, nuclear waste, etc. acts like an anchor, keeping us from moving ahead not only physically, but also, perhaps, spiritually.

Society is headed toward the year 2000 with the accelerator mashed to the floor. Yet, the voice in our head says, "Consider the consequences." We are too paralyzed, like in a dream, to remove our foot from the throttle; like lemmings to the sea.

The Speedster is an excellent example of the benefit of thinking light when using electric propulsion. With only 72V of battery pack, a 4.5 HP motor, and a single-ratio rear drive, the 600-lb speedster is "brisk" from a standstill and quickly reaches a 50 mph speed.

Fig. 4-97: Richard Rahders helped build the Speedster.

Photo: Michael Leeds (R. Rahders)

Speedster Two

Following its debut at Phoenix in 1992, the Speedster toured several schools in California. While the Speedster was a great demonstrator and a delight to experience, it lacked room for a passenger. To let someone experience it, then, meant letting them drive it. The Speedster's quiet elegance disguised its powerful acceleration, as many a novice discovered. Also, with its frame and suspension designed for solar racing, the Speedster was quickly becoming "thrashed" with street use and the antics of a large number of inexperienced drivers. Clearly, a major overhaul would be needed.

With these conditions in mind, I put together a project proposal to transform the Speedster for a new mission in life: safe for the street and able to carry a passenger. The result was Speedster Two (Application A45).

Beyond the Speedster

The Speedster is a proof-of-concept vehicle. It is also a good first draft of a street machine in the 800-lb (running weight)

Fig. 4-98: How was the test drive? Rose's smile says it all.

Fig. 4-99: Brett Hackleman is next in line for a spin in Speedster Two.

Fig. 4-100: The rear seatback hinges down for access to the charger, and plastic covers remove to access the batteries for maintenance.

Fig. 4-101: All controls and instruments are wrapped around the driver position.

Speedster Two

I was way down the line of people that "borrowed" the Speedster following its racing career. The vehicle was fun, but it was clearly dangerous to use on the street. While the overall ergonometry of the vehicle was intuitive, it bump-steered (took another line when it hit a bump) because the steering system was worn. The Speedster lacked reverse (gear), real suspension and stable mirrors, and had no rollbar.

I submitted a proposal to upgrade the Speedster, it was accepted, and I began work. Over the course of several months, a street-savvy machine, the Speedster Two evolved.

I had these observations and made these changes:

Rear Wheel Assembly. The moped rear wheel assembly was too small for a vehicle this fast and heavy. Frequent tire blowouts, a noticeable lean in turns, and the easy burn outs from a standstill suggested that something stronger was needed. I adapted a larger, huskier wheel/tire/rim from an Auranthetic. The wider wheel could be run at lower tire pressure, softening up the otherwise unsuspended rear end. Also, the smaller overall diameter of the wheel decreased the drive ratio, too, minimizing the tire-spinning.

Front Suspension. The parallel A-arms (front wheel support) were designed for that of a solar racer, and too small for street use. The vehicle "bump-steered." Increasing wheel castor eliminated some of this. Nevertheless, front wheel alignment constantly changed with use as the undersized components bent and flexed. (Replacement of these components was not funded.) I installed larger front spring-shocks. The old ones were almost fully compressed for drivers weighing over 150 lbs. This relieved some of the stress on the lighter suspension components.

Rear seat. A rear seat was installed, providing a means to give rides to children and adults in an educational setting. The seatback was designed to pivot forward and lay flat against the seat bottom. This gave access to the battery charger and charging extension cord. It also improved the aerodynamics when no passenger was aboard and increased the cargo-carrying ability.

Battery Pack. The original 24 C3 batteries were worn out. These were replaced with more robust 27TMH Trojan batteries and divided into two saddle packs. Mounted on (and secured to) extensions off the frame on either side, this arrangement created the rear passenger space. A plastic cover, removable for maintenance, was installed over each pack to keep curious fingers away from battery terminals.

Steering Support. The upper support for the vehicle's steering post, weakened and sloppy from the loads imposed on it, was replaced with a new one and structurally reinforced. A lock was installed on the lower steering support to keep the arm from popping out (as it did occasionally, turning a casual cruise into a steering adventure).

Control panel. A control panel was built and positioned for better driver visibility and reach. Switches like run, horn, headlights, and turnsignals, originally mounted in the steering post upper support, were re-mounted on an aluminum panel. A reversing switch was added, all switches got labels, and indicator lights were added for nighttime operation.

Emergency brake. An emergency brake, adapted from a 280ZX, was installed and connected to the rear wheel brake assembly.

Roll bar. A roll bar, fashioned from 2-inch muffler tubing, was added to the vehicle. (Ugh. Stronger tubing is called for.)

Reversing circuit. An electrical reverse "gear" was added. I took a low-budget approach, using four 12V starter contactors, to reverse the field winding relative to the armature winding. This is essentially a double-pole, double-throw operation. (Another mistake. This was more time-consuming, and less safe and reliable, than if I had just purchased and installed a reversing contactor for $175.)

Miscellaneous. The vehicle was rewired, and many components re-located. I recessed and shock-mounted the headlight assembly to avoid the frequent damage it had sustained when the vehicle front end would tap something. The turn signals and brake light were made operational. I installed motorcycle tires on the front end. The front seat was redesigned for better ingress/egress and better back support. The charger was installed onboard. The hydraulic brake cylinder was overhauled and the disc brakes adjusted.

Wiring Diagram. Once I completed the vehicle rewiring, I drew up a complete wiring diagram for the vehicle from my sketches. I also drafted a system schematic. These were designed to aid mechanics or electricians in troubleshooting and repair.

Operations manual. I also put together an Operator's Manual for the Speedster, listing location and function of all vehicle components. Besides helping the novice operator understand vehicle features, this manual is a good place to give appropriate warnings about the limits of vehicle operations.

Register, License, Insure The Speedster is street and highway legal. Because it is a three-wheeler, it falls into the general classification of a motorcycle. (It is in a new class that is bigger than a motorized bicycle.) Like any motorcycle, it is expensive to have comprehensive or collision coverage, unless a high deductible is taken. A relatively inexpensive insurance rate provides good liability coverage.

Helmet. The motorcycle classification means wearing a helmet. The roll bar and seat belt offset the need for a helmet but— the law is the law. Besides, without engine noise, it's easier to hear other traffic.

Fig. 4-102: The Speedster II is ready to deliver to its owner— Dr. Paul Lee.

Photo: Donna Worden

Fig. 4-103: Can you tell that I enjoy driving the Speedster II?

class. However, the existing vehicle design is too lightweight in its basic construction to consider further improvement without major design changes.

What's the next evolutionary step? I estimate that a stronger vehicle would cost $5K in parts and $6K in labor (150 hours at $40/hr) to construct (TechTalk T37).

Anything larger than this vehicle brings us to the crossroads of designs like the Sylph, Doran, and Vortex, all discussed in Chapter 3.

License and Register

Design and build to your heart's whim, but if you want to put your creation on the road and be legal, you must give some thought to how you can register, license, and insure the finished product.

A scratchbuilt 4-wheeled vehicle will run into a snag here. Even if you do not intend to sell it, motor vehicle regulators in many states have no way to red-flag the vehicle and prevent you from selling it to someone else. They have the authority to reject it. If they do register it, it must meet

their criteria. Your next stop could be a bureaucratic twilight zone.

When it comes to prototypes, three-wheels have something a four-wheeler does not—*identity*. Again, by definition, a motorcycle can have two or three wheels. If your creation has three wheels, then, it *must* be a motorcycle. It's the law.

The primary reason most scratchbuilt EVs have only three wheels is to aid in the process of registering, licensing, and insuring. So, find a used or damaged motorcycle *with* the license plate and, if it's there, the paperwork. Find out where the ID number is stamped onto the frame (and engine, if any).

Position the driver and passenger in a tandem-offset seating arrangement above *the battery pack, ensuring good visibility for the driver.*

Fig. 4-104: An ideal profile for a 2-person street machine.

Drawing: Bruce Severance

Check this out with the DMV (Department of Motor Vehicles). Tell them you want to restore it and want to make certain there are no warrants or other issues that would interfere with re-registering it. If the machine comes from a salvage yard, get a bill of sale, and a bill of sale.

Once your EV motorbike is roadworthy, go in and register it. A re-registered or "modified" motorcycle is usually a ho-hum, fill-out-the-form process. Motorcycles are currently exempt from smog inspections and certificates. Still, someone may want to inspect the vehicle. This is when all that work you've invested in making it look clean and strong will pay off. If the inspector is looking at a contraption or if you come in with an attitude, a stamp of approval may be in jeopardy.

Insurance

Prototypes can be difficult to insure. It's not that insurance companies are unwilling to take your money. Rather, it's a sure bet that they'll cover themselves well in the process, and that means the premium will be *high*. In the old days, you could walk away, forgoing the insurance. Nowadays, it's illegal to drive without insurance.

Fortunately, the law only insists that you carry liability insurance. That covers damage to property or people you hit.

Liability insurance for a motorcycle is a *fraction* of the liability insurance for a car. It makes sense. A compact car has many times the damaging power (it is five times the weight) of a medium-size motorcycle at a given speed. Motorcyclists are aware of their relative vulnerability in close encounters with heavy metal. Per mile driven, they are less likely to be involved in an accident.

Liability insurance, then, for a "modified motorcycle" is no big deal.

What do you want? To be legal? To be covered? To be compensated? Make your choices, write the check, sign the paperwork, and walk out.

Minimum Safety Equipment

Browsing the California Vehicle Code will show that much less equipment is required for motorized bicycles and motorcycles than cars. You've got options when it comes to things like windshields, heaters, and defrosters.

Don't skimp on safety-related items. It's easy to look at the list as all the things you can leave off, but lights, turnsignals, mirrors, and horns are important on a scratchbuilt EV. It's rough out there on the street and highway. You might be hard to see. You'll need to drive defensively. See and be seen. And heard. Stay safe.

---

*T*echtalk

T_{37} Profile of a Street Prototype

Based on my experiences with lightweight EVs, I have the following recommendations for a high-performance, long-range street machine.

• Design for a 1200-lb running weight (including 175-lb driver. Add passenger weight). Use 120V pack. For example, using the 27TMH series, the ten batteries will weigh 600 lbs. This leaves a body and frame weight of 425 lbs to stay within design limits.

• Fit an all-weather, aerodynamic shell. Sketch it in some detail. All components will need to fit inside. The canopy-roof should remove for touring. Integrate a roll-bar into the rear bulkhead support. A high-threshold door for ingress and egress on one side will give a sporty access but maintain overall, lightweight structural support.

• Position the driver and passenger in tandem-offset seating *above* the battery pack. This ensures good visibility for the driver. The high profile helps other people see this vehicle, too. This design positions the battery weight low, center, and forward for stability. This "stacked" arrangement minimizes vehicle width and length.

• Consider an exchangeable battery pack. The pack can be split into two identical, 300-lb "modules" of 60V each. These may be saddlepacks or extend, side by side, across the width of the vehicle. A community service center can be built to maintain the packs, leasing them (yearly) to owners for home charging, and exchanging the packs when extended range of the vehicles.

• A 10 HP series motor and electronic controller would make up the propulsion package. A 4:1 (fixed) gearbelt drive will power the vehicle to 60 mph, but ensure good low-end performance. Electric reverse and regen braking should be included.

• The vehicle can be arranged as a standard 4-wheeled EV or as a motorbike (3-wheels). In the 4-wheeled configuration, the FRW (front-to-rear weight) ratio is 1:1, with the rear wheels driven through a simple lawnmower (seated type) differential. In the 3-wheeled layout, the two front wheels are both steered and powered. Maintain a FRW (front-to-rear) ratio of 4:1 for good stability. With this low a vehicle weight, the rear wheel supports too little weight for good traction during acceleration or regen braking, hence the front-wheel drive.

Chapter 5
Solar-Powered Vehicles

It excites the imagination. Wheels and propellers spinning from light. A vehicle achieving speeds of 55 mph on the sun's energy alone. Driving or flying across a continent, silently and efficiently. Design so good that, with careful attention to aerodynamics and weight, one horsepower goes a long, long way. Zero emission in nature, no other system of propulsion offers such high purity of operation.

Electric propulsion is an ideal partner for solar power. Working anywhere under the sun, vehicles of all types can sail the land, water, and air on the energy of the solar wind.

Fig. 5-1: Student team leader Ricardo Espinosa finishes a test run in Cal State L.A.'s Solar Eagle.

Photo: Stan Carstensen (CSLA)

In this chapter, you will see the many ways that solar power has already been harnessed in moving cars, boats, and planes.

SOLAR CARS

The solar car has been a prime mover in bringing the electric vehicle into such prominence in the past decade. A flurry of races and rallies involving solar-powered cars has swept the planet. Initially started in the Tour de Sol in Switzerland, the sensation spread to the Australian continent and then to the USA (Application A46).

Why the interest? Solar cars are anything *but* practical. The combination of electric propulsion and solar technology is an unlikely marriage, expensive and fragile when the panel is actually mated to the vehicle. Some people believe that automakers encourage solar racing to show how expensive and impractical electric propulsion is!

What is the value of the solar car? Solar cars turn people's heads. Anyone who walks up to a solar car for the first time will find that their inner child is alive and well! Solar cars are the stuff of dreams and fantasy. Sleek, delicate machines that run on the free fuel of the sun.

Upon closer inspection, it is clear that solar cars demonstrate the practicality and simplicity of EVs in three ways. First, spectators are frequently amazed by the acceleration and speed these vehicles achieve working with only one horsepower. Second, the solar component of the car drives home the idea that solar is a power source that works anywhere under the sun. Finally, a solar car project is a fun way to design solutions that consider a scope beyond mere machinery. Coupled with lightweight, aerodynamic bodies, electric propulsion offers an elegant solution in the face of smog-ridden basins throughout the U.S. continent, declining oil reserves, and other issues that affect the quality of life.

Most of the existing solar cars were built at the college and university level. A solar car project sensitizes students to environmental issues by exposing them to technologies based

Fig. 5-2: A winner of the Tour de Sol in Switzerland.

on a non-fossil fuel. Engineering knowledge, then, may be applied to designing solutions to today's problems.

At this point, racers are the only electric vehicles that use solar energy as a primary source of propulsive power. EVs designed to operate on the road may have solar cells attached to them, but these are *solar-assisted*. This definition will become clearer as the reader delves into the world of events surrounding solar-electric cars.

How Does a Solar-Powered Car Work?

In principle, solar-electric cars are fairly simple. Sunlight striking solar-electric modules on the vehicle is converted directly into

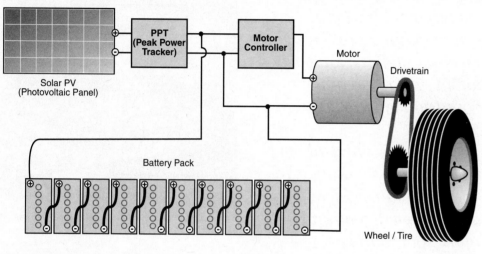

Fig. 5-3: Components of a solar car.

Fig. 5-4: James Worden sits beside the Solectria 5 he has driven to victory.

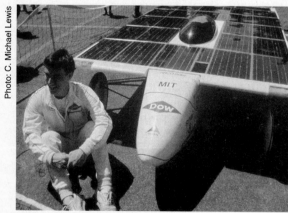

A pplication

A 46 The Solar Cars are Here!

World awareness of the potential of electric vehicles, particularly ones that can be powered from the sun, started in the mid-80s. Here's a brief summary of this history to date:

1985. Tour de Sol. Switzerland starts the popular Tour de Sol, a race event that challenges the vehicles over the course of 5 days, including a stretch over the Alps! The event is held annually and attracts entrants worldwide. The first race drew a crowd of 500 spectators, the second saw a gathering of 3,000 and the third drew a crowd estimated at 20,000. Today's races draw many tens of thousands of people.

1987. World Solar Challenge. Australia expands the solar racing circuit in a grand scale with the World Solar Challenge, challenging its entrants to a transcontinental race, north to south, of over 2000 miles across the starkness and heat of the)outback.

1988. Solar Cup USA. California hosted the Solar Cup in Visalia, launching the first solar car race in the USA.

1989. Race veteran James Worden piloted his Solectria 5 on a 22-day transcontinental (west-to-east) USA run.

electricity and routed to the electric motor (Fig. 5-3). Typically, a small set of batteries is carried onboard to help with high loads — acceleration, hill climbing and higher rates of speed. The batteries also assist with propulsion when the panel can't receive much sunlight, i.e., during the early morning and late afternoon hours, and through overcast and shaded conditions.

A strict rule in the racing format, of course, is that the energy that comes out of the battery must be replenished with electricity generated from the sun's energy. How much is captured, how well it is put to work spinning a wheel, and what the wheel is attached to are all important factors (Techtalk T38).

Analysis of the winning entries in transcontinental races reveals the essential design factors for any solar-powered car. In order of importance, the five major factors are: power input, drivetrain efficiency, aerodynamics, weight, and rolling resistance. Riding shotgun over all these factors is reliability and strategy. Vehicle breakdowns and poor execution of race strategies will adversely affect otherwise highly-competitive designs.

Several books review the entries in previous transcontinental races in great detail. For more detail on scratchbuilt vehicle design, refer to Chapter 3 (review Techtalk T10)

There is the energy of 1,000 Watts falling on an area 3 feet square (a square meter) on a clear day at high noon.

T_{38} *Techtalk* — How Much Energy is Available?

There is the energy of 1,000 Watts falling on an area 3 feet square (a square meter) on a clear day at high noon. Commercial grade solar cells yield efficiencies of 12-14%, or approximately 100 Watts of electricity per meter after losses. Solar-powered racers get a 25% overall increase in power from their panels by using more expensive solar cells. With a 17% conversion efficiency, space-quality cells produce 120 Watts of power from each square meter of sunlight.

Drivetrain efficiency — including solar panel, power conditioners, motor and controller, and transmission — is essential when the power source is so restrictive. Aerodynamics, or slicing through the wind without expending much energy to do it, is also vital. Winning solar-powered cars are lightweight. Accelerating the vehicle to some speed, particularly from a standstill, consumes much more energy than it takes to maintain a steady speed. Climbing a hill, even at a constant speed, consumes power in big gulps.

Successful solar-powered cars utilize a peak power tracker (PPT), like the Maximizer or LCB. High temperatures, varying light intensity, and changes in the panel's orientation —all affect panel output. The PPT's job is to maintain the best match between solar input and the vehicle's battery or motor "bus" voltage.

1989. Tour de Sol USA held its first USA event. It provides organizational support to similar interests all over the country each year.

1990. (July) Sunrayce. GM-sponsored Sunrayce pits vehicles from 32 colleges and universities in the USA against each other and the elements in an 11-day, 1800-mile transcontinental run through 7 states from Florida to Michigan.

1990. (Aug) SEER (Solar Energy Expo and Rally). A gathering of solar cars participate in a road rally, and alternative energy technology and products from the Western USA are displayed.

1990. (Nov) World Solar Challenge, second transcontinental Australian race. Over 40 entrants participate.

1993. Sunrayce '93. The 2nd transcontinental USA race (Texas to Michigan). The University of Michigan won.

1993. World Solar Challenge, Australia. Honda Dream wins this 3rd race across the Australian continent and beats the Sunrayce record of 1987.

1995. Sunrayce '95. The 3rd transcontinental USA race (Indiana to Colorado). MIT won.

Fig. 5-5: The reflective coating on the inside of this canopy keeps the driver cool on sunny days.

Photo: Richard King

Let's Race!

There's no better place to learn about solar cars than at the start. Of a transcontinental race, that is. Richard King is the Sunrayce Program Director at the U.S. Department of Energy. In 1988, the Sunrayce Program was responsible for soliciting proposals from colleges and universities throughout the USA, selecting thirty-two (32) of the best, and helping them get to the starting line. The prize was simple: the top three teams would be sponsored in the Australian transcontinental race, going up against entries from all over the world! The rules varied slightly from (but generally did not conflict with) those of the Australian race.

What's it like to build a solar car? Michael Seal of Western Washington University briefly describes the process (Application A47) of undertaking a project of this magnitude, and various aspects of the WWU design .

Fig. 5-6: Viking XX at Western Washington University.

Fig. 5-7: It's not often that a solar car has to worry about jaywalking camels.

All photos:
Vehicle Research Institute
(Western Washington University)

Fig. 5-8: Solar cars are a big hit with crowds that gather along the transcontinental route.

"All ideas, no matter how outlandish, were recorded without comment during the first brainstorming session."
Dr. Michael Seal

Fig. 5-9: Viking XX is a familiar sight near the Vehicle Research Institute.

Viking XX Design

A 47

Michael Seal, Ph.D.

In 1988, the VRI began the design of a solar-powered race car capable of winning the GM Sunrayce and being a viable competitor in the World Solar Challenge in Australia, both scheduled for 1990.

How do you begin a project of this magnitude? You break it up into small, manageable pieces. A major fundraising campaign was initiated.

A simple solar-powered car was built quickly to gain experience and credibility with potential sponsors. A previously-built Viking super-mileage marathon car formed the basis for the new car. An electric motor from an automobile cooling system fan drove a rear wheel with a direct friction drive to the tire. A simple flat solar panel 4' by 12' was mounted above the aerodynamic body shell to provide power. No battery was fitted to the system. The vehicle would achieve 15 MPH on the level in bright sunlight. A video of this car and previously successful Viking cars helped with the fundraising effort.

A reliable machine would be of the utmost importance. So, we resolved to only build components that we understood thoroughly, and to buy anything that was beyond our capability. Testing was a must.

Milestones were set (these dates must be perceived as real), and the first trial of the complete car was tied to an irrevocable media event. The time line will slip, but new ones were substituted and posted. Otherwise, despondency would set in and progress stop.

The prime design consideration was solar power. Many designs assume ideal solar conditions and prove inferior at 0.7 (7/10ths) sun. The second most important consideration was aerodynamic drag, for speeds above 30 MPH. Low vehicle weight was the third most important.

Many competitors seem to have their priorities mixed up and build extremely fine vehicles for some other power source than photovoltaic. Although it is very important for most vehicles to have good road-holding characteristics, a solar racing car can assign a relatively low priority to them.

A brainstorming session was held on overall vehicle design. All ideas, no matter how outlandish, were recorded without comment during the first brainstorming session. In the second session, we analyzed the different designs to see which one had the most positive features and the fewest negative ones.

We chose the configuration which eventually evolved into the Viking XX design — a two-person vehicle, drivable in either direction, with fore and aft symmetry instead of side to side. It certainly satisfied the first criteria: it would be difficult to imagine any way of providing a greater solar strike area within the 2 meter wide by 6 meter high design limits!

There were obvious difficulties. As the car must drive in either direction, the controls must be duplicated, although the removable steering wheel can easily be transferred to the other end. The 50% increase in solar strike area which was allowed in the rules for a two-person vehicle must be paid for by the additional weight of a passenger and the attendant structure to hold the passenger. The frontal area due to the passenger would not increase at all, however, in the Viking XX design. The aerodynamic compromise due to the requirement that the vehicle travel in both directions was investigated. Preliminary analysis suggested that weight increase would be less than 50% over previous best single-seaters.

We built a 1/10 scale model of the GM Sunraycer and a 1/10 scale model of Viking XX to test in our wind tunnel. The Sunraycer has a superior Cd, but its frontal area was substantially greater than Viking XX. The overall drag aero of Viking XX was only 8% higher than the Sunraycer. Further analysis showed that if Viking XX were equipped with 13.25% efficient terrestrial grade solar cells, the performance would be slightly better above 30 MPH and somewhat worse below 30 MPH than the Sunraycer. As we had no hope of obtaining satellite grade solar cells at this time, we determined to build our car to this design — using lower-grade solar cells — as it was the only design that looked to be competitive with Sunraycer.

A silver-zinc battery in the maximum allowable Watt-hour size (5kW hours) was chosen, as it appeared likely that in good sunshine the full capacity could be regained during allowable evening and morning charging time. This power could then be expended during the day climbing hills, outrunning bad weather, or simply driving faster than input sun would allow. The relatively modest weight (118 lbs) made this a viable option, particularly as ballast was needed on that side of the car to avoid overturning. Light drivers and passengers were recruited as their ballast weight could be carried behind the front wheel where it was most needed to provide side wind stability.

In the interest of providing maximum reliability, we managed to drive the car 850 test miles before the Sunrayce USA. During testing, a number of components failed. We were able to design more reliable components or find supplies of better units which improved reliability of the whole system. We determined that we would make or buy a spare part for every component in the car except the main monocoque structure. These parts were stored in a truck that followed, complete with the tools necessary for replacing each part.

We spent quite a bit of time practicing part replacement until we felt confident that we could carry out any repair in minimum time. A number of design changes were incorporated to facilitate rapid repair. As we live in a wet part of the world, it seemed necessary to weatherproof everything. This turned out to be a substantial advantage over other teams as it always seems to rain during a solar car race.

We were second overall to the University of Michigan "Sunrunner" in the GM Sunrayce. For this, we received GM sponsorship for the World Solar Challenge. We placed fifth in the transcontinental run across Australia.

Fig. 5-11: The Solar Eagle's panel was divided into three segments.

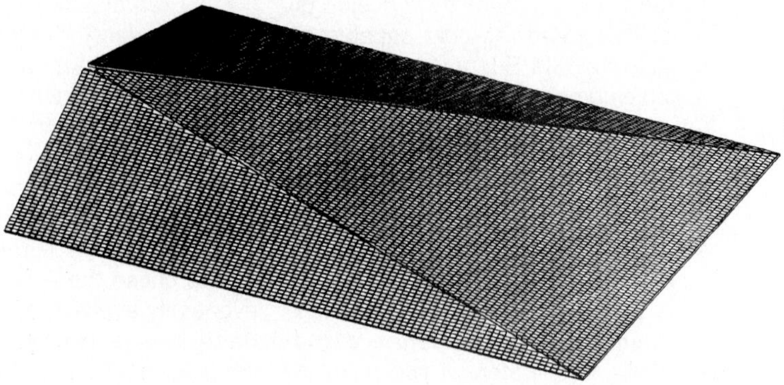

Designing Your Own Panel

How about designing your own solar panel?

Here is a very brief description—in photos and CAD renderings—of the process of design and construction of a solar array for a solar car.

This comes from a personal experience as part of the design team for the Solar Eagle (1988-1990), the entry designed at CSLA (California State University, Los Angeles) for the GM-sponsored Sunrayce USA. In the first transcontinental race of solar-powered vehicles in the USA (1990), the Solar Eagle placed 4th out of 32 entries. Four months later, the Solar Eagle placed 10th (out of 42 entries) in the 2nd World Solar Challenge, a similar race across the continent of Australia. Both races involved distances greater than 1,700 miles in length.

While the size, type, shape and scope of a solar array *you* build for a stationary or mobile application will vary considerably, easily 85% of the process used to build the Solar Eagle's solar array would have direct application.

2

1

8

Photo: Bill Stellmacher (CSLA)

Fig. 5-10: After windtunnel tests reduce the design possibilities to one, a rule-compliant design is drawn.

Fig. 5-17: Before and after each race day, the solar panel is removed and oriented for maximum solar gain.

Fig. 5-12: Armando Garcia and Richard Benevides solder cells into strings.

Photo: Stan Carstensen (CSLA)

3

Fig. 5-13: Richard solders the cell strings into modules over a CAD-generated template.

Photo: Stan Carstensen (CSLA)

4

Fig. 5-14: Richard and I wire the modules together into strings on the substrate.

Design and construction cycle of a solar array for a transcontinental solar-powered race vehicle.

5

Photo: Stan Carstensen (CSLA)

Fig. 5-15: The panel undergoes testing in direct sun.

6

Photo: Bill Stellmacher (CSLA)

7

Fig 5-16: CSLA's Solar Eagle was the result of a lot of work by many people. Dean Ray Landis (tie) spearheaded the project.

Photo: Stan Carstensen (CSLA)

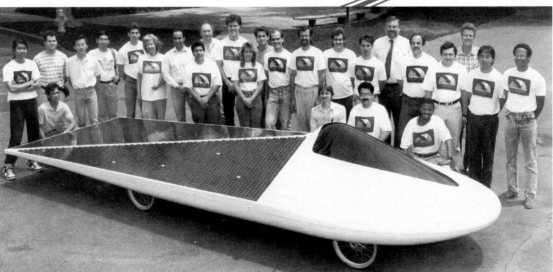

*A*48 SunCoaster
Tom Bennett

What has three wheels, can carry 220 pounds of driver and baggage, has a top speed of 19 mph, and gets the electric energy equivalent of 2,667 miles per gallon of gasoline? SunCoaster.

In 1990, some of my students and I visited the Siemens solar cell production plant in Vancouver, Washington. We saw processes for making solar cells and met the people involved. (I arrange field trips to add flavor to the General Physics labs I conduct at Lewis and Clark College.) The visit generated a lot of discussion about solar energy on the trip back in the van. Wouldn't it be great to build a solar car? That was the start of the SunCoaster project.

Two of my students and I submitted a solar car proposal that was funded by the Student Academic Affairs Board of Lewis and Clark for $2,250, to be built in the summer of 1991. One of these students graduated and left the project, so Eileen Niedermann and I proceeded. We visited Western Washington University and were inspired by the projects involving Michael and Eileen Seal.

While we were gathering information for our design, we modified a go-cart frame as a test platform for our growing collection of possible electrical parts. It was unsafe at any speed but a necessary learning experience for our solar vehicle.

Eileen and I attended SEER '91. We thoroughly enjoyed our Willits visit and came back loaded with

Oregon) did all the custom welding in his go-kart racing shop. We fitted components to the welded frame, including two solar panels we had purchased. We sent a photo of the vehicle to Siemens and they generously donated the remaining two panels we needed for the SunCoaster's power source.

Eileen began her senior thesis work on a hybrid solar cell-thermoelectric device, and I proceeded with the solar vehicle and the design and testing of a dependable speed controller. My 17th version worked great and has continued to work without problems for the past two years! SunCoaster runs very smoothly on good surfaces. It is stable, partially because of its low center of gravity. There's no flex in the suspension, so bumpy surfaces are unpleasant to some drivers. We had the vehicle running before SEER '92.

SEER '92 was fun, the vehicle ran well, and we enjoyed having it on display. With our lightweight driver, Toni Van DeKop, we successfully drove the rally course, taking first place in the Innovative "A" Solar-Electric category.

In 1993, our physics department hired a new machinist, Steve Attinasi. Along with student Marc Saxowsky and myself, the three of us spent some effort in refining the vehicle and improving the safety features. SunCoaster has been in several alternative energy fairs and auto exhibits, including the Portland Roadster show.

Benefits from the project include valuable experience in machine work for a student, the construction of a well-engineered solar vehicle (that focuses interest and much discussion concerning solar energy), and school interaction with many local businesses.

What would we do differently? Use a three-speed hub for more durability, increase the capacity of the solar panels, and add disc or drum brakes.

Tom Bennett works in Lake Oswego, Oregon. Eileen Niedermann graduated and is in the Peace Corps in Tanzania.

Fig. 5-18: Tom Bennett initiated the Suncoaster project.

Photo: Tom Bennett

*T*39 SunCoaster Specifications
Tom Bennett

Turning Radius: 6 feet.
Speed: Top: 19 mph. Cruise: 10 mph, 150 Watts consumption, or 15 Watt-hours/mile. Gasoline equivalent: 2,667 miles/gallon.
Range: batteries only, 11 mph to 70% DOD (depth of discharge), 17 miles.
Range: summer (calc), 120 miles.
Weight: 220 pounds
Dimensions: Length (7.5 feet), Width (4 feet), Height (4.5 feet), max load: 220 pounds.

notes, photos, product information, and contacts. An after-dinner sketch on a napkin looks remarkably similar to our final design! When we got back, we transferred this design to chalk on the floor, and then to the table trace. We kept the width and length of the vehicle to something that would fit inside a pickup truck, for transport purposes. We bought our aluminum frame material and machined it to fit the worktable trace. An early contact, Don Holmboe of CMC (Tigard,

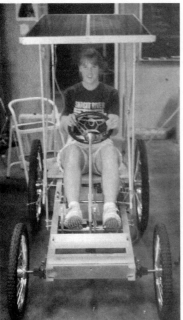

Fig. 5-19: Eileen Niedermann helped design and build the SunCoaster.

Photo: Tom Bennett

SunCoaster

The Suncoaster is a street version of principles learned with solar racing vehicles (Application A48). SunCoaster's components (Techtalk T39) and specifications (Techtalk T40) let the vehicle use energy at a rate better than an equivalent 2,000 miles per gallon of gasoline. Want to compute the equivalency of your own vehicle? (See Techtalk T41)

Getting Started in Solar Energy

It helps to start young when it comes to solar energy. The ways that solar energy can assist us now and in the future are varied and exciting. A good start is putting one little piece of the sun to work. After that, like the sun, it is self-sustaining!

Fig. 5-20: Students find racing a solar car challenging and exciting.

Photo:C. Michael Lewis

T_{40} echtalk —— SunCoaster Components
Tom Bennett

Guiding Philosophy: simplicity, low weight, low cost, unified design.

Motor: Pacific Scientific, 1 HP, 90 V.
Controller: Homebuilt PWM (pulse-width-modulated), 555 Timer, 9 power Darlington transistors.
Operator Control: Hand-operated, spring-return potentiometer throttle.
Battery Pack: Powersonic, 12 A-h lead-acid gel cells, five propulsion (60 VDC), one for Aux (12 VDC).
Photovoltaic Modules: Four Siemens M75 (50 W) solar panels, series-wired, 72 V output, 3 Amp output.
Drivetrain: Motor hub, nine-tooth sprocket, to a 53 tooth chain ring on a five-speed Sturmey Archer wheel hub, free-wheeling hub.
Tires: ACS tread tires, 100 psi, 20 inch by 1.75
Brakes: BMX bicycle brakes, all wheels. Two operator levers, one for front and one for rear brakes.
Frame: 1 x 1.5 inch aluminum 6063 rectangular tubing. Seat frame, uprights and bracing: 1 x 1 inch.
Panel Mount: Tiltable, 25-degree total arc, ratchet pull-down working against two auto pneumatic tailgate lifters.
Instruments: Simpson Wattmeter for solar panels (0–300 Watt), wattmeter for motor (0–1500 Watt), motor voltmeter (0–100 Volt), bicycle speedometer.
Safety Features: Roll bar, three-point harness, lap belt, padded tiller, turn signals, hazard flashers and brake lights, horn, electrical disconnect switch, keyed speed controller, two independent brake controls.

T_{41} echtalk —— Gasoline/Electric Equivalency
Tom Bennett

Here's a handy formula for converting mpg (miles per gallon of gasoline) to W-h (Watt-hours) per mile:

$$\text{(\#)} \frac{\text{Watt-hours}}{\text{mile}} = \frac{4.0 \times 10^4 \text{ Watt-hour/gallon}}{\text{(x) miles/gallon}}$$

Plug x number of miles per gallon to get the number of Watt-hours. For example, an EV with a performance value of 50 Watt-hours per mile, such as the Horlacher electric, gets the equivalent of 800 miles per gallon.

Fig. 5-21: Glenn Hackleman originated the design of a solar-powered linerunner.

Water & Air

The ultimate test of a propulsion technology is its ability to perform in the two environments where reliability is the dominant design factor: the ocean and the air. When the weather is wet and stormy, land vehicles are rarely impeded in their functions. The same conditions make travel by water or by air a more difficult venture, perhaps downright risky. The water and the sky are not hostile to the intruding electric ships, just horribly unforgiving of mistakes.

Here are a number of projects and adventures involving electric propulsion in the two environments of water and sky.

Fig. 5-22: Burton Gabriel sets a new world record for electric displacement boats.

Photo: Jerry Gay

Fig. 5-23: Winning is always a good feeling.

Photo: Jerry Gay

Fig. 5-24: The SEVA team sweats out the last minutes of the race.

Fig. 5-25: Many boat styles participate in the electric races.

Photo: Jerry Gay

Photo: Jerry Gay

Application A 49

Electric & Solar Boat Races
Andrew Muntz

There were no roostertails and certainly no ear-splitting roars, but competitors in the newest form of boat racing still managed to put on a show that proved every bit as exciting as race boats that go many times faster and consume much more energy. Here are the highlights of the 2nd annual Electric Boat Regatta held in late July and early August 1993 near Everett, Washington.

New Speed Record. Burton Gabriel of Port Ludlow, Washington, established a new speed record when he made two runs through a one-kilometer speed course at an average speed of 41.187 miles per hour, nearly doubling his own record established last October. The course was set on Spada Lake, a pristine alpine lake located in the foothills of the Cascade Mountains east of Everett.

Endurance Boat Racing. A field of fifteen battery-powered boats competed in the six-hour Delco Voyager Battery Marathon race on Silver Lake near Everett. Most entrants came from the Pacific Northwest with a few from as far away as Milwaukee, Wisconsin.

David Mischke of Edmonds, Washington won the event for the second year in a row. He held a narrow advantage over a boat campaigned by a group of electric vehicle enthusiasts from Port Townsend, Washington that call themselves the NOPEC (North Olympic Peninsula Electric Craft) Racing Team, in a not-so-subtle reference to the oil cartel.

One of the intriguing aspects of competition between battery-powered boats is the strategy that results because the boats can

Electric Watercraft

In the water, we find solar boat races, the Esther restoration, and the SolExplorer.

Solar and Electric Boat Races

In its second year, the Electric Boat Regatta was presented by Snohomish County Public Utility District, an electric utility serving the area immediately north of Seattle, Washington. Held in late July and early August 1993 near Everett, Washington, the three-day event featured competition for battery-powered and solar-powered boats. Out of it came a new world speed record, a down-to-the-wire marathon race and a near doubling of performance by the competitors from the previous year. Andrew Muntz, a customer relations manager for the utility *and* the race director, wrote up a comprehensive tour of the Regatta (Applications A49).

Fig. 5-26: A bridge is a good place to watch a solar boat race.

Photo: Michael Bittman

only use a limited amount of energy. For example, the boats in the battery marathon race use only the energy that can be stored in no more than 125 pounds of batteries. During the event, therefore, competitors pay close attention to how much energy remains in their batteries, carefully calculating the best rate of consumption in an effort to use all the energy available to them, but not so much that their boat can't finish.

The boats showed a tremendous improvement in performance this year. In 1992, Mischke's winning SEVA averaged 5-1/2 mph. This year, Mischke's boat covered 56 miles during the six-hour race, an average speed of over 9 mph! Had the propeller not broken (consuming 20 minutes repair time), the average would have exceeded 10 mph easily.

Compared to other forms of racing, the boats consumed virtually no energy. The winning boats were able to race all day using an amount of energy equivalent to a *cup* of gasoline.

Fig. 5-27: Craig McCann piloted the Photocomm Skimmer to victory in the 4-hour marathon. Nice design!

Photo: Jerry Gay

Solar Boat Racing. The next day, only the sun's energy was consumed during competition between boats. Qualified boats for this six-hour race are restricted to solar panels of terrestrial-grade cells not exceeding an area of 40 square feet.

The winner was Michael Bittman of Port Townsend, another member of the NOPEC Racing Team. Bittman's NOPEC II led the race wire-to-wire, covering an impressive 40 miles before time ran out. Averaging almost 7 mph, the NOPEC II handily improved on the 5 mph average set by the 1992 winner.

The day's only incident occurred about four hours into the race when the Marquette University boat caught a gust of wind and capsized. The boat, named Sun Warrior II, was taken back to shore, repaired by the engineering students, and reentered in the race, completing four more laps before time expired. It finished second.

The winning boats were able to race all day using an amount of energy equivalent to a cup of gasoline.

Fig. 5-28: Solar panels in some boats were designed for tracking the sun independent of orientation.

Photo: Michael Bittman

Fig. 5-29: Solar panels work well in a water environment.

Photo: Michael Bittman

Photo: Otmar Ebenhoech

Fig. 5-30: Otmar Ebenhoech pauses lakeside by a boat he helped design and build.

What's it like to race in a boat powered by electricity from the sun? Michael Bittman of UROWN Power Company piloted NOPEC II craft in both the battery marathon and the solar-only race (Application A50). In the first event, he took sixth place after traveling 46 miles in six hours, with 1st place honors in the practical, non-racing hull category. The next day, Bittman piloted the NOPEC to a first place victory in the solar race.

Electric Launches

How do electric boats stand the test of time? The front page of the Nov. 1893 issue of

Photo: Michael Bittman

Fig. 5-31: Michael Bittman guides NOPEC II back to shore after winning the six-hour race.

Fig. 5-32: The smile says it all!

Photo: Michael Bittman

Application A50

A Sunlight Cruise

Michael Bittman

The NOPEC II is a converted rowing boat, build by co-pilot Gerald Douglas of Catspaw Kayaks. A 1/4 HP motor turns a ten-inch prop via a chain. I helped design the solar rack with Burton Gabriel of Gabriel Marine, holder of the Electric Boat Displacement world record, and Burton built it.

The propulsion system was designed and constructed by Tim Nolan of Tim Nolan Marine Designs. The solar panels, twelve Solarex 36-Watt panels, were donated by Creative Alternative Utilization of Sustainable Energy (CAUSE), a non-profit organization. A Cruising Equipment digital amp meter is used to monitor current flow between the panels and motor. The array is adjustable fore and aft, and port and starboard. The pilot adjusts for maximum amps.

In the race, NOPEC II traveled 40 miles in six hours around the one-mile-plus course, averaging 6.64 mph, with some laps over 7 mph. Our lead was never threatened.

Photo: Michael Bittman

Fig. 5-33: Co-pilot/boat builder Gerald Douglas helps with NOPEC II.

Scientific American magazine was devoted to the new electric-powered *ELCO* craft:

"No electrical feature at the World's Columbian Exposition was entered upon with more uncertainty than the introduction of electric launches on the lagoons. Up to this time, such launches had not been made use of in this country except in an experimental way. In spite of these uncertainties, however, the launches were among the first electrical features that were ready. And they have fulfilled their requirements during the entire period that the Exposition has been open. With gratifying results. They have carried over one million passengers. They have earned $314,000.

The launches were in constant use from 12-14 hours per day on a single charge. The greatest test was on Chicago day when the fifty (50) electric boats made a total of 623 trips, each 3 miles in duration. Six of these boats averaged fifty miles each — another twenty of them averaged over forty miles — carrying 40 people per trip.

... the batteries are of 150 ampere hours' capacity. Each boat has 66 cells. These are arranged in three groups of 22 cells, or two groups of 33 cells each for propulsion. One lever alongside the steering wheel selects four speeds forward and two backward."

No, that isn't a "typo" on the date. This project happened more than 100 years ago!

Restoring an ELCO Boat

The success of the ELCO (Electric Launch Company) boats at the Exposition in 1893 encouraged the Navy to use them as gigs for its major warships. In 1988, Bruce Herron, Richard Orawiec, and LeRoy Wolins found one of the few surviving ELCO boats from that period, the *Esther*, abandoned in a boat yard. Despite the fact that it was fitted with a Chrysler engine and had superstructure changes, *Esther* was quickly identified as an old ELCO boat. The long, rich history of its origin and service began to unravel. Joe Fleming, a marine engineer with experience on the ELCO craft, provided some insight into what kind of system would work for *Esther* today (TechTalk T42)

The Good Ship Esther Foundation was formed, and the restoration of hull and electric powerplant was begun (Application A51).

Richard gave me a copy of *Launches and Yachts* by William Swanson. For the most part,

Fig. 5-34: An Electric Launch Company (ELCO) boat at the turn of the century.

Techtalk

T42

The ELCO Boats
Joe Fleming

Cruise speed on the ELCO boats is 5 to 5.5 knots. Restored, I'd recommend a 15/11 prop (15 inches diameter, 11 pitch). It will want to turn at 1,000 rpm.

The system will use 20 Amps for each horsepower the propeller will want. Horsepower is determined by multiplying Volts x Amps x system efficiency. Figure 80% efficiency. Divide the product by (the conversion factor of) 750 Watts, which equals one horsepower. Thus, 48 Volts x 20 Amps x 80% efficiency — divided by 750 Watts equals 1.024 horsepower.

(I recommend during trials that you) put a voltmeter and ammeter on the batteries. Steady your speed at 40 amps draw. That should be 2 horsepower. (Note the speed.)

Twelve 8D-type batteries (12V, 220Ah), wired in three strings of four batteries will give you 48 volts at 660Ah. At a 40-Amp rate, *Esther* should go 660/40, or 16.5 hours. Converting knots to speed, that's 5.7 mph for 16.5 hours, or a 94-mile range."

(Editor's note: 94 miles represents a 100% discharge. A better service life will result from only 50% DOD, or depth of discharge. This still gives a 47 mile range — with a safe 100% reserve. Also, 8D batteries are too heavy and not a deep-cycle type. Choose another battery, like the 27TMH.)

Fig. 5-35: The *Esther* is re-worked with solar-powered tools.

$A_{51}^{pplication}$ Good Ship *Esther*

Richard Orawiec

Our Foundation is named for the *Esther*, delivered to the Navy by the Electric Launch Co. (ELCO) at the Brooklyn Navy yard in 1896.

The electric power plant was pulled from *Esther* in 1909. Thereafter, *Esther* received a long series of INFernal combustion engines, serving as a ferry and a tugboat for a fifty-year service. During the 1970s, she was on display at a maritime museum in South Haven, and later, abandoned.

Rescue came in 1988 at the hand of Bruce Herron of Blue Star Woodwork. Herron was looking for an old boat to restore. When Leroy and I realized *Esther*'s history, we knew it was time to turn back the clock to restore the electric propulsion—and power it with non-polluting sunlight. We joined the project.

Esther was stripped and we replaced her keel. We used batteries and an inverter to power our tools during this period.

Esther has a displacement hull, designed for entry and exit from the water. Imagine flipping the hull over, upside down, and sitting it on axles. You'd be looking at an electric car with good aerodynamics. The master shipbuilder had his own version of a personal computer to help as he sighted down his thumb from 20 paces at *Esther*. It was quite a lesson to learn what our forefathers knew — how to shape a renewable resource, trees, into a hull that moved quickly and easily through the water.

*Esther*s original powerplant was probably 6 HP. The 1902 launches had a "radius of action" of up to 80 miles with maximum (long-range option) batteries. *Esther*s new power plant will be essentially the same as the one used in 1896. A pulse modulation controller will be substituted for the mechanical control relays. The original launch had the motor midship. Ours will be positioned over the shaft with a sprocket and chain reduction. We have a 5 HP Baldor electric motor, rated 48V and 2200 rpm. It's Amp-hour curve suggests that, at 1250 rpm, it will drive *Esther* through the water at 5 knots at a discharge rate of 40 Amps.

Five "strings" of four PV modules (48 Volts at 50 Watts) will fit easily on the launch roof. This photovoltaic canopy will generate 250 Watts of peak power toward the propulsion effort. A tracking array would work best dockside, trimmed underway to maintain a low profile.

The only way for us to know for sure what prop will work best is to complete *Esther* do shakedown cruises, and fine-tune the system. Prop diameter and pitch, motor rpm, load, cruising speed — all will be balanced to an optimal solution.

Fig. 5-36: The engine comes out.

Fig. 5-37: An electric motor is installed in *Esther*.

$T_{43}^{echtalk}$ Electric Boat Design

What about system voltage, battery capacity, motor speed control, and solar-charging in electric boats like *Esther*?

Low Voltage. High voltage and saltwater don't mix. The "below 50 Volts" rule for marine electricity (mentioned by Swanson, Techtalk T44) recognizes that low voltage reduces the shock hazard. It's all the better that it avoids a lot of bureaucracy, too.

Battery Capacity. From data in the original ELCO manuals and the Scientific American article, it's clear that a launch the size of Esther, at 48 Volts, would want a battery capacity of 300-450 Ah.

I recommend the use of 6V batteries instead of 12V batteries for a pack the size of *Esther*'s. It is true that 12V batteries are the fastest, most space-conserving means of reaching high voltages. However, voltage is not an issue here. Capacity is. A 12V battery has proportionately higher internal resistance, delivering fewer watts per pound of battery, than a 6V one. Typically, then, a 12V battery sacrifices energy density for power density. In high rpm motor applications with limited space (like cars), this is justified. *Esther*'s system has different requirements. A big prop wants low rpm. Low rpm and low voltage are a good match, direct-drive or geared.

Let's assume *Esther* is now outfitted with a 48-Volt system. Using marine deep-cycle batteries, we can get 48 Volts with eight standard 6-Volt batteries, each 220 Ah in capacity. At 60 pounds each, eight batteries will weigh 480 pounds.

This is the *minimum* size of pack. *Esther* originally had much more capacity than this. If we double the pack size (described above) to 16 batteries and put the two (48V) packs in parallel with each other, this larger pack's capacity will increase to 440Ah. Better yet, the paralleled batteries *share* the motor current. The lower discharge rate per battery will increase battery efficiency and service life.

Motor Control. Swanson's claim for the efficiency of the electronic controller is generally accepted knowledge. It gives infinite speed selection and corrects any mismatch (in voltages) between batteries and motor.

Solar Charging. It is true that a PV canopy on *Esther* will generate power at a fraction of the amount consumed, even at cruise speeds. And that power will come expensively. Twenty modules represents a minimum $6K investment. The good news is that only two days of sun will power *Esther* more than an hour at cruise speed.

As Richard Orawiec has commented, "The plug for this thing is there," pointing toward the sky.

this is a reprint of the original 1902 catalog for ELCO (the Electric Launch Company). I found myself engaged with Swanson in a technical discussion of refitting the *Esther* with today's electric powerplant technology. I addressed various design issues—low-voltage, battery capacity and type, motor control, and solar charging—from a propulsion viewpoint (Techtalk T43). William Swanson added his own design notes from a marine viewpoint(Techtalk T44). Combined with the "rules of thumb" derived from Joe Fleming, these notes suggest a design approach that should help electrify any type of watercraft.

Fig. 5-38: New life is breathed into an electric launch.

Fig. 5-39: Bruce Herron and Richard Orawiec attach a solar panel to *Esther*'s bilge pump.

Photo:Richard Orawiec

Photo:Richard Orawiec

Techtalk
T44 *Esther* Drivetrain Design
William Swanson

In a displacement boat like *Esther*, you want the largest possible propeller that will fit in the aperture (cutout). So, measure the maximum possible clearance, and subtract about 2 inches for the maximum diameter of the prop. Consult a naval architecture manual. Cross reference prop diameter and engine rpm on the nomograph for finding the prop pitch to order from a prop manufacturer. For example, a 15/11 prop is 15 inches in diameter and has a pitch of 11 inches, and rpm will be in the hundreds, maybe a thousand. For a big prop, the lower the rpm, the better. Low rpm means less "slip" (loss of efficiency), less cavitation (air bubbles), and generally less wear-and-tear.

A three-blade prop is the safe, sane choice. A two-blade would be too little in surface area, and a four-blade is good if you've got the dollars. It doesn't have to be anything fancy or "high tech." Get quotes from Michigan Wheel, Federal, and other prop manufacturers for making the prop.

The prop must be bronze. *Esther* would have too many electrolysis problems with an aluminum prop. Consult a thrust bearing manufacturer for size and installation.

Displacement Hulls, Power-plants, Controls. I'd say an electric motor in the 5-7 horsepower range is about right. Unlike cars, displacement boats have a very low "maximum" speed, so that even if you put, say, a 100 HP motor in *Esther*, you're still only going to get the same performance as a 10 HP motor. It's a different story for planing powerboat hulls. Expect to pay as high as $100 per horsepower over the counter.

All powerplant calculations should be at 75-80% of maximum speed. Use this formula: 1.2 x square root of waterline length (in feet) = maximum speed of *Esther*. Now, multiply this number by .8 (80%) to get your "cruising" speed. "Cruise" is the speed you'll use in *any* calculations involving motor rpm, battery capacity, etc. Finally, *Esther* should use a "chopper" (motor control) system. It'll deliver 20-50% more operating time.

I believe there is a U.S. Coast Guard boatbuilding regulation somewhere that divides systems above 50 Volts and those below. If I were you, I'd do whatever was necessary to keep *Esther*'s system at a maximum of 48 Volts. Above 50 Volts, you have a ton of specification requirements. Below 50, you're golden.

A whole mess of batteries can be wired in either series or parallel. You can come up with any voltage (and capacity) you want. There's no real advantage to 6-Volt batteries when your operational choices are in 12-Volt increments: 12, 24, 36, or 48.

Batteries in Boats. There are 5 issues for batteries in a marine environment: type, cost, weight, maintenance, and replacement.

NiCd, sodium-sulphur, lithium, and similar batteries—it's all hooey. Someday, maybe, one or more, but not right now. There's only one option here: the bread-and-butter, garden variety, lead-acid deep-cycle battery.

In the "real world", you're interested in dollars per Amp-hour ($ per Ah). Pick the cheapest, but reasonably reliable name-brand of battery. Also, if a single human being can't reasonably lift the damn battery in and out of its slot in the boat, the battery is too big. If this means you have to design in forty small (group 24 or 27) batteries instead of six monster batteries, do it.

Batteries will need maintenance. Sealed batteries aren't required. If the boat is going to be upside down (or even 90 degrees over) for any period of time (say, oh, three seconds), you've got much bigger troubles than electrolyte slopping around. What you've got basically is irreversible sinking!

Finally, the batteries need to be easily replaced. If your battery isn't sold at Sears, K-Mart, or your local car battery store, it's not worth whatever other advantages it may have.

Solar Charging. Electric boats use energy at the rate of 50 to 100 Amps per hour. A solar charging system that supplies a small fraction of this is just an expensive toy. A month of sunlight for an hour's running time is not currently practical.

A Solar-Electric Catamaran

The first *good* example I saw of a watercraft outfitted with electric propulsion was the SolExplorer, built by Pete and Mike Stevenson. This prototype is 6th-generation, if you count the larger catamaran to which they affixed a few thrusters in a quick experiment to test a fledgling idea. Willing to start over as many times as it took, the Stevenson's integrated the good in each new attempt. Like any good proof-of-concept vehicle, the SolExplorer is a winning design (Application A52).

Fig. 5-40: The SolExplorer quietly checks out a waterway.

Fig. 5-41: With two motors, SolExplorer is snappy and maneuverable.

Fig. 5-42: Directional thrusters make for tight turns at speed.

Fig. 5-43: The solar panels constantly recharge the batteries, even when the vehicle is being trailered.

Fig. 5-44: An early design of SolExplorer.

All photos: Stevenson Projects

Fig. 5-45: Larger "cats" have room for solar panels.

150   *The New Electric Vehicles*

SolExplorer Saga

Pete Stephenson

We first got interested in using quiet electric power for boats about ten years ago. Up until then, we had been building project prototypes for magazines like Popular Science, Popular Mechanics, Home Mechanix, *Better Homes and Gardens*, Family Circle, and others — mostly out of lumberyard-available materials.

Design One. Our first step was to borrow a Hobie 14 and clamp on our motors. With the batteries taped precariously in place and no place to sit, we controlled the motors separately. It was quite the Chinese fire drill, but we managed about 4 mph (brisk walking speed) and we had fun.

Design Two. Our next effort was a plywood tender. At this point, we were convinced that "scale effect" would favor the tiny twin. Three canoe-kayaks were linked together with solar panels screwed to the crossbars. Deep-cycle RV batteries on either side powered the T-3 motors. We spent many fun days cruising the jungle river on Kauai (one of the Hawaiian islands), exploring new-to-us areas opened up by the little boat.

This boat seemed to bring out a better side of humanity at beaches and launch ramps. Maybe it was the solar panels. Everybody seemed to be "on its side." People were clearly hopeful of a new alternative to the smells, frustrations, and costs of gasoline-fueled outboard power.

Design Three. Thinking "product," we decided to try another, more optimized design. We ordered larger thrusters and some urethane foam. We shaped a really efficient, elliptical-bottomed, ultra-high aspect ratio hull with plumb bows for max waterline per boat length, ensuring minimum draft. Everything was faired, and flexible gills smoothed in the rudder boxes.

Now we had speed—a strong 5 mph. Suddenly the rivers were shorter and we found ourselves throttling back in the narrow, winding parts. Fitted with an underwater viewer, the boat opened up the reefs and marine life to our regular cameras. With precise control to pick our way around stream rocks, or hold station over a reef even in a good current, it was a fun boat.

Shipped back to the mainland to make molds, the new boat suddenly seemed huge. It proved bulky and balky for squirting around the confines of docks and heavily-populated channels. The wide open spaces of the reefs and the lack of traffic on the rivers had lulled us into a goof.

Design Four. We scaled down our next design. With a boat this small, especially a catamaran, every inch and pound can make a difference. The process is more like "board-shaping" than boat-building. It's a challenge to eke practical performance out of voluntarily small motors. We wanted a whole, interconnected organism rather than a linear drivetrain.

A glassed wood prototype was built pretty close to what we wanted to end up with. It proved quick to maneuver, planed well for surfing wakes and beach use, and worked the shore well with its reduced draught. It had plenty of bow rake for rougher waters, which was also helpful for shedding water plants and kelp. This prototype taught us a lot about steering and throttle integration. Steering moved from a handlebar design, to a steering wheel, and finally to push-pull sliders.

Design Five. We liked the layout of the Design #4 prototype enough to grind out a plug to get the female mold for an all-glass version. The new boat looked liked the prototype, but structural components were reworked for best use of the new material.

Named *SolExplorer*, this design performed better in every way than any of the previous boats. Clearing 6 mph with twin motors, and five with a single, she's capable of over 20 miles in a five-hour run—*with no* solar input!

From the first, we've been struck by the practical way solar energy (recharging) and boating work together. We rarely sit down and count out how much a boat gets used, or even how much it's actually underway on a day when it does get used. When we trailer the boat to a lake or marina, she's refuelling all the way down the freeway. Once launched, we go for a two-hour explore, and then have lunch — and the boat's refuelling all the time. After another two-hour run, we take her home.

Battery levels are never as down as we're expecting them to be.

Cruising easy at around 4, we're using 12-15 Amps. And with four panels we're getting back around 6 Amps at 24 Volts. So, for every hour underway, we've got about 3 hours of "sunning" time (a 3:1 ratio) to keep levels up. And if one of those refuel hours is also a running hour, then the ratio is even less.

Even if you don't care about escaping for a while, finding fuel-docks open, or fiddling with fouled plugs, the feature we like best is the silence and smooth control. The lack of vibration and noise allows a blending with the surroundings. The boat permits the experience of getting up close and being personal with wildlife. Animals flee with engine noise or paddle movement. Sitting still, you are allowed to approach in SolExplorer.

In the new boat, we've kept the basic, knock-down modular layout of the first boats. This way, the boat can be car-topped or shipped compactly. Also, it can be rigged with different options for different days. The underwater viewer is fold-away. We add it when we want to peer at marine life as well as shore birds and the like. The same space fits a pair of extra solar panels for a quicker recharge.

The boat actually turns more tightly with only one motor attached, so the twin-screw set-up is needed only for a little extra speed, and the reliability of redundancy. More speed is possible with higher-pitch props, of course. The trade-off is less range. We've found that 4-6 mph is just right for getting around without becoming frustrated.

The SolExplorer showed a lot of talent for hooking onto fish. On days when no other fishermen in the area were getting any action, we hooked onto one after another with the boat cruising silently without a wake. After four straight hours of running our "Stealth Solar-Troller," the batteries were down less than ten percent!

Altogether, SolExplorer's power is translated into fun performance. Not crash-and-bang thrill-craft stuff, but a quiet-enough-to-be-relaxing, and fast-enough-to-prevent-frustration kind of operation that let's you cover more ground and get much closer to wildlife than possible with a paddle boat.

Electric Aircraft

In the sky, we find electric propulsion in the Sunseeker and the return of the airship.

The Sunseeker

In 1980, Eric Raymond had a dream. Ten years later, on July 1, 1990, Eric climbed into an electric ship that he had designed and constructed and begin an incredible journey. It was a transcontinental flight across the USA in the Sunseeker, a plane powered only by the sun (Application A53).

Up close, the Sunseeker *is* a dreamship. Solar cells flexible enough to adhere to the curvature are mounted on top of each wing's surface. A small electric motor mounted in the inverted tail section spins a lightweight, 8-foot propeller. The motor is powered by hundreds of rechargeable NiCd batteries, like those you might use in a standard flashlight.

The Sunseeker uses battery energy to fly off the ground on its own and climb to altitude. There, the motor is switched off, the propeller blades fold backward in the slipstream, and the solar cells commence a 90-minute recharge of the depleted battery pack. In the meantime, Eric flies the ship on another form of solar power: thermals. Whether solar-electric or solar-thermal, then, the Sunseeker's transcontinental flight was definitely solar powered the entire way.

There were many challenges in designing and building the Sunseeker (Techtalk T45). There was also the flight itself. An accompanying chase plane relieved Eric of many functions — navigation, long-distance communication, and weather-radar operations. Camera stills and videotaping provided sponsors and photographers with breathtaking close-ups of the Sunseeker. The chase plane's presence discouraged any behavior of other aircraft that might endanger Eric's flight.

Eric's flight demonstrated the benefit of thinking big, and building light and clean. It is one more example of the merits of hybrid technology — utilizing two or more sources of power — to offset the disadvantages inherent in

---

Techtalk T45

Features of the Sunseeker

The flight of Raymond's Sunseeker was simple in theory but difficult in execution. Depending on thermals means building a high-performance, hybrid aircraft. To do this, Eric concentrated his efforts in two critical areas: lift and drag. The Wortmann airfoil he chose for the wing ensured good laminar flow. The variable camber trailing edge combined low-speed lift with a flat, high-efficiency cross-section at speed. A mixer adjusted flaps and ailerons simultaneously to get this effect. The initial 38:1 glide ratio was reduced to a 30:1 ratio with the solar cells and propeller added.

Eric reduced the overall drag in three ways. First, he designed for a very low frontal area. Second, he chose a slippery shape for the main fuselage, a pod-and-boom design, preserving laminar flow for most of its length. Finally, the pod concept also reduced the overall surface area, minimizing aerodynamic losses to skin resistance. The combined effect, along with the folding prop, made Sunseeker a super sailer.

The main function of electric propulsion was to get Eric and the Sunseeker airborne and up to a respectable altitude. After that, it served him whenever the lift (from thermals, slope lift, or wave activity) became spotty, or Eric needed to maneuver to land at his overnight spot.

Most people don't understand how sailplanes work. They see sailplanes towed to altitude using a power plane. Once released, they assume it's all downhill, that the airplane "glides" to the ground. Even with glide ratios of 60:1, this doesn't account for sailplanes staying up so long, for many hours, or even all day. Like hawks, vultures, and eagles that effortlessly gain altitude, sailplanes find and then circle in thermals.

A thermal is an invisible but gentle tornado of warm air that is formed from the sun's heating of the ground. Pilot skill is very much a factor in finding a thermal, and using it to best advantage. Eventually, the thermal expands with altitude and "thins" out. At some point, then, the experienced pilot will leave the thermal, and head off in a chosen direction of flight. This is the glide portion of the flight, where lift dances with gravity, bleeding off altitude. In this fashion, Eric sailed Sunseeker across most of the USA on solar power.

Electric propulsion helped Eric power away from thunderstorms that he couldn't go over, under, or through. Or anytime he was running out of altitude. Still, he always rationed this power carefully. Low weight was important. The low-weight battery pack had the capacity to power the motor for only 10-15 minutes in the climbout. At day's end, it must be fully charged for liftoff the next morning.

The Sunseeker was equipped with a built-in safety chute, a carryover from Eric's experience with hang gliders. While the aircraft was stressed for 6.6G's, it was possible to experience a lot more if Eric got caught in a wind sheer or storm conditions. The canopy was too tight for Eric to extract himself very easily, and a parachute was too bulky to wear all day. If anything went wrong, Eric could pull a handle, and the rear section of the pod would calve open. A rocket would then launch (and fully extend) a parachute—sideways, back, and up. This would get it clear of the tail section, bringing airplane and pilot down to a safe landing.

any one source. As well, it proves the usefulness of natural and sustainable energy sources. Finally, it gives wings to the power of personal expression and belief.

The Return of the Airship

Born in an age of airplanes, most people do not realize the enticing merits of returning to the use of airships. There are so few surviving witnesses to one of the grandest forms of transportation by air. Earlier this century, peaceful giants in the sky logged millions of freight and passenger miles.

Newer materials, the use of technology developed in other arenas, and increasing reasons to look to less-polluting transportation in the air — all help hasten the time to reassess the role of the airship in the world at large. There is no doubt that, at a fraction of the cost of other technologies, a modern, safe, fast airship can be built.

Fig. 5-46: Lightweight solar cells are laminated to the wings.

Fig. 5-47: Sunseeker is truly solar-powered, using solar energy stored in batteries or thermals to stay aloft.

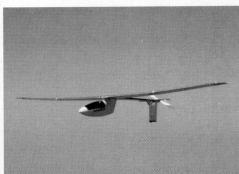

All photos:
Eric Raymond

Fig. 5-48: Eric Raymond banks Sunseeker in search of thermals.

Fig. 5-49: Sunseeker's inverted tail ensures that the propeller will not strike the ground.

Fig. 5-50: (next page) Eric Raymond flies Sunseeker.

Sunseeker Saga

Eric Raymond

The possibilities for solar-powered flight have held my interest since 1979. My earlier experiences with internal combustion engines made me wonder why people put up with these dirty, noisy, unreliable devices. The concept of taking one or more of these infernal machines up on a small aircraft, in the close proximity of flammable liquids, seemed dubious at best. Of course, this configuration has been made relatively safe on large aircraft such as airliners. Statistics for private and sport planes, however, show that engines are the leading cause of accidents.

Less obvious to the casual observer is that a pilot's all-important senses are impaired by an engine. The sense of hearing is lost in the never-ending racket. A view forward is usually compromised by the pilot's position directly behind the engine. The sense of feel is numbed by the vibration, which also fatigues structural parts of the aircraft.

Gliding, as an alternative, is perceived by most to be a continuous, downhill slide, like a ski run. However, invisible updrafts (thermals) are almost everywhere, and the art of riding these is called soaring. Gliders, then, are more aptly named sailplanes. Sailplanes have climbed to over 53,000 feet and flown more than 1,000 miles at a time. Although they may weigh as much as 2,000 lbs, they only require a few horsepower from the updrafts to sustain altitude. Migrating birds use this secret energy source to fly from Canada to South America. They could never store enough energy in their bodies to fly such a distance.

To design for gliding is to design for low power. Using sailplanes and man-powered aircraft as a starting point, I calculated that a one-seat aircraft could be built that would meet the international standards for strength and be capable of flying 100 mph — and require only one horsepower to sustain flight. The Sunseeker prototype meets these goals.

Although the structural and aerodynamic goals were easily met, the electrical system required considerable innovation to make it functional. The aircraft was intended to carry 35 pounds of NiCd (nickel-cadmium) batteries from the outset, to provide the power to take off and climb rapidly. These are recharged in flight for use at any time. Their weight is actually an asset in gliding flight, increasing speed.

Since my long-term goal is to make solar-powered aircraft affordable, I judged the amorphous PV (solar-electric) cell to hold hope for the future. This belief was reinforced by a manufacturer's claims of 13.7% efficiency. The true efficiency of the cells on my prototype is only 2.1%, which did not afford enough power for continuous cruising as intended. I had expected to cross the USA in a week or less. Still, by climbing in thermals up to 14,000 feet of altitude, I made it to the North Carolina coast in 23 flights.

The initial powered test flights were made using two DC motors of one horsepower each, in tandem. At 80% efficiency, they required more cooling than I could provide, and I never got the impression that they would last long enough to cross the country. Instead, I opted for a hollow-core, brushless DC motor. It is a marvel of efficiency and reliability, weighs only 4 pounds, and is capable of running at 5 HP continuously. It required another 4 lbs of electronics to generate the pulse-width-modulated AC.

The Sunseeker was built using the best technology that was available at a reasonable cost. The structure is all oven-cured, unidirectional carbon fiber prepreg (prepregnated). All major parts were made into a sandwich structure. The fuselage has a Nomex honeycomb core, and the wings and tail surfaces have a thin Rohacell foam core. The wings have been load-tested to 6.6g without damage. The test flights were made without power, as a glider, with the aircraft weighing 100 lbs. The installation of solar cells, batteries, motor and propeller added another 100 lbs. The added weight improved both speed and control.

Even at 204 pounds, the Sunseeker includes many amenities for such a small plane. It is equipped with a ballistically deployed parachute, which can bring down the airplane with pilot. It has gyroscopic instruments for flying in clouds. It is equipped with an oxygen system and a drinking water system. Pilot cooling is accomplished with an adjustable air vent. The canopy can also be opened in flight without sacrificing much performance, and this provides both cooling and a closer contact with the sky itself.

For the flight across the continent, I had planned to wait for a super soaring day, with strong west winds. The weather forecasts never even looked average. I planned to make it to New Mexico the first day, but the headwinds limited my distance to 247 miles or just past Phoenix, Arizona. After that I was able to cross about one state per day, weather permitting.

I was escorted by a conventional light plane, whose pilot, Klaus Savier, did the navigation work by Loran. We avoided major airports, preferring quiet country airports. The people who greeted us each evening were always very friendly, and were always willing to make room for the Sunseeker in a hangar for the night. My wife, Aida, followed on the ground. She towed the airplane's trailer, navigated with aeronautical charts, and listened to us on the airband radio in order to stay up with us.

I wish I could say how beautiful it was to see the Atlantic come into view under my nose. However, when I arrived, I was greeted by visibility of less than a mile, driving rain, and NE headwinds of 30 mph. The wind had been against us for more than 90% of the time of the transcontinental flight. In retrospect, it would have been much faster to fly from east to west.

As the relevant technologies progress, the speeds and carrying capability of electric aircraft will increase. The potential for an aircraft equipped with a reversible hydrogen fuel cell looks very promising. In the next century, I predict that even airliners will go electric, storing their fuel in a non-combustible form. Safety will be further increased by the inherent reliability of electric motors. The current research in more efficient airliner engines has concentrated on propellers turned by turbines. These supersonic propellers would convert readily to electric power, reducing the costs of energy and maintenance.

Photo: Eric Raymond

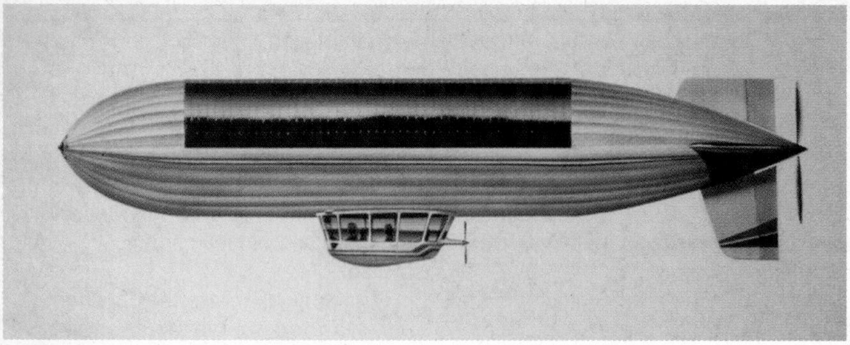

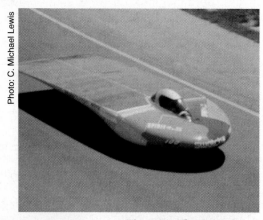

Fig. 5-51: One design for a solar-powered airship.

A World of Solar Vehicles

A tantalizing idea, then, is the solar-powered airship. Sunlight may intercept solar cells on the upper skin, as in Eric Raymond's design (Fig 5-51). Or it may penetrate a transparent glazing and be focused on high-efficiency cells. Altogether, very little energy storage (batteries, fuel cells, etc.) is needed onboard. Like solar cars, when a solar airship is not consuming energy, it is storing the incoming energy for those moments when thrust is needed.

I'll end this chapter the way it began—with solar cars.

Photo: C. Michael Lewis

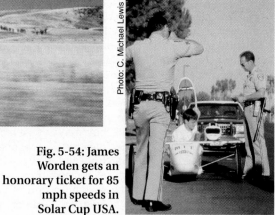

Fig. 5-52: The Swatch car won the Solar Challenge in Australia in 1990.

Photo: Viking Research Institute (WWU)

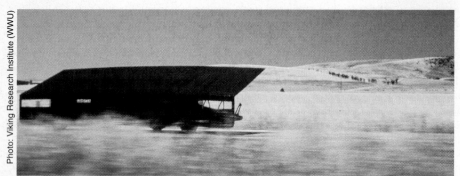

Fig. 5-53: Viking XX runs across the Australian outback.

Photo: C. Michael Lewis

Fig. 5-54: James Worden gets an honorary ticket for 85 mph speeds in Solar Cup USA.

Photo: C. Michael Lewis

Fig. 5-55: Overhead solar panels supply lots of shade.

Photo: C. Michael Lewis

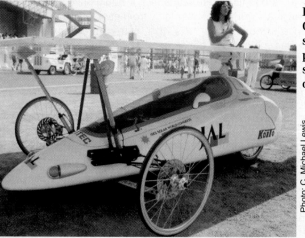

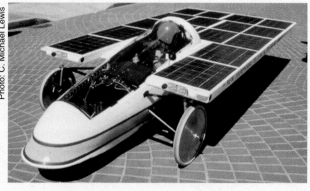

Fig. 5-56: A solar car looks for a recharge site during the American Tour de Sol event.

Fig. 5-57: The Solar Eagle takes a spin around the CSLA track.

Fig. 5-58: The CalPoly Pomona team races Solar Flair at PIR.

Fig. 5-59: MIT leads the pack as Tour de Sol USA begins.

Fig. 5-60: Artistic expression is found in many solar cars.

Fig. 5-61: Jonathan Tennyson's Mana La is at home in the islands.

Fig. 5-62: SolTrain climbs the grade outside Willits, California on solar-powered batteries.

Chapter 6
Infrastructure, Energy, & Fuels

*T*he electric vehicle is only as good as the system that supports it. Thus, the EV industry faces the same four challenges that the new gasoline-fueled cars did after the turn of the century. First, access to "fuel." Fortunately, many sources of energy will power the EV. Second, standardization of plugs and receptacles and the ampacity of service outlets. Third, an integration of the technology. And, four, public confidence in the new stuff under the hood.

Fortunately, most of the infrastructure for EVs is already in place!

Fig. 6-1: Electric vehicles can be "fueled" from many sources.

Photo: Victoria Lenda (MendoMotive)

This chapter will make it clear that most of the infrastructure for EVs is either in place already, or just around the corner. It will look closer at the energy sources that supply electrical energy for EVs. Finally, it describes ways to include an energy partner in the EV itself in a hybrid configuration.

Powering the EV

The electric vehicle can be recharged at home and at work, at convenience points or in regular parking areas. The EV can also be fast-charged or have its battery pack swapped for a freshly-charged one.

Home Charging

Unlike a car with an engine, an EV can "refuel" at the owner's home. Just plug it in (Application A54). Even the largest chargers require an ampacity and voltage not greater than that used by the service outlet for an electric range or clothes dryer. Smaller chargers need nothing more than a standard wall socket.

Surprisingly, the biggest challenge with using the utility grid for refueling an EV at this point is access to the wall socket. In urban areas, less than 35% of the population lives in a dwelling with a garage or carport. Vehicles parked on the street, in an apartment complex, or in a large parking structure simply do not have access to a dedicated wall receptacle for an overnight charge of the EV.

Access to electricity is critical to EV success. Nighttime charging of EVs utilizes an untapped power source. An estimated 30 million EVs in the USA may be recharged overnight without the construction of even one new powerplant. There's that much "excess" electricity (capacity) from existing power plants "off peak" (7pm-11am). This is also the cheapest rate of electricity available. So, it's a natural—an infrastructure that is ready to springboard EVs into an immediate victory in the fight against pollution.

An estimated 30 million EVs in the USA may be recharged overnight without the construction of even one new powerplant.

Worksite Charging

Worksite recharging is the next best thing to charging at home. Where this is available, the effective range of an EV is *doubled*. While the average commute in cities like Los Angeles is less than 20 miles, worksite recharging makes it possible for an EV owner to "full-range" the vehicle getting to work. The 8-hour workday is enough time to fully recharge the vehicle.

At this point, worksite recharge is novel and is easily accomplished for a small number of EVs. It represents very little power drain. Where outdoor sockets are not currently available, installing a charging station incurs only the cost of a breaker, a length of Romex, an all-weather receptacle, and the labor to add it.

Why would an employer provide such a service? In California (and other states), an EV can help a company meet its carpooling mandates. Since it goes three times as far as a fuel-efficient ICE car (on the BTUs of the original energy source), an EV is effectively a "carpool" by itself!

Worksite recharging adds somewhat to the peak load. However, EVs arriving before 8am will have 3 hours of bulk charging completed before the 11am peak load period starts. For most EVs, recharging adds no more to the peak load than would the operation of a coffeepot.

Fig. 6-2: This sign designates an EV charging space.

EV CHARGING STATION

... recharging a car adds no more to the peak load than would the operation of a coffeepot.

Opportunity Charging

Innovative EV owners have always found ways to extend their operating range. One way is through the "opportunity" charge. At every opportunity, the EV is plugged in. With permission, of course. This has rarely been a problem in small communities or rural areas where businesses and friends alike have been glad to lend a hand, or more appropriately, access to a wall socket.

Even people who drive "all day long" are usually parked more often than they are on the

Photos: Stephen Heckeroth

Fig. 6-3: PV panels power home and electric vehicle.

Fig. 6-4: The EV plugs into the solar-electric system.

Application

A54

Home Charging an EV

Stephen Heckeroth

As an architect, I have channeled my concerns regarding the environment into refining residential passive solar design. I drive a Type III Karmann Ghia I converted to electric propulsion. Opponents of electric cars argue that emissions are only transferred from the tailpipe to the smokestack or the nuclear power plant. This argument can be put to rest when PV charging stations are integrated into the roofs of our homes.

I recently installed laminated-glass panels—capable of producing 400 Watts per 100 sq ft—on the south-facing roof of my barn, replacing a leaky metal roof. The integrated PV installation cost $8/sq. ft., including the avoided cost of new material ($2/sq ft). The 3,000-Watt array provides all the power for our house, an apartment in the barn loft, and my electric car.

The barn's 700 sq. ft. array produces a steady three kW for seven or eight hours a day in the summer and 1.5 kW for four or five hours on a cloudy winter day. This yields a yearly average of 15 kWh a day. Combining the new California net metering law—the utility must pay the same rate for my home-generated power *fed* into the grid as they charge for electricity *consumed* from the grid—and time-of-use rates, I expect the array to produce about $7.50 worth of electricity per day in the summer and a low of 75 cents per day in the winter. This means an avoided expense of approximately $4 a day or $1,500 a year. The system, including the Trace synchronous inverter and batteries, will pay for itself in less than seven years. Over its 30-year expected life, the PV roof will generate $45,000 of "avoided" utility bills even in the unlikely event utility rates remain constant.

road. Opportunity charging is a smart idea whose time has definitely come. Parking garages, restaurants, and stores are all possible locations for opportunity chargers. In Switzerland, a power outlet is integrated with a parking meter, allowing EVs owners to pay for both the space and the electricity they use.

As with worksite recharging, opportunity charging need be neither expensive nor complex. A receptacle on the outside of a building or in a parking garage will do. Outdoor Romex, an all-weather box, and a standard receptacle will supply enough capacity for an onboard 110vac charger. This is automatically current-limited by the GFI outlet, reducing the impact on utility peak loads.

EV Service Stations

The general public is accustomed to refueling their vehicles in a service station. Infrastructure to support EVs, then, will benefit from a facility similar to the service station (Application A55). However, it will likely be very different from the ones used to dispense gasoline and diesel fuel.

Photo/Drawing: Bruce Severance

Fig. 6-5: Solar energy helps with peak load in charging EVs.

When it comes to "refueling" an EV, a service station can perform one of two battery services: fast-charge or battery exchange.

The Fast-Charge System

Fast-charging an EV's battery pack is the current rage in technology. An 8-12 hour recharge period for EVs is unacceptable to a general public that is used to

Fig. 6-6: Solar panels recharge an electric motorcycle miles from grid power.

A*pplication* 55

EV Solar Charging Station

Ruth MacDougall

On August 5, 1992, the Sacramento Municipal Utility District (SMUD) unveiled the first solar-powered EV charging station in the Western USA. By utilizing advanced photovoltaic (PV) panels, energy from the sun supplied the power for (up to) sixteen EVs.

The free-standing structure, measuring 8 feet wide and 130 feet long, provides 16 shaded parking spots reserved for the SMUD fleet of EVs. The 1,000 square foot array develops 12kW and an average daily energy production of 68.4 kWh of power. This is enough energy to drive a compact pickup 30 miles *and* four sedans 30 miles each *and* ten NEVs (neighborhood EVs) 25 miles each.

The PV array utilizes a tracking mechanism, automatically orienting the panels with the sun's position and providing maximum power, even on cloudy days.

SMUD has one of the largest fleets of EVs in existence and continues to discover new ways to utilize the full potential of their widespread use.

Photo: Sacramento Municipal Utility District

Fig. 6-7: Inside the SMUD solar charging station.

Techtalk *T46*

Battery Fast-Charge Tests

Fast-charging rates of my electric Honda VX (EVX) during the 1992 Phoenix Races were based on tests conducted at Trojan Battery Company several months before.

The test setup. A "source" battery pack of 24 Volts was wired up to a 12 Volt battery (a 27TMH battery, the type used in the EVX) through control equipment (a carbon-pile controller). A strip chart recorder was connected to data (time, volts and current), a thermometer was inserted into a vent cap to measure battery temperature, and the crude setup was enclosed in shatterproof plastic shields.

The first fast-charge. My calculations—based on the Coderre model, the previous year's race with the Lead Sled and an analysis of the winning entries—suggested an average charge current of 400A into each of EVX's paralleled packs. When the switch was thrown, an initial 425A charge rate was observed. This rate dropped to 375A after three (3) minutes. The temperature rose 10 degrees F. in the battery. No gassing was observed.

Pack Discharge Tests. Following the fast-charge, the test battery was placed on a controlled discharge machine, with an 85A setting. After 18 minutes, the batteries were down to 100 Volts. So — a 1,200 Amp-minute (400 Amps multiplied by 3 minutes) recharge rate had given the battery a 50% recharge. A 10 degree F. gain in temperature was recorded during discharge.

Test to Destruction. An attempt was made to find the upper limit of current the battery could survive. A direct connection was made between the 24V pack and the 12 V test battery. An initial 525-Amp charge rate had dropped to 475A when, at 2 minutes and 15 seconds into the test, a negative terminal of the test battery melted, opening the circuit. There was no spark, flame, or explosion. The terminal melted just below the plastic cover, at its narrowest point, just above the electrolyte level.

getting 150-300 miles of "gasoline" after less than five (5) minutes of pumping at a service station.

Existing technology can perform a quick-charge rate of an EV battery pack in 10-15 minutes. This *is* fast when compared with the recharge time of most EVs. It requires a special charger (justified only in a station because of its cost) and a high-ampacity utility tie-in.

One problem with a fast-charge facility is that, compared with refueling a gas car, a 10-15 minute time period is *slow*. Even if the fast-charge rate is refined to work faster, it still expects too much patience from today's drivers. As well, it's likely to occur during daytime hours, impacting the utility peak load.

Application *A56*

Fast-Charging at the Races

The EVX, a 1992 Honda Civic VX converted to electric propulsion, was designed to race in the stock category of the Phoenix races in 1992. Toward this end, its battery pack consisted of *two*, paralleled packs of 120V, each composed of ten 12V, 27TMH (Trojan) batteries.

Tests conducted at Trojan Battery Company confirmed that the 27TMH battery could withstand a 400A recharge rate for three (3) minutes. With two packs onboard, each charged at the 400A rate from one of two offboard 180V battery packs, the needed 1,200 Amp-minute rate would safely provide a 50% recharge in a three-minute pit stop.

The two onboard packs were isolated from each other when the car's circuit breaker was opened. Four sections of 00 (gauge) welding cable brought the positive and negative leads from the onboard packs out to connect with the offboard battery packs (a miniature power station) through a homebuilt controller, the ShuntFET (Fig. 6-8). This design worked like two fill tubes into one gas tank, allowing a 800-Amp charge rate (400 amps per pack) into the car.

Race day arrived and the EVX took the lead with its ambitious pace. The EVX, with Tim Considine at the wheel, racked up 46 miles before the readout dropped to 100V and he zoomed into the pit. The recharge cables were attached. With a total current of 700 Amps at 168V, we stretched the charge time to four minutes before we stopped, disconnected, and resumed racing.

After 23 miles, it was time to pit again. (Sure enough, we had transferred a 50% charge!) With a higher voltage from the offboard packs (we could tap higher or lower in 12-Volt increments), we got our 400 Amps average per pack. Much sooner this time, the Honda VX was again out making speed.

We managed to pull up to 2nd place before we made our last pit stop. It was at this point that the first-place car, a Solectria entry, spilled zinc-bromine, spinning to a stop near our pit crew. We abandoned our recharge to help pull James Worden from an ugly cloud of poisonous gas, the race was red-flagged, and the rest is history.

Our EVX took second place, proving that a fast-charge system could work and be competitive.

Fig. 6-8: The ShuntFET was built to control 800-Amp charge rates.

The faster the fast-charge rate, the greater its impact on peak load.

A clever fast-charge system that averted peak loading was one used by Joe Coderre for his own electric car. In 1975, as the owner of a series of rebuilt-battery outlets, he wanted to drive his electric at freeway speeds between each store. To do this, he set up a means to recharge the onboard battery pack at each site during his hour-long stay.

Standard chargers would not be able to handle this job. Instead, Joe Coderre set up a series of battery recharging "stations." Each store had a stationary battery pack that was recharged slowly from the utility grid over a period of days. When he visited that store, he connected the depleted pack in his car *directly* to the fully-charged one. At this high a transfer rate, Coderre's EV was almost fully charged when he was ready to leave.

The Limits of Fast-Charge Systems

Are there any limits to the rate at which a battery pack be recharged?

To find out, Otmar Ebenhoech and I entered an old EV in the 1991 Phoenix stock car race. Affectionately named the Lead Sled, the vehicle had no hope of competing directly with other lighter and more aerodynamic vehicles in

Fig. 6-9: The Lead Sled used fast-charge in the 1991 Phoenix races.

the 120-mile race. Encouraged by Coderre's experience, I calculated the probable success of a similar technique of rapid charging from an offboard battery pack. Consequently, our team was successful with a 50% recharge during the race in a bit more than seven (7) minutes, allowing the Lead Sled to place 6th out of a field of 12 entries (instead of last!).

This experience suggested that a lightweight, streamlined car could be competitive in a similar race. A post-race analysis and some projected qualifications launched a new project for the 1992 races (Techtalk T46). A 1992 Honda Civic VX was electrified and wired to interface with a charge-rate interface, the ShuntFET. The EVX entered by the Hackleman-Schless team received a 50% recharge in three (3) minutes repeatedly (Application A56) in the 120-mile endurance races, placing 2nd in the 1992 race and 4th in the 1993 race.

The EVX...was 50% recharged in three (3) minutes repeatedly in the 120-mile endurance races.

Fast-charging at these rates was justified in a race environment. However, these charge rates are harmful to the battery packs involved, and will decrease their service life.

As the technology of batteries *and* chargers improves, even higher charge rates may eventually be safe. At this point, however, fast-charge rates like those demonstrated in the Lead Sled and the EVX exceed the limits available in off-the-shelf technology.

Fig. 6-10: The EVX at Phoenix.

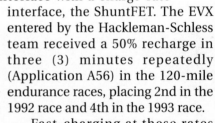

Fig. 6-11: The ShuntFET connected the offboard battery pack to the EVX through large cable connectors.

Fig. 6-12: Tim Considine gets a hug from son, Chris, after driving the EVX to victory.

Fig. 6-13: The Hackleman-Schless pit crew awaits the Formula E's arrival.

Fig. 6-14: The racer stops short of the fresh pack and the side doors are opened.

Fig. 6-15: Depleted modules are lifted from the vehicle.

Fig. 6-16: The racer is pushed forward and a new pack is inserted.

Fig. 6-17: The doors are closed and a ram makes contact with the modules.

Fig. 6-18: The Formula E speeds back onto the track.

Battery Exchange Technology

Another option for the EV service station is to exchange a vehicle's depleted battery with a fully-charged one. Isn't battery pack exchange difficult? For some time, I believed it was. Experience has changed that.

Battery Exchange in a Racer

Two years running (1992-93), the Hackleman-Schless team had a perfect record with its Formula E racer, grabbing four 1st-

*A*pplication
A57 Formula E Battery Swap

The Formula E racer was built around a modified Formula 440 racing chassis. Ten 12V batteries made up the battery pack, divided into two 250-lb, 60V modules. A stock Trojan 24C3 battery was chosen for its power density and weight. The weight factor was critical. We planned to run fast and pit often, exchanging depleted modules with fresh ones. With two people per module, four teammembers would briefly lift a 125-lb load.

We wanted a 10-second exchange time. After considerable discussion and experimentation, we opted for human-power over machinery for the swapout. A major challenge was the electrical disconnect and connect with each swap. Almost immediately, Ely hit upon the idea of strapping a copper plate to each end of the module that held the batteries inside a Lexan "case." This transformed each module into a monster version of a standard D-type (flashlight) cell.

Ely installed a CO_2 ram to the rear of the module area on each side. With the flip of a cockpit switch, the ram would close a gap of several inches, pushing a "hot" lead against the module's plate. This made positive contact *and* shoved the pack forward, pushing the copper plate at the front end of the pack against a stationary contact. The setup was repeated on the other side of the vehicle.

With this arrangement, teammembers could throw modules into the vehicle like a sack of potatoes. Once the ram acted, each module completed the circuit and the pack was securely sealed in the vehicle. For the planned two-and-a-half-hour Open Class race , we assembled 15 battery sets (30 modules), with Trojan Battery employees helping to build the packs.

How did it go? Our fastest recorded swap time was 14 seconds. Combined with the vehicle's low running weight and good aerodynamics, the fast-swap scheme worked flawlessly. We had no serious competitor. The Formula E grabbed 1st place trophies in both the 25-mile heat and 90-minute endurance races in 1992 at Phoenix.

The Formula E returned to Phoenix in 1993. With a new paint job, a bubble canopy, a battery pack increased to 144V, and homebuilt dollies to move the greater module weight, the Formula E was able to stay ahead of its only real competition, the SnoWhite entry of Bob Schneeveis and Otmar Ebenhoech, two of our former teammates. Our fastest swap was 12.6 seconds!

Again, in 1993, the Formula E won both first-place trophies in the Phoenix races, and was retired from racing undefeated.

place trophies in the Open class at the annual Phoenix Solar & Electric races in Arizona.

What was its secret? Four people exchanged two battery modules (total: 500 pounds) *eight* times in pit stopswith an average time of 15 seconds (Application A57).

Battery Exchange in a Car

After the 1992 wins, we wanted to apply our fast battery swap scheme in a standard car.

I helped acquire a '92 Geo Metro and Ely converted it to electric propulsion. It was equipped with a steel battery receptacle (Application A58). Several battery "modules" were built. A gadget that could raise and lower the battery pack was added. The Geometric's 1,200-lb battery pack could be exchanged for a fresh one in 42 seconds' time.

Battery Exchange Technology

There are many virtues of fast-swap *battery exchange technology,* or BET (Techtalk T47). Swift commercialization is assured because the hardware and practices are a part of existing industrial processes. The BET system involves the standardization of battery modules and receptacles and other off-the-shelf technologies. The initial deployment of the BET design in service stations can even be semi-mobile. A semi-trailer rig delivers a modified trailer to any paved area. It contains battery-swapping hardware, several sizes of battery modules and electrical wiring to link it to the

---

*T*echtalk
*T*47 Battery Exchange Technology

The BET (battery exchange technology) system involves the following components: battery pack, receptacle, battery transfer system (BTS) and data terminal.

Battery Pack. The battery pack contains conventional (stock) lead-acid batteries configured to the desired ratings (voltage, current, amp-hour capacity, etc.). Modules are available in several standardized sizes and contain the batteries, interconnects, power receptacle, and gas exhaust system. Insulation and battery warmers are available in colder climes. The module's top is removable for maintenance (watering, hydrometer checks, etc.) and cell exchange. A small microprocessor is located in each module to monitor battery functions and report the module's service readiness or initiate a maintenance cycle.

Battery Receptacle. The receptacle for a battery module is also standardized in size and depth. It is custom fit to the vehicle, used or new. Its under-vehicle position preserves vehicle handling and stability, and it eliminates shock hazard by keeping the pack away from the consumer. It secures the battery module until released by the BTS machinery.

Battery Transfer System (BTS). The machinery to exchange battery modules may be one of two types: portable or permanently installed. Either system aligns the EV and extracts the depleted battery, selects and installs a fully charged battery, and releases the EV.

The Data Terminal. This interacts with the EV owner and communicates options to the BTS hardware. This unit bills the user for the exchange service, and applies a credit where energy remains in the discharged module. This unit also queries the module's microprocessor for charging and maintenance decisions.

---

*A*pplication
*A*58 Geometric Battery Exchange

The Geometric is a 1992 Geo Metro that provided the first demonstration of an EV equipped with a BET system.

The vehicle was first converted to an EV in the conventional way. Then, its seats were removed and a rectangular hole was cut through the bottom of the vehicle. A steel receptacle for a battery "module" was welded in place, and the seats were custom fit atop it. Thirty, low-profile Trojan batteries (three paralleled 120-Volt strings) were arranged inside an open-top module made of sheet steel.

A stock 12-Volt winch was installed in the trunk and, through a clever arrangement of pulleys, steel cables were routed to four anchor points on the module. Terminated in T-pins, these cables secured a clevis fixture on the module. By operating the winch, the battery pack could be raised, lowered, or held in place.

Lacking infrastructure, the Geometric was designed to swap its own battery pack. Applied commercially, a BET (battery exchange technology) system would be installed in a service station and the vehicle would drive in for a battery exchange.

How would it work? Once a credit card had identified the vehicle's battery pack and queried the driver about any options, the system would move the vehicle forward and position it. One scenario would have a hydraulic lift rise and take up the battery weight. The car's battery-retaining anchors would be released, and the pack would be lowered and sped on its way to the service or recharge area. A new, fully-charged replacement pack would be cycled onto the lift, pushed up in place, and secured. The EV would now be "refueled" and ready to go on its way.

Fig. 6-19: The Geometric exchanges a depleted pack for a fresh one.

nearest utility pole. It also has a human interface much like the cash-dispensing machine used by banks. As the technology matures, special-built facilities—set up like a car wash (battery swapping *is* just a process)—will streamline the process. The Geometric's pack was exchanged manually in less than a minute. How much better would any system have to be than that!

What would it be like to drive into a service station equipped with a battery exchange technology (BET) system?

First, align your vehicle with the exchange track and insert your E-card in the terminal to initiate the BET process. This communicates your pack type to the system, and gives you options on the size (range) of the replacement pack. The system credits your account with any electricity remaining in the pack that you've returned, perhaps simply deducting it from your next electric bill!

Your vehicle now moves forward (you may or may not be in the vehicle). The battery pack is released and lowered on a lift. A new pack is inserted into the under-vehicle receptacle. That's it. You're now ready to drive out. The BET process takes less than a minute.

The Implications of Battery Exchange

Four major virtues addressed by a BET system are range, maintenance, affordability, and timing.

• Range in an EV based on a BET design is without limits. While "refueling" an EV might require more frequent stops (initially), it can be done quickly.

• Maintenance of BET battery packs is transferred to qualified service personnel, minimizing liability issues and ensuring reliable operation.

• EVs using a BET system have a lower purchase price, too. The BET batteries are leased, not owned, reducing the upfront cost of going electric.

• Finally, the BET design makes EVs work *now*. Imperfections in batteries in the BET system remain totally transparent to the driving public. Long before a battery pack experiences a problem, it is detected and remedied by the battery service agency.

Energy Sources

One of the primary virtues of the electric vehicle is that the electricity to power it is available from *many* sources. As transportation shifts from ICE technology to electric propulsion, what criteria do we use to rank these potential energy sources?

Two factors normally associated with any energy source are pollution and resource depletion. Carbon pumped into the atmosphere contributes to global warming by better than fifty percent. And, however abundant now, fossil fuels *are* a finite resource.

The potential energy sources for EVs, then, are listed below in descending order (within their classes) according to their sustainability and pollution-free nature.

Of the sustainable energy sources, we have solar (solar-thermal and solar-electric), wind-electric, hydroelectric, and biomass (alcohol and ethanol).

In the non-renewables, there are the fossil fuels (petroleum oil, oil shale, gas, and methanol) and nuclear energy.

Sustainable Energy Sources

Utility-scale power plants using solar and wind energy abound in California. Hydro-thermal, hydrogen, and biomass sources have also been effectively demonstrated as energy sources despite an uneven playing field.

Solar Electricity

A resident living with SCE (Southern California Edison) as the local utility is likely to be one of 500,000 people that get their electricity directly from the sun.

With the completion of SEGS-9 (Solar Electric Generation System IX), facilities built by LUZ located in the Mojave Desert totalled over 354 megaWatts of energy to SCE and its customers. This is enough energy to power a city the size of Albuquerque, New Mexico or Austin, Texas directly from the sun.

Before its bankruptcy from political hanky-panky, LUZ International was the world's leading developer of commercial solar power plants. LUZ was a privately-owned firm headquartered in Los Angeles and responsible for the design and construction of the world's nine largest SEGS. These account for more than 92 per cent of the world's solar electricity generated from utility-scale plants.

The award-winning, LUZ-designed solar thermal plants use electric-generating systems powered by steam turbines. Sunlight is the primary energy source (Techtalk T48). To ensure uninterrupted power to the grid, a supplemental natural gas system is used, driving the same turbines. Technically, then, the LUZ design is a hybrid system. When there is adequate sun, the system is solar. On cloudy or rainy days, and at nighttime, the plant uses the natural gas backup. Energy brokers at utility control centers, then, can rely on power, at any time of the day or night from a SEGS facility.

LUZ International

Fig. 6-20: Collectors at Harper Lake, California, use the sun's energy directly.

Fig. 6-21: A SEGs power block generates electricity from the sun or natural gas.

LUZ International

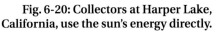

*T*echtalk
*T*48

LUZ Solar Power Plants

The solar field at a SEGS facility is composed of reflector assemblies in the shape of parabolic troughs. These individually track the sun with sophisticated microprocessors and light-sensing instruments. The reflector assemblies focus the sun's light onto specially-coated steel pipes which are mounted inside vacuum-insulated glass tubes. The glass tubes prevent heat losses and protect the pipes from the environment. Inside the pipes is a heat transfer fluid, or HTF, made from synthetic oil. Heated to 735 degrees Fahrenheit by the sun, the HTF is routed through a heat exchanger, generating superheated steam for a turbine generator.

The collectors themselves are 95-97 percent efficient! Each reflector is made up of hot-formed, mirror-glass panels, supported by a steel truss system which gives the units strength against torsional loads exerted by winds. The width of the parabolic reflectors is 5.76 meters, about 18 feet across. A typical solar "field" collects 535 square meters (approximately 5,000 square feet) of sunshine. The quality and accuracy of the panels yield a reflectivity of 94 percent and a geometric accuracy of 97 percent. This means that 91 percent of the incoming radiation impinges on the receiver.

The rest of the system is "boilerplate." The HTF (heat transfer fluid) circulates through the solar field and generates steam via a bank of shell-and-tube heat exchangers. The steam then enters a reheat turbine at 1450 psi and 700 degrees F. The turbine has six extractors supplying the deaerator and five feedwater heaters. Mechanical-draft cooling towers are used to eject power cycle waste heat into the atmosphere. (This is no more heat than would be given off by the solar energy impacting the ground. It does, however, give a good boost in altitude to the hawks that come to investigate the shiny contraptions!)

LUZ International

Fig. 6-22: Collectors bring a life-giving element in the reclamation of the desert—shade.

T49 Solar-Thermal or Photovoltaic?

The energy in a square meter (nine square feet) of sunshine at noon (on a clear day) is nearly 1000 Watts. This energy can be converted into electricity in two ways: solar-electric and thermal-electric.

T50 LUZ Fuel and Emissions Savings

Once in operation, each square meter of mirrors in the LUZ systems saved a barrel of oil per year. At current SEGS capacity, 2.2 million barrels of imported oil have been saved. Over the expected 30-year lifespan of a LUZ plant, this amounts to 66 million barrels. This reduces the U.S. trade deficit by $55 million per year.

Another benefit of the LUZ design is the "avoided emissions" value. All operational SEGS plants displace, per year, the equivalent of 1.2 billion pounds of CO_2 and 750,000 pounds of NOx (nitrous oxide, the major component in smog). This saves $19 million per year in pollution costs, too.

Terrestrial-grade (low-cost) silicon solar-electric panels—like those used in a number of facilities installed by ARCO Solar two decades ago—convert 12-14 per cent of these 1,000 Watts into electricity. The newer, less-expensive amorphous solar panels convert 6-8 per cent of this power into electricity.

The LUZ design uses the sun's energy directly, supplying thermal energy to produce steam for conventional Rankine-cycle reheat steam turbine systems. This conversion (system) process is 30-35 per cent efficient. Design improvements could be expected to increase this figure to 40 per cent in the immediate future. Up to 50 per cent efficiency was forecast for newer plants, as the heat transfer fluid was eliminated and super-heated steam was available from the collectors directly.

Fig. 6-23: LUZ technology is simple and environmentally benign.

T51 Solar EV Charging Station

A solar EV charging station would consist of (excluding structural or architectural components) a solar array, array power conditioner, DC and ac bus, power storage (battery pack), vehicle battery modules (Battery Exchange Technology), battery charger, and a line-tie (to utility grid).

Solar Array. The solar array would consist of commercial-grade 12V modules. A fixed array will work best where early morning and late afternoon sun is not available (shading, mountains, fog, and smog). The system would shift for seasonal changes in the azimuth and declination angle. Panels will provide shade and storm shelter for vehicles under charge, or office and industrial space).

Power Conditioning. Peak power trackers (PPTs) will match the solar array to the DC bus. A low-voltage or high-voltage array will work, since each has its merits and liabilities. However, if a fast-charge system is

planned, a high-voltage DC bus will make power transfer easier to packs of lower voltage.

DC and AC Bus. A DC bus shunts the PPT output from the array and nighttime utility power. It is the source for fast-charge or a battery exchange technology (BET) system.

Utility Line-Tie. A 220/440 vac, three-phase line-tie (connection to utility grid) will easily supply any additional power required for battery charging, day or night. The utility line-tie recognizes that a station that tries to use 100% of the available solar energy will cost ten times the system that aims for 90% solar usage. A synchronous inverter is an expensive option to the battery charger in the SEVCS, unless the utility recognizes net billing (buys solar at daytime rates and permits buying grid-power at night at night rates—a win-win situation.)

Battery Storage. On-site battery stores array power or utility power, for those times when the array cannot deliver power, i.e., excessive recharging needs, nighttime, heavy cloud cover, etc.

Pack Exchange. Includes BET hardware for exchanging battery packs, and automatically begins recharging depleted packs from solar or nighttime utility power.

Fast-Charge. Includes hardware to fast-charge batteries in EVs using the facility, direct from the DC bus.

Battery Charger. An ac charger that converts utility ac into DC voltage applied to the DC bus.

Interface Hardware. A custom-built monitor unit to be used by a customer or station attendant. The unit monitors, displays, and logs station operations (voltage, currents, grid interface meters, etc.) for verifying proper system operation. It also centralizes array, battery, and grid disconnects for inspection or maintenance of array, battery pack, and utility interface. This unit houses fuses, breakers, fuses, relays, etc. for station operation.

Customer Display. Includes display units to inform drivers that recharging is initiated, underway, or completed. Also, may allow user input for pack type and size.

The LUZ technology is more simple and less expensive (per installed kiloWatt hour) than solar energy systems that use photovoltaic panels (TechTalk T49). The existing plants deliver power at rates cheaper than new nuclear plants and are competitive with conventional peaking facilities.

The LUZ design was environmentally benevolent from the start, saving on imported fuel and increasing avoiding emissions (Techtalk T50). Ground-breaking to online startup was usually no more than 18 months. Solar thermal plants really shine during peak load periods. They deliver 80% of their power during periods when customer demand is highest.

A SEGS facility (of the current design) that is sized 80 miles square would generate all the power consumed in the USA right now.

Solar PV Stations

An idea that works anywhere under the sun is the solar EV parking station. Most parking areas have a large amount of roof area. A massive solar array would provide the same shade *and* also supply (or supplement) the energy needed to recharge EVs. Unlike the solar-thermal principle used in the LUZ power plants, this array uses photovoltaic (PV) arrays, converting the sun's energy directly into electricity. A solar parking area was built by SMUD (Sacramento Municipal Utility District) for their growing fleet of electric cars and trucks.

In 1992, I was asked by an automaker to look at the feasibility of a solar-powered EV recharging station. Both a fast-charge and battery exchange system were analyzed for use with a PV solar array and a utility line-tie (Techtalk T51). Fewer components and less expense were involved in the design involving a BET system. Depleted packs not recharged from solar charging by day's end would be serviced overnight from the utility grid at off-peak rates.

Photo: Sacramento Municipal Utility District

Fig. 6-24: Solar stations work anywhere under the sun.

Photo: Zond Systems

Fig. 6-25: Wind power is derived indirectly from sun energy.

Photo: Zond Systems

Fig. 6-26: Wind is usually highest in the winter, when solar energy is at a minimum.

Fig. 6-27: The SkyRiver facility.

... a new turbine manufactured today produces enough electricity each year to offset 600,000 pounds of carbon dioxide (a "greenhouse gas").

Fig. 6-29: Land use is still multi-functional with windturbines.

All photos: Zond
Systems

Fig. 6-28: A truck drives into the mountains with blades for a wind-turbine.

Fig. 6-30: Human-made flowers complement natural flowers.

Fig. 6-31: Big and powerful, windturbines are gentle giants.

Wind Power Systems

In the early 1980's, aided by tax incentives (1981-1985), energy in the wind was industrially harnessed, growing in leaps and bounds. Companies like Zond Systems and U.S. WindPower gave substance to the idea that sustainable energy sources could make real power (Application A59).

Unlike the petroleum and nuclear industries, the wind energy industry today receives *no* tax credits nor government subsidies of any kind. While the midwest (USA) offer some of the most energetic wind sites, most wind energy installations have been made in California (TechTalk T52).

The New Windmachines

The template of wind farms is easily applied to new sites, and new wind energy technology is emerging (TechTalk T53). The biggest breakthrough in this past decade is the variable-speed turbine.

Application

A59   Wind Power in California

Kevin Cousineau

In 1981, Zond Systems and U.S. WindPower began their first wind projects. These projects gathered small individual turbines and clustered them onto areas which have become known as wind farms or wind parks. Zond's first wind farm went online on Christmas eve of 1981, producing the first commercially-generated electricity to be sold to Southern California Edison from wind power. In 1985 alone, Zond installed over 1000 turbines, in less than six months (an industry record that still stands).

After the demise of the Federal Tax credits in 1985, many people believed that this industry would disappear. Not only did the industry survive, it progressed. Today more than 45% of all commercial wind turbines operating have been placed into service since the loss of those tax credits (Techtalk T53). Without subsidies or tax credits, the wind industry still helps support us all by its tax payments at the end of each quarter.

Most Americans are not aware of the operational excellence of our modern wind turbines. In 1989 and 1990, and to a larger extent in 1991, the wind industry in California generated nearly 1.5% of California's entire electrical energy demand (over 2.5 billion kilowatt hours in 1990). This may seem small when compared to the national usage, but with California the seventh largest economy in the world, it is a significant amount of electrical energy. In fact, it is equivalent to the energy required to operate a city the size of San Francisco or Washington, D.C. And all of this energy came from the wind.

The Virtues of Wind Power

Wind power is renewable energy. By this we mean that it is a resource of where the availability is not depleted through its use. Unlike coal, oil, and natural gas, the availability of wind power is virtually limitless. As long as the nearest star, our sun, continues to shine—and scientists tell us that is for another 4 to 5 billion years—there shall be wind. Why? Wind power is solar energy that has already been converted to mechanical motion. This explains why wind machines are so efficient. Depending upon wind velocity, present-day turbines can convert better than 40% of the entire energy available in the wind to electrical power. Modern photovoltaic arrays operate with efficiencies approaching 12%. At best, diesel engine-driven generator systems have a 20% conversion efficiency.

The Future of Wind Power

Even though wind power is now hitting its stride, there is a political stalemate. Marked by protest and the non-availability of power purchase contracts, we will not see further wind power development in California for years to come. There has been press that windmachines represent a visual pollution which is not offset by the air and water pollution that windmachines avoid. Although each new turbine manufactured today produces enough electricity to offset 600,000 pounds of carbon dioxide (a "greenhouse gas") each year, some people only see its effect on their skyline.

Wind power alone could easily provide 25% of our nation's entire energy needs by farming only wind sites of the highest potential. Clearly there is a place in our country's energy mix for wind power.

Fig. 6-32: Windmachines at the Victory Gardens facility.

Fig. 6-33: Running water is 24-hour power.

Existing windplant design is forced to match the rpm of the generator (and, hence, the rotor blades themselves) to the utility line frequency of 60 cycles. Windspeeds that exceed the 20-30 mph range of windplant design, then, cannot be effectively utilized. This is unfortunate, since the power in the wind goes up with the cube of the velocity, and very small changes in windspeed, including those of a gust, result in large energy yields. As well, this untapped power from higher windspeeds must be safely dissipated by braking or spoiling (if the windplant is to survive), increasing the load factor and requiring a stronger structure and a higher cost for the windmachine itself.

The variable-speed turbine dissolves the association of rotor rpm and line frequency "electronically." DC-to-DC technology matches a wide range of input rpm to the grid. The result is more power, lighter windmachines (decreased structural loads) and longer-lasting components in the new turbines.

Techtalk

T53 New Sites and Windmachines

Kevin Cousineau

During the early 90s, Zond Energy Systems completed the 77 MegaWatt Sky River project (Tehachapi, CA), which includes the installation of a privately-owned, 73-mile, 230,000-Volt transmission line dedicated solely to wind power. However, the primary thrust of California wind developers' has been projects outside California. Kenetech completed a 19 MW wind farm in Alberta, Canada, a 25 MW wind farm in Minnesota, and a 35 MW wind farm in Texas. Zond also developed a 6 MW facility in Texas. In the Midwest, projects are planned for Iowa, Wyoming, Texas, Minnesota and Montana as utilities want to supply clean, renewable power without polluting the water or air.

New turbine technology developed for these projects:

Vestas V-39. Designed, developed and manufactured in Denmark by Vestas A/S, this turbine has a blade diameter of 127 feet and produces 500 kiloWatts (kW) of power in winds exceeding 30 miles per hour.

Zond Z40. Designed, developed and manufactured by Zond Energy Systems (Tehachapi, CA), this turbine has a blade diameter of 130 feet. At full output, it produces 550kW in winds exceeding 30 miles per hour. A testament to its rugged design is the survival of 12 of these turbines during a wind storm in western Texas with peak gust velocities exceeding 117 mph. The turbines operated, paused for high wind speeds, and returned to operation when the wind had subsided, automatically (without human intervention).

Kenetech 33k VS. The 33k-VS wind turbine has a blade diameter of 33 meters (108 feet). It is a variable-speed turbine developed by a consortium of the Electric Power Research Institute, Pacific Gas & Electric Company, Niagara Mohawk, and Kenetech. The turbine's power electronics first rectify and excite the induction generator, then convert its rectified output to a constant frequency AC voltage for power line operation at 480 VAC, three phase. The Kenetec 33k-VS has been installed in western Texas, Minnesota, and California. (Operation of the power electronics is similar to the GM Impact electric vehicle.

Enercon E-40. Enercon, a German company, is currently manufacturing the E-40 wind turbine, a variable speed machine. It is also a direct-drive turbine that does not use a gearbox to increase the hub speed. Instead, it utilizes a special design, low-speed synchronous generator and power electronics—a unique approach to wind power technology. Like the Zond Z-40 wind turbine, this turbine has a 40-meter rotor diameter. It produces 500 kW at full output.

Hydroelectric Energy

Hydroelectric means making electricity with water that has potential (flow or pressure). Almost 15% of the energy generated in the USA comes from hydroelectric power. It is a sustainable energy source that can grow safely from developing smaller water sources.

Even seasonal sources of electricity from waterpower have one advantage over solar energy and wind energy: they work 24 hours a day. So, a hydroelectric generator with one-fourth the output of a solar PV array will, in a 24-hour period, generate as many kWh of electricity. Waterpower is also not adversely affected by cloudy or stormy weather.

A difference of temperature of only 36 degrees F. is enough to generate electricity from the ocean.

Fig. 6-34: A closed-cycle OTEC system.

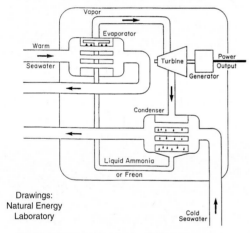

Drawings:
Natural Energy
Laboratory

Fig. 6-35: An open-cycle OTEC system.

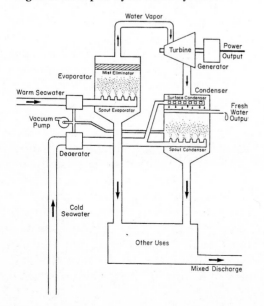

Hydrothermal Energy

A difference of temperature of only 36 degrees F. is enough to generate electricity from the ocean (Application A60). This is found in the difference between the temperature of water at the ocean's surface and the water located several hundred feet below the surface. When the two are connected through an ocean thermal energy conversion (OTEC) plant, the result is generated power. (An OTEC unit operates very much like a refrigerator "running backwards.")

One of the most promising development sites is located off the big island of Hawaii. Noteworthy is that the experimental plant has byproducts which are beneficial to a whole host of community businesses (Techtalk T54). When was the last time a powerplant was such a blessing to a community!

Application

A60 Ocean Thermal Energy Conversion
Luis Vega

In the most recent operation of the ocean thermal energy conversion (OTEC) plant at Keahole Point, Hawaii, desalinated water has been added to the long list of beneficial byproducts of the process. The facility, which has been operation since December 1992, now produces 7,000 gallons of desalinated water per day, a world record for OTEC production.

The principle of OTEC operation is simple. There is energy in the difference of temperatures between surface water and deep water in the oceans. As little as 36 degrees F is needed (in large volume) to generate electricity from the two temperatures of water. Via a 1,000-foot pipe, the OTEC plant brings water from the depths and processes it alongside water from a shallow depth.

There are basically two approaches to the extraction of thermal energy from the oceans: "closed cycle" and "open cycle".

A closed-cycle plant will use warm surface seawater to vaporize a working fluid, such as ammonia, which drives a turbine-generator to produce electricity. The cold deep seawater condenses the same working fluid.

In the open-cycle plant, surface seawater is flash-evaporated in a vacuum chamber. The resulting low-pressure steam drives a turbine-generator. Cold seawater condenses the steam after it has passed through the turbine. It is this feature of the open-cycle system (demonstrated in the Hawaiian OTEC facility) that allows a configuration which will produce desalinated water.

The OTEC facility produces as much as 250 kW of power. Of that, 150 kW is consumed in plant operations, yielding a net 100 kW. Of course, the cold seawater is put to other community service, besides delivering fresh water, before being discharged at several hundred feet of depth in the ocean.

Project personnel at the Pacific International Center for High Technology Research (located at the OTEC facility in Hawaii) now want to build and operate a 5 megawatt OTEC plant to bring this benign technology into the utility mix.

T54 Tapping the Ocean's Energy

OTEC technology generates power on the difference between the temperature of water at the surface of the ocean and water at great depths. This technology is environmentally benign, yet consistently underfunded.

The lack of funding has provided one positive result: lean power. OTEC advocates have had to discover financially beneficial uses for *every* byproduct of the OTEC process. For example, the cold water brought up from the depths is still *very* cold as it exits from the electric power-generating cycle. Routed through pipes in greenhouses, this cold water will condense moisture from air, supplying "drip" irrigation to the greenhouse plants. Routed through aquaculture tanks, the water has enabled the growth of species that would not survive warm Pacific waters. In fact, the water is cold enough to provide non-electric refrigeration of perishables, too.

The newest benefit of the "open-cycle" OTEC plant, beyond the net electric power it generates, is desalinated (fresh) water (review Application A60). Water from deep in the ocean is rich in nutrients and elements. Experimental processes to extract these byproducts are underway.

The benign side-effects of OTEC technology and its usefulness in meeting other needs in the community clearly favor its continued development. Hopefully, more and more people will become aware that it is possible to generate power on the planet without a host of toxic byproducts, such as those found in generating electricity from coal, petroleum, and nuclear sources.

Photo : Reynaldo Cortez

Fig. 6-36: Electrolyzers use electricity to break the water molecule into hydrogen and oxygen.

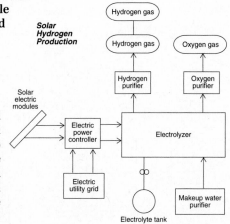

Solar Hydrogen Production

Fig. 6-37: With water and sunshine so abundant on the planet, a "hydrogen economy" is the perfect solution.

T55 Hydrogen from Sun and Wind

Kevin Cousineau

There are bright possibilities for wind and solar energy. Wind power can be used to supply another non-polluting fuel—hydrogen—through the electrolysis of water. Unlike the refining and drilling of oil, the refining of hydrogen from wind turbines also produces oxygen. Freely vented, the oxygen would help offset the carbon dioxide now causing a global rise in temperatures. Furthermore, when burned in the cylinders of an engine, this hydrogen is recombined with oxygen to produce water vapor for exhaust. Such an automobile would be a "zero emission vehicle," producing no air pollution. In the fuel cell, the conversion efficiency is higher and cleaner yet.

Hydrogen produced from wind and solar energy offers a believable promise — ending the present cycle of pollution from the refining and combustion of oil and fossil fuels. Oil reserves, then, would be left for more important uses such as plastics. Imagine the impact on air pollution, 70% of which comes from burning oil (or gasoline)!

Hydrogen

One of the most underrated energy sources is the hydrogen stored in water. A water molecule, or H_2O, is two parts hydrogen and one part oxygen. Electricity can split the bond in this molecule, releasing hydrogen and oxygen. When burned, hydrogen recombines with oxygen to make—water.

Energy sources like the sun and wind will make hydrogen and oxygen from water (Techtalk T55). On a volume basis, hydrogen has only 1/3 the heat of combustion as methane. However, on a weight basis, it has 2.4 times the heat of combustion of methane.

Burned in an engine, only 10% of the hydrogen's energy can be put to work. Turbines like the Nomac design (review Application A62) yield 2-3 times the work from the same quantity of hydrogen. The greatest yield occurs when hydrogen and oxygen are fed into a fuel cell. A *fuel cell* is a unique kind of thermo-chemical chamber that produces electricity from hydrogen and oxygen (or air), and has the byproducts of heat and water. A fuel cell is 3-5 times more efficient in using hydrogen than an IC engine. In mobile applications, the challenges of safe, lightweight storage of hydrogen are addressed with new materials.

Biomass

Fuel that you could "grow" has been a favorite fantasy of many people for a long time. Alcohol is one such fuel, and it comes from biomass, i.e., crops. Biomass is not a new idea. Quite the contrary, biomass was the source of most liquid fuels prior to the development of petroleum.

Since it is hard to stuff a bundle of cornstalks into a gas tank and expect a car to move, biomass is typically converted to a more useful form — methane, ethanol, or methanol.

• *Methane* is produced by biochemical decomposition of the biomass.

• *Ethanol* is derived from fermentation of biomass that is rich in various carbohydrates, i.e., grains, fruits, molasses, etc.

• *Methanol* is derived from destructive distillation of agricultural by-products; i.e., "cracked" from cornstalks, sugarcane, hemp, and other cellulose. Methanol can also be made from fossil fuels. However, it adds highly-toxic formaldehyde to the exhaust emissions when burned in engines.

Methane

Methane is one fuel found in biogas, a fuel derived from the decomposition of manure and biomass in the absence of oxygen. Large amounts of biogas are required to produce significant amounts of methane, the most useable portion of biogas. H_2S (hydrogen sulfide), another component of biogas, is highly corrosive. If the biogas is burned directly, the effect of H_2S (and its rotten-egg odor) is eliminated. Many municipal waste treatment plants power their entire facility from the methane "byproduct" of decomposition.

Methane is difficult to store and use for mobile applications. It needs a pressure of 2,200 psi to be "liquefied." By comparison, propane needs only 300 psi for liquefaction.

Alcohol

Alcohol, in the form of ethanol, is derived primarily from biomass. It is a relatively clean-burning fuel that produces CO_2 as an emission. It is unique, however, in that it "recycles" CO_2 in the atmosphere through photosynthesis. That is, when burned, alcohol from biomass only returns what it has taken.

Alcohol is not a new fuel. Indeed, it was used by farmers and auto drivers in tens of thousands of autos, and farm and military vehicles, from the 1890s through World War II (TechTalk T56)

As a fuel, alcohol has had a troubled history. Prohibition stifled its continued development, as did attacks by the NPI (National Petroleum Institute). Today, alcohol is used as a fuel in the midwest USA. For a long time, Brazil has had a national plan that mandates alcohol use for fuels. Ignorance about its benefits and availability form the primary reasons why it is not more extensively used (Application A61).

T_{56} *Techtalk* — A Brief History of Alcohol Fuel

(1860) Fuel costs per gallon (for steam engines, home heating and lighting): Alcohol, \$.54, whale oil, \$1.62.

(1861) Congress levies civil war tax: \$2.08 on alcohol, 10 cents on kerosene.

(1906) Theodore Roosevelt repeals "whiskey tax," attempting to break up the powerful influence of the Standard Oil trust on the U.S. economy.

(1920) National Prohibition begins. Outlaws the manufacture, sale, or transportation of intoxicating liquors.

(1921) T.A. Boyd, a GM research scientist, declares that "alcohol is the most direct route for converting energy from its source, the sun."

(1926) William Jay Hale, an Ohio chemist, alarms the oil industry with "chemurgy," demonstrating how to make fabric from milk, paper from cornstalks, plastics from soybeans, and fuel from grain.

(1926) Henry Ford builds an automobile body from soybeans.

(1933) National Prohibition ends.

(1922-72) Oil prices remain at \$2 to \$4 per barrel for fifty years.

(1972-80) Oil prices increase to \$32 per barrel in an 8-year span.

(1972) Bureau of Mines study shows high-compression engines modified to run on alcohol give the same power, per gallon, as gasoline, and that alcohol blended with gasoline increases octane rating.

(1973) A Harvard Business School study indicates that the "social" price of oil is \$65-100 a barrel.

(1972-75) The 1970s' oil embargo reduces oil consumption by 6%, through conservation measures adopted by the American public, the purchase of fuel-efficient cars, and a shift to coal for power generation.

The oil industry was embarrassed in 1936 when it was demonstrated that, at the same time they continued to *ridicule* gasohol (a gasoline-alcohol mix) in the USA, they were *touting* its benefits in mixes they were selling overseas in England!

Alcohol from Fossil Fuels

Alcohol, in the form of ethanol or methanol, may also be derived from petroleum. However, a petroleum-based source for alcohol suffers two major problems. First, sulphur is emitted when the fuel is burned. Second, alcohol made from petroleum "adds" to the CO_2 imbalance on the planet. Like any fossil fuel, it releases carbon locked up in extinct plants. The loss of forest growth and millions of acres of rainforest—two of nature's most prolific CO_2 "scrubbers"—diminishes the planet's ability to absorb the carbon contained in fossil fuels. More than 80 percent of our airborne pollution comes from fossil fuel sources.

Photo: MendoMotive

Fig. 6-38: Henry Ford felt that engines should use alcohol fuel so that farmers could grow the fuel to run their tractors.

Fuel from Crops

Rudolph Diesel held the same vision for his powerplant, the Diesel engine, as Henry Ford had with alcohol and the ICE. Diesel designed his engine to run "on a variety of fuels, including vegetable and seed oils." (Rudolph Diesel disappeared at sea off an ocean liner in calm seas.) A number of projects in recent years have revived an interest in powering the diesel engine from biomass-derived fuels.

Non-Sustainable Energy Sources

Fuels that rely on finite (limited amount) energy sources and demonstrate a high pollution index for organic life are called non-sustainable. There are two types here: petroleum and nuclear energy.

Petroleum

The use of petroleum (fossil fuels) has been the predominant source of energy and fuels worldwide for almost a century. (It shows, too!) It comes in many forms: oil, gasoline, diesel fuel, oil shale, coal, propane, methanol, and oil shale are all part of the petroleum family.

The basis for the proliferation of petroleum is simply stated. Oil has a high energy density, access to it can be controlled by a relatively small number of people, and there is virtually no investment involved in locating, extracting, refining, and distributing it. That it continues to be used at the exclusion of almost every other type of energy source is a black mark in the evolutionary history of humankind on the planet.

---

*A*pplication

A 61   ### Biomass to Fuel

"California is the 3rd largest transportation fuels market in the world," says Alma Williams, an ethanol fuels consultant. "The state is also a major agriculture center, producing fruit, grain, cotton, and rice in large quantities. It is uniquely poised to produce *and* use alcohol fuels. Yet it has virtually no ethanol production facilities and industry. Agriculture waste is treated like garbage."

Alma Williams, at one time the executive director of the California Renewable Fuels Council, says that the Midwest-based ethanol fuels industry was surprised to see that California had not initiated an ethanol program. The Council was started to supply information to legislators and regulators, the farming community, and the general public about the potential, particularly in light of the changing transportation fuels market, and the existence of flexible-fuel vehicles. Farmers in the "grain belt" states thrive on the added value this gives any crop. Many produce "fuel" crops like corn, the source of 85% of the alcohol in the Midwest.

Williams contends that most people in California don't even know what she's talking about. "I see rice farmers struggling to dispose of rice straw, now that the Air Resources Board restricts their burning it," Williams says. "Rice straw is a perfect candidate for ethanol fuel production, particularly in light of new technologies developed through the Solar Energy Research Institute (SERI)."

What other materials qualify for conversion to ethanol? "Culled fruit," Williams says. "Also, sawmill residues, wastepaper, slash, and other agricultural residue. Regulators awash in solid waste will stand there and tell me it's not cost-effective to turn the biomass into fuel. They seem to think that if fuel doesn't come out of a barrel from the Middle East, it's not fuel. When was the last time these guys were on a real farm!"

With what is now known about the unhealthy side-effects of fossil fuels on life and the planet, their use today is justified in only one context—the development and widespread conversion of all energy-generating devices to sustainable technologies.

Nuclear Energy

Nuclear energy taps the energy that holds matter together. Once touted as the energy source too cheap to meter, it has fallen on its financial face.

Shadowed by the use to which this awesome power was first put (atomic bomb), nuclear advocates were blinded to the problems inherent in extracting and refining it, using and recycling it, and disposing of the waste generated at every one of these stages. Heavily subsidized and with such a monstrous investment, the nuclear industry has underplayed the breadth and magnitude of these problems. It is still trying to revive itself.

Years ago, I heard a quote that summed up the situation. "God showed humankind how to do nuclear power in the example of our own sun—use only the fusion process and locate it 93 million miles away from all life."

After a childhood dream to be an "atomic scientist,", I was only seven weeks into studying to be a nuclear engineer when I uncovered the truth about nuclear power. It was a major blow. I initially worked to expose the deception of the nuclear power industry, but soon transferred my energy into developing and using sustainable technologies

The Hybrid EV

The battery pack in an EV stores a finite amount of power. However large this amount is or how efficiently it is converted into propulsion, the time will come when the vehicle will require a recharge.

Facilities that will fast-charge or exchange a depleted battery pack with another are needed to make the "pure" EV as workable as cars with gas engines. Until this infrastructure is set in place, there is an alternative that will undoubtedly come into play: the "hybrid EV."

What is a Hybrid EV?

A *hybrid* EV is an electric vehicle that uses two or more power sources. With a battery as one of these power sources, many energy sources compete for a role in the hybrid

"partnership." Solar (PV). Flywheels. Fuel cells. Turbine-generator. An engine-generator.

Of whatever type, the job of this alternate source in the hybrid EV is to augment battery power. This should add to the overall range, performance, or other operational aspects of the EV. Many factors favor a hybrid configuration (Techtalk T57).

Hybrid sources always increase the complexity, initial cost, and overall vehicle weight. It is important to honestly assess their real benefits against their real costs.

The Hybrid Partner

Since the available energy may vary considerably with the type and design, a closer look at these alternatives is in order. Solar cells, the flywheel, the fuel cell, the turbine-generator, and the engine-generator are all possible hybrid partners in the EV.

There is a specific qualification the energy partner will be asked to contribute in an EV's operation. More often, a slow, steady energy rate is expected. Batteries are very good in handling peak loads. So, batteries will handle "sprints" while the energy partner is expected to be there for the long haul.

Series or Parallel Hybrid?

Most hybrid EVs operate in a "series" arrangement. That is, the energy partner is designed to produce electricity and work in series with the electric motor. Let's refer to it as the *auxiliary power unit*, or APU.

How does the APU work? Anytime the APU is operating, it supplies steady, consistent electricity. When you're stopped at the light or stop sign, all of the APU's power is going into the batteries. When you're traveling down the road at 15 mph, some of the APU's power goes to the motor and the remainder goes into the battery pack. At some speed, say 35 mph, all of the APU's output goes into the electric motor. At 50 mph, the batteries supply the additional power (above the APU's output) needed to reach and hold that speed. Generally, battery output will exceed APU output during acceleration, hill climbing, and high speeds.

An alternative to the series hybrid is the "parallel" hybrid. Here, the energy partner produces mechanical motion which it imparts to the wheels in parallel with the electric motor. A vehicle with the engine powering one axle and the electric motor powering the other is an example of a parallel hybrid.

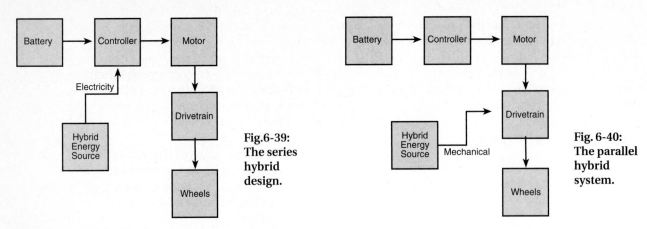

Fig.6-39: The series hybrid design.

Fig. 6-40: The parallel hybrid system.

Virtues of the Hybrid EV

Many factors contribute to the popularity of the idea of using two or more energy sources in the hybrid EV.

•Hybrid EVs address two fears held by the driving public concerning electric vehicles in general: low performance and getting stuck somewhere with a dead battery pack. Pure EVs deliver high performance (speed, acceleration, and hillclimbing ability) at the expense of range and battery life. The presence of an energy partner in the hybrid EV, then, is perceived as a backup energy source that helps overall performance, and provides some insurance against getting stuck in the "boonies" with a depleted battery pack.

•All sources have inherent advantages and disadvantages. Utilizing two or more sources often adds the good features of each source, and offsets the shortcomings inherent in any one source.

•Different energy sources are both available and most useful at different times. You know how far you're going, and can select the appropriate source for the task.

•Hybrids may increase vehicle reliability. You can drive on battery power alone or on the auxiliary power unit (APU), perhaps at a reduced speed. Like any good partnership, both the batteries and APU work well together or independently of each other. If either system fails or becomes inactive, the other may get you home.

•In the hybrid vehicle, the batteries usually handle "peak" loads and the hybrid energy partner is there to provide a smaller but steady flow of power toward propulsion or recharging the battery.

•A hybrid EV is another point for the validity of using lead-acid batteries in the battery pack. Today's lead-acid batteries may demonstrate low power density and low efficiency compared with other battery types. However, they are inexpensive, readily available, and have a recycling industry behind them. Coupled with an energy partner, their disadvantages are offset.

•The hybrid configuration may minimize the *number* and *depth* of charge/discharge cycles the batteries must endure. This increases battery longevity, may permit the use of batteries that cannot survive deep discharge, and limits the exposure of the battery to the effects of sulfation.

•A hybrid relieves the battery of the need to store a large amount of power at one sitting, and to ladle it out over the range of the vehicle in operation.

Solar Cars

Most solar cars are hybrid vehicles (see Chapter 5). In transcontinental races, the energy of sunlight supplies a constant flow of electricity, propelling the vehicle or recharging the batteries. With a practical limit of 100 Watts per square meter (approximately nine square feet), solar cars must be extremely light to work even at speeds that would be safe in street traffic.

Will we be seeing solar-powered cars on the street anytime soon? Not likely. Injecting a gossamer, fragile machine into the midst of fast, heavy, solid, unforgiving cars and trucks on bumpy roads has its shortcomings. To other vehicles, such a vehicle is a moving street bump, unseen, or simply unrecognizable as something to worry about hitting.

In today's EVs, the main virtue of solar energy in a hybrid street machine may be in operating cooling fans or keeping the vehicle's 12V AUX battery topped off. Its contribution to propulsion even in small vehicles is more likely to result in a damaged panel, ineffectual operation (from shading), or outright theft of the solar panel.

The Flywheel

A flywheel is a kinetic energy storage device. A lightweight mass turning at very high rpm in a vacuum can hold an amazing amount of energy. For example, a flywheel module weighing less than 15 pounds can store 1 kWh of electricity and deliver it to a propulsion motor at a rate that generates over one hundred (100) horsepower! A 300-lb bank of flywheel modules equals the output of a 1,200-lb lead-acid battery pack

Flywheel technology is advancing rapidly. Present designs make the flywheel itself an ac motor that is spun up to speed when plugged into utility power. A system similar in effect to a regenerative braking circuit allows power to flow from the flywheel toward the propulsive effort.

Proponents believe that flywheels will altogether substitute for the EV battery pack. Initially, the high cost will limit this possibility to fleet or industry applications. Flywheel modules should be available for hybrid EVs within the next decade.

The Fuel Cell

A fuel cell is unique combustion chamber where hydrogen and oxygen are combined in a thermochemical process to produce heat, water, and electricity. Combining the same two ingredients (hydrogen and oxygen) in an engine, by comparison, produces only one-third the work value and no electricity. Constructed somewhat like a battery, the fuel cells consists of electrodes and separators (membranes) that allow the unique catalytic operation to occur.

There are several types of fuel cells, some of which have demonstrated 40% conversion efficiencies in producing electricity.

Fuel cells do not work with any type of fuel other than hydrogen. However, there must be a source of the hydrogen gas. Hydrogen gas may be stored onboard, in pressurized form or bonded with metal hydrides.

A more common technique to supply hydrogen without storing it is to use a "reformer" to extract hydrogen and oxygen from other fuels, like alcohol, methanol, gasoline, etc. This process is fairly efficient, but it produces emissions. A benefit of the reformer-fuel cell combination is that the heat given off by the fuel cell may be applied to the reformer to, in turn, more efficiently extract the hydrogen from fuels. A major challenge in fuel cell technologies today is the contamination of the fuel cell when "air" is used as the reactant rather than pure oxygen.

The virtue of the fuel cell is its projected role in the solar/hydrogen/electricity cycle that would provide the ultimate, sustainable global energy technology that no corporation or country could monopolize.

Fig. 6-41: Solar cars use electricity from batteries and solar cells.

Photo: National Renewable Energy Labs

Fig. 6-42: Flywheels store electricity as momentum and supply electricity as needed from the motor-generator.

Drawing: U. of Texas (Center for Electromagnetics)

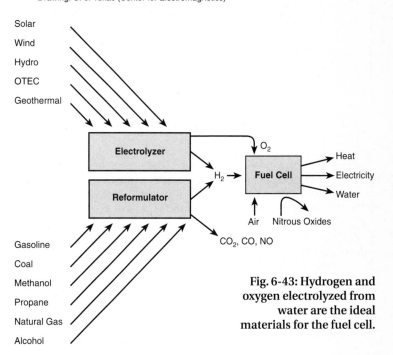

Fig. 6-43: Hydrogen and oxygen electrolyzed from water are the ideal materials for the fuel cell.

The Turbine-Generator

A turbine connected to an electric generator is another energy source for the hybrid EV. The electricity produced from the turbine-generator is connected directly to the DC (battery) bus. Neither the turbine nor its generator are coupled to the drivetrain mechanically.

Many earlier problems with turbines — cost, complexity, size, weight, etc. — are addressed in more recent designs, like the Nomac turbine (Application A62).

The IC Engine

A standard IC engine is a common hybrid energy partner. An engine that powers the wheels directly is at its highest efficiency when the vehicle is at a constant speed and load, i.e., cruising at freeway speeds. Where an electric motor is also able to power the wheels and handle acceleration and hillclimbing in stop-and-go traffic, the combination is a beneficial one.

Arranging both an engine and an electric motor on the same axle gets complex. This explains the popular arrangement in the parallel hybrid of the electric motor powering

---

*A*pplication
62
Nomac Turbine

The Nomac is a gas turbine-driven generator set that will produce 25 kW continuous (35 kW intermittently) with a thermal efficiency exceeding 30%. The complete generator set is 14 inches in diameter and 22 inches long. It has one major moving part, requires no oil or water, and has extremely low emissions.

The Nomac system is a radical departure from previous efforts although the actual technology is extremely conservative.

To appreciate the Nomac approach, first consider a conventional, simple-cycle gas turbine. It consists of a compressor, combustor, turbine, gear box and accessories. First, air is compressed. Then, fuel is added and burned to heat the air. Finally, the air is expanded through the turbine. The turbine produces the power to drive both the compressor and (through the gear box) the output shaft. Add a starter, generator, lubrication system, control system, filters and silencers. The result is a gas turbine.

When this turbine is used in aircraft, the pressure ratio and the turbine inlet temperature would be increased dramatically. This would call for multi-stage components, exotic materials, complex internal cooling systems, etc. The result would be reasonable efficiency but at high cost!

Automobile versions require a recuperator (static) or regenerator (rotating) to reduce fuel consumption by using the heat of the exhaust to preheat the combustion air. However, recuperators are expensive and bulky and regenerators have seals that leak and a short service life.

Nomac starts with a radically new, proprietary concept for a recuperator (patent applied for). It is all prime surface, uses no welding or brazing and cannot leak. Most important, it is inexpensive. It is also hollow, so that the gas turbine can be installed inside. This eliminates most of the ducting, reduces radiated heat losses and results in a very compact package.

As a hybrid partner in an EV, the Nomac turbine drives a generator on a common shaft with air bearings, eliminating additional turbines, bearings, gear boxes, and a lubrication system. The high-frequency output of the generator is rectified to direct current, and the firing angle of the rectifying devices provides the basic electric control. The fuel control is designed to hold a constant turbine inlet temperature over a wide range of output, which maintains high efficiency even with partial loads. The Nomac turbine is inherently multi-fueled, burning unleaded gasoline, #1 diesel, #2 diesel, kerosene, jet fuel, methanol, ethanol or any mix of these fuels.

The final product is a mechanically simple device. There are only two moving parts, the compressor-turbine-generator rotor and the fuel-pump rotor. Manufacturing techniques will be similar to those of a turbocharger when the turbine is produced in large quantities. The complete package should cost less than a reciprocating engine-powered generator, while yielding the range, performance and air conditioning equivalent at low cost and reduced emissions.

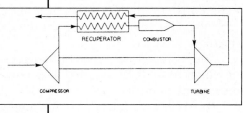

Fig. 6-44: A standard turbine generator.

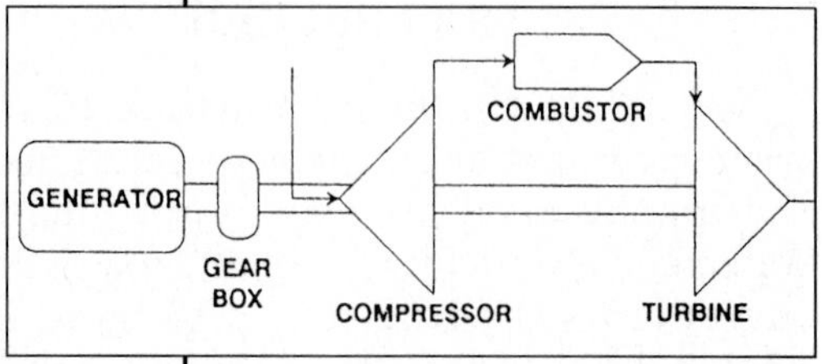

Fig. 6-45: Nomac turbine design.

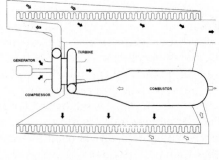

Fig. 6-46: Turbine construction.

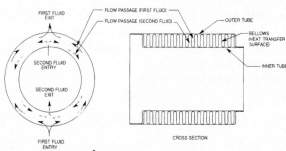

Fig. 6-47: NoMac design details.

one axle (front or rear) and the engine powering the other one. Each power source, then, operates independently of the other, and the vehicle's operator selects either one of them (or both) to use.

Automakers find the parallel hybrid with engine an attractive combination. This type of vehicle will be marketed as an LEV (low-emission vehicle). Electric drive on city streets and engine operation on the freeway could raise the engine's fuel economy and lower its "per mile" emissions. Where the electric drive has a regenerative braking feature, it will recharge the battery pack during stops or downhill driving. If the battery pack is depleted, the regen circuit can supply a constant recharge current while the vehicle operates at freeway speeds. This will act as a "load" to the vehicle in the same way that an air conditioning unit is powered, except the road itself acts as a kind of "V-belt" between the front and rear wheels.

The parallel-hybrid LEV is a valid technology that is, unfortunately, wide open for abuse. With the selection left to the driver/owner for engine or electric drive, there is no way to enforce compliance with mandated air quality standards.

The Engine-Generator

The engine-generator is one of the most widely used energy partners in the hybrid EV. Ideally, it combines the best features of the electric motor with the best features of the ICE. The electric motor contributes its flat torque curve and variable-load characteristics, short-term high-power endurance, and high efficiency. The engine contributes its high power density and fuel availability. In the process, each offsets the disadvantages inherent in the other.

This is not theory. The engine-generator system is new to cars, but it's not a new idea.

Fig. 6-48: An engine-generator helps power this EV.

Actually, it was successfully demonstrated during World War II in submarines! Further testament to its success is the hybrid technology (without the batteries) used in the diesel-electric locomotive, the mainstay of our railroad system.

Limitations of the Engine-Generator

The hybrid EV equipped with an engine-generator is an idea that is more popular with people who don't drive EVs than it is with ones who do. With few exceptions, EV owners that have tried an engine-generator are disappointed with the cost/benefit ratio and eventually abandon it. When questioned, they rarely oppose the idea of the hybrid idea itself. In fact, they often express their willingness to try flywheels and fuel-cells, even turbine-generators.

What reasons do these individuals give for eliminating the engine-generator?

• *Noise and vibration*. While this may be attributed to poor mounting methods, the engine's inherent inefficiency is also suspect. Noise and vibration are two expressions of inefficiency. Turbines, fuel cells, and flywheels are inherently "quiet" because they yield higher efficiencies in converting fuels to mechanical or electrical energy.

• *A high pollution index*. The small engines used in hybrids typically pollute more per kWh produced than the larger engine in a gas-powered car. Small engines, then, spell big pollution.

• *Fears subside*. As these owners used their EVs, their fears of poor performance and range, or getting stuck out, subsided. Soon, they appreciated the substitution of an equal weight of batteries for the APU, on maintenance issues alone!

• *Modified driving habits*. EV owners discovered alternative ways to handle long-distance travel, i.e., bus, rail, and airplane. Renting an IC-engine'd vehicle for the occasional long-distance excursion avoided the cost of a backup vehicle sitting at the curb for its occasional use.

Despite these objections, there is little doubt the engine-generator will find its way into the coming hybrid EV mix. It is also clear that it will exist for political reasons rather than technical, sociological, or environmental ones.

Chapter 7
Inside the Electric Vehicle

Do you need to know "what's under the hood" in order to drive an electric vehicle? Absolutely not. The modern EV is more similar to than different from operating a gas-fueled car. Many people operate cars without the slightest knowledge of how they work. To them, opening the hood of a car would be as alien an experience as taking the back off a TV set.

Photo: David Chung (M. Hackleman Collection)

Fig. 7-1: There's lots of extra space after this vehicle is converted to electric propulsion.

Despite its long history, electric propulsion is new to most people. So, until knowledge about it becomes more widespread, you may be the most knowledgeable person about your own vehicle! A basic understanding of the workings of an EV, then, could be very helpful to a driver or owner at this stage of its evolution.

Don't worry. You won't have to become a mechanic or electrical engineer. Compared with an ICE, EV technology is downright simple. With fewer moving and interdependent parts, EVs are less likely to experience a problem and when they do, are easier to troubleshoot and fix.

This chapter is aimed at familiarizing the novice with EV components and their functions in the overall operation of the EV. Scan the Techtalk sidebars if you are hungry for more details. The next chapter, Chapter 8, will continue this treatment, focusing on component selection, installation tips, operational idiosyncrasies, and maintenance issues.

The variety of ways that EV components may be applied is best revealed in the Applications. Duplicating the layout of an application that is similar in size, weight, and scope to your own is likely to result in a successful design.

Major EV Components

An electric car is composed of four (4) major components: electric motor, batteries, controller, and charger. There are also four major categories of support hardware for the EV system: interface hardware, control and safety circuitry, AUX power, and monitoring (Fig. 7-2).

Briefly:

The *electric motor* performs the same function as an engine. It is a prime mover. It converts energy into mechanical motion. In the ICE (internal combustion engine), the energy source is a fuel like gasoline, diesel fuel, LPG, alcohol, or hydrogen. In the electric motor, the energy source is electricity. It can be produced from fuels like coal and oil, or it can come from solar cells, windmachines, and hydropower. The electric motor is bolted to the transmission or drivetrain through an adaptor plate.

The *batteries* are both the "gas tank" and "fuel" in an electric vehicle. In a sense, batteries store the electricity that the electric motor needs. In reality, batteries are electro-chemical devices. When charged from a source of electricity, a chemical solution changes "state." When connected to a load (i.e., the electric motor), the chemical solution reverts to its previous state, and electric current flows.

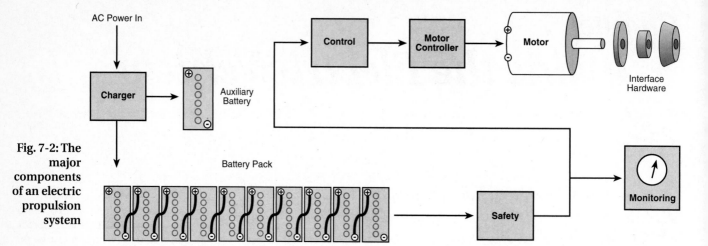

Fig. 7-2: The major components of an electric propulsion system

The ***controller*** is an electronic device that controls the flow of electricity from the batteries to the motor. The controller acts somewhat like a monster light-dimmer switch, and is linked to the accelerator pedal through its potbox. The controller supplies the motor with current in the same proportion that your foot depresses the accelerator pedal. When your foot is off the pedal, no electricity flows whatsoever.

The ***charger*** is another electronic device. Its job is to replenish the batteries after their energy has been consumed by the motor in operation. A charger has an input side and an output side. The input side plugs into an energy source which may come in a variety of forms. Solar farms. Wind turbines. Hydroelectric generators. The utility grid. The output side of the charger is connected to your EV's battery pack. The charger's job is to match voltage, current, frequency and duration so that electricity flows from the source to the battery pack and recharges it.

Interface hardware involves mechanical devices that fit the electric propulsion machinery to the vehicle itself. The adaptor plate mates the electric motor to the vehicle's transmission or drivetrain. The motor mount supports the electric motor, using old engine mounting points or new ones. The battery frame supports battery weight by tying into the vehicle's own structural members. The battery box encloses the battery pack to contain fluids and gases, maintain battery temperature, and permit access for maintenance. (More detail on interface hardware will be found in Chapter 8.)

Control and Safety equipment. A variety of components add control and safety features to the electric drive. Some work to enhance control. Others are designed, in the event of a problem, to prevent widespread component damage or operator injury. The contactor allows the vehicle's operator to enable or disable the propulsion system from a keyswitch. Fuses protect the battery pack (and you) against the hazard of a short circuit. A circuit breaker helps isolate the battery pack from the electric drive during servicing and maintenance. Interconnects wire the batteries together in the pack and cables electrically join the major subassemblies together into working circuits.

Auxiliary loads and 12V power. Horn, headlights, windshield wipers, turn signals, brake lights, and many other electrical devices are designed to work on 12VDC. These auxiliary loads are just as important in an EV as they are in an ICE car. An auxiliary battery, like the one found in most cars, is one possibility for supplying this power. Since the alternator (or generator) is missing in the EV, the auxiliary battery is replenished during charging. Or a DC-DC converter is used, supplying 12VDC by using the larger voltage of the propulsion battery pack as a source. Your system may use both an AUX battery and a DC-DC converter.

Monitoring equipment. Instrumentation and other other indicators enable the operator to monitor the operation of the electric propulsion system. A voltmeter will display pack voltage; a dual-scale unit will keep tabs of the 12VDC system, too. An ammeter shows the amount of motor current. The Amp-hour meter is the closest thing to a fuel gauge in the EV, showing the amount of energy contained in the battery pack. Indicator lights and other instruments may further extend the capabilities of monitoring the EV system.

EV COMPONENTS

In this chapter, EV components are discussed in subsections under their general function. The process is repeated in Chapter 8, showing components selection, installation, and use. Further detail about EV components is scattered throughout the book. Again, the best way to understand the importance and function of components is through their interaction with one another, as revealed in the Applications themselves.

Basics first! Let's look at the four (4) major components found in the EV: the electric motor, batteries, controller, and charger.

The Electric Motor

The electric motor is the heart and soul of the electric vehicle (EV). The electric motor's job is to convert energy from one form into another. In this case, electricity (from batteries) is converted into mechanical (rotational) motion, and transferred, often through a drivetrain, to the wheels (Fig 7-3).

The objective of this section is to ensure that the electric motor you choose in a conversion or a scratchbuilt will give you the most value for your dollar. Whether you know it or not, you want a motor that works well for the dollars you invest. Almost any motor may "work." By the time you've finished with this section, you will be armed with the information that will allow you to select a motor that "works well."

Motor theory or motor principles will not be described in any detail in this section. There are probably a hundred books on the subject of electric motors. If you want to know more, check the local library. Sources & References lists a few books I've found particularly helpful.

There are three words of importance in the selection of an electric motor for an EV: match,

mate, and cost-benefit. First, the motor must match the application. Second, it must mate to the rest of the machinery. And, third, it must meet your personal cost/benefit ratio.

Motor Types & Ratings

Motors are defined by their type, characteristics and ratings. Series, shunt, and brushless DC are examples of motor types. The characteristics of a motor are strongly influenced by their type. Torque vs rpm, cw or ccw rotation, and low-end vs high-end performance are examples of characteristics. Voltage and current ranges, HP values, and weight are examples of motor ratings.

A Basic Motor

A basic motor may be described as a wire rotating in a magnetic field. Through clever application (or manipulation) of the laws of physics that apply to electricity and magnetism, the wire chases the field in the same way a dog will chase its tail. Only, in the case of the motor, useful work is accomplished.

Motors are composed of stators, rotors, frames and a commutation system (Fig. 7-4). By definition, the stator is the stationary portion of the motor and the rotor is the rotating part. Either the stator or the rotor may constitute the "wire" or "field" of the motor's workings. The frame forms the structural shell of the motor, supporting the stator directly and the rotor indirectly through bearings. The commutation system may transfer power or describe the relationship (or phase) between the stator and the rotor. If the phase is too great (the dog can't see the tail) or too little (the dog catches the tail), the circle is broken, the motor stops, and work (or entertainment) ceases.

Categories of Motors

There are two general categories of motor: ac and DC. This describes the kind of electricity the motor uses. Alternating current (ac) may be found at the standard household wall socket. Direct current (DC) is the kind of electricity a battery will supply.

In the DC category, there are five types of motors: series, shunt, compound, permanent magnet, and brushless DC. In the ac category, there is one type of motor we'll consider: induction.

Fig. 7-3: The electric motor is bolted to an existing transmission.

DC Motors

The DC motor is designed to work with DC current, which includes chopped (pulsating) DC, like that produced by modern controllers. The primary differences between the five types of DC motors has to do with *how* the magnetic field is produced (Techtalk T58).

In the remainder of this section, we'll look at the characteristics peculiar to each of these motor types, and what works best, under what circumstances, in the EV. Refer to the motor chart (Techtalk T59) for more detail on the torque, horsepower, speed control, direction of rotation, reversal of rotation, and regenerative braking of each motor type.

The Series Motor

In the series motor, the electric current that flows through the armature also passes through the field (see Fig. 7-5). The armature and field, then, are wired in series. If you opened up one of these motors, you would see that the field windings are composed of a very few windings of wire that are very large in diameter. Where the field coils are passing the full motor current (hundreds of amps), only a few windings of wire will produce a strong magnetic field.

Generally, the series motor is widely used in EVs of all sizes and types. In low-speed applications, such as industrial trucks and golf cars, it is considered a workhorse motor. In street and highway cars, it is strong, economical, and available in a variety of horsepower ratings.

The Shunt Motor

In the shunt motor, the field windings are paralleled with, or shunted across, the armature windings (see Fig. 7-6). In this case, the field coils will draw their current separately from the batteries. Here are several characteristics of shunt motors.

Generally, the shunt motor works best at the high end of the speed range. It has a natural inclination to maintain a constant speed. In EV applications, the added complexity of controlling both the field and armature makes the shunt motor less popular than the series motor. As well, its proportional torque-current relationship makes startup under load more difficult at low rpm, requiring a clutch and more gearing than a series motor.

The Compound Motor

The compound-wound motor (or compound motor) is a hybrid, deriving its name from the existence of both series and parallel field coils within it (Fig. 7-7). The compound motor combines the best features of both the series motor and shunt motor. The "series" windings give good torque at low motor rpm during startup, acceleration, and hillclimbing. The "shunt" bias gives good no-load speed control at high motor speeds, and higher overall efficiency at "cruise" speeds.

Generally, the compound motor would seem a better candidate for use with EVs than the series motor. However, the extra set of windings (and control circuitry) adds

T_{58} *echtalk*

Types of DC Motors

There are five types of DC motors. They differ primarily in the way in which the magnetic field is produced or wired.

In three of these motor types — series, shunt, and compound — the field is generated electro-magnetically. This means that the magnetic field itself comes from electricity flowing through a wire that is wound into a coil. These coils are referred to as field windings, or simply fields.

The way the field coils are wired electrically in respect to the armature's windings defines the type. A *series* motor has its field winding in series with the armature. A *shunt* motor has its field winding shunted across (or paralleled with) the armature. And the *compound* motor has, as the name implies, two field windings, one in series and one wired in shunt.

In the remaining two DC motor types, PM (permanent magnet) and brushless DC, the magnetic field is generated by magnets. In the *PM* motor, the magnets are stationary and surround the rotating (armature) windings. In the *brushless DC* motor, the main (armature) windings are stationary and the magnets are affixed to the rotor.

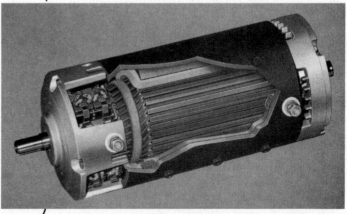

Fig. 7-4: A cutaway of a series motor

additional cost and complexity to the motor. The compound motor's only hope of future use is the increasing competition from ac drives. It may force the DC motor manufacturers to absorb the additional costs of constructing compound motors for the benefits of high-end performance and efficiency they promise.

The Permanent Magnet (PM) Motor

The PM (permanent magnet) motor develops its field flux with permanent magnets instead of electromagnetic field windings. The PM motor, then, supplies a constant field without any consumption of field current.

PM motor operation falls squarely on the control of armature current and voltage. The lack of field coils somewhat simplifies the construction of the PM motor, resulting in a lower cost and lower pricetag. To ensure a strong field, the heavier magnets are stationary and the armature winding spins. Brushes and a commutator are used to route motor current to and from the motor.

The Brushless DC Motor

The idea of a brushless motor has intrigued motor designers for years. The brushless DC motor is similar to a standard PM motor but is different in that the position of the windings and magnets are reversed. That is, the main windings are stationary and magnets are affixed to the rotor. The advantage? The brushes are eliminated.

The characteristics of the brushless motor combine the benefits of the series motor with those of the PM motor. Coupled with the more simple design and fabrication of fixed power windings, the virtues of the brushless DC motor are smaller size, lighter weight, and improved efficiency for the same horsepower of other DC motors.

The brushless DC motor does more than eliminate brushes and increase the HP/pound ratio. It blurs the distinctions between DC and ac motors. Modern electronics has made high-power electronic switches (like the mosfet) available inexpensively. For example, Uniq Mobility uses three-phase stator windings in its brushless DC motor, much like the ac induction motor counterpart. Six (6) times the number of output circuits are needed in the brushless DC motor's controller compared with one for a comparable series DC motor. The higher cost of electronics, then, is justified in the light of a higher power-to-weight ratio and the simplicity of manufacturing processes for the motor. In mass production, electronic devices become less expensive, too.

AC Motors

Today, the electricity for the motor in an EV comes from a battery pack. Since the battery's chemistry produces DC electric current, a DC motor seems the obvious choice in an EV. Yet, for a very long time, many people have sought a way to use an ac motor in an electric vehicle. Why?

The "limitations" of the DC brush motor are as obvious to the ac motor crowd as they are to the brushless DC motor crowd. In stationary applications, the ac motor had surpassed the cost/benefit ratio of the brush DC motor by mid-century. With higher voltages and frequencies, the parts got proportionally smaller in ac motors for the same horsepower and torque. This translated into less weight and higher rotational speeds. Obstacles aside, the potential benefits were tantalizing: better overall motor control and performance, less weight, and simpler construction.

Even in the 1980s, using an ac motor in an EV was a "bridge too far". The obstacles were formidable. An inverter was needed to change the DC into ac. First, the DC had to be "vibrated" into ac. While high frequencies were desired, the switching power supply was in its infancy. The electronic power devices of the day were temperamental, relatively low-power, expensive, and switched (turned on and off) at low speed. So, early ac controllers were big, bulky things that were expensive to build and worked marginally, when they weren't blowing up!

Things have changed. Twenty-five years ago, it was an engineering feat to reduce a room-size computer into something the size of a filing cabinet. Today, the same performance is available from a few computer chips. After a decade of application, inverter technology has evolved to its present rugged and reliable state. With the obstacles removed, the idea of an ac motor that runs off a DC battery pack is not so odd at all. In fact, the electronics have reached the point where the advantages of ac motors—light weight, high efficiency, simple assembly, and compactness—can begin to compete with their DC counterparts.

In the ac category, actually a number of motor types are available. Synchronous ac. Variable reluctance. Induction. Synchronous

Characteristics of DC Electric Motors

Motor Type	Torque/Current	Horsepower	Motor Control
Series	Torque rises with the square of current. At *twice* the current, there is (2)², or *four* times the torque. As the load increases, the series motor digs in and delivers raw power—it has a reputation of a real workhorse. Less efficient at high rpm and large variations in load.	Rating is continuous (100%). A 20 HP unit—common in EVs weighing 2,500-3,500 lbs—is likely to deliver 95% of work of engine rated at 100 HP. Will safely deliver 4-6 times its rating for short periods. 10 HP yields 55 mph; more helps with startup and hill climbing.	Use electronic unit. Motor speed regulated by varying voltage or current to the field and armature. Depends on external loads for speed regulation. "Unloaded," it will overspeed (and damage or destroy motor). Avoid, or install an rpm limiter.
Shunt	With fixed field, torque varies proportionately with armature current supplied by electronic controller. Able to maintain a constant speed independent of load, but sluggish when started under load. Will not overspeed. Not recommended for use with larger EVs.	Available in a wide range of HP ratings, all continuous (100%). Depends on full field strength, particularly at low rpm. Use an electronic controller on armature and a separate controller (simple or electronic) on field for high-end adjustment.	Use electronic unit to control armature. Maintain constant field strength up to upper rpm. Weakening field (less voltage and, thereby, current) at high rpm will increase motor speed (rpm) by 25%. Use full field strength as load increases or rpm drops, or may overheat.
Compound	Averages best features of series and shunt motor. Windings have "bias" to work more like series or shunt motor at time of manufacture. Good low-end torque, but less than squared factor of a series motor current.	Delivers both low-rpm torque and high-rpm efficiency. It requires high-current control circuitry of the series winding and armature. Simple circuitry helps "tune" the shunt winding for high end efficiency. efficiency at cruise speeds. Hard to find for EV usage.	Use *two* electronic control units—one for series field and armature, other for shunt field. Series coil may be bypassed somewhat after startup to use shunt field for good benefit at higher rpm (vehicle speed). See characteristics of series and shunt motors.
Permanent Magnet	PM motor has a starting torque that is greater than the more common compound motors and less than that of a series motor. RPM increases with voltage, current increases proportional to load.	Lack of field coils makes the PM motor an attractive, low-cost solution for fractional horsepower applications. Motors using permanent magnets (excluding brushless DC motors) with ratings above 2-3 HP are rare.	Motor speed (rpm) related directly to voltage supplied to it. Constant field flux makes simple control circuits (i.e, series-parallel) work but offer more 'drag.' Use electronic controllers for best vehicle operation.

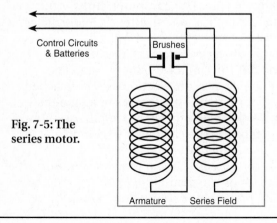

Fig. 7-5: The series motor.

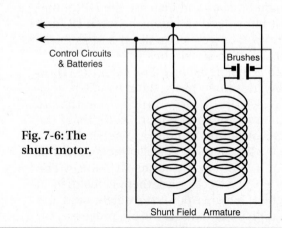

Fig. 7-6: The shunt motor.

Direction/Rotation	Reversal of Rotation	Regen Braking	Notes
Look for factory clockwise (CW) or counter-clockwise (CCW) rotation. Re-settable. May use as much as a 20^0 degree timing advance. Some engines (i.e., Honda) rotate in a direction opposite that of other engines.	Use a DPDT contactor to reverse polarity of armature windings relative to field windings. Helps back up a vehicle with single-ratio drive. Posts A1 & A2 are armature, F1 & F2 are field. Observe design rotation direction.	Difficult to accomplish in smooth, safe way with external contactors and separate field excitation. EVs operated in hilly country should use an electronic controller with a built-in regenerative circuit. See notes.	Motor of choice for conversions. Lightweight vehicles have less need for regen feature. If regen is used, install to work partially off release of accelerator pedal, the rest by depressing the brake pedal.
Shunt motors may be biased (by brush plate position) for cw or ccw rotation. As with series motor, the direction of rotation is determined by the position of the field windings relative to the armature windings.	Reversed by shifting the field windings relative to the armature windings. Since the field windings use small amounts of current, a relatively small DPST relay may be used for electrically reversing the motor,	Shunt motors without an electronic controller can have a controlled regen feature by varying field strength. However, use with a controller with built-in regen and keep normal field strength.	Shunt motors may be found in older EVs. If their controller still functions, this is a good deal. Otherwise, don't expect to find a shunt motor offered today for an EV application.
Has a designed direction of rotation. Look at the nameplate or contact the manufacturer to determine if it is cw or ccw. Motor will heat excessively in operation if rotation is incorrect.	Important that both of the field windings, series and shunt, maintain the same relative orientation with each other. DPDT contactor should shift the polarity of the armature with respect to the series and shunt windings.	Regen braking in the compound motor is similar in every way to regen braking a series motor. Ensure that any field-weakening feature (for high speed operation) gives normal field strength to motor during regen.	Some older EVs used compound motors. These are good units to use in an EV if they were manufactured with bias to the series field. Use standard electronic controller on series field & armature.
Omnidirectional, rotating cw or ccw with equal efficiency. Although the brushes could be biased to run in either direction, the 2-3 Hp limitation of size makes this unnecessary.	The direction of rotation of a PM motor is easily reversed by switching the polarity of the power supplied to it. Use a DPDT relay with contact ratings equal to highest current.	Constant magnetic field makes PM motor ready to supply regen. Induced by shifting into a lower gear, re-wiring pack from series to parallel, or going downhill—unless controller lacks regen option.	The magnets in a PM motor can be de-magnetized (permanently) with excessive current or heat. Use an electronic controller in high-load applications to minimize this effect.

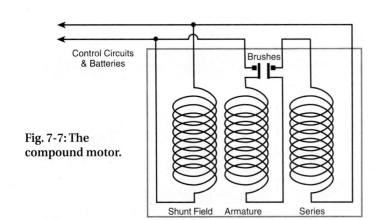

Control Circuits & Batteries

Brushes

Fig. 7-7: The compound motor.

Shunt Field   Armature   Series

Notes:
• Reversing circuits for these motors. Review Techtalk T68 and Fig. 7-22 through Fig. 7-25, page 203.
• Finding and selecting motors. Review Chapter 8.
• Regenerative and dynamic braking. Review Techtalk T65 through T67.
• Controllers for these motors. Review Chapter 8.

and variable reluctance motors are still in the prototype stages. They have not appeared in any vehicles that demonstrate their potential benefits. For this reason, only the induction ac motor will be discussed.

Induction AC Motors

The induction motor is one of the most efficient and simple motors in existence. It

rivals the modern transformer in its capacity to handle enormous power with few losses. The reason is simple. The induction motor *is* a transformer. By design, the primary windings are wrapped into a cylindrical shape and *induce* voltage and current into the secondary windings.

The most obvious benefit here is that the induction motor eliminates the need for both commutator and brushes. Like the transformer, steel laminations are bound and wrapped with copper to make a lightweight, rugged rotor.

AC motors offer many benefits (review Techtalk T59). As a "rotary transformer," the induction motor inherits all of the benefits of the transformer itself.

The Importance of AC Power

Even when it was first introduced, the transformer was a marvel of simplicity and efficiency. With the vision brought to this technology by Nikola Tesla, the ac generator was invented and perfected. Coupled with the transformer, the AC generator made the transmission of electrical current over long distances possible (Techtalk T60).

DC vs AC Drives

Which system will you use in your EV? AC or DC?

As of the mid-1990s, you can purchase a DC system (motor and controller) for 30-50% of the cost of an ac system. AC drive systems are more electronic-intensive and generally less available as off-the-shelf hardware.

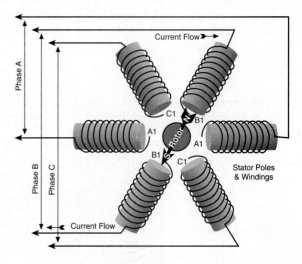

Fig. 7-8: Inside the induction motor

This imbalance is likely to end within the next decade. There are definite limits to commutating electric horses through brushes! AC motors are demonstrating higher operational efficiencies and better horsepower-to-weight ratios than their DC equivalents.

Electronic hardware gets cheap in mass production, benefiting both DC and ac motor drives. However, the ac drive system uses a simpler and cheaper motor than a DC one, and it is this factor that will align off-the-shelf ac and DC drive systems in price by the year 2005. As the demand for lightweight, high-power propulsion systems increases, the use of ac systems will gain prominence, although it may take decades.

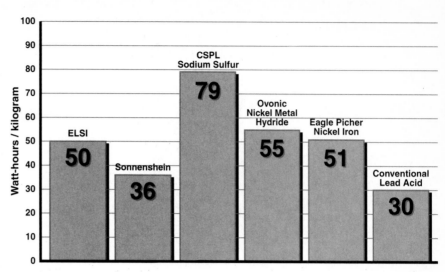

Fig. 7-9: Types of batteries available for use in EVs

Batteries

The selection of the batteries for the EV is one of the most important decisions you will make. This will dictate the payload and performance — acceleration, speed, and range — an EV will deliver. Batteries influence (and are influenced by) the vehicle's operating weight.

In the first part of this chapter, the basics, ratings, and characteristics of batteries will be covered. Ratings include voltage, capacity, weight, cycle depth. Characteristics include energy density, power density, operating temperature, etc. In the next chapter, we will go shopping for batteries, design their placement in the vehicle, install them, and learn how to use and care for them.

The Basics of Batteries

The batteries used in most EVs are similar in some respects to the lead-acid battery used in an ICE car to start the engine. Lead-acid informally describes the chemical action that absorbs electricity, "stores" it, and produces electricity as needed.

Other combinations of electrolytes and materials—nickel-metal hydride, silver-zinc, nickel-cadmium, sodium-sulfur, etc.—have similar reactions to electricity as the lead-acid battery. In fact, these terms define them as types of batteries. All of them can be (or have been) used in electric vehicles (Fig. 7-9).

Lead-acid technology has been the battery of choice for EV use for more than a century.

Lead is plentiful and cheap. The lead-acid battery is simple to construct. It is also 100% recyclable.

With the renewed interest in EVs as the propulsion system of choice for the 21st century, other battery types will compete with lead-acid technology. Some will find a niche in the EV market, even in this decade.

Which type will dominate and find itself in the mass-produced EVs of the 2010 models? Ultimately, the one that offers the best cost-benefit ratio will survive. In 1995, all of the alternate battery types are still undergoing testing, are generally unavailable for purchase and are more expensive than the lead-acid battery battery pack.

For these reasons, this chapter will focus on the use of lead-acid batteries in the EV. Even if you eventually use another type, you'll find that most of this information still applies. A battery is, after all, a "black box.". What's inside is less important than what it *does* for you and your EV!

What is a Battery?

A battery is a group of electrochemical cells that are packaged together in a tough rubber or plastic case (Fig. 7-10). In the wet lead-acid battery, a cell is composed of alternating layers of two types of rectangular-shape lead "plates" sandwiched together. Each type of plate is terminated in an interconnect that is either positive or negative and is connected to all other plates of its type in the cell. A very thin insulating material is inserted in the lead sandwich between each plate in the stack to prevent the different types of plates from

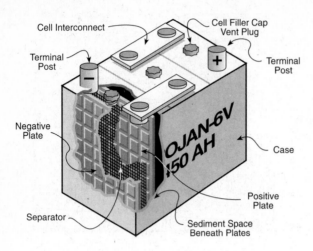

Fig. 7-10: The inside of a lead-acid battery

shorting out against one another. The packaged plates are then submerged in electrolyte, a very weak sulfuric acid solution.

As in all types of cells, these "plates" are electrodes. The positive (+) one, or anode, is mostly lead-peroxide (PbO_2) and the negative (-) one, or cathode, is sponge lead (Pb). The dilute sulfuric acid ($H2SO_4$) electrolyte provides a path for the electrons between the cathode and anode, and the reverse, as part of the charge or discharge cycle.

Cells are packaged into two convenient voltages: six-volt (6V) and twelve-volt (12V). Each cell produces a bit more than two volts (2.1V) of potential. Thus, a 6V battery is comprised of three cells and a 12V battery has six cells. If the battery is not a sealed-type, the 6V battery is identified by its three vent caps, and the 12V battery by six vent caps.

Lead-acid batteries are delivered to the retail store without the electrolyte added, to ensure a long shelf life. Still, each battery has been given a positive, dry charge. When purchased, the battery is activated by adding the electrolyte and is ready to go to work.

How does a battery work? Briefly: during discharge, as electricity leaves the battery, acid is absorbed by the plates. When nearly exhausted, the battery's electrolyte solution becomes as close to water as acid rain. When recharged, as the battery absorbs electricity, acid is driven out of the plates, the specific gravity of the electrolyte increases (becomes more acidic), and the battery fills up with energy.

Battery Ratings

There are three major ratings to consider for your EV's batteries—capacity, voltage, and cycle depth.

Capacity

A battery's capacity describes the amount of energy it will store.

Note the word "energy" instead of "electricity." A battery does not store electricity. Rather, the electricity that is put into a battery during charging causes a chemical reaction, and a change of "state" occurs. This is a reversible reaction. When a "load" is connected to the battery, the chemical reaction is reversed, releasing electricity.

A battery is not a bucket. True, electricity can be pumped into a battery until it reaches a "full" condition. Conversely, electricity can be taken out of a battery until it is "dead," or completely discharged. Still, when filled and emptied quickly, some of the energy will get lost. Many other factors will affect how much useful electrical energy is actually there. Temperature, the rate of charge and discharge, age, and battery type will all affect a battery's true capacity.

Manufacturers have developed several rating systems to help quantify a battery's capacity. Ampere-hour, reserve capacity, and kWh are three of these systems (Techtalk T61).

The *Ampere-hour* method defines capacity by its ability to deliver a constant current over a long period of time (i.e., 20 hours).

The *reserve* method measures capacity as the number of minutes a battery will deliver a specified discharge rate (i.e., 75 Amps).

The *kWh* method defines capacity as the amount of energy (Volts x Amps x time) pumped into a discharged battery to bring it to a fully charged state.

Interpreting Capacity Ratings

A battery doesn't know its own rating. It delivers current, to the best of its ability, at the rate specified by the load itself.

Each rating system (Ah, reserve, and kWh) gives you a general idea of capacity. What happens if you discharge it at a greater rate? Or, as in driving an EV, at variable rates? Discharge rates of 100, 200, and 400 Amps are typical in an electric vehicle during acceleration, higher speeds, and hill climbing. You will not find batteries with rating systems that reflect these discharge rates.

Is the battery a fuel tank of indeterminate size? Yes and no. Yes, you will find it difficult to predict a vehicle's range with any of these rating systems. And, no, it's not impossible to predict capacity. Here you must rely on rules of thumb and experience.

Don't be alarmed. You have very few choices in the matter of selecting a battery that will work in an EV. The standard battery pack of an EV will have ratings of 110 Ah for 12V units, and 220 Ah for 6V units. That's because, at 60-70 pounds each, this is about as much weight as you'll want to be juggling when building your electric vehicle!

Voltage

By definition, a battery consists of two or more cells wired together. A lead-acid type cell produces approximately 2.1 Volts. Thus, a six-volt battery has three cells (6.3 Volts) and a twelve-volt battery has 6 cells (12.6 Volts).

Most 6-Volt batteries and 12-Volt batteries use fill caps. Thus, a battery's voltage can often be determined at a glance. There are three (3)

---

*T*echtalk

T 61 Battery Capacity Rating Systems

Manufacturers have developed several rating systems to help quantify a battery's capacity: Ampere-hour, reserve capacity, and kWh.

Ampere-hour. The oldest system that describes a battery's capacity is the Ampere-hour. Or Amp-hour. Or, if you've got to write it a dozen times, Ah.

The amp is a unit of measure of current flow. Hour, of course, is a measure of time. Multiplying the two together gives the Amp-hour value. In the rating, the number preceding the Ah is this value. 60 Ampere hours and 205 Ah are examples. The larger the value, the greater the capacity of the battery.

The Ah rating, by itself, is useless. A battery designed to deliver 3 Amperes for 20 hours will *not* deliver 20 Amperes for 3 hours, or 60 Amperes for one hour, or 120 Amperes for 1/2 hour. Yet, if you multiply the Amperes by the hours for each of these examples, you'll get a 60 Ah *value*. Chemistry and heat losses (due to internal resistance) are two reasons why higher discharge rates result in less capacity.

Battery manufacturers, then, specify the Ah rating for a discharge rate in hours. C/20 is one such standard, where C is capacity, and 20 is hours. The SLI (starting-lighting-ignition) battery in an ICE car, for instance, is given a 20-hour rate. Dividing the Ah rating by 20, then, yields the rate of discharge. A manufacturer will guarantee that a 60

Ah automotive battery will deliver 3 Amps for 20 hours.

Batteries designed for applications like golf carts or marine propulsion systems are sometimes given C/6 or C/8 ratings.

What's wrong with this system? It's odd to rate an SLI battery at an Ah capacity with a C/20 rate when, in fact, it is really designed to deliver a walloping amount of power, like 300-500 Amps, for a few minutes. In an ICE car, the battery has one main function: to start the engine. And it won't do that at the rate of 3 Amps in 20 hours!

In this light, it is important to realize that Ah capacity is less a measure of what the battery will *do* in service and moreso a method of standardization between battery types and sizes. Obviously, if you don't know what rating system is being used, a battery with an advertised C/20 value will appear more attractive than one with a C/6 value even when they're identical. Know your battery ratings!

Reserve Capacity. Another rating system is "reserve capacity." It is a variation on the theme of the Ah rating. It is expressed as the number of minutes the battery will deliver power at a specific rate.

For the SLI battery in a gas car, the reserve capacity acknowledges a discharge rate of 25 Amps. This rate approximates the "average load" a battery in an ICE car might experience when there's alternator trouble. For example, a reserve capacity of 35 minutes means you have that much time to get your car to a service station, with the headlights and windshield wipers on, before the car

will stop for lack of ignition energy.

Batteries designed for use in golf carts typically use a 75-Amp rate for the "reserve capacity,". For example, a six-volt battery rated at 220 Ah at a C/20 (20-hour discharge rate) is likely to have a reserve capacity of just over an hour.

kWh Capacity. A third way to describe the amount of energy contained in a battery pack is the kWh rating. A kWh is a unit of measurement of energy and work. A thousand watts (or 1 kW) consumed in an hour's time is one (1) kWh. Two thousand watts in a half-hour period and 250 Watts in a 4-hour period also equals one kWh.

The kWh rating of a battery pack reflects the amount of electricity that must be put into it to bring it to a 100% SOC from a depleted state. A 12V battery is considered discharged when its voltage drops to 10.5 Volts. A 6V battery has a discharged voltage of 5.25V.

Recharging a battery pack will require a number of amps for a number of hours. Not surprisingly, the Ah rating of a battery, particularly at the C/20 rate, lacks only the voltage element in describing the amount of energy a pack contains in the kWh rating system. A 120V pack using batteries rated at 220 Ah, then, has a capacity of 26.4 kWh.

As with the other rating systems (Ah and reserve capacity), the kWh rating system does not guarantee that 26.4 kWh will be delivered to the load, particularly at C/1 rates. It only describes how much energy it will take to refill the battery.

caps on a 6V battery and six (6) caps on a 12V battery.

A maintenance-free battery will not have fill caps. Use a multimeter on batteries of unknown voltage.

Battery Pack Layout

The battery pack in an EV is comprised of many batteries that are wired together to produce some higher voltage and, in some cases, a higher overall Ah capacity.

The basic building blocks of a battery pack are the 6-Volt battery of 220 Ah capacity and the 12-Volt battery of 110 Ah capacity. Both types are approximately equal in weight and they have nearly identical kWh ratings.

[Note: A battery pack of interconnected 6V or 12V batteries may itself be referred to as a "battery". More often, the phrase "battery pack" is used. Either usage is correct.]

To help you understand voltage and battery packs, let's build a battery pack. Imagine that we had ten 110 Ah, 12V batteries sitting on the floor, and a bunch of interconnecting wires. How can they be wired into a battery pack for an EV?

Packs can be wired in series, parallel, or both (Techtalk T62). In series wiring, battery voltage is accumulative (Fig. 7-11). In parallel wiring, battery capacity is accumulative (Fig. 7-12). A combination of the series and parallel wiring (Fig. 7-13) is the best way to achieve both high voltage *and* capacity without increasing the weight of individual batteries in the pack.

Voltage versus Ah Capacity

What is better — a battery pack of higher voltage or higher Ah capacity?

Generally, in an EV it is better for a battery pack to be configured for as high a voltage as possible. There are three factors that favor higher voltage systems: line losses, motor speed, and the nature of modern DC-DC controllers. Line losses, for the same amount of power transferred, are higher within low-voltage systems. Motor speed is linked to voltage; the higher the voltage, the higher the motor speed. Finally, a DC-DC controller will turn excess voltage into current, as required by the motor.

Of course, factors like the voltage ratings of the motor and the controller may limit the maximum voltage of the battery pack. In general, voltage is served first, and additional Ah capacity is added, if needed.

Cycle Depth

There is only one type of battery to get for your EV and that's the "deep-cycle" variety. Here, a cycle is defined as a full charge and a deep discharge of the battery.

Deep-cycle refers to the battery's unique design: an ability to withstand discharge to a very low value, say 15-20% of its capacity, repeatedly, without damage or destruction. Do that a few times to an SLI battery (like leaving the car's headlights ON), and you'll be in the market for a new battery!

One of the characteristics of the deep-cycle battery is thick plates. Thick plates resist physical damage due to the warping that can occur with deep discharge. By comparison, the plates of a SLI battery are paper-thin. This allows more surface area of active material in the cell's enclosure, enabling it to deliver the hundreds of amperes a starter motor may want

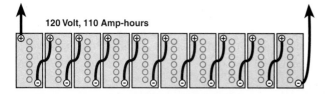

120 Volt, 110 Amp-hours

Fig. 7-11: Series wiring of batteries increases voltage.

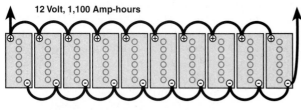

12 Volt, 1,100 Amp-hours

Fig. 7-12: Parallel wiring of batteries increases capacity.

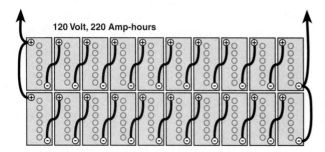

120 Volt, 220 Amp-hours

Fig. 7-13: Series and parallel wiring adds voltage and capacity.

to start an engine. The SLI battery gets in trouble quick if it is deep-discharged. Its plates can warp, causing irreversible physical damage.

The deep-cycle battery, with its thicker plates, is able to withstand the duress of high discharge rates to very low capacities. Deep-cycle batteries are available in both 6V and 12V configurations.

Energy and Power Density

A deep-cycle feature gives a battery *energy density*, since more of the battery's energy is available for use. The ability of a battery to deliver power at high discharge rates reflects its *power density*. The energy density, then, is like the size of a fuel tank whereas the power density is the "octane of the fuel" it contains.

A deep-cycle battery is designed for good energy density, then, while an SLI battery is designed for power density. Deep-cycle battery packs will also provide good power density if the pack voltage is high enough. The higher the voltage, the smaller the current value the motor draws for the same work. At 400A, today's deep-cycle batteries are at the "limit" of what they can supply in the EV.

Depth of Discharge

Deep-cycle batteries may be discharged to a very low *depth-of-discharge*, or DOD. A standard DOD value is 80%, where 80% of the pack's rated Ah capacity is used, leaving a 20% reserve. Deep discharge, repeated often, is stressful to a battery pack of any type and will decrease its useable service life.

A sensible precaution against a short service life is to establish a conservative DOD for your battery pack. At 80% DOD, you might expect a service life of 300 cycles. By comparison, a more conservative DOD like 50% might yield 600 cycles. An onboard Ah meter is indispensable for monitoring the battery pack's DOD. It will help you abide by the DOD percentage you select for your vehicle.

Many EV owners elect to use the 80% DOD. Otherwise, the vehicle carries around a lot of unused capacity. When there's a choice between performance and service life, many people prefer performance.

The unused energy in your pack (below the preset DOD), whether it's 20% or 50%, may be just the ticket for getting you home sometime. If you use any of your reserve, make certain that you immediately recharge the battery. Letting a battery sit idle at a low state-of-charge, or SOC, will shorten its service life.

Temperature and Sulfation

The performance of all types of batteries is affected by temperature and sulfation (Techtalk T63). The lead-acid battery is "happiest" at 85 degrees F.! Above 125 degrees F, the battery is in danger of physical damage. At temperatures below 72 degrees F, its performance begins to suffer. The greater the temperature drop below this amount, the greater its sluggishness in doing useful work.

Due to the high water content of the electrolyte, the lead-acid battery is susceptible to freezing. A full SOC is the best insurance against this happening, protecting the battery to well below 0 degrees F.

A low SOC can bring about another harmful state for lead-acid batteries: sulfation. Sulfation is chemistry gone bad, where the lead crystals formed during discharge are too large, and resist dissolution when charged. Batteries that sit unattended for a long period of time are likely to suffer this condition.

The effects of temperature and sulfation are not easily remedied, but they can be avoided. Battery warming (and cooling) will ensure that the battery remains in a zone where it will perform as expected. Sulfation is avoided by ensuring that the battery pack is not left in a discharged state. The urgency of recharging the battery pack is inversely proportional to its DOD. The deeper the discharge, the sooner the charge cycle should be initiated.

The selection, installation, use, and maintenance of batteries will be discussed in more detail in the next chapter (Chapter 8).

Controllers

Control of a vehicle is subtle. Control of an EV is the same. If you already drive, your first experience in an electric vehicle will feel familiar in some ways, very different in others. It won't be as mysterious and panicky as learning to drive a car for the first time. Many of the controls of the EV are similar in location, function, and appearance to those of an ICE car.

Techtalk T63 — Battery Temperature and Sulfation

A lead-acid battery is designed to work in moderate temperatures. Most wet-cell lead-acid batteries supply optimum performance at 95 degrees F. Most humans (and their cars) are designed to like ambient temperatures of 72-85 degrees F. At these temperatures, batteries in ICE cars are running below optimum temperature most of the time.

High Temperatures. Temperatures above 125 degrees F will physically damage the lead-acid battery and shorten its service life. It is possible to approach this value on a summer day in the desert at high discharge rates, during high charge rates, or during accidental overcharge. If you cannot adequately cool the batteries to keep their temperature below this point, halt the charge or discharge once this limit is reached or exceeded.

Low Temperatures. As temperatures drop to freezing (32 degrees F), unprotected batteries in an EV will be sluggish when operated. This is perfectly normal. When lead-acid batteries get cold, their chemistry and internal resistance is adversely affected. The normal delivery of battery power is reduced. The battery has not lost capacity. It is simply unable to deliver it. The chemistry is restrained.

Batteries can also freeze. A fully-charged battery can typically survive temperatures 40-50 degrees below freezing. However, a depleted battery will freeze and suffer irreversible internal damage at temperatures as high as 30 degrees F. Since water expands when it freezes, batteries in a pack that freeze are "dead lead", and will require replacement.

As soon as current starts flowing through a battery, it will warm up. However, it is unlikely that the warming cycle during EV operation will heat the battery significantly. Lead is very dense, and a battery pack represents a large thermal mass. When warm, the pack tends to stay warm. When cold, it tends to stay cold.

In colder climes, add insulation to help keep the battery pack warm. A source of heat will be needed to help offset losses through any insulation. Over the years, EV owners in these areas have evolved a number of ways to do this. Electric blankets, banks of light bulbs, heating coils, thermal plates, and ac charging have all been applied. These are treated in detail in Chapter 8.

Sulfation. Sulfation is an extreme condition of the normal chemical process in a lead-acid battery. It coats the lead plates with a crystalline barrier that inhibits charge and discharge. It spells irreversible death to a battery. It is usually triggered when the battery is left at a low SOC for a prolonged period of time. The effect is more pronounced the lower the SOC. Repeated delays in recharging the battery pack, even for higher SOCs, will produce sulfation.

There is controversy over the effect of some additives you can buy to treat the condition of sulfation. There is little substantiated evidence of additives reversing the battery's condition and restoring its service life. Like the human body, the best remedy seems to be prevention. Maintaining a high SOC when the battery pack is not being used, and immediate recharging of a depleted battery pack will prevent the onset of sulfation.

Control Functions

Every EV—regardless of size, shape, and function—will have two distinct components of control: operator controls and power switching. One fits the operator, the other the function.

Operator controls are the switches and levers, wheels and pedals an operator manipulates that, in turn, activate slaved devices that handle power switching. These are virtually identical to gas car operation.

Power switching translates the operator's input into action, smoothly regulating motor current. Relays, solenoids, SCRs, and MOSFETs are power-switching devices. One or more of these devices may be present in the controller and overall system.

In the smallest EVs, the controller may be a switch that turns the motor ON or OFF. For this size, power switching values are small, so the devices are simple. As the EV gets bigger, system voltages, currents, and motor factors like horsepower, torque, and rpm get larger. The sophistication of the system also enlarges to handle these tasks responsibly.

These controls must work, be efficient, and act in a fail-safe manner. There is no greater terror than the loss of control. It is not fun to be caught up in a big, fast machine that has just stopped listening to you.

Is EV Control That Different?

As the EV industry matures in this decade, it will unravel the subtleties of electric propulsion. After an initial frenzy of experimentation, EVs will feel more intuitive to operate. Automakers are ponderous industries, responding slowly to change and innovation, so this process will take time. For this reason, your EV may be somewhat of a mystery to you *and* people around you.

We all want the "warm tummy feeling" when it comes to transportation. The sooner you cozy up to the basics of EV control, the sooner you will understand all the noises and nuances. This is important. Until the infrastructure for EVs evolves, a garage mechanic may not understand anything about what's under the hood, much less what's wrong with it!

Fortunately, a basic understanding of EV components will demonstrate, once and for all, how little there is to go wrong in an EV. There are few parts, they perform simple functions, and if you can balance a checkbook, you can probably point to an offending component in case of failure. This technology is *simple*.

Basic Control Requirements

There are things that we want our EV to do. Go when we want it to go. Stop when we want (or need!) it to stop. Reverse directions, for backing up the vehicle. These are basic control requirements.

There are some subtle aspects to these functions. First, we want them to happen at specific rates. We don't want to peel out at every start, or skid to a stop every time we hit the brakes. When we say we want the EV to "Go", we mean at a rate which we will select each time we want to "Go". And we want to have the option of braking slowly, or fast, or in between. The rate of acceleration or braking, then, is one of the implicit definitions of "control."

A second aspect of control is that we don't want these things to happen when they shouldn't. If you're boppin' down the road at 25 mph, you do not need the EV to go suddenly into reverse. In the design process, you learn that control circuitry is very literal. For this reason, you must often ensure that something cannot happen so that it will not—by accident or through improper operation—occur at the worse possible moment!

"Go" and "Stop" functions involve fairly intuitive control techniques in electric vehicles and involve well-known operator controls, ie., the accelerator pedal and the brake pedal. However, EVs are different than gas-powered vehicles. Consequently, motors, batteries, and control circuits require special consideration in light of this new technology.

The Evolution of Motor Control

Electric vehicles manufactured in the early part of this century used control techniques that varied the voltage to the motor in ways that were simple in principle and effective. Resistive, voltage tap, and series-parallel all had their merits. Each had its disadvantages, too, particularly in larger EVs. Today, electronic controllers are the mainstay of EVs, varying the duration of high-frequency pulses to limit current to the motor.

The Electronic Controller

In a sense, *all* of these early systems appeared practical primarily because the alternative—the direct control of high current and high voltages—was a formidable challenge. Even as late as 1970-80, buying an electronic controller was an expensive experiment. As well, simple switches and contactors were no match for the destructive properties of the arc generated whenever the flow of high power electricity was interrupted.

Early departures from voltage and resistive control of DC currents took the path of diodes, SCRs (silicon controlled rectifiers), and transistors. The desirable features of a good electronic controller were known. Infinite variability. Reliability. Inexpensive.

Over time, advances in the power devices used in controller technology have made it possible to control higher voltages and currents. The major key was high frequency. Earlier in this century, it was Nikola Tesla that pointed the way. The higher the frequency of switching, the greater the efficiency, the less dangerous it was, and the greater the capacity to control large amounts of power.

Fig. 7-14: Resistive control is used on older golf carts.

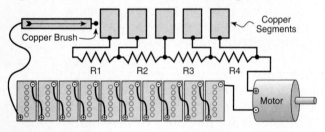

Copper Segments

Copper Brush

R1   R2   R3   R4

Motor

Fig. 7-15: Voltage tap is used to avoid jerky operation.

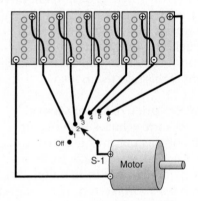

Off
S-1   Motor

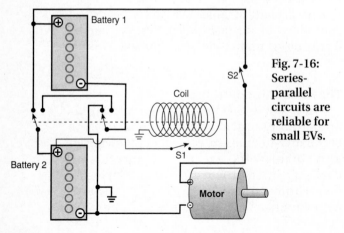

Battery 1

S2

Coil

Fig. 7-16: Series-parallel circuits are reliable for small EVs.

S1

Battery 2

Motor

The trick was to get the power devices to switch on and off at a rate of *tens* of thousands of times a second. The motor would see full voltage but, by varying the duration of the ON time relative to the OFF time, the *average* current was controlled. Simple motor control techniques, by comparison, manipulate the voltage to the motor in steps or limit current in resistors, both inefficient processes.

Electronic control techniques exist for both DC and ac motors. DC motors have the advantage of simpler control methods, including some non-electronic ones. These will be reviewed first.

DC Control Techniques

DC Motor control in the EV is limited to four techniques for series, shunt, compound, and PM magnet motor types. The techniques are resistive, voltage-tap, series-parallel, and electronic.

Resistive control uses current limiting as a motor control technique (Fig. 7-14). *Voltage-tap* regulates motor current by limiting the voltage that the motor "sees" (Fig. 7-15). *Series-parallel* improves on the voltage-tap method (Fig. 7-16) by arranging the batteries in series and parallel configurations, always ensuring that every battery is equally discharged. The electronic controller converts battery power into a set of pulses and varies the pulse duration of a specific frequency to control motor current (Fig. 7-17).

Small and very simple applications using a PM motor, particularly where cost is a factor, may benefit from using a combination of resistive and series-parallel control techniques. The electronic controller is the preferred controller in today's larger EVs.

The control system of a modern EV makes provisions for motor speed, coasting, dynamic or regenerative braking, and reversing the motor's direction of rotation.

The Pulse Width Modulated Controller

The PWM controller works like a fast-acting on-off switch, connecting the batteries with the motor at a rapid rate. The controller acts at some constant frequency and varies the *duration* of the pulse. In turn, the duration of the pulse follows the degree to which the driver depresses the accelerator pedal, increasing in width (time) with more pedal. Of course, a mechanical switch would be quickly destroyed with so much arcing.

Older PWM circuits employ SCRs or high-power transistors in their design to handle rapid switching. Newer controllers use MOSFETs (metal-oxide silicon field effect transistors) or IGBTs (isolated gate bipolar transistors). Switching frequency has leaped, too, moving from a range of 1-5kHz to a range of 15-20kHz, or higher..

How Does It Work?

The closest analogy of the PWM circuit is the light dimmer switch used in many households. While it's not visually noticeable, light bulbs lit with standard wall socket current (120 vac, 60 cycles) are turning ON and OFF very quickly. At 120 times per second, to be precise. (That's the 60-cycle rate multiplied by the two portions found in one cycle.) At such a high rate, the bulb appears to burn steadily. If it didn't, it'd drive us crazy in a short time.

A light dimmer, inserted between the wall socket and the light mounted in the lamp, lets you adjust a knob to dim the bulb to your satisfaction. How does it work? The 60-cycle rate is still delivered to the bulb but the triac inside (a double SCR) 'chops' off some of the time the bulb is ON during both the positive and negative portion of the cycle. The bulb sees the full voltage, but less average current, dimming in the process. In good units, the light dimmer's knob adjusts this rate infinitely between full ON and full OFF.

The PWM controller is a sophisticated version of the light dimmer switch, but it's designed to handle more power. A Curtis PMC 1221, for example, will handle 400 Amps of current at 120V. That's 48,000 Watts! Or nearly *fifty* 1000-Watt light bulbs!

The PWM controller circuit can be used with any of the four DC motors that we've discussed — series, shunt, compound, and permanent magnet. This "black box" is mounted near the motor itself. Some brands have fans mounted in them. Others rely on external cooling techniques.

The accelerator pedal is linked to the PWM controller through a variable resistor, which is usually external to the controller housing. A potentiometer, or pot, is another name for a variable resistor. So, the unit is called a potbox. The potbox is bolted to the chassis and is designed to secure the other end of the cable that attaches to the accelerator pedal.

There are several manufacturers of electronic EV controllers. One such controller, the Curtis PMC Model 1221B, with which the author is familiar, will be discussed in the following sections.

A Curtis PMC Controller

The Curtis PMC # 1221B is a MOSFET controller a little larger and longer than a cigar box (Fig. 7-18). Like the motor, contactors, and shunts mounted in the "engine" compartment, the controller is a sealed unit. This means it can be "hosed" down of accumulated dust with water and the car driven shortly thereafter.

This controller is dominated at one end by four large electrical posts. To these are attached the lugs at the ends of large electrical wires (the size of welding cables) from the battery and the motor (Fig. 7-19). There are three smaller terminals here, too. Leads from the potbox connect to two of them.

How does it work? The degree to which the pedal is depressed (mechanical) is reflected in

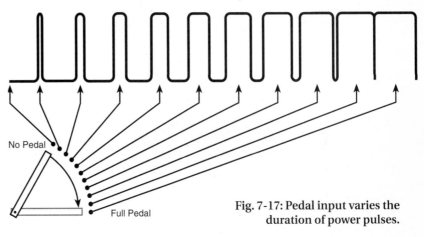

No Pedal

Full Pedal

Fig. 7-17: Pedal input varies the duration of power pulses.

the rotation of a potentiometer (in the potbox) that sends a signal (electrical) to the controller, varying motor current.

The third pin is "enable." If this pin does not see pack voltage, the controller will not work. Connecting 12VDC here (from the AUX battery or supply) will not work. Some wiring diagrams use a jumper between this pin and the B+ lug of the controller. Circuits that exclude a contactor may switch it on via a relay from the key.

Like most electronic controllers for EVs, the Curtis PMC is very efficient (96-98%). Since it controls very large currents, even the 2-4% losses can amount to a significant amount of heat. So, typically the controller is bolted up anywhere there is some cooling air (Fig. 7-20). Or it may be bolted to a large heatsink and mounted in an airtight compartment. Some designers may add a 12V cooling fan to help move heat away from the controller.

If the Curtis controller's ratings are exceeded and it begins to heat, it will protect itself in two stages. In the first, the circuitry switches to a lower operating frequency. The jump from 20kHz to 1 kHz has two effects. One is a reduction of power. The other is an audible tone. Human ears can detect a 1kHz signal. So, the driver feels a sudden drop in power, and hears it, too! This is a signal to the driver to "back off", and slow down.

If the overloading continues, the controller will enact the next stage of protection against damage by shutting itself down. The EV will lose all power. Only after the controller has cooled sufficiently will it reset itself and once again function normally.

The controller does have a few adjustments (Fig. 7-21). These are hidden behind set screws

that will discourage any casual "tweaking" by operators. These are preset at the factory to a standard setting.

The simplicity of the exterior of this controller belies the complexity of the circuitry within (Techtalk 64) The bulk of the electronics is consumed by power-switching devices. Since each MOSFET device can only handle a small amount of current, many of these devices are mounted in parallel until the final peak rating is achieved. The remainder of the electronics is devoted to controlling these output devices and protecting them under a wide range of operating conditions.

Hobbyists may want to build their own PWM controllers. It is a formidable job. Scout around in the EV community for some circuit diagrams. The primary advantages of the commercial units are that they're time-tested, available off the shelf, and warranted.

Coasting

The internal combustion engine in a car helps the car to slow down when the driver's foot comes off the accelerator. This is called compressive braking.

In an electric vehicle, taking your foot off the accelerator removes the power from the motor, but the motor will freewheel. Aerodynamic drag, and friction in the motor, bearings, and gears will eventually stop the vehicle, but the effect is like having the vehicle in neutral. It just wants to go on and on. This is called coasting.

EV owners capitalize on this coasting effect by anticipating the flow of traffic or signal light timing, stretching out the distance the vehicle will travel. After all, it takes a lot of energy to build the momentum in a vehicle. Why throw it away? In a gas-powered car you achieve the same effect by putting the transmission in neutral or pushing in the clutch. Either procedure is highly illegal, too. In an EV, it occurs naturally, without any shift of gears or action of any kind on your part.

Coasting adds great economy for the power expended, but it takes some getting used to. Very quickly, it seems second nature. With practice, you'll bring your EV to speed and use coasting intentionally to save energy and increase range. The next time you drive an ICE car, you'll notice how inconvenient it can be to have the vehicle slow down so much when you come off the accelerator.

Fig. 7-18: The Curtis PMC Controller

Photo: Curtis PMC Instruments

Photo: ElectroAutomotive

Fig. 7-19: The controller installed'; nearby, the contactor and potbox

Fig. 7-20: This controller is cooled by airflow through the heatsink.

Fig. 7-21: Controller ramp and current rates may be adjusted.

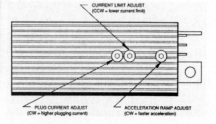

CURRENT LIMIT ADJUST
(CCW = lower current limit)

PLUG CURRENT ADJUST
(CW = higher plugging current)

ACCELERATION RAMP ADJUST
(CW = faster acceleration)

There are times when this coasting effect is not so handy in an EV. What happens when you drive down a steep grade? What will limit the speed of the vehicle? Here, you must use the brakes excessively to compensate for the lack of compressive braking. What happens when you park on a hill? Putting the vehicle's transmission in low gear won't keep the vehicle from rolling away. You must learn always to use the parking brake in an EV.

The Curtis 1221 controller offers a mild form of compressive braking, called plug braking. It requires that you wire up the fourth large lug of the controller. It will "load" the motor and dissipate some of the vehicle's momentum as heat.

Dynamic and Regenerative Braking

A stronger, controlled braking effect in an EV occurs when regenerative and dynamic braking circuits are added to the control circuits (Techtalk T65).

Regenerative braking (or "regen") lets the motor act as a generator," converting the vehicle's momentum into electricity. As the batteries absorb this electricity, the vehicle is slowed down. While often touted as a "range extending" or "energy recovery" technique, regen's greatest virtue is that it saves on brake jobs.

Dynamic braking loads the motor with a resistance, dissipating electricity produced from momentum as heat and slowing the vehicle.

Regen and dynamic braking are really complementary techniques. Regen is used first. Dynamic braking is engaged when the vehicle has slowed to the point where the voltage of the electricity is too low to charge the batteries. It is also handy when the battery pack is full (as when the vehicle is used after a fresh charge) and the battery pack can't take any more electricity.

EVs using a PM motor can easily take advantage of regen and dynamic braking. Other motor types require special circuitry to affect regen and dynamic braking. As desirable as either feature can be, it is not necessarily easy or inexpensive to use regen or dynamic braking (Techtalk T66).

There is also the question of how to integrate it into the vehicle (Techtalk T67). Do you flip a switch on the dash? Should it engage when you lift your foot off the accelerator

---

Techtalk

T64   Inside the PWM Controller

Daniel Pliskin

A variety of solid state switches exist to handle electric power but MOSFET switches are the device of choice in EV controllers. It can be described as a voltage-controlled resistor. When no voltage is applied to its gate, a MOSFET looks like an open circuit (it's off). When voltage is applied to its gate, it turns on.

To the power source, the MOSFET really looks like a low value resistor (0.1 ohms, for example) when it's ON. At high current rates, this adds up to a lot of waste because the losses are proportional to the square of the current. Use the power formula, P=I squared x R, or power equals current squared x resistance. Therefore, 300 Amps through a 0.1 ohm "switch" would force the "switch" itself to try to dissipate 9,000 Watts of heat!

Fortunately, multiple MOSFETs can be wired up in parallel to share the current. Twenty MOSFETs in parallel, then, would limit the current in any one of them to 1/20th of the value. Since the effective total "on-resistance" would only be 0.005 ohms, working the same equation yields only an overall dissipation of 450 Watts. The more MOSFETs you use in a controller, then, the more efficient it is (lower "on" resistance) and the more current you can draw through it (lower heat dissipation). As you might expect, the controller gets much more expensive, too.

MOSFETs are basically "current devices" but they are also rated for how much voltage they can handle without being internally damaged. Typically, the higher the voltage rating of a MOSFET, the lower its current rating. Thus, a controller designed to operate at higher voltages will require a larger number of MOSFET devices to ensure the equivalent current draw.

Other control circuitry inside the controller itself usually operates at very low voltages. Where the controller is designed for medium-to-high voltage applications, an internal power supply is needed to convert the higher voltage to a lower one for control devices with limited input voltage range. This power supply should work over a large range of input voltages so it can "track" the MOSFETs, which can handle voltages under their rated maximum levels.

Lastly, for a controller to operate at its maximum rated current all the time, it would need to dissipate significant amounts of heat. Fortunately, peak current usually occurs during acceleration. Once up to speed, an EV will draw a fraction of the current that it draws when it is accelerating from a stop. Manufacturers give their motor controllers two current ratings: maximum and continuous. This way, the heat-sinking capability of the controller can be designed for some point between continuous operation and full loads.

Techtalk
T65 Dynamic and Regenerative Braking

All electric motors have the potential of being a generator. So, when the control circuit disconnects the battery from the motor (you take your foot off the accelerator), the motor can be "re-wired" as a generator and "loaded" to produce electricity. Since it takes energy to make energy, the vehicle's momentum (energy of moving) is consumed and the vehicle slows.

The immediate benefit of this process is that it simulates the compressive-braking (slowdown effect) feature of gas engines, reducing the brake wear normal to most cars.

There are two ways the generated electricity will represent a load to the "generator": dynamic and regenerative braking.

• Dynamic braking dissipates motor electricity as heat in resistors. This is just an electric version of the heat generated in disc and drum brakes. This works for low-grade electricity (too low in voltage to charge a battery).

• Regenerative braking, or regen, recovers useful electricity by putting it back into the batteries. Hence the term, regenerative. To regenerate is to be "formed or created again, restored to a better, higher, or more worthy state, to utilize by special devices heat or other products that would ordinarily be lost."

Sounds like perpetual motion, doesn't it? It isn't. The vehicle's momentum will be used up in the process, slowing the vehicle.

Techtalk
T66 Design Issues of Regenerative Braking

EV designers know that regen braking is beneficial. That it is not more widely done is testimony of the complexity involving in doing it safely, except in very small controllers using PM motors.

Here are the relevant issues:

•Energy reclaimed. Regen braking may only yield 25% of the energy reclaimed after losses in the DC motor and batteries.

•Braking effect. The braking effect is strongest at the onset of regen braking, and then drops off. (Today's AC motor/controllers provide strong regenerative braking all the way down to zero speed.)

•In the series motor, the field winding must be separated from the armature winding and separately excited to generate electricity.

These factors represent challenges that will be circumvented in the years to come, with smarter circuitry and (perhaps) the re-emergence of compound-wound motors. Regen braking is important if your driving day takes you up and down a lot of hills, or if your vehicle is fairly heavy. Learning how to coast and the use of lightweight EVs will minimize the *need* for regen braking.

In the smaller EVs using PM motors, consider the idea of incorporating dynamic and regen braking together. The reason is simple. Regeneration ceases when the voltage of the motor/generator falls below pack voltage. This also results in a loss of the braking effect. The next detent on the brake pedal, then, could connect the motor to resistive coils. Energy is energy. Just because the electricity isn't high-grade doesn't mean you can't do something with it! When dumped into resistive coils, this electricity will buy you a braking effect, and save wear and tear on your hydraulic brakes. Further depression of the pedal can engage the wheel brakes.

Techtalk
T67 Integrating Regenerative Braking

Regen braking with ac motors and controllers is often tied to the accelerator pedal. If the pedal is backed off just a bit, the vehicle goes into "coast" mode. If the foot is further lifted from the pedal, regen braking begins. The more the pedal pressure is released, the more a braking effect is felt.

Adjusting a knob on the dash or console often sets the level of regen that can occur, allowing the driver to control the braking rate to a level that feels comfortable. At a dial setting of 2, regen could be as gentle as the compressive braking one feels in a car with an engine. At 5, the feeling is much stronger. At 9, regen could rapidly decelerate the vehicle, feeling like strong brakes.

To a novice, acceleration and "electric" braking on the same pedal might seem strange and scary. However, it only takes a few minutes to get used to this feature. It is surprisingly intuitive, and very quickly feels natural.

The main drawback of regen on the accelerator pedal is that it is easy to forget that it works that way. In a panic stop, it is unnerving, as you jerk your foot off the accelerator and aim for the brake pedal, to have the vehicle brake hard before you've even hit the brake pedal! Also, what happens when you drive a *different* car afterward? One where there is *no* braking available at the pedal!

Engineers can add circuitry that compensates for these conditions. For example, releasing the pedal quickly might disable regen. For a panic stop, then, you get only regular brakes. Still, smart electronics rarely compensate for ignorant or inattentive drivers. The liability issues alone are awesome in attaching regen to the accelerator pedal, no matter the merit of the concept.

pedal, as compressive braking does? Or should it be part of the brake pedal? Or mounted on the steering wheel?

Design engineers recognize that this morning you may be driving an EV and this afternoon you may drive a car with an engine. Like anything else, regen braking must be intuitive to use or an accident can result.

Until the controllers of DC motors come with a regen option, it is left to the EV owner to design and install regen braking as an "add on."Many EV builders opt not to use it. Very soon, this may no longer be a choice. The virtue of compressive braking in an ICE is that it works like a "dead man switch", slowing and stopping a car even if the driver is incapacitated. At some point, a similar feature is likely to be legislated for EVs.

Reversing a Motor

In an ICE car, backing up or moving a vehicle in reverse requires that you shift gears. Mechanically, the direction of rotation for the engine's driveshaft (respective to the engine) is changed in the gearbox. This is necessary because engines rotate

in one direction, irrespective of the car's motion, backward or forward.

An EV that uses (or retains) a transmission can use the same method of reversing the vehicle. However, an EV can also shift into reverse "electrically" (Techtalk T68) after it has been brought to a stop. Unlike an engine, an electric motor can run in either direction.

Some motors are designed to operate in one direction. This is usually a factory setting. Like an engine's timing (which advances the spark to permit high speed efficiency), the motor brushes are advanced a specific amount (i.e., 20 degrees). Temporarily reversing any motor will have no effect, but the motor will

---

*T*echtalk

T68 Electric Motor Reversing

EVs without a variable-ratio gearbox (stick shift or automatic transmission) reverse the EV's direction of travel in another way—electrically. If it's a DC motor, all you have to do is reverse the motor electrically. This involves a little bit of wire-switching, with solenoids or a heavy switch handling the job. Which wires are switched depends on the type of motor.

The simplest reversing-switch uses a DPDT (double-pole, double-throw) toggle switch that energizes a hefty relay equipped with "normally-open" and "normally-closed" contacts. In the de-energized position, the "normally-closed" contacts wire the motor for travel in the forward direction. Energizing the relay closes the "normally-open" contacts, reversing the motor for backing up.

Use a DPDT switch with a center off position, between the forward and reverse positions. This is a safety feature, since you must accidentally

elbow it through two positions to have your forward-moving vehicle go bananas. A more "fail-safe" method is to use a military-style toggle switch. You can't bump this into another setting because you must pull *out* on the toggle and push it down or up to get it to clear small detents. This arrangement baffles children, too.

The permanent magnet motor is the easiest motor to reverse (Fig. 7-22). Simply reverse the polarity of the wires coming from the batteries. Reversing a series (Fig. 7-23), shunt (Fig. 7-24), or compound (Fig. 7-25) motor involves reversing the polarity of the armature windings with respect to the polarity of the field winding and batteries.

Avoid the easy solution of reversing the field windings respective to the armature and battery. It can result in field discharges (collapsing inductive coils), losing field control (resulting in runaway or overspeed problems), with the loss of potential dynamic-braking during the interval the field is open.

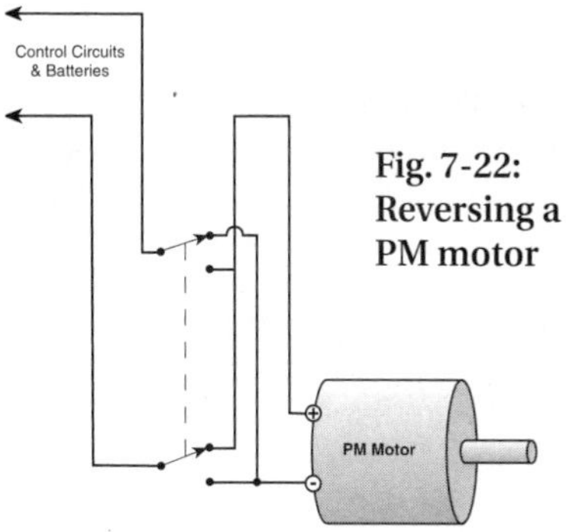

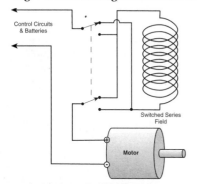

Fig. 7-22: Reversing a PM motor

Fig. 7-23: Reversing a series motor

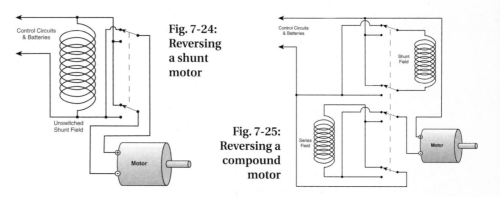

Fig. 7-24: Reversing a shunt motor

Fig. 7-25: Reversing a compound motor

perform poorly and may be eventually damaged if wired to run in this direction all the time. Check with the manufacturer to find the motor's standard direction of rotation

Electric reversing may seem complicated, but it's a blessing in vehicles where a fixed-ratio drive is used instead of a transmission since it avoids the need for a reversing gear.

AC Motor Control

The controllers for ac Motors and the brushless DC motors are electronic in nature and more complex than their DC motor counterparts (Techtalk T69). The bulk of the controller is the many additional sets of power devices needed for three-phase operation. For this reason, the controller is more expensive than the motor it controls. Additional control circuitry is required in the ac controller to detect shaft position and smoothly operate the motor through its many modes.

Like the DC controller, one mode of an ac controller is translating accelerator pedal position into propulsion. Where the DC motor usually has a fixed "timing" of rotor-stator position, the ac controller can shift this phase. The ability to continuously tune the motor over a wide range of speed and loading ensures good efficiency for whatever conditions the ac drivetrain might experience.

Another mode of operation in the ac controller is responsible for shifting phases to accommodate regenerative braking. While this is technically challenging, it is a much less clunky method of getting regen than most DC motor circuits. As with DC motors, there is some question yet about the best way to integrate regenerative braking into the vehicle.

Charging

At some point, an EV's battery pack will become depleted, or its owner will come home and want to replenish the batteries. It's the job of the battery charger to match an energy source to the EV's battery pack, control the recharge rate, and shut down when finished.

A *major* virtue of the EV is its ability to use electricity from many different sources. However, no matter what source(s) you choose

---

Techtalk T69

Design Notes for AC Controllers
Daniel Pliskin

There are additional costs in building both the ac motor and the 3-phase controller. Much of this money is spent for FETs (or one of the bipolar technologies) to lower the voltage drop across the drivers (and the resulting losses). Overall, three-phase controllers are significantly more sophisticated than controllers used for split-commutator motors, and they use six times as many silicon FETs or bipolars in their three half-bridges. Rare earth magnets for the motor's rotor are expensive, too.

While there is much controversy over which 3-phase motor (brushless DC or induction ac) is best suited for a particular application, the controllers that drive these motors are essentially the same.

Three-phase controllers generate three pseudo-sinusoidal outputs that are 120 degrees out of phase with each other. By sequentially driving each of the terminals either up to battery plus((+), letting them float or driving them down to battery minus (-), the three phases are generated. In the motor, there are as many pairs of magnetic poles on the rotor as sets of 3-phase windings on the stator (6 windings per set). In operation, the controller sequentially energizes the stator windings, creating an electrical "rotating" magnetic field which, in turn, mechanically pushes and pulls the rotor poles around.

As such, 3-phase motors are synchronous motors, and the controller needs to "know" where the rotor poles are, in order to keep the stator poles "rotating" in sync with the rotor. Three shaft position sensors (usually Hall-effect type) "tell" the controller when it is time to electrically advance the stator to its next stage. A 3-phase controller routes power to the motor by pulse-width-modulating the 3-phase outputs.

The circuitry that advances the stator poles runs independently of the PWM section of the controller. It decodes the shaft position sensor outputs directly and encodes it into one of the six stages of 3-phase.

Both "open loop" and "closed loop" designs exist. Open loop circuits control motor speed by the amount of power fed to the motor via the accelerator. Closed loop circuits compare the rpm of the motor with the output of a tachometer circuit, using the difference (error) to feed extra power in order to maintain that motor rpm. The vehicle's accelerator acts something like a cruise control, with pedal position corresponding to a specific (desired) motor speed.

A major advantage of closed loop operation is that it allows controller configurations that allow regenerative braking (recharging the batteries) when the driver eases off the accelerator.

The revolution in motor technology is being led by an ongoing evolution in the components that make up motor speed controllers. The power density of FETs is getting better every year and IGBTs have come of age. Several 3-phase controller chips are already on the market. Motors and controllers we ogle today will soon be commonplace.

---

to use, the battery pack has specific needs. Understanding these needs, in turn, will help you use an energy source that's available to you, even if it's not a straight plug-in, like the wall socket most people will use for their EV.

What Does the Battery Need?

To be recharged, a battery needs DC current, the correct charge voltage, a charge profile, and time. In more detail:

• *Charge Current.* A lead-acid battery produces DC (direct current) during discharge and that's what it wants in order to recharge itself. AC (alternating current) won't charge batteries. The DC current can be steady but is more often "pulsating." Line chargers typically supply 120 "pulses" per second. Switching-type chargers will provide thousands, even tens of thousands of pulses per second.

• *Charge Voltage.* The voltage of the charger must be higher than the pack voltage for current to flow. The greater the voltage difference (between charger and pack voltage), the greater the value of charge current.

• *Charge Profile.* The recharge curve of a battery is anything but flat (Fig. 7-26). For this reason, the charger must be capable of supplying energy in a manner that "tracks" the charge profile. Failing to do so, at least, wastes energy in heat and dissociated water, and increases the size of your utility bill. At worst, it can undercharge or overcharge the battery, shortening its service life. It will also adversely affect EV performance and reliability, forcing a premature replacement of the pack.

The ideal process of battery recharging can be likened to pouring coffee into an empty cup. You start slow (so the liquid won't ski back out of the cup), increase the rate (the accumulating liquid absorbs the inrush of new coffee), and slow down near the end (surface chop causes spills over the brim).

Read five books on batteries and you will see five *different* charge profiles for lead-acid batteries. Pick one.

Generally, the charge profile of a battery pack is served by a battery charger that can respond to three distinct portions (or percentages) of the charge cycle. This is the 5-75-20 plot. A 100% recharge, then, has an initial (5%) phase, the bulk (75%) phase, and the taper (20%) phase (Techtalk T70).

• *Time.* It takes time to recharge a battery pack. A depleted 20 kWh pack will take as much as 6-14 hours to recharge. If we use a 10-hour time period, the three phases described above (100% total) can be roughly translated with one hour equaling 10%. Initial charging, then, consumes 30 minutes, bulk charging takes 7.5 hours, and taper charging works out at 1.5 hours.

The most efficient and economical recharge is essentially an overnight process. This neatly complements the excess electricity available from the utility grid at night. Many EV owners are able to obtain discount rates for recharging their EV at night.

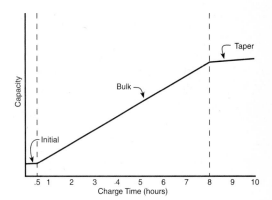

Fig. 7-26: Charge cycle of the lead-acid battery

Techtalk

T70 — Phases of the Charge Cycle

There are three phases of charge cycle: initial, bulk, and taper.

The *initial* (5%) phase of recharging a depleted battery pack wants to see a maximum C/20 rate of charge. For the stock 220Ah battery pack, this represents eleven (11) Amps of current. A depleted battery has a very low internal resistance. While it can absorb huge amounts of current, anything above the C/20 rate is wasted and is rough on the battery.

The *bulk* (75%) phase of charging will accept a higher charge rate. The internal resistance of the battery climbs onto a step after the initial charge phase. At this point, the battery is awake and is making "better chemistry." Some chargers increase the charge rate to C/10 (or 22 Amps, for a 220Ah pack) during the bulk phase. This is a bit more wasteful than the C/20 rate. However, if the vehicle needs to have a shorter recharge time, this is the best phase in which to accomplish it.

The *taper* (20%) phase of charging, as it name implies, must taper the charge rate. As it nears full, a battery's internal resistance increases rapidly. Even a C/20 rate will cause gassing (bubbling) as some of the electricity is dissociated into hydrogen and oxygen. At this point, the charge rate should decrease, dropping to a C/40 rate (5.5 amps) before the charger is shut off.

If the battery pack is *not* depleted (80% DOD or deeper) when the recharging cycle is started, the bulk charge (phase) rate can be initiated immediately.

Where the EV must be pressed into service ASAP (as soon as possible), it's possible to get a 75% recharge in as little as six hours with standard chargers. New charging technology has refined this technique, claiming an 80% recharge in 15 minutes.

Reduction of service life is often acceptable in recyclable technologies where there is a performance gain. Only time will put numbers to the factors involved in trade-offs. Fast-charging technology has great potential where the reduction in service life and efficiency is not too great.

The jury isn't in yet on the idea of super-charging. At the Phoenix races in 1992, my Honda VX got a 50% recharge in 3 minutes' time, repeatedly (review Chapter 6). The service life of the batteries was certainly affected, but there are no numbers to suggest how much.

Sources of Power

Unlike ICE cars, EVs use electricity which is available from many sources. The battery charger is not itself an energy source. To work, it must plug into an energy source. The type and extent of internal processing the charger must perform depends very much on the form of the electricity fed to it. So, it is here that we must focus our attention next. Let's examine the electricity available from the utility grid, standby generators, and sustainable energy sources, like solar, water, and wind energy.

Utility Home Power

For many people, the energy source for their EV will be the ac power found in their homes. It come in two flavors of 60-cycle power from the utility grid. One is the 110v found at a standard household wall socket. The other is 220v, like that supplied to an electric clothes dryer or an electric range. The receptacles are different so that you can't inadvertently plug into the wrong voltage!

Chargers that use an input of 110vac or 220vac (or both) are manufactured for a wide range of output DC voltages found in EVs. The limiting factor is the standard wall socket itself, which is limited in its ability to supply high wattage (15-16 amps) of ac power (Techtalk T71). Higher amperage is available from 110vac with the proper (NEMA-type) plugs and receptacles. Battery packs of higher voltage or higher transfer rates are best served from a 220vac source.

Fig. 7-27: Match NEMA sockets/plugs for your charger.

Industrial Power

Industrial sites also use the utility grid, but they have a slightly different standard. If an EV is going to be plugged into a receptacle at a shop or other commercial facility, expect a voltage of slightly lower value. A standard wall receptacle in a shop may read only 110v, whereas a household socket will read 115-120v. The most significant change is in the receptacles for big machinery. Here, only 208v will be available (it is one leg of 3-phase power).

Don't worry. Your battery charger will still work here. However, its charge rate will be proportionally lower (about 10%). Also, at a setting where your charger precisely finishes the charge at home, it will undercharge the EV's pack when plugged into 208vac.

Standby Generator

Electricity that is nearly identical to grid power is available from standby generators. A commercial standby generator is an engine-driven generator fueled with gasoline (Techtalk T72. These are used at off-grid and remote sites, in RVs (recreational vehicles), in EVs configured for hybrid power (see Hybrid EVs, Chapter 6), and in backup generators for emergency use. EV owners afraid of getting stuck out, or wanting to occasionally go a long distance can bolt a standby generator to a small trailer and head down the road (Fig. 7-28).

Most standby generators are designed to produce 110v or 220v, 60-cycle AC. Of course, a charger that plugs into a wall socket can be plugged directly into this system and begin charging. As well, late in the charge cycle, the charge rate to the batteries must be backed off. Where several charging sources are available, it makes sense to use a standby generator for only the bulk phase of charging. Save the taper charge for later.

Sustainable Power Sources

An exciting prospect for every EV owner is plugging the EV into a sustainable energy source. Solar power is a natural energy source for EVs because it is available when transportation loads are at a peak: during daylight hours. Wind-generated and hydroelectric energy are also sustainable energy sources.

Increasingly so, plugging into the utility grid gives an EV owner the possibility of using solar, wind, and hydroelectric power. In the "mix" of generated power a utility company may buy from the many sources available to it, sustainable energy sources are on the increase.

EV owners may also make their own power using these energy sources. Indeed, my first encounter with electric propulsion technology (twenty years ago) came about as I searched for an alternative to gasoline to power my car and truck. Consequently, my first EV plugged directly into the wind-electric machines I had installed on my farm (review Application A15).

Independently-owned, sustainable energy technologies produce their power as DC current. Since they store their power in batteries, they are specifically designed to charge 12V batteries.

Photo: AC Propulsion

Fig. 7-28: A generator can be towed behind an EV for extra electricity.

Fig. 7-29: An electric motorcycle gets a sunny refill.

Fig. 7-30: A bridge rectifier.

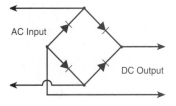

AC Input

DC Output

Techtalk
T71 What's Available at the Wall Socket

Chargers are available with DC outputs of 12V, 24V, 36V, 48V, 72V, 96V, 108V, 120V, and 144V. These should fit most EVs manufactured today. Charging rates of these chargers are typically 15A (15 Amps) when plugged into a 110vac source and *double* that when plugged into a 220vac source. Careful! Battery charger (DC) Amps are *not* the same as utility line (AC) Amps. This is a *common* error in thinking, by the novice and professional alike.

How much current is available from the two possible input voltages—110vac and 220vac? Household 110vac sockets, wiring, and circuit breakers are rated at 20 Amps. However, a rate closer to 14A is available *continuously*.

Each leg of household 220vac (electric range or clothes dryer) circuits will supply as much as 30-50A of current.

To get some idea of how much charge current is available to the battery at these values, start with the voltage of the EV battery pack. Let's look at three pack (DC) voltages: 72V, 120V, and 144V What charge rates are available to each of them them at 110vac and 220vac?

A rough idea of charge rates is obtained by dividing the wattages (volts x amps) available at each of ac voltages. Here's the result:

Battery Voltage	DC Amps at 110vac	DC Amps at 220vac	AC Amps drawn at 15A DC
72	23	46	9.8
120	13	27	**16.4**
144	11	22	**19.6**

(These figures assume a 100% efficiency in the charge; derate accordingly.) So, a 72V battery pack could draw as much as 23A (DC) on a 15A,120vac circuit without tripping the AC breaker. A 144V pack, however, can only draw 11 Amps without a circuit breaker trip.

See how much higher the charge rates can be for all of these packs when plugged into a 220vac source!

Finally, I have included a column that describes how many ac Amps are drawn when a 15A (DC) charge rate is applied to each battery pack. These values are obtained by multiplying the pack voltage by 15A and dividing the product by 110vac. Note that the 72V pack is only drawing 9.8 Amps of AC power for a 15A charge rate. A 120V pack is likely to trip the breaker at the same 15A charge rate, and the 144V pack most definitely will!

Your charger does not have to live with the limits imposed by *standard* wiring. Receptacles and plugs rated for several values in the 20-50A range are available for 110vac *and* 220vac. Of course, they must be service wired with a larger gauge of wire to the "mains" (power distribution panel) and a circuit breaker (or fuse) of similar amperage installed.

The pattern of plug and receptacle is different for the different amperages. Each has its own NEMA number. Again, this is insurance against a 30A load being plugged into a circuit (receptacle, wire, and breaker) rated at 15A. At least, this it will cause a nuisance trip. At worse—a fire.

T72 Charging with Standby Generators

Standby generators are designed to produce 110V or 220V, 60-cycle ac. A 6kW (6,000-Watt) generator is capable of supplying 50A at 110vac or 25A at 220vac. If the stock EV charger has a fixed output of 15A or 30A (respectively), then, only a fraction of the standby generator's capacity is utilized. In this case, it would need to run twice as long to charge the pack. That's a lot of noise and fuel consumption.

There are several ways to circumvent this blockage. Where the standby generator is only occasionally used, a special high-rate charger can be built. This is easy and inexpensive for a 120V battery pack. Other EV pack voltages may be better served if the 110V or 220V generator is replaced with a generator of a voltage that matches them directly. Hybrid EVs will use these and other methods to match voltage and wattage.

Late in the charge cycle, the charge rate must be backed off. For this reason, use a standby generator for only the bulk phase of charging. Save the taper charge for later.

This is perfect for EVs! The technology (notably solar) is modular in nature. Modules may be wired in series (like batteries) to serve virtually any voltage of EV battery pack. DC-DC technology can step up (or step down) any voltage. Thus, any differences of voltage between a stationary storage system and an EV's battery pack may be matched.

I was quick to realize that my farm EV was not just another appliance that consumed energy from my windmachines. In fact, I discovered it was just the "mobile" portion of the windplant's battery pack! It was able to move itself to the job, eliminating the need for a long extension cord.

Off-grid energy producers are already beginning to store electricity by producing hydrogen. Electricity can be generated from hydrogen and oxygen in the fuel cell. Hydrogen is a combustible fuel and can be burned in engines or turbines. Coupled when generators, this is another way to make electricity.

Charger Processes

By now, you know what the battery pack needs and what various energy sources can supply. What happens inside the charger itself? What processes does it undertake to match the source and the EV pack?

A charger will perform one or more of the following processes: AC-DC conversion, voltage matching, current regulation, and charge-rate adjustment.

Converting AC to DC

Where the charger is plugged into an energy source such as the utility grid, it must convert ac into DC. Remember—a battery needs DC current to recharge. Making DC out of ac requires a rectifier. Also called a *diode*, the *rectifier* is an electronic check valve about the size of a fat grape.

With one diode, 60-cycle ac power is converted into DC power pulsating at a 60-cycle rate. This works but it's a bit bumpy and inefficient. With two diodes, the result is DC power pulsating at a 120-cycle rate. This is actually smoother power, but it's still rough. Four diodes arranged in a pattern called the *bridge* (Fig. 7-30) is more versatile and efficient in making DC from an ac power source. Packaged in an epoxy box with terminals, two for the ac input and two for the DC output (plus and minus), the result is a bridge rectifier module. A unit the size of a walnut and costing $5 can convert (with adequate heatsinking) 4,000 watts of ac power into DC current.

Diodes and diode bridges have ratings. The voltage rating is PIV (peak inverse voltage). A 200PIV rating is the minimal value for use with 120vac and a 400PIV rectifier is needed for use with 220vac. Amperage is the other rectifier rating. Allowing for current spikes and a design safety factor of two, a bridge rectifier rated at 35A is good for a charge current of 20 Amps.

Diodes get warm when the work. A diode will typically "drop" 0.5-1.0 Volts. At a 20A rate, this produces heat and explains why rectifiers are mounted to heatsinks. A heatsink is a shaped metal or aluminum surface designed to dissipate waste heat. To install, coat the mating surfaces of bridge and heatsink with thermal compound (a gooey substance that helps heat transfer) and mechanically secure the join.

Voltage-Matching

One of the battery charger's jobs is to match the voltages of source and battery pack. Recall that, for current to flow, the source voltage must be higher than that of the battery pack. For moderate current, the voltage difference is slight. This gap increases for higher current rates.

Where there is *no* difference in voltage between the source and the battery pack, this task can be simple. A commercially-manufactured solar module, for example, is designed to charge a 12V battery directly. A 36-Volt battery pack, then, is easily charged by three 12V solar modules wired in series.

A 120V battery pack is also easily charged from a 120vac source voltage without the need for any voltage-matching (Techtalk T73). The "pocket" charger is a good item to stuff away in a glovebox (Fig. 7-31).

Where the difference between the voltages of the source and battery pack is greater than about 5-10 Volts, the only efficient voltage-matching technique to use is the transformer. A transformer is two (or more) closely coupled, independent windings arranged around a core material, like iron. A voltage fed in one winding (the primary) will "induce" voltage in the other winding with *no* direct electrical connection. The proportion of the number of "turns" of primary and secondary windings affects the voltage, stepping it up or down. To keep things right with the laws of conservation of energy, the current decreases or increases (respectively).

The transformer, then, converts ac of one voltage to another voltage. What does it look like? If you were to open up your TV set or stereo amplifier, it's the ominous black, lumpy thing. A smaller version of this gizmo is contained in the little black module you plug into a wall socket to power a tape or CD player, a calculator, or other small devices that normally operate from AA or C-size batteries. Transformers are used *everywhere*.

Transformers have three ratings: input (primary) voltage, output (secondary) voltage, and secondary current.

In most chargers, the operation of voltage matching is performed *before* converting ac to DC. Transformers work only with ac. DC makes them smoke!. So, the transformer first steps down (or up) the voltage, and then the rectifier or diode converts the ac into DC.

Type of Charger

High-power transformers, like those used in EV chargers, are separated into two groups: line chargers and switching chargers.

Line chargers use transformers that work at the line (utility) frequency of 60 cycles. This results in a large and heavy transformer (and, thus, a heavy charger) where the power transfer is 2,000-4,000 watts in capacity.

A *switching charger* converts line (utility) power directly into DC, then oscillates it into high-frequency (5,000-20,000 cycles) ac power at the same voltage. This is fed into a transformer that steps the voltage down (or up) to match the pack voltage, and rectifies it into DC current. High-frequency transformers are

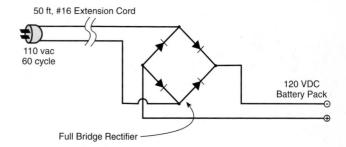

Fig. 7-31: The pocket charger.

very light in weight compared with line (60 cycle) chargers.

Onboard vs Offboard Chargers

The bulk and weight of the line charger makes it difficult (and undesirable) to carry inside the EV. It is often installed offboard. An *offboard* charger is any charger that is installed separate from an EV. To use it, the EV must return to the garage or shop where the charger is located.

An *onboard* charger is one that is installed in the EV and connected to an energy source via an extension cord. Since switching chargers tend to be lighter, they are often installed as the onboard charger. Homebuilt chargers based on the autotransformer are also light enough to be carried onboard.

An EV owner may own both an offboard and onboard charger. A common configuration is to use an offboard charger plugged into 220vac for high-rate recharging at home. An onboard charger (110vac), then, is useful anywhere the EV might travel.

Current Regulation

Energy sources can (or will) deliver power at various rates of current. In their charge cycle (initial, bulk, and taper phases), batteries require current at various rates. Alas, supply and demand do not always coincide.

So, another task assigned to the charger is to provide the right *amount* of current at the *right* time. As previously discussed, there may be a big difference between the input and output current of a charger.

Generally, 110vac is used for battery packs of 120V or less, with overnight charging cycles. Higher power transfer is available from 220vac, which also serves pack voltages of 120V or higher. These are not hard and fast rules. Carefully consider what you need and what will work.

As (the battery) nears a full SOC (state of charge), a constant voltage circuit tapers the charge rate and avoids gassing.

Automated Charge Cycle

Chargers can control current automatically or through adjustment, or both. Circuits exist that can control preset values of current and voltage.

A constant current feature helps the charger maintain a preset (or adjusted) charge rate (i.e., 10 amps). This works well for the initial and bulk phases of charge cycle.

A constant voltage feature (preset or adjusted) allows the charger to maintain a preset (or adjusted) voltage value (i.e., 146V). This is critical for the final phase of the charge cycle, since it looks ahead to where the battery pack should be when fully cycled. A battery's internal resistance continues to climb as it nears a full SOC (state of charge). Engaging a constant voltage circuit tapers the charge rate and avoids gassing.

A "smart" charger is one that combines constant current and constant voltage circuits. It lets you dial in start and finish values, plug your EV's battery pack into an energy source, and walk away.

However, things are not that easy. Many factors can influence these settings. What happens if you add 50 feet of extension cord between the charger and the wall socket? What is the finish voltage of your pack? What happens when you want a faster charge rate? Are you

---

Techtalk
The Owner-Controlled Charge Cycle
T74

Whereas a simple charger cannot detect a battery's SOC, its owner will have a pretty good idea of what it is. How far was the vehicle driven? Was the trip easy or rough on the pack? Did the vehicle feel low (on charge) toward the end? Answers to these questions can place the percentage of DOD within ten percent of its actual value.

The Base Charge. When the recharge will take place at the standard home base, the last setting of a variable rate charger is probably a good starting point. At most, for a depleted pack, the charge rate might need to be turned down. Then, after 15-30 minutes, it can be kicked back up.

If a faster charge cycle is desired, charge current may be adjusted as high as the source will allow at the beginning of the bulk phase. Thereafter, periodic checks (hourly) will reveal if a further upper adjustment is needed. The timer should be used here to ensure that things shut down, either as the pack nears the taper phase or as insurance for the absent-minded. If the knob's pointer hasn't exceeded the position noted for normal finish charging, the charge rate will taper eventually and the timer will shut down the charging process.

On-the-Road Charging. If the onboard charger must be plugged into another source that is not the home base, the EV owner is advised to make no assumptions about what is required. Here's a checklist I use in this event.

• Does the owner know if the line is dedicated or if there are other appliances on the same circuit? Make certain that nothing like a computer is using the same circuit! Switch wall sockets, if necessary.

• Where is the fuse (or circuit breaker) panel? Does it use fuses or circuit breakers? If fuses, are there replacements, if you blow one?

• How old is the wiring? Older households use fuses. Newer ones use circuit breakers.

• Is your charge rate adjustable? Dial it down, and if things look good, start with a maximum of 10A at first. Boost it to 15 Amps after ten minutes if there is no problem. Keep rechecking, to make certain a fuse hasn't blown (or a circuit breaker hasn't tripped). In older structures, check that wires and plugs are not getting hot.

• What is the cost per kWh at this site? Offer to pay for the charge, at twice the kWh rate. Usually, the kWh rate is 6-15 cents per hour. A quarter for an hour's charge is cheap infrastructure. If you blow a fuse, pay for it or replace it.

plugged in at home or the shop? Is it summer or winter? How old is your battery pack?

In fact, today's chargers aren't smart enough to handle the job completely and reliably. Like the VCR, the most popular onboard charger comes with adjusting knobs and a meter. You must ride shotgun over them if you want to be certain you don't undercharge or overcharge your battery pack.

Of course, as EVs become commercially available, chargers will get smarter.

Adjustable Charge Rate

With so many variables to consider, today's "smart" charger is a simple one controlled by a human being. No kidding! A maze of electronics is always needed to do what humans do with little training and virtually no effort. Armed with the basics, most people would find themselves adept at maintaining their EV's battery pack in good operating order with even a homebrew charger. Anyone competent enough to operate a soldering iron can build a unit.

In a short time, new owners will settle into a routine when it comes time to plug in, whether at home or on the road (Techtalk T74)

One of the greatest fears people have about EVs is getting "stuck in the boonies." This can happen in an ICE car, too! A little mental preparation will do a lot toward reducing the fear and, if it actually happens, minimizing the effect it will have on your life (Techtalk T75)).

Maintaining Equal SOC

One challenge in a series-wired battery pack is maintaining a similar state-of-charge (SOC) in each battery of the pack, and even *between the cells of each battery*. Some variance is natural and tolerable. If the variance between the SOC of cells grows from an average value, overall battery performance will degrade and the electric vehicle's operation will be adversely affected.

The same amount of current flows in each cell of a battery in a series-wired pack during charge *and* discharge. This suggests that everything should stay fairly equal. However, the *effect* of current flow in each cell is not the same. Many factors, like manufacturing variances, the amount and level of electrolyte, temperature, and age will affect any cell's SOC. Over time, the interplay of these factors will allow the SOC of some cells to drift far apart.

A battery pack is no greater than its weakest component. Unidentified, low-performing cells

and batteries will affect the battery pack throughout its service life and prematurely end it.

The first step in maintaining an equal SOC across the cells and batteries in a pack is preventing the spread of variance. Understand the nature of conditions that contribute to SOC variance within the cells of the pack (Techtalk T76). Caring for the battery pack will postpone the moment when other action must be taken.

The traditional method of "equalizing" the SOC throughout a pack is the *equalizing charge*. The equalizing charge is a periodic

Batteries are Not Created Equal

Several factors affect the SOC of cells in a battery and explain why they differ initially and eventually. Manufacturing variances. The amount and level of electrolyte. Temperature. Age. The last three are "moving targets," changing through the battery's service life. However, understanding the nature of these factors will help an EV owner to mitigate their impact.

Manufacturing Variations. All batteries are not created equal. Nowadays, it is more difficult than ever to maintain quality control in the mass-production of batteries. To avoid the hazards in transporting batteries (fire, spills, explosion, shock, etc.) and to assure the best shelf life, most batteries are not "activated" (electrolyte added) until purchased. For this reason, there is no way to effectively "test" the battery before it's put on the shelf. As well, to avoid overstock, batteries of different types are produced in limited production "runs" at the factory. As with other types of products, greater differences are likely to show up between items of different runs than between items in the same run.

The quality control of battery production, then, is the "pro-rated guarantee." If the battery fails shortly after purchase, the manufacturer will usually replace it. Of course, if a battery is only slightly defective, it may go undetected for some time. Once revealed, the user may recover some portion of the original cost, or credit toward the cost of a replacement if abuse can be ruled out. Of course, a weakness may never be conclusively identified.

Electrolyte Variations. The amount and level of electrolyte in each cell of each battery in a pack affects a cell's SOC. Batteries are filled with a stock solution of electrolyte with the correct specific gravity (1.260). Once activated and pressed into service, each cell is electrochemically affected by the charge and discharge of current. Heavy states of charge and discharge, along with the periodic "equalizing charge" (more on this soon), will cause some of the water in the electrolyte to dissociate into its elements, hydrogen and oxygen. These gases will be either vented to the atmosphere or recombined and retained in the battery.

There are many opportunities for the SOC of some cells to get out of sync with others during activation, manhandling, and operation. If possible, activate the cells yourself or oversee this operation. If the cells are not filled to exactly the same level throughout the batteries, the SOC will be off from the beginning. Take great care not to spill or overfill the cells during handling or watering. This will throw off the ratio of sulphuric acid to water, and the cell's specific gravity. Remember, in normal operation, *only* water is added to a cell. The remedy for a spill or overfill is complicated and time-consuming. Most remedies are more likely to seesaw the specific gravity the other way than to restore it to the original state. Avoid this problem!

Hydrometer checks and a careful record of the amount of water added to each cell during servicing are two of the best ways to detect the unequal SOC of cells in the pack. Over a period of time, weak, damaged, and

...where a major difference of SOC exists between cells in a battery, there will be a difference in the service life of individual batteries in the pack, too.

shorted cells in the pack will reveal themselves through this record-keeping. More on this in the next chapter.

Temperature. The efficiency of the electrochemistry of a battery is temperature-sensitive. This is most noticeable in cold weather, when a pack's performance will feel sluggish. This happens even if only a few batteries are cold.

Many EVs split the battery pack into two (or more) portions to help maintain the vehicle's original front-to-rear weight ratio. Predictably, batteries in an exposed region of the vehicle (i.e., under the hood) will have a temperature different from those mounted in a protected (i.e., enclosed battery box) location. As the ambient (air) temperature swings through the short cycle of day and night, through stormy weather, or the longer swing of averages through the seasons, it affects pack sections differently. The temperature of exposed batteries will respond (and vary) more quickly than those that are protected. Charge *and* discharge currents are both affected by cells (and batteries) of different temperatures. The relative SOCs will begin to pull apart.

Battery Age. The life story of a lead-acid battery may contain some adventures but it is, for the most part, dull. Contrary to popular opinion, peak performance of a battery is a flat curve that plateaus after about 30 cycles (discharge-charge) and gradually drops off after 85% of the battery's service life. After this, the slope becomes progressively steeper. Weakened performance and poor efficiency will dictate a replacement.

A host of factors can accelerate the useful service life of a battery. For this reason, where a major difference of SOC exists between cells in a battery, there will be a difference in the service life of individual batteries in the pack, too. Often, the entire pack may be faulted when it is only a few of its batteries that are responsible for poor performance. Unfortunately, the entire pack may have to be replaced.

A simple swapout of bad batteries for new ones is rarely a good idea toward the end of the pack's service life. This introduces wildly different SOCs in a pack. New ones will only get stronger. Old ones will only get weaker. Imagine ten people pulling along the length of a rope, each pulling at different times and rates. In both cases, overall performance will suffer.

overcharge of the battery pack. Like a prescription for medicine, it requires a specific dosage (of overcurrent) at a specific frequency (typically, 25-50 times a year for an EV). It is performed at the end of a standard charge cycle. However, instead of ending the charge current, it is sustained, usually for a prescribed period of time (1-2 hours). At the end of the equalizing charge, batteries (and their cells) will be at a full SOC (Techtalk T77).

The equalizing charge is convenient and expedient in some applications, but wastes energy and is harmful. Newer, more efficient methods are being employed in the fight against unequal SOC, too (see Chapter 8).

Control and Safety

A variety of components add important features to the electric drive. Some work to enhance control. Others are designed, in the event of a problem, to prevent widespread component damage or operator injury. This list includes the contactor, circuit breaker, fuses, interconnects, power cables, and interlock (Fig 7-32).

Keyswitch

For the sake of convention, in an EV conversion, the keyswitch should be made to turn the car on and off. In many EVs, this engages a power relay (the contactor) that will apply propulsion voltage to the controller and motor.

At first, operating the key switch will feel odd. After all, there is no engine or motor noise. At most, if a contactor is used, you'll hear the contactor's thunk. Then, silence. (The momentary (start) position of the keyswitch has no effect. There is no starter circuit to engage in an EV like there is in a car with an engine.) An EV operates only when the pedal is depressed. Then, quietly, the EV begins to move!

Main Fuse

A fuse is a a sacrificial component designed to protect the battery pack (and vehicle) against the hazard of a short circuit in the main propulsion wiring. It is rated to pass more current than the vehicle will normally experience under its toughest conditions, but to interrupt battery power quickly when amperage climbs above this value.

T_{77} *echtalk* — The Equalizing Charge

There is no question about the value of maintaining a constant SOC throughout a pack. The main virtue of the equalizing charge is its simplicity. Once you get used to plugging in the EV, it is no big deal to do the occasional overcharge.

How often is the equalizing charge applied? Longtime EV designers and owners will tell you, if you use an EV daily, that the best service life results from a bulk (85%) charge each time the EV is used, and an equalizing charge each week.

A good maintenance schedule will compensate for the gassing effect that occurs with the equalizing charge. At this rate, the batteries must be re-watered approximately every 4-6 weeks. Hot weather will demand this anyway, since it also evaporates water from a battery's electrolyte. Water replacement is always higher in summertime than wintertime.

How long is the equalizing charge applied? The objective is to bring the battery with the lowest SOC to a full SOC. The equalizing charge is sustained until this happens.

The charging process today defines this as a period ranging 30-90 minutes in duration. An older method measured the pilot cell. The pilot cell is the cell with the lowest SOC in the pack. It is identified when a technician takes a hydrometer reading of every cell in the battery pack. The cell with the lowest measured (or recorded) value of specific gravity is labeled the pilot cell. Thereafter, the equalizing charge is terminated when this cell, as measured by a hydrometer, reads "full."

Periodic hydrometer checks might, in the course of a year, transfer the title of "pilot cell" to other cells in the pack.

A fuse is usually installed as the *first* component at the most positive post in the pack. For this reason, it is literally bolted to the battery post itself, protecting the pack from any short-circuit condition beyond this point (Fig. 7-33).

Conversions typically use a 400A fuse. Even if your controller will permit a 400A rate, that's motor current, not battery current, and it's usually not sustained. A 400A fuse may take seconds *or* several minutes to "open" the circuit, allowing for intermittent 400A current. There are "fast blow" and "slow blow" fuses. Get the charts for each and select the amp/time trip level you want. With both, the time period drops as current values increase above the rated ones. Short circuits usually (but not always) result in high currents.

Carry a spare fuse. Unlike the circuit breaker, the fuse is a one-shot deal. If your vehicle uses a DC-DC converter only (no AUX battery), you'll need a flashlight to install the new fuse at night on the road. If it blows, nothing electrical is going to work.

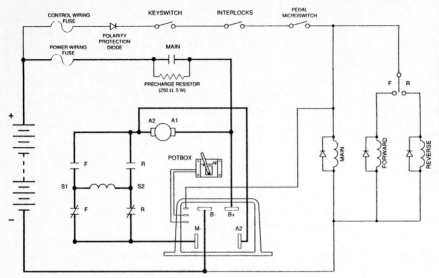

Fig. 7-32: An EV propulsion system wiring schematic

Fig. 7-33: The fuse is connected directly to the battery pack.

Fig. 7-34: The main contactor

Contactor

The contactor is a power relay that allows the vehicle's operator to enable or disable the propulsion system with a simple, small switch (Fig. 7-34). In a conversion, the contactor is often energized by the keyswitch.

The contactor will pass full battery current for as long as the key is on and the vehicle is in use. However, its design function is to *interrupt* full battery current, in the event the operator wants this to happen. When de-energized (keyswitch off), the large contact area snaps open, creating a big gap that will open the circuit under full load. For this reason, use only contactors rated for DC current *and* EVs. They use one (or more) techniques of suppressing the arc that other contactors may find difficult to quench.

Some EV conversions wire the contactor's coil is series with a microswitch that is part of the potbox assembly of the controller (Fig. 7-35). With this arrangement, the contactor is energized when you put your foot on the throttle and de-energized anytime you remove it. Wired in series with the keyswitch, it takes both conditions (key on *and* pedal depressed) to energize the contactor. Thus, either condition (pedal up *or* key off) will de-energize the contactor.

Other EV owners find it objectionable to have the contactor clunking ON and OFF with accelerator pedal action. It's your choice. If you want extra protection without the thunk, wire the potbox microswitch to supply (and interrupt) power to the controller's enable pin

(Fig. 7-36). This will disable the controller whenever the accelerator pedal is released.

A growing number of EVs (some conversions and most prototypes) do not use a main contactor (Techtalk T78). In those circuits, the controller's enable pin is operated from the keyswitch through a small relay that is not part of the main power circuit.

Circuit Breaker

A circuit breaker is a manual on-off switch (Fig. 7-38). Also, it interrupts the flow of motor current in an overload by automatically "tripping" and opening the circuit. It often works faster than a fuse. The unit is inserted between the battery pack and the propulsion system.

The circuit breaker fills many functions nicely. It's fast-blow feature protects the propulsion system against stall motor current and saves replacing fuses. It may be turned off manually, too, if something appears to be wrong, backing up the key-switched contactor. For servicing and maintenance, it is switched OFF, removing voltage from the controller and motor area. If it is unlabeled, it will offer protection against a thief stealing the EV!

Like the fuse, a 400A circuit breaker is designed with a delay that lets it take 400A for many seconds. At a 500-Amp rate, it might pop in a few seconds. This feature provides some

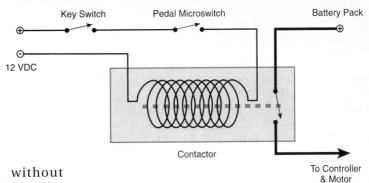

Fig. 7-35: The contactor may be operated from the microswitch on the potbox.

leniency for high currents without compromising the protection afforded for shorts, and has typically a shorter time period than fuses, popping before they do.

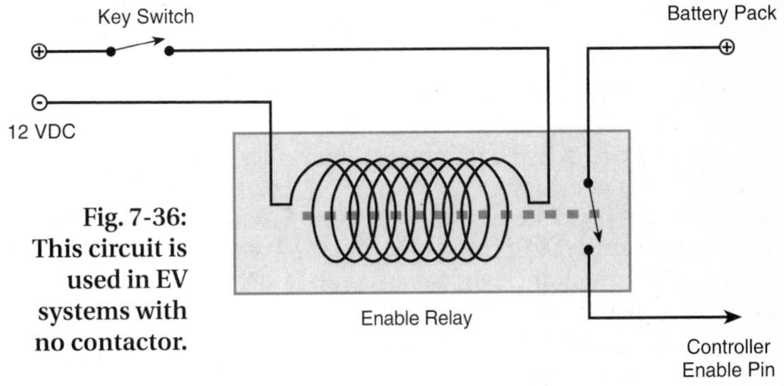

Interconnects

An interconnect is the term associated with electrical links between the batteries in a pack. Flexibility is important for the tight turns an interconnect may need to make if it is to avoid blocking vent caps, other battery posts or interconnects, and battery tie-downs.

An interconnect may be one of several types, depending on the types of posts the batteries use (see Chapter 8). Where the posts of the two batteries (to be connected) are in close proximity, a copper strap (or several layers of thin copper flat stock) may do. Greater spans are bridged with a short length of battery cable terminated at each end in lugs (or some other connector type). Use the special tool (Fig. 7-39) to install these lugs or get it done.

An interconnect must be able to handle full motor current. It should be insulated to protect against shorts. It will need to be coated with an anti-corrosion compound since it is so close to the batteries.

Fig. 7-36: This circuit is used in EV systems with no contactor.

Fig. 7-37: Mount the control hardware on the sidewall.

Fig. 7-38: Circuit breaker and fuses.

Photo: ElectroAutomotive

Photo: ElectroAutomotive

Cables

Cables electrically join the major subassemblies together into working circuits. Currents as high as 400A may flow as energy moves from batteries to the motor through the controller. Cable sizes are large to minimize energy lost as heat in the cables. Cables with hundreds (or thousands) of strands of copper are preferred. Where the gauge is 00 (double 0), flexibility is important. Welding cable is a common choice for propulsion system cables in EVs.

While cable typically has a strong rubber insulation, the cable must be protected against chafing against metal edges that, over time, may result in a short. Rubber grommets may be used to line the edges of holes through which cable passes. Sheathing and custom-built brackets (Fig. 7-40) offer the best protection for high-capacity cables.

Interlock

An interlock is a means of insuring that something can or cannot happen (Fig. 7-41). An interlock in the charging circuit (Fig. 7-42) disables the EV propulsion system when the charge cord is plugged into the vehicle (Techtalk T79). That way, no one can drive the EV away, ripping up the charge cord or receptacles, and damaging the charger and EV.

T78 Redundant Protection

Most EV systems use a contactor, circuit breaker, and fuse(s). All three components are wired in series, all are designed to interrupt high current, and two of them work manually and two work automatically. Why use all three?

The question is actually a good one. Newer EVs, particularly prototypes, often do not use a main contactor, relying instead on the system's fuses and circuit breakers to handle short-circuit conditions. Manual shutdown, then, works by turning off the key or throwing the circuit breaker to the off position.

There are arguments against and for this line of thought.

For the pro side, with all three, the propulsion system has maximum protection through redundancy, even double redundancy. High-voltage DC current is considered more dangerous than ac. Any component can fail. Contactors can fuse closed. Breakers may not respond to low-current shorts. Fuses can blow too fast or not fast enough. An extra $200 buys extra security.

An argument against the use of all three is: "enough is enough." Security is a state of mind. What's enough and what's too much? Early EV components were not as reliable, or were improperly understood (and under-rated) for the level of protection single components would give. Often, these systems used low-voltage packs and higher currents were at work. Early EV controllers were prone to shorting out and meltdowns. Finally, homebuilt EVs rarely used *all* of these components initially. One bad experience could make someone a convert, leaping from little protection (or none) to lots of redundancy.

Today's EV circuits use components that are sized to the application. This correct matchup, along with industrial quality control, makes for greater reliability. Combined with the presence of circuitry in today's controllers (i.e., the "enable" pin for keyswitch operation, the fuse and circuit breaker provide sufficient and redundant protection. The contactor, then, is the most expendable component in the EV propulsion circuit.

Where a contactor is absent from the EV's circuitry, the keyswitch should be set up to energize a relay with contacts rated for 120VDC and one Amp. Its 12V coil should be wired in series with the potbox's microswitch (Fig. 7-36). The relay's contacts will, with key on and pedal depressed, enable the controller for operation.

Some controllers (like the Curtis PMC) will not turn on initially if they sense a high-pedal condition. This prevents the EV from bolting if the key is turned on while the pedal is partially depressed. To work, the pedal must be released and then pressed again to permit motor operation.

Can any of the other components be eliminated instead of the contactor? No! Fuses are well-designed and inexpensive insurance against shorts. The circuit breaker is irreplaceable because it is so versatile. First, it pops faster than a fuse and is resettable. Second, when positioned near the operator, it's easy to shut things down if the keyswitch doesn't do it. And, third, it will remove battery voltage from the drive system during maintenance and repair.

If you eliminate the contactor, make certain that the alternate wiring is clearly indicated in a wiring diagram (or operator's manual) in your car. Troubleshooting an EV is easier where a technician is able to look over a schematic or wiring diagram. Like math, these speak a "universal language." The sooner an experienced EV tech knows about a deviation from traditional circuitry, the faster a problem can be isolated!

T79 Charging Interlock

A charging interlock is a good idea. Even if the charge cord is in plain view, it requires very little distraction to try to drive off in an EV while it is still plugged in. Even if you wish to delude yourself into believing *you* would *never* do this, consider that someone unfamiliar with the vehicle could.

The interlock circuit may be wired up in several ways. One simple technique is to use a relay with SPST contacts and a 110vac coil (Fig. 7-41). The NC (normally closed) contacts are wired in series with the keyswitch circuit and the coil is wired to the ac input of the onboard charger (Fig. 7-42). When the charge cord is plugged into the charge source, the interlock relay is energized, opening the keyswitch circuit. The keyswitch, then, cannot energize the contactor and controller for vehicle operation. As long as 110vac is applied to the vehicle, the EV cannot be driven off.

This circuit works for vehicles equipped with onboard chargers. It will need to be modified to work with offboard chargers. As well, the interlock will not work if the ac charging source is somehow turned off.

An alternate interlock technique is to use a microswitch that is physically "tripped" when the charging cord (or plug) is connected.

Auxiliary Power

In a gas-powered car, the SLI (starting-lighting-ignition) battery helps to operate many "accessories"—lights, turn signals, blowers, windshield wipers, horn, etc. When the engine is running, all of these functions are powered by the engine's generator or alternator.

In an EV, there is no engine, generator, or alternator. Yet, all of the accessories remain. There are new ones, too, like contactors, relays, instruments, and other control functions. How are they powered?

First, let's look at how we'll generate the 12V power to run accessories. Then, let's look at accessories an EV is likely to need.

Fig. 7-39: Use the right tools to attach lugs to big cables.

Fig. 7-40: Protect battery cables with sheathing and brackets

There are four ways to power accessory loads in an EV: pack tap, an auxiliary (AUX) battery, a DC-to-DC converter, and a hybrid setup.

Pack Tap

Power for accessories in an EV can be "tapped" from one battery in the propulsion pack (Fig. 7-43). In no-frills EVs, like an Electrathon racer and electric scooters, particularly those with a series-parallel control system, the pack tap may be the only expedient method of getting a 12V supply voltage.

Pack tap is *not* a recommended technique for anything but very small EVs for several reasons (Techtalk T80).

Fig. 7-41: An interlock prevents someone from driving off while the EV is still plugged in.

The AUX Battery

An auxiliary (AUX) battery is the traditional way that accessory loads are powered in the EV. It is similar to the SLI battery found in ICE cars, and may occupy the same location. However, in the EV, the Aux battery must be a deep-cycle type. Why? Unlike the SLI battery in the ICE car, it cannot be recharged from a nonexistent generator or alternator. Thus, it must withstand deep discharge in the normal operation of the EV. As well, it must always retain a reserve for lights and emergency flashers just as cars with engines must.

During the charge cycle, the AUX battery is charged at the same time the main pack is being replenished. Older-style chargers often have a built-in, 12V charger for this purpose. If not, a separate charger must be included. It must be sized to fully recharge the AUX battery within the same timeframe as the pack. A depleted AUX battery can disable an EV (even one with a fully-charged propulsive battery pack) when the contactor is de-energized.

A virtue of the AUX battery is its independence from the propulsion battery pack. A problem with the main battery pack, then, isn't going to interfere with an ability to supply "juice" for warning flashers and lights, or a call for help via a CB or cellular phone.

The rating of the AUX battery is situational and deserves some thought. The EV has a limited range before its battery pack, and the AUX battery, must be recharged. With EV operation limited to 1-2 hours at a time, it's possible that the AUX battery could have a low Ah rating. EV owners like to minimize onboard weight, so a smaller and lighter AUX battery helps. But — don't guess. Note the ratings of all operational loads and the frequency and duration of their use. Some calculations and summing will help find the approximate Ah rating for the AUX battery.

It's a good idea to include some means of monitoring the AUX battery, voltage and current. Matching dual-scale ammeters and voltmeters can do this with the flick of a switch. Otherwise, a digital meter will do the job.

Fig. 7-42: An interlock circuit.

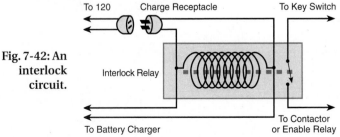

To 120   Charge Receptacle   To Key Switch

Interlock Relay

To Battery Charger   To Contactor or Enable Relay

T80 — Pack Tap

In the smaller EVs, power for 12V accessories can be supplied by a "tap" on the main pack (Fig. 7-43). In this setup, the positive terminal of the 12V battery closest to ground is wired to the accessories fuse panel. In a pack comprised of 6V batteries, it is the second battery closest to ground that will supply the needed 12V power.

Pack tap is important in simple EVs, ones using a 12V or 24V battery pack, particularly if a series-parallel control system is used. This ensures that the "tapped" battery will be replenished during the recharge cycle, since it is in parallel with the other one.

Pack tap is *not* a recommended technique for larger EVs for four reasons. First, to work, the main battery pack and the 12V system must *share* a common ground. This is a major no-no in large EVs. Second, as the propulsive pack is depleted, the 12V supply will drop lower and lower, eventually disabling the EV. Third, accessory loads in a vehicle can represent a fairly hefty load. Tapping power from one battery in the main pack will discharge it at a faster rate than the others. During vehicle operation, this battery will be depleted before the others. This will, in turn, limit the output of the battery pack, degrading EV performance and range. Finally, how is the "tapped" battery assured of a full recharge when its SOC is so different from all the others?

One merit of pack tap is its utility in an emergency. If the EV is disabled because the battery for the accessories is depleted, pack tap can energize the 12V supply (and the contactor and propulsion system relays) for the time it takes to get home.

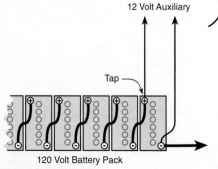

12 Volt Auxiliary

Tap

120 Volt Battery Pack

Fig. 7-43: Pack tap is used in small EVs.

Fig. 7-44: This DC-(to)-DC controller is found in many EVs.

Fig. 7-45: The hybrid system uses both a battery and a DC-DC converter.

The DC-to-DC Converter

The DC-to-DC converter (or DC-DC) is an electronic gizmo that powers accessories in the EV directly from the propulsive power pack (Fig. 7-44). As its name implies, it connects across the battery pack, converts the high-voltage DC into 12VDC, and supplies power to the accessories. In most designs, it *replaces* the AUX battery.

Select it carefully (Techtalk T81). Reliability is essential for a stand-alone DC-DC converter. Imagine you're in a storm at night and a semi-trailer truck starts to pull out in your path. You've got the headlights, defroster, and heater

T81 — Selecting the DC-DC Converter

The DC-DC converter uses low-cost, high-frequency conversion electronics to do its job. Inside, the DC input is "switched" to ac, stepped down to 12 Volts, rectified back to DC, and passed through the voltage regulator.

The DC-DC converter's input is available in several ranges of input voltages. Select a unit with an upper value close to the EV's pack voltage. The unit must faithfully power a full load of accessories, even when the pack voltage drops as it nears depletion. Here's a shopping list.

•Select an output current rating of 30A or more for a car.

•Output voltage should be 12.6V at full rated current.

•Input voltage range should have a high-end rating that is equal to or slightly larger than the pack's voltage at full charge. It should still deliver 80% of rated power when the pack voltage falls to a low value.

• The output current rating must handle the largest operational load. To figure this, you must determine the ratings of everything used onboard — lights, turn signals, horn, wipers, blowers, relays, etc. (Here, a 50A/50milliOhm shunt is handy. Inserted inline in the 12V supply, it can be monitored with a digital meter as each load is switched on. Write down the current draw.)

Establish three values: minimum, nominal, and surge. The *minimum* current rating of the converter is one that equals the largest single load. The *nominal* current rating represents a combination of loads — i.e., relays, blowers, headlights, and horn — that might be used simultaneously. The *maximum* current rating (peak or surge) represents the sum of all loads used briefly. The specification sheets for a converter will indicate values for continuous and surge ratings.

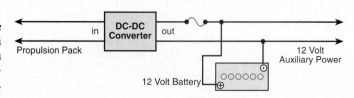

in — DC-DC Converter — out

Propulsion Pack

12 Volt Battery

12 Volt Auxiliary Power

on. With all those loads on, you're still going to want a *big* sound from the horn.

The DC-DC converter's input is wired directly to the battery pack (through its own fuse), bypassing the main pack fuse. This way, the pack's main fuse may blow (or the breaker can trip) without also disabling the 12V supply. It's bad enough to blow a fuse zooming up a hill at night without also going into a total blackout at speed!

The main advantage of the converter is that it is light (1-3 lbs) when compared with an AUX battery (30-60 lbs). It is about the same cost as the deep-cycle AUX battery *and* the 12V charger it replaces. A good converter will keep producing 12V power even when the battery pack is too depleted to operate the vehicle.

The use of a stand-alone DC-DC converter has one major disadvantage. In EV circuits that include a contactor or control relays, the vehicle will be disabled if this unit fails.

A Hybrid 12V Supply

A hybrid 12V supply system combines a DC/DC converter with a small AUX battery for control circuitry and accessory loads. The two are wired in parallel (Fig. 7-45). In a hybrid 12V circuit, the AUX battery's job is to handle *peak* loads. The converter's role is sustained loads, and AUX battery recharging.

The primary virtue of the hybrid 12V supply is safety. With this setup, if the DC-DC unit fails, the AUX battery is there to take up the slack (for a while). A second virtue is that, with such teamwork, both the battery *and* converter ratings may be reduced, resulting in smaller, less expensive components.

The main disadvantage of the hybrid setup is greater weight (than a stand-alone DC-DC unit) and, perhaps, a higher cost than either the AUX battery/charger technique or the stand-alone DC/DC system.

With the right combination of components and conditions, the hybrid 12V setup may be employed to help equalize the SOC of individual batteries in the main pack *without* overcharging the whole pack (see Chapter 8).

AUX (12V) Accessories

Many 12V accessories are affected when a vehicle is made electric. Here are some thoughts relative to each accessory.

Horns. All EVs, no matter the size, need a horn. Legal is good, but get a big one so that you'll be *heard*. The silence of EVs makes it hard for people to hear them coming. A little beep works for shopping malls. A big horn help with bigger objects (trucks?) that want to cross your path.

Wipers. A wiper motor is a high-current device. If it goes slower than normal, the 12V supply (DC-DC converter and/or battery) is too weak. Fix it.

Headlights. Headlights, tail lights, brake and turn signal lights, and a license plate light add up to 15-20A at 12V. Don't skimp on them. Your EV may have a big horn, but a little extra boost in the lighting category will help, too.

Battery Vent Blower. Heavy discharge currents will dissociate water in the batteries and release oxygen and hydrogen. A vent blower sucks air out of the battery compartment and exhausts any gases outside the vehicle. It should be ON any time the vehicle is in operation.

Gases may take a while to get clear of the interior of a battery after prolonged operation. A timing circuit (or timer switch) will keep the blower working for a while, in much the same way as the engine fan in some gas-powered cars continues to cool the radiator after a vehicle is stopped. A timer that can be adjusted by the driver on exiting the vehicle is one way to safely vent gas for as long as it is necessary.

Recharging an EV should begin as soon as possible following use. The vent blower should operate during the recharge process. Following an equalizing charge, it should work for a while to clear the compartment of the gases that will otherwise accumulate.

Blowers venting gases should be of the brushless type. These do not produce a spark that could ignite gases.

Defrost and Cabin Heat. Electric vehicles operated in colder climates lack the engine heat that can be routed into the driver and passenger compartment. Even if the owner is content to wear more clothing, the lack of heat for defrosting the windshield is dangerous.

I've seen EV owners defrost the windshield and heat the EV's interior with two methods.

• *Floor Heater.* Use a floor heater to operate directly off the battery pack. This is straightforward. Substitute an electric heater for the water-coolant heater (used with engines) inside the blower assembly. In severe cold conditions, these heaters did not use more than about 10% of the battery pack's capacity when full-ranged. That's about 5 miles' worth under the worst conditions. Add a timer to *preheat* the vehicle cab from utility

Fig. 7-46: A PTC coil is one way to provide both cab and defrost heat in an EV.

power, while it is still plugged in. Once underway, the heater need only make up for heat losses.

• *PTC Unit.* Install a PTC (positive temperature coefficient) unit. This is a solid-state heater that becomes more resistive to electric current as it heats. Combined with a heavy flow of air, it will transfer heat very quickly. Its design makes it self-limiting. If airflow is cut off to it, it cuts back to a very low heating value. When installed in the vehicle, the relay which routes power to it (from the propulsion pack) is energized only when the defroster fan is on high.

PTC units are designed to fit the space normally used by the heater coil coupled to an engine. Remove the entire heater blower assembly, remove the old coil, and insert the PTC unit. Re-wire the fan switch to energize the power relay that powers the PTC unit when there's maximum air flow.

Monitoring

How do you know what is happening during the operation of any vehicle? You see movement, you hear wheels and motor sounds, and you sense vibration in your hands. Sensory input, then, communicates action.

Other conditions are not so easily detected with our senses. In an EV, at what rate is power being consumed? How much energy is left in the battery bank? How hot is the motor? Ultimately, we must rely on monitors to extend the reach of our senses, and supply the answers to these and other questions.

A monitor is a device that detects, processes, and communicates data or information. A well-designed monitor communicates this at a glance. Fuel and temperature gauges, speedometer and tachometer, and oil and generator lights are all examples of monitors.

Monitors in an EV are of a different type than those used in an ICE car. In a conversion, the fuel gauge, water temp and oil pressure sensors, and generator lights will go away. In their place are instruments to monitor voltage, current, battery capacity, and temperature.

Most monitors fall into one of three kinds: indicators, gauges and meters. For almost any function, an indicator (light) and sensor may be substituted for a gauge (or meter), and vice-versa. There are advantages and disadvantages in using either (or both) of these monitors (Techtalk T82).

Typically, the EV will benefit from a combination of gauges and indicators. The voltmeter and ammeter (Fig. 7-47), Ah gauge and tachometer cover the likely gauges, besides the speedometer. Indicators are good for system activation, turnsignals, and notification of high motor temperature.

This section will further detail the functions of the instruments monitoring the electric propulsion system. In use, they will help you operate and better understand your EV.

Voltmeter

A voltmeter is an electric (or electronic) device that displays EV voltages (Fig. 7-47). The most important voltage to monitor is that of the propulsion battery pack. Of secondary importance is monitoring the 12VDC (AUX battery) supply. Some EVs have the ability to read the voltage of every battery in the pack. In practice, one meter can monitor all of these functions, although it cannot display them simultaneously. Toggle and rotary switches are handy for selecting the voltage you want to watch at any given moment.

The reading on the voltmeter affords one of the best ways to know a battery pack's SOC (state of charge). A reading can be made in a static state (no battery current flowing) or in a dynamic state (a specific rate of motor current is flowing). As the battery pack discharges, the average voltmeter reading (static or dynamic) will drop. Over time, the attentive EV owner will learn how to "interpret" the voltmeter, converting its data into useful information regarding battery pack SOC (Techtalk T83).

The voltmeter can be analog or digital in nature. An analog meter is usually a needle that deflects across the face of a scale. Over a wide range of issues, there are many factors to consider in choosing the correct analog meters for the EV (TechTalk T84).

A digital voltmeter displays numbers with LEDs or liquid crystal technology.

Ammeter

An ammeter shows the amount of battery current that flows to the controller and, eventually, the motor. Its readout displays

Indicators and Gauges
T82

Monitors can take the form of indicators, gauges, or meters.

Indicators. Indicators are a simple and inexpensive way to know the ON-OFF state of a function. For example, a glowing light will help you remember to turn something OFF that you've forgotten was ON.

Years ago, automotive manufacturers began installing more indicator lights and fewer gauges. They felt that drivers didn't use the gauges. So, while a gauge might clearly indicate, with its needle slowly rising, that trouble was on the way, if it went unnoticed by an inattentive driver, it wasn't doing its job. Indicators offered a good alternative. No lights? Everything's okay. A light ON? Solid or flashing, this spells "trouble-trouble-trouble."

Indicator lights are also known as idiot lights. An indicator light in a standard car that indicates a hot engine, a loss of battery voltage, or a loss of oil pressure is good, but it suffers severe limitations, too. One is that it doesn't give you any real

warning. Once ON, you are supposed to know what that means and take immediate action. Two, it has a nasty habit of coming ON too late to be of much use. And, third, if the filaments of the bulb have burned out, you will never get a warning! Without a means of testing the bulb, then, you'd be an idiot to use them.

Increase the effectiveness of an indicator by choosing the correct color for the lens or bulbs. You are more likely to use (or appreciate) an indicator if it doesn't bother you. So, if it will be on a lot (system on, fan cooler on, etc.), use green or blue colors. Yellow is good for turn signal lights. Reserve red for danger. Use a flashing light for daylight use (so you'll notice). Equip indicator lights with a dimmer (rheostat). Something bright enough for daytime use may blind or distract you at night.

Gauges and Meters. Gauges and meters fill the gap between knowing nothing (no light) and still not knowing much (light ON) but knowing that something is wrong. A meter shows you the degree of something. Long before an indicator labeled HOT starts

glowing or flashing, a temperature gauge will show you when things are cool, warm, and hot. You can see a needle creep up. In a gauge, then, you can estimate the immediacy of doing something about a rising needle. Can you make it to the top of the grade, or should you take the next exit?

Gauges and meters require your attention and an understanding of what is being represented. An occasional glance will do, with more frequent scans when conditions (hill climbing or low battery state) warrant them.

The terms gauge and meter are often used interchangeably when referring to an analog device. An analog meter has a needle that moves through an arc against a calibrated scale. A meter can also be digital. A digital meter displays numbers that correspond to the values you might read where a needle points on a scale.

Fig. 7-47: Fuel and temp gauges are modified to read volts and amps in instrument cluster.

amperes (or Amps, or A), showing the *rate* at which your EV is using power.

The reading on the ammeter is generally proportional to how far the accelerator pedal is depressed. More pedal equals more amperage, and more power to the motor. Want a lower current flow? Back off the pedal!

How is this current actually measured? Ammeters do not pass the kind of current they measure. Instead, the meter reads current that flows through a "shunt." A *shunt* is a calibrated device that looks like a block of brass or bronze (Fig. 7-48). The shunt is inserted directly in-line (in series) with the heavy cables between the battery pack and motor controller (Techtalk T85). Small sensing wires attached to terminals on the side of the shunt are routed to the ammeter itself.

Ammeters, like voltmeters, can be either analog or digital in nature.

Analog vs Digital Meters

A common division in EV circles occurs around the question, "Which is better? Analog

or digital meters?" A case can be given for either type (Techtalk T86). Weigh carefully the factors of importance to you.

After many years of using both types of meters, I find myself content with using an analog device for reading current, but prefer the accuracy and resolution of a digital display for reading voltage. This creates a dilemma because I like matched meter sets, too! More recently, I have been using an aH meter.

The Ah Meter

The Amp-hour meter is the closest thing to a fuel gauge in the EV (Fig.7-49). It is designed to display the amount of energy taken from (or still remaining in) the battery pack.

Circuitry behind the display unit does all the work. Both voltage and current are monitored (and may be displayed, via

T83 Relating Voltage and State of Charge

A battery pack's voltage, after charge, will display a specific reading. As the EV is operated, this voltage will drop. At some point, the pack will be depleted. What will the voltage reading be at this point?

There is a relationship between the voltage reading and the pack's state of charge (SOC). One range of voltages will be displayed if the readings are taken when no current is being drawn (i.e., the vehicle is at rest). Another range of voltage will be displayed at various values of motor current. What are these ranges?

A voltage reading taken at "no load" (no motor current) will vary for some period of time *after* the load has been removed. Thus, it is important *when* you note the voltage reading.

For this reason, I prefer to take voltage ratings at a specific rate of motor current. A motor current of 75A has proven to be a good sampling zone. Steadying the motor current to 75A is as simple as modulating the accelerator pedal. Note the voltage rating as the motor current steadies on 75A. Compare it with this chart for one 12V battery.

Voltage at 75A discharge rate

12.0V	100%	Charged
11.8V	75%	
11.5V	50%	Half
10.8V	25%	
10.5V	0%	·Discharged

Halve these values for battery packs made up of 6V batteries.

A 120V battery pack, then, at a 75A discharge rate will display 120V at 100% capacity, 118V at 75%, 115V at 50%, and 108V at 25%. The pack is depleted when the reading is 105V.

For battery packs of different voltages, divide the pack voltage by 12V, and multiply the resultant by the values above. Type or write up this list on a small piece of paper, and glue it to the dash near the meter. A quick comparison after taking a reading will establish the approximate SOC of the battery pack.

A fully-charged pack will read, per 12V unit and after about 15 seconds at no load, about 12.6V. (Add 0.6V per 12V unit to the values above to get the no-load voltage readings.) Therefore, under the same conditions, the readings will be 12.4V at 75% capacity, 12.1V at 50%, 11.4V at 25%, and 11.1V for a depleted pack.

Below 10.5V at 75A, a 12V battery will still contain some energy, but it also can be damaged by continued discharge.

T84 Analog Meters

Value, accuracy, size, type, power consumption, and the relative polarity in various circuit operations will affect the selection of the analog voltmeter and ammeter.

• *Value.* An analog voltmeter is less expensive than an analog ammeter. A voltmeter takes its reading "across the battery pack." By contrast, an ammeter takes its reading across a shunt that is in series with the current flow from the battery pack. An ammeter, then, adds the cost of a shunt to the investment.

• *Accuracy.* Accuracy is important in an analog meter. Typically, an analog meter reads the most accurately in the center of its scale (the needle is halfway across the face). It is least accurate at both ends. This explains the scale on the speedometer that read up to 120 mph in cars. Readings around 60 mph, then, are more accurate.!

Before installation and use, check the accuracy of the analog ammeter and voltmeter against against a digital voltmeter. Reject anything that is off by more than 5% at center-scale.

• *Meter size.* The larger the meter movement (in inches across the face), the better the resolution and the easier it is to read quickly. Scale divisions that read to the nearest 10A or 5V will do.

• *Type of meter.* Meters designed for mobile applications (auto-style) are "dampened." This lets the needle remain relatively steady even when the vehicle is experiencing rough terrain. Instruments designed for stationary applications, undampened, are hard to read, and the needle may damage itself, too. Road-test meters before you commit to their use, i.e., drill out their mounting holes.

• *Power consumption.* The voltmeter works even when the vehicle is stationary. In contrast, the ammeter reads only when there is current flow. Since the voltmeter consumes a small amount of power, it is customary to wire it into the key switch circuit so that no reading occurs when the key switch is off. Where dual-scale meters are used, a center OFF position is another way to turn off (or leave on) the voltmeter's reading.

• *Polarity.* Analog meters, volts or amps, are polarity-sensitive, showing current flow in *one* direction. If you wire the meter up backward, the needle will deflect against the stop to the left. Repeated polarity mistakes will damage the meter's needle and inner workings.

There *are* ammeters designed to show current flow in either direction. Usually, the zero point is halfway across the meter face. Flow in one direction deflects the needle to the right, and reverse current flow deflects the needle to the left. Center-zero meters are tempting to use because they are inexpensive, and uncomplicated. However, they offer poor accuracy and resolution. Avoid them.

• *Reversal, regen braking, and charging.* Various operations will electrically *re-wire* sections of the electrical circuits. If you electrically-reverse your EV, make certain that meters are wired to points that don't experience reverse flow (polarity). The same rule applies for regenerative braking. Arrange meter circuits for the correct polarity whenever in this mode.

For charging, position the ammeter so that it will have the correct polarity when charging commences.

switches) by this unit. Frequent sampling of these values is accumulated as the EV changes speeds. Since the product of volts multiplied by amps equals power (wattage), the recorded data represents actual power consumed in propulsion. Irrespective of the battery rating, then, the driver of an EV knows the pack's state of charge.

The data the Ah meter collects may be displayed in other ways. One brand uses a vertical bar of LEDs (light-emitting diodes) to display battery capacity. Full capacity may light all of the LEDs, with individual segments (from the top down) winking out during discharge. One brand lights just one LED, which shifts from segment to segment during discharge, down through the array.

Another brand of Ah meter puts numbers on a liquid crystal display. It is set up in one of two ways. The most common is for zero to represent a fully charged pack. As the pack discharges, the value of Ah removed is a negative unit that grows in value. A less common technique reverses the numbering system, with the pack's kWh capacity displayed when full. Discharge, then, counts down, reaching zero when depleted.

Recharging the EV's battery pack reverses these processes. So, a full recharge relights the LEDs, and returns the Ah display to zero or a specific capacity value. Partial recharges reach midpoints. With all three systems, the user has some idea of the battery's SOC at any time. All three units allow extra energy in each charge cycle to compensate for battery and charging inefficiencies. The actual amount is preset, but is often user adjustable.

Combined Ah Meters

Since the Ah meter *must* monitor both voltage and current to keep track of Ah usage in the battery pack, very little extra circuitry is needed to help display these value manually or automatically in just one package (Fig. 7-49.)

---

*T*echtalk

T 85 The Ammeter's Shunt

When a current flows through a shunt, its small resistance causes a small drop in voltage across it. A sensitive meter, with its wires attached to each side of the shunt, can detect and display the value of this voltage. In analog meters, it is most correct to say that a small bit of that current is deflected, or shunted, to the meter by the shunt, causing a needle's deflection. The meter's dial, perhaps calibrated to read 500 Amps of current, then, is only experiencing milliamps of current itself. Since the shunt is calibrated to drop a specific amount of voltage for a specific amount of current, the scale will represent the bulk of the current flowing from battery to controller through the shunt.

Shunts are not polarity sensitive. They will handle reverse current and will provide an accurate reading of current flow in either direction.

Shunts have ratings. They are designed to work with specific meters. For example, a 50mV (milliVolt)/500 Amp shunt will deflect a 50mV meter. If the scale displayed on the face is "graduated" in five divisions, each division represents 100A. Full deflection of the needle, then, will indicated a 500A current flow in the shunt.

A 50mV/50 Amp shunt (traditionally used for the 12V circuit in the EV), will deflect the same meter full scale with only 50A of current flow. This explains how one meter can have two scales with big differences in the amount of current they display. With both of these shunts wired to a switch, the EV operator can monitor battery current or aux (battery) current.

A mismatch of shunt and meter will lead to false readings. Ensure that you have the correct shunt and meter combination.

The Internal Shunt

An older style of current meter may include the shunt inside the meter case.

Except in smaller EVs and unless you're experienced with them, avoid meters with internal shunts. There are several reasons why. First, picked from a pile of meters, there's no way to tell if an ammeter has an internal shunt. Rarely is there any printed notice of it, either. A meter designed for an external shunt, will, when connected in-line directly with a power cable, die violently in the space of a microsecond. Check!

Second, a meter with an internal shunt is generally not a good choice for an EV. Since the meter must be visible to the driver, it forces the routing of heavy battery cables to the mounting location for the meter, i.e., the dash—both inconvenient and power consuming. Remember those I-squared-R losses! Good layout design for the EV's power cables suggests the shortest distance between motor, controller, and battery pack. An external shunt lets you put the shunt where these big cables are, adding small wires to reach the meter itself.

Finally, a meter with an internal shunt cannot easily be wired to display both propulsive and AUX battery currents. This forces the use of *two* meters.

Fig. 7-48: An ammeter shunt.

Photo: ElectroAutomotive

"Smart" meters are on the way for EVs. These will use a microprocessor to monitor a large variety of conditions, store data, and supply more information to the user than is provided at this point (TechTalk T87).

Temperature Monitoring

Compared with the ICE engine, electric propulsion generates very little heat. Still, the motor, controller, charger, and batteries will get warm in normal service. Under extreme conditions, they might get hot. Today's motors are designed to work at temperatures twice those of engine parts. Still, how do you detect high-temperature states? Temperature gauges and thermoswitches are available for this job.

Temperature Gauge

The temperature gauge is similar to the one found in most cars to monitor engine heat. To work, the gauge is connected to a sensor called the "sender." The sender is a thermistor, or a resistor with an NTC (negative temperature coefficient). So, as the temperature *increases,* the sender's resistance *decreases,* increasing the deflection of the needle of the temperature gauge toward the *hot* side. In a water-cooled engine, the sender is in contact with the coolant (water or glycol). In an air-cooled engine, the sender is in contact with oil.

Monitoring the temperature of an electric motor requires a sender similar to the one used with engines. It *is* possible to adapt the engine

---

T86 Techtalk — Analog vs Digital Meters

When it comes to meters, is analog or digital better?

• **Readability.** Analog meters are considered easier to read than digital meters. Understanding them requires no computation. Like gauges that show fuel level in the gas tank, temperature, or pressure readings, an analog voltmeter or ammeter gives a relative reading—low, midrange, high. Digital readings involve a different part of the brain, requiring recognition, and a comparison to some standard to impart a "relative" meaning.

• **Accuracy.** Relatively inexpensive digital meters give the same accuracy as expensive analog meters. In the case of the ammeter, virtually any digital voltmeter will work with a standard shunt.

• **Resolution.** Digital meters give a precise resolution of voltage and current where analog meters, as the range of values increase, lose resolution. An *expanded scale* voltmeter mitigates this issue by limiting the range of voltage it displays. For example, a 120V system will often use an expanded-scale meter of 100-150V. This meter will not display voltages below 100 Volts or above 150 Volts. For a 120V pack, 146 Volts is the highest charge voltage and 105 Volts is the lowest discharge point. A difference of only 50V across the face gives this reading three times the resolution of the meter with a 150V difference (0-150V).

• **Range.** Analog meters, particularly voltmeters, have specific "ranges." To use them requires the selection of the most appropriate scale. Most digital meters have an "auto-ranging" feature. Simply touch (or connect) the meter leads to *any* voltage. The meter will find the correct range, shifting the decimal point and displaying the value.

• **Polarity tolerance.** Analog meters of *any* type are sensitive to polarity, where digital meters are not. The digital meter's leads are usually red and black, but reversing them only brings a negative (-) or positive (+) sign on the display.

• **Sample rate.** A digital meter "samples" voltage (and current) to work. Where the meter samples too slowly, what it displays may be old news. During rapid acceleration, the reading of volts or amps will lag behind the values of each. If the meter samples too quickly, the display will be shifting too rapidly to read. Sample rate is more of an issue with current than it is with voltage.

• **Decimal point.** Today's digital multimeters, even with auto-ranging and auto-reverse, will put the decimal point at the wrong point. For example, a 260A current will read as 26.0 on the display. This is not a deficiency, but simply an oddity. It's easy to get used to, and is no reason to reject a specific meter unless other factors demand it.

• **Illumination.** To be used at night, meters must be illuminated. Digital meters using LEDs make their own light. They're great at night (and sometimes hard to see in daylight!). Automotive gauges often are backlit or include a built-in bulb to illuminate the faceplate. Panel meters and digital meters with liquid crystal displays rarely include this feature, and you must add the needed illumination. Most metering, digital or analog, designed for use in EVs includes night illumination.

• **Noise.** Digital meters can get confused by transient noise. Modern electronic controllers operate at high frequencies. Motors generate CEMF (counter electro motive forces) and EMP (electromagnetic pulses). Either may "freeze" the display. Cycling the meter (off, then on) or releasing the accelerator pedal momentarily will usually "unlock" this condition.

Digital meters usually get a cleaner signal from a Hall-effect sensor in EV motor circuits. This device detects tiny changes in the electromagnetic fields around wires as the current in them varies. These signals are routed to amplifying circuits and work for analog or digital meters. Unlike shunts, circuits based on Hall-effect detection do not come into direct contact with large electric currents, and may avoid much of the noise they carry.

• **Cost.** The biggest advantage of a digital meter is the resolution and accuracy you can buy at a low cost. A common analog ammeter with a 0-500 amp scale is 3 inches across and costs $70. A quick look will indicate that your motor is drawing 300-400A. A digital meter ($22 from Radio Shack) across the same shunt will tell you that the motor current is precisely 355A.

sensor for use with the EV's motor. The benefit here is that it retains the stock instrumentation cluster that can't accept a different gauge.

Scratchbuilt vehicles have it a little easier here. Gauge/sender packages are available from automotive parts houses. Units designed for monitoring cylinder head temperatures are a good bet.

A temperature-sensing circuit is also within the grasp of any hobbyist that knows the working end of a soldering gun. It is built around a thermistor available from electronics supply houses, runs off the 12V AUX battery, and may be precisely calibrated. The addition of a rotary switch allows one meter to monitor senders attached to different heat sources.

Senders positioned at several points in the battery pack and one at the electronic controller would be helpful, too. Select a thermistor for a working range of 30-130 degree F. for batteries, and 70-200 degrees F. for the controller.

Thermoswitch

Another device that will monitor various components for heat buildup is the thermoswitch. The *thermoswitch* is a "thermal switch" with a preset design "threshhold." When it reaches a specific temperature, it acts like a switch and turns on.

It is easy to wire up a thermoswitch. Connect up one side to 12V. Connect the other side to whatever you want it to switch on when activated. The thermoswitch will light up an indicator, sound a buzzer, or start a blower motor! Or all three!

Thermistors are available in a wide range of temperature ratings. Select one with a current-handling capacity to drive a bulb, buzzer, fan, or a combination of these. Or select one with a rating that will let it energize the coil of a relay that will handle these loads, or larger ones.

Fortunately, manufacturers are realizing the importance of including thermoswitches in their motors. For example, a motor from Advanced DC Motor Company includes one. Connect the small protruding wires to make light or sound, or move cooling air!

Tachometer

Another common gauge in many instrument clusters is the tachometer. With a swing of its needle, you can see the motor's speed—which is especially important when you can't hear it!

T_{87} *echtalk*

Smart Meter Features

A single computer chip or microprocessor can store and process an amazing amount of data. What might we ask of it in making smart meter for EVs?

- Give us a fuel gauge that's accurate and intuitive!
- Adjust displayed values to compensate for the effect of battery temperature.
- Adjust displayed values to compensate for battery inefficiencies at various discharge rates.
- Record and compare routes that are repeated (i.e., several different ways to work). Learns mileage of repeated trips (work, stores, town, battery exchange station, etc.). User can query system if SOC is sufficient to accomplish specific trip.
- Display miles-to-discharge at current discharge rates.
- Suggest a speed to extend range if needed.
- Detect and warn of performance variations.
- List probable causes of variations in SOC—efficiency, temperature, battery age, sulfation, and low electrolyte.
- Self-tests. Isolate problem areas and display.
- Track battery info—age/# of cycles/efficiency/maintenance dates.
- Forewarn of upcoming maintenance check or maintenance overhaul.

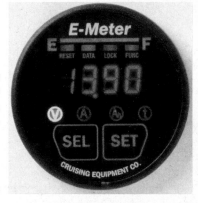

Fig. 7-49: One meter will indicate voltage, current, and Ah capacity.

Photo: Cruising Equipment, Inc.

A tachometer's sender is frequently designed to monitor an engine, so it is unlikely to work directly with an electric motor. Hobbyists know to install a disk on the rotor that has magnets embedded in it. A sensor or Hall-effect device will detect this pulsating signal and drive the tachometer. The trick is to calibrate it to work the tachometer in your vehicle.

Again, auto parts houses sell tachometers with presettable senders, and this should give a good fit for the EV

What now?

The next chapter integrates what this chapter has presented. Even if you're not ready to convert yet, look it over for what is involved!

Chapter 8
Find, Fit, Use, and Maintain

*T*his chapter is about doing it. It assumes that you are
ready to transform an interest, an idea, or a fantasy
into an EV parked in your driveway. While Chapter 7 gives
you the EV's building blocks, this chapter
is about putting them together.

Here, you will select and install the
motor and batteries. You will also learn
how to operate and maintain the EV.
Conversion or scratchbuilt, ninety
percent of this chapter applies to both.
The theme of this chapter is integration—
getting everything working well together.

Fig. 8-1: The electric motor,
mated to the transmission, is
ready to install.

Photo: ElectroAutomotive

I will stop short of getting into too much detail
about EV conversions or scratchbuilts. These
have been detailed in earlier chapters. Still, as
you explore further into conversions and
scratchbuilts, you will need to come back to
this chapter to get useful help.

What Do You Want?

The clearer that you can be about what you
want in an EV, the better.

Do you need something to get you into
town, to buy a few groceries, to visit friends? Do
you need a rugged, tough, farm vehicle? Do you
want something that will commute to work and
back? Is this a street, highway, or freeway
machine?

You may want a vehicle to do all these
things, but it may be asking for too much.
Versatility in any vehicle is nice, but it's lousy
for efficiency. It's the same as packing a
month's worth of stuff for a weekend journey.
Like a station wagon, it will do many things but
not any one thing very well.

After all these years of designing and
building EVs, I've discovered that there really
are only a few *classes* of vehicles. Off-road,
street, highway, and show.

• **Off-road** is the work vehicle, designed to
work mostly off pavement. It is 2WD or 4WD,
carries stuff, and is geared low to pull a load or
climb terrain.

• **Street** is a local machine, 20-30 mile range.
Zippy but only reaches 30-45 mph. Carries two
people, plus groceries.

• **Highway** is a long-distance cruiser, meant
for the commute. It is able to reach freeway
speeds, and maximum range is very important.

• **Show** is some glitzy, slick, sharp, agile,
has-the-"look" machine. Off-the-line
performance is critical, as is strong acceleration
up to speed. Seats two so a friend or a stranger
interested in EV technology can get the feel.

Does one of the classes fit you? A
specialized vehicle is definitely the answer. Be
honest with yourself. What do you want? Or
really need. You are making a substantial
investment in time, money, and effort. Make
certain you get what you want.

Local vs Distant Travel

It helps if you narrow down your thoughts
to local versus distance travel. Local means

around the place (a 40-acre farm), a few miles in the city, 10-15 miles one way maximum. Distant means wanting (or needing) to go to a distant town, visit friends all over the place, something that is 20-30 miles one way.

If you're not certain what you want, don't worry. I'll bet that you'll have a good idea after you've read this book!

Homework?

Do your homework. Review the Applications found in this book that most closely match the vehicle that interests you. Note the size and ratings of the components they use: motors, batteries, and chargers. Armed with that information, compare it with the following sections on selecting, installing, using, and maintaining that hardware.

THE MOTOR

The following sections detail the selection, installation, use, and maintenance of motors in EVs.

A. Selecting the Motor

Even a decade ago, finding and selecting the motor for an EV was a real hit or miss proposition. Today, it is much easier to access a list of motor manufacturers and write for their specifications. Or consult a local distributor. Periodicals, books, and computer networks are also easily accessed for this information.

Electric car clubs are a longtime resource for EV information. It's a good place to mix with designers, builders, and EV owners, get a ride, and even test drive an EV. It is an experience worthwhile pursuing. Don't be afraid to ask for help. Listen, be skeptical, and stay true to the idea you have.

Where to Look for Motors

There are a number of places to find motors. Send for specifications, a list of local reps or dealers, and prices. Generally, motors can be new, used, or surplus.

New Motors

Many people will be interested in a brand-new motor. There's merit in this idea. Charts and graphs show how the various motor ratings interact with one another over a wide range of operating conditions. The warranty is a feature many people will want. If you have a problem or question, it's nice to know that someone will

be there. Finally, motors specifically built for EVs are manufactured in significant quantities to be affordable.

For most conversions, *use* these sources. In any case, check out the price. It will give you some means of comparison if you're looking at the value of used and surplus motors.

Used Motors

A used motor is another option. For example, the old Prestolite motor is a good option if the price is right.

More likely, a used motor may be in an EV that someone is selling. Expect it to be an older style, and a lower voltage unit, too. An older EV might sell for a price well below what you'll pay for a whole system. Experience is a must here, to evaluate the condition and overall ratings. Technical sheets rarely accompany the motor. A tin label affixed to the motor may contain the essential information you'll need. Used motors are a good option for medium-size vehicles and prototypes.

Surplus Motors

A surplus motor is one found through a surplus outlet. Or one a dealer has modified to work with EVs.

An aircraft generator is an example of a surplus motor. Build for aircraft, it is lightweight and tough. It tends to be a relatively low-voltage unit, but works well with prototypes. It is not as efficient as a motor that is purpose-built for use in EVs.

With used *or* surplus motors, replace the bearings if possible. Installation is an involved process and it's no fun to immediately remove the motor just to replace bearings. Check the brushes, too. Replace them, if need be, or order spares.

Parts vs Kits

A motor can be purchased as part of a kit. This may be a generic kit (Fig. 8-2) or one designed for a specific vehicle (Fig. 8-3). If you already need everything that's in the kit, it may be the best value. A motor-only purchase from the same dealer will have the highest price tag.

If you do not plan to use a high-voltage system, shop around for the motor! Many first-time EV owners undersize the motor for their vehicle. When they upgrade, they will want to sell the old hardware. EV club members list hardware through computer bulletin boards and club newsletters.

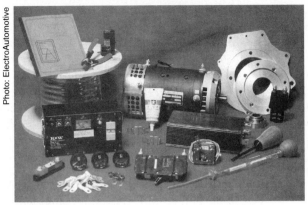

Photo: ElectroAutomotive

Fig. 8-2: Some kits will work for most vehicles.

Fig. 8-3: This is the complete kit for this truck.

Photo: Solar Car Corporation

What to Look For

Every motor has its ratings. A successful EV uses a motor with all of its ratings aligned. Everything must match and nothing must be compromised. Type, horsepower, speed (rpm), current draw, voltage, duty cycle, weight, shaft size and type, cooling requirements, bearing and mounting positions—all share the value of a good fit.

Refer to Chapter 7 for more information on motors and their attributes.

Type of Motor

In the mid-1990s, for the dollar, the motor of choice for a conversion of a standard size car is the series motor. The primary decision factor will be, "What horsepower?" Under 2HP, PM motors dominate.

AC motors will be seen more and more in this market in the next decade. Automakers will choose this technology for its long-term benefits. Complete systems will become available, offering attractive features (like regen) to justify the higher cost and price.

Horsepower

Vehicles weighing over 2,000 lbs (as an ICE) demand the bigger EV motors, like the 17HP and 20HP units from Advanced DC Motors Company. Compacts can use motors down to 10HP in size if the EV's curb weight doesn't exceed 2,500 lbs. Prototypes weighing 500-900 lbs will find a 4.5HP motor adequate.

Voltage

Motors should have a voltage rating equivalent to two-thirds the battery pack voltage. Thus, a 72-Volt motor can be used with a system voltage of 72-108V with the proper controller. The manufacturer should be consulted where the pack voltage is double the motor's rated voltage.

A motor is inefficient if used at a voltage less than its rated one, and it will have difficulty reaching good speed. Too much voltage will saturate the windings, overspeed the motor, and cause arcing and heat buildup at the brushes and commutator.

Current

New motors have current ratings. Used and surplus motors may have their current rating typed on the motor's ID label. If not, compute the horsepower and voltage ratings. To offset losses, one horsepower at the shaft wants a one (1) kWh rate. Twenty HP wants a 20kW rate. For a 120V pack, this represents approximately 85 Amps. With a peak output of 100HP, the motor will want every bit of the 400-Amp rate the controller will deliver. (Note: Only test a series motor under load.)

Motor RPM

Knowing the rpm rating is very important with fixed-ratio drives. The motor wants to be operated at, or near, its rated speed. Rated rpm is often printed on the metal tag. Or check with the manufacturer. At half this rating, horsepower rating may be less than half. Motor speed affects efficiency, tendency of the motor to overheat, and available torque.

Motor Weight

Make certain the motor is designed for mobile applications. If the motor housing looks molded, reject it! Note the weight of motors of different horsepower (Fig. 8-4). Above these values, the motor is too heavy.

Shaft Type

Somewhere along the line, you're going to to connect the motor to the gearbox or a drive axle. What kind and size of shaft is coming out of the motor? At one or both ends? (It's usually just one). Is it splined or does it have a keyway or space for a key? How long is the shaft? If a gear or pulley is attached to it, will this do or will you need to replace it?

When looking at used and surplus motors, it is easy to ignore these factors, putting off dealing with them until later. Fight this urge. Adaptors can be a real bear to find. True, a motor shaft can be machined to accept a standardized fitting, coupling, gear or pulley, but it can be expensive. Wherever you're getting the motor, the "missing link" might be nearby. If you are familiar with the kind of drivetrain you'll use, this will help in looking for the motor. If not, bring it with you to check. Don't force-fit this. If you can't gather the pieces, put the motor down and walk away.

Mounting Position

Motors are designed to operate in different positions. You want one designed for horizontal operation. Vertical mountings demand thrust bearings. Find one, adapt one, or stay horizontal.

Bearings

What supports the motor (armature) shaft—bushings or bearings? Check both ends. Little motors intended for an EAB (electric-assist bicycle) may use motor bushings, but anything over 1/6 HP in an EV wants ball bearings. Check the bearing type. Is it a sealed bearing? Or is there a lube (zerk type) fitting? If so, add lubrication to your maintenance schedule.

Electrical Connections

Does the motor have posts, or large wires dangling out of a hole? If you don't know what's what, trundle that motor and yourself down to the nearest generator or motor repair/rewinding shop and have them tell you whatever they can. A sharp motor man can tell you a lot—make, manufacturer, application, rpm, types of fields, voltage, and current ratings, etc. Listen to what he has to say. Write it all down. Without notes, things you barely understand will slip away, beyond mental recovery.

Motor Rotation

Most motors are designed to rotate in a specific direction. (This is a design issue. You can't *solve* this by electrically reversing the motor!) Notations are clockwise (cw) or counter-clockwise (ccw), facing the shaft end. If shafts protrude from both ends of the motor, notations usually apply facing the shaft at the end opposite the brushes.

An inspection may reveal shaft rotation in one of three ways.

• Motor's rating tag, if it has one.

• Observe internal or external fan. Correct rotation is one where the fan or blower efficiently expels a flow of air.

• Brush rake or drag relative to the commutator. Brushes mounted at an angle suggest a preferred direction of rotation. A perpendicular mounting angle *may* mean that the direction of rotation doesn't matter.

Cost

Can you afford the motor? When the ratings match, buy it. Why? If there's no risk and no unknowns, how can you afford not to buy it!

Don't pay more than you have to. Everything is a question of value. Don't be disrespectful of your luck, either.

More likely, there is *some* risk of a used or surplus motor's working properly, and some

Fig. 8-4: Weight versus horsepower of a series motor

Motor/ Diameter/ Weight	Time On	Volts	Amps	RPM	H.P.	kW
L91-4003 6.7: Dia **82** lbs 38 kg	5 min	87	280	3650	26.4	20.0
	1 Hr	91	150	4950	15.0	11.4
	Cont	92	130	5100	13.6	10.3
	5 min	112	260	4650	31.0	23.4
	1 Hr	115	135	6200	17.9	13.5
	Cont	116	122	6500	16.0	12.0
203-06-4001 8" Dia **107** lbs 49 kg	5 min	86	322	3600	31.5	23.8
	1 Hr	90	190	4800	20.6	15.5
	Cont	91	178	5000	19.0	14.4
	5 min	111	300	4650	37.0	28.0
	1 Hr	114	180	6200	24.0	18.0
	Cont	115	165	6500	21.7	16.3
FB1-4001 9.1" Dia **143** lbs 65 kg	5 min	88	360	3300	35.0	26.5
	1 Hr	89	210	3600	23.0	17.3
	Cont	90	190	3900	20.0	15.0
	5 min	109	340	3520	43.0	32.5
	1 Hr	114	205	4800	27.5	20.8
	Cont	115	182	5200	25.2	19.0
	5 min	134	320	4200	48.8	36.8
	1 Hr	138	185	5700	30.4	22.9
	Cont	139	170	6000	28.5	21.5

unknowns. Ask about warranty. Offer a deposit, get a receipt, make certain it permits a full refund, expect a time limit, and check it out right away. Can't come to an agreement? Walk away. It serves two purposes. First, it gives you time to think, cool off, breathe again, and check out anything you need to check out. Second, it lets the owner know you are able to walk away if the thing isn't right. Resist the urge to "buy now or lose it forever." Good luck!

B: Motor Installation

Installing the motor, whether converting an ICE car to electric propulsion or scratchbuilding an EV, involves several tasks. Once checked for fit (adequate space), the motor must be interfaced with the transmission or drive system, and mounted securely to the chassis. Any cooling needs must be met, as well as motor reversing, if there is no mechanical reverse. Finally, the motor must be protected from road debris and dust. This is a good time to think about adding a thermoswitch (if one doesn't exist), to warn of heat buildup in the motor when it operates in hotter climes.

Do It Right!

Fashioning the motor mount(s) and adaptor plate requires a level of experience and a quality of fabrication beyond those of the average hobbyist, tinkerer, engineer, designer, or JOAT (jack of all trades). Don't be fooled into thinking otherwise. A poorly mounted and badly aligned motor will eat up your money and time, and create a hazard to anyone near it. This is simply no place for OJT (on-the-job-training), particularly with conversions. It cries out for genuine experience. Plan to get help.

A step-by-step look at the conversion process as outlined in several EV books will quickly reveal the challenges of installing motor and batteries in an EV. Collect this material. And—read and heed. Remember, while some books will supply more detail than presented here, don't expect them to tell you more than *what* needs doing. Few will reveal precisely *how* it is accomplished. Either buy this hardware prefabricated or order it done from shops that specialize in it.

Mounting the motor in a conversion requires fewer decisions than mounting a motor in a scratchbuilt vehicle. After all, the vehicle *had* an engine. And that engine used up

space, bolted up to a drivetrain, and was supported. The electric motor needs the same three things—space, a drivetrain, and support.

Is There Room for the Motor?

When compared to an engine, an electric motor is *small*. Engines have lots of things hanging onto them: alternator, carburetor, air cleaner, fuel filters, water pumps, compressors, etc. Of course, once the ICE-related hardware—engine, and fuel, cooling, and exhaust systems—is removed, there should be lots of space for the electric motor.

Watch out! While even a 20HP series motor is relatively small in diameter, it may be *longer* than the original engine. This is particularly true for engines with their crankshafts mounted perpendicular to the vehicle's centerline.

While it's easier to "check the fit" once the ICE stuff is removed, it could be an expensive mistake to put off doing it. First, measure the room that's available in the engine compartment. At one end is the seam of bell housing and engine. At the other is the sidewall of the engine compartment. Of course, part of the sidewall can be removed to fit a motor. If it's tin, no problem. If it's part of the suspension support for the front wheel, don't do it!

Now, measure the length of the motor. Or note this measurement from the motor manufacturer's specification sheets. Allow an extra 2-5 inches for the adaptor plate. Okay, look at the two totals. Is there a problem? If no, proceed. If yes, determine precisely the space the adaptor plate will need *and* look at the feasibility of cutting into the sidewall. Not sure? Get help!

Once the engine is removed, test fit the motor in the drivetrain space right away.

Building the Adaptor Plate and Hub

In most conversions and many prototypes, the electric motor will interface with a stock transmission's bell housing. This is the flared portion that contains flywheel, clutch, clutch plate, throwout bearing, etc. You will need all of this stuff, some of which must be removed from the engine before you junk, sell, or recycle it. If you bought a glider (ICE-related stuff was already gone), you must obtain this hardware used (or new) to complete your conversion. Do it now. You must have it in hand to mate the motor to the drivetrain.

Most conversions retain the clutch feature. It is possible to adapt the motor to a transmission directly. And it is possible to operate an EV without a clutch. However, this installation is the exception. I recommend that you retain the ability to shift the gears in your vehicle while running.

Mating the motor to a drivetrain requires the construction of two components: the motor hub and the adaptor plate (Fig. 8-5).

The motor hub is a chunk of metal that slides onto the electric motor's shaft. It is "keyed" to resist rotation about that shaft and is secured in position by set screws or a locking mechanism (Fig. 8-6). The hub has the same bolt pattern as the engine's crankshaft end, enabling the flywheel to be bolted directly to it. As in the original vehicle, the clutch and pressure plate are secured to the flywheel (Fig. 8-7).

The adaptor plate mates the electric motor to the vehicle's transmission or drivetrain. It is precision-machined to perform four jobs:

• matches some (or all) of the bolt holes of the bell housing.

• matches the threaded holes in the motor's faceplate.

• precisely aligns the transmission shaft with the motor shaft.

• provides for motor hub and shaft clearance.

The adaptor plate assembly *always* uses more space than the original engine. How much is the big question.

Adaptor plates are typically manufactured on industrial-grade machinery. Ones designed by a novice and built on a drill press are unlikely to successfully fulfill all four of the jobs required of it.

Due to the complexity involved, an adaptor plate may consist of two or more parts. The extra spacing required between motor and clutch housing (to accommodate the motor shaft and hub) is the only odd requirement here. It may be accommodated by using several 1/2-1 inch plates or standoffs.

Whether a flat plate or a standoff is used, retain some method of "keying" the plate to the bellhousing. Any traditional positioning method (like pin and hole) will do. Bolt holes have a built-in clearance that, through accumulation, will misalign the transmission and motor shafts. The interface of motor, adaptor plate, and bell housing *must* hold a tight tolerance if the finished assembly is expected to work for years. Misaligned shafts generate noise and eat bearings.

Fig. 8-5: This kit adapts the electric motor to the existing drivetrain.

Fig. 8-6: The hub is attached to the motor shaft.

All photos: ElectroAutomotive

Fig. 8-7: The flywheel bolts to the hub. The clutch-and-plate assembly is next.

Fig. 8-8: A special motor cradle bolts up to the original engine mounts.

Many automotive machine shops specialize in building adaptor plates. These serve a large market of people wanting to adapt non-stock engines to various cars. Literally, they can adapt any motor to any drivetrain. Often, they will have the "blueprints" of engines, transmissions, and bell housings in their files. If you walk in with the electric motor specs, they can build you an adaptor plate.

The one thing a machine shop doesn't normally build is the motor hub that the EV requires. And their adaptors don't allow for the extra space between bell housing and motor that it will dictate. If someone there will take the time to work this out with you, great. If you have the motor specs and they have the transmission specs, that's all of the information needed to do the job. Offer to pay for this service. When the shop is involved in the design, they're likely to redo the part for free when a mistake is made. If they build to your design (drawing or numbers), right or wrong, you've bought the part.

Until EVs become more widespread, the adaptor plate for your EV is likely to be a custom-built part. When you add in the complexity inherent in any adaptor plate, it adds up to an expensive part of an EV conversion. At this point (mid-90s), expect to pay $800. Shop around. Get quotes in writing.

Securing the Motor

Bolting the motor to the drivetrain is *not* the same as mounting the motor in the vehicle! Engines and transmissions are shock-mounted to the chassis. The transmission's mounts, by themselves, are *not* strong enough to support the electric motor. While it is true that the electric motor is lighter than an engine, it will still need its own motor mount. The motor mount supports the electric motor, using the original engine mounting points or new ones.

Motor mounts come in different configurations. Some cradle the electric motor between two points (Fig. 8-8). Others bolt to the motor's brush plate (the opposite end of the adaptor plate) and tie to a nearby support point. Since almost any arrangement will use one or more of the original mount points for the engine, get these fittings before the engine goes away! Also, as conversion books will tell you in detail, make certain that you establish reference measurements between the bell housing or transmission and the vehicle chassis. The completed electric motor installation must honor these clearances.

Again, if the vehicle came to you as a glider, search out and find used or new motor mounts or mounting hardware. Some fabrication will be involved in *any* case, but you might as well keep it minimal. Even if you don't understand the importance of this, the person who will be doing the job for you will. Since you can't make reference measurements on a glider, find a vehicle of the same year, make and model, and take them off of it.

A number of EV component suppliers have stock motor brackets for sale. These will make the conversion of a specific vehicle, i.e., a VW Rabbit, a straight bolt-up. Nevertheless, investigate the possibility of adapting a bracket to your own use. At least it fits your motor! Coupled with your vehicle's mounting hardware, it's a start. If you're lucky, each will get a minor cut, and some welding will finish the job. Beforehand, make certain you can return the bracket (within a reasonable amount of time) for a refund if you can't figure out how to make it work.

An electric motor installed in a car needs one component that the engine mounting probably didn't have: a torque bar. From a standstill, a series motor can develop torque that only racing engines will demonstrate. So, just as the armature leaps into rotation, basic physics wants to rotate the motor housing, transmission, and whole car in the opposite direction. It usually loses, but the strain is enormous.

If the electric motor is solidly supported to as many places as the engine was, everything will probably be okay. However, if you skip supporting the motor to any mounts located perpendicular to the motor shaft, install a torque bar between the motor and one of them. Or some other point on the chassis. The torque bar can work in compression or in tension.

The Virtues of Benchwork

The motor is heavy. How will you support it while you take measurements, adapt it to the drivetrain, and figure out the motor mounts? All of these processes will suffer if you are constantly hassling with its weight as it it's moved in and out of the drivetrain compartment, or are supporting even part of this weight during test fits. It may be rough on your body, too! Also, where will you do all this work? Draped over a wheel well? Consider the merits of a motor hoist and benchwork!

An engine hoist with a hydraulic jack can be rented from an equipment outlet. The A-frame will move across the floor, and position the motor over its mounting point in the engine compartment. A block-and-tackle secured to an eyebolt in an overhead joist works, too. Ones that run in a track—so that you can move it from vehicle to bench and back—are great!

Initially, this process helps check the fit, take measurements for the adaptor plate, and determine motor mounting points. In vehicles with front-wheel drive, consider removing the transmission. Mating the motor to the drivetrain is an involved process, much better performed at a bench than in the confines of an engine compartment. Also, it is easier to mate the motor to the transmission on the bench and drop it into the vehicle as an assembly, with motor mounts attached (Fig. 8-9). That's the way it's done on an assembly line! There are many phases to this process. It takes a big weight off your hands (and mind) to be able to move through it without a lot of grunting.

Fig. 8-9: Electric motor and transmission are re-installed in the car.

Cooling Needs

Will your motor need cooling? A motor which is 75-85% efficient is also 15-25% inefficient. And something must happen with that inefficiency. It's got to go somewhere, disguised as something. Some of it will end up as vibration, some as light, some as noise (audio vibration), but most is heat. Excessive heat melts insulation, expands and contracts parts beyond tolerance, and thins the lubricant in the bearings.

A well-designed, efficient motor generates little heat and usually has no problem in dissipating it. But even a good motor in an EV is going to be running inefficiently at times (starting, for instance) and it may not, in itself, be able to easily rid itself of its own heat. Give some attention to cooling that motor!

Cooling a motor may be as simple as leaving it exposed to airflow. When the vehicle is moving, will it get air movement? Expect the motor to need cooling the most on a hot day on a steep uphill section. What happens if you stop? What happens to your cooling system then?

If it looks like the motor won't get much natural circulation, add a cooling system. Both passive and active methods exist.

A passive cooling system assists the motor by increasing the surface area of the motor housing, helping it to radiate or convect away heat. For example, Roy Kaylor drilled and tapped holes in the shells of a motor he refurbished, bolting on extruded aluminum channel lengthwise, all around the circumference of the motor.

An active cooling system assists with fans or blowers that move air. Motors with grillwork (or inlet and exhaust ports) probably have a cooling fan inside. It runs at the same speed as the motor shaft, explaining why it may need help at low vehicle (and motor) speeds. Identify the existing inlet and outlet. Install a blower to pull or push air in the same direction. A high cfm (cubic feet per minute) blower will consume 100 Watts or more.

Sealed motors may also get assistance from blowers that pull or push air over their surfaces. It's best to try to passive cooling first. Then, if more cooling is needed, a shroud around the motor (using the passive cooling fins as standoffs) will direct forced air along the motor's housing surface for maximum benefit.

Motor Reversing

All motor types can be "reversed" in their direction of rotation, for reversing the vehicle's direction of travel. Different methods apply to different motors. Will your vehicle use a transmission with a manual (mechanical) reversing gear? If not, all motor leads must be brought out to a DPDT contactor for reversing.

Dust and Debris Shields

Electric motors with inlet and outlet ports must be shielded against road debris, dust, and sand. Ingesting a pebble will destroy a motor.

Screens that come with the motor are good for rocks and pebbles but provide no protection against sand and dust. Add a finer mesh of screen to the existing one. Several brands of air filters (for engines) will neatly fit around several sizes of series motor for this job. Adding an underpan to the vehicle (perhaps of Corruplast, a corrugated plastic) will deflect a lot of road debris. A smooth underpan on my EVX improved vehicle range by 6%, too!

A forced-air cooling system may be needed for excessive dirt or off-road vehicle use. Its inlet can be positioned for maximum protection, and the forced airflow will compensate for the restricted airflow of paper filters. The underpan I've added in my conversions is a good shield against road debris, but I also don't travel many dirt or gravel roads!

C. Motor Operation

There are no special operating procedures for EV motors, particularly brand-new ones. Like engines, you don't want to lug them (work at too low an rpm under heavy load) or overspeed them (it's easier to do because they're quiet). Unlike engines, motors don't start when you turn on the key (you have to push the accelerator pedal), and they won't slow down the vehicle with downshifting.

Initial Operation

As with any new engine or new assembly, be alert to unusual sounds, vibration, and smell. This is important where the motor is a used or surplus one. Isolate the sources or cause, if possible. Bearing rumble is a good indicator of motor-to-drivetrain misalignment, particularly if you installed new bearings. Metal-on-metal sounds usually indicate interference. Don't freak out. It may be minor, handled by filing off an edge.

Check motor case temperature after a normal run. And, again, after a long run at speed or with lots of hill climbing. Electric motors exhibit a higher resistance to heat buildup than engines. What's hot to an engine is warm to a motor. A thermoswitch or temperature sensor is critical for knowing when motors are really getting too hot. Spit that sizzles and leaps on a motor housing means "hot."

Series DC motors are rugged and reliable, but are different to operate than vehicles with engines in a number of ways. This includes shift points, number of gears used, cruise throttle, and overspeed.

Shift Points

Series motors of higher HP seem to be the most happy around 2,500 rpm. Below this, they will consume more power for the same load in a lower gear. When shifting gears, try to achieve 4,000 rpm so that the shift up drops motor rpm not much below the 2,500 rpm value.

Shift-up points for EV motors are 5-10 mph higher (on the speedometer) than they are for engines. Shift down a gear when motor rpm drops below 1,800 rpm.

Number of Gears Used

Electric motors have a flat torque curve. For this reason, they operate efficiently over a wide range of rpm. In a vehicle equipped with a 5-speed transmission, it is normal only to need the first three gears. So, while an engine will want to see 4th gear at 60 mph, it won't be needed for an electric motor until as high as 85 mph is reached! Never mind about 5th gear!

Cruise Throttle

Series motors will consume power at cruise speeds, even if they aren't doing much work. So, on level ground, bring the speedometer up to 2 mph above the speed at which you want to cruise, then release the accelerator pedal altogether. Allow the vehicle to slow to 2-3 mph under this value (it will take a while), then re-apply power and repeat this process. A lower overall Ah consumption will result for the same stretch of road (per mile or over a specific distance) than if the vehicle was held a constant light throttle at the cruise speed.

Overspeed Protection

Series motors can't limit their own speed. Bolted to a transmission with the clutch in or the gearshift in neutral, they can be revved up and overspeed. Even if you wouldn't do it, someone using your vehicle could! In a fixed-ratio drive, breaking a gearbelt would also have the same effect. Before a reaction is possible, the motor (at partial or full throttle) would quickly exceed its maximum rpm and possibly self-destruct. Internally, the commutator would probably fly apart, catch on the brushes, and initiate a violent chain reaction.

A relatively new product offers some protection against series motor overspeed. This gizmo monitors motor rpm. When it exceeds a preset value, it de-energizes the main contactor, shutting power off both to controller and motor. If the vehicle has no contactor, the unit can de-energize a relay that will shut off power to the controller's enable pin (re-examine Fig. 7-36). The unit automatically resets and restores power when motor rpm drops to a safe value.

D. Motor Maintenance

Electric motors have one moving part. They require little or no maintenance. After 20K miles, the brushes and bearings in my Advanced DC motor are fine. The motor is washed of accumulated dust at the same time the batteries in the front engine compartment are washed. A flashlight (or a sun-reflecting mirror) helps me inspect the commutator. A blackened commutator spells trouble. "Chocolate brown" is okay.

When the vehicle's clutch is replaced eventually, I will probably install new brushes and motor bearings. I doubt that they will need it, but it's an opportune time to do it. It's one way to ensure that the motor will require no further work until the clutch is again replaced.

THE BATTERY PACK

The following sections detail the selection, installation, use, and maintenance of the battery pack in an electric vehicle.

A. Selecting the Battery Pack

Many factors compete for your attention in selecting the battery pack for an EV. What type of battery technology will you use? What are your performance and range expectations? How big and heavy a pack will your EV require? Will the pack be built around 6V or 12V batteries. What kind of posts will they have?

Types of Batteries

When it comes time to select the battery pack for a project in the years 1996-97, the average EV designer and builder will find any battery type other than the lead-acid battery too expensive to use.

While there is a lack of choice of battery technologies at this point, the lead-acid battery would win out over much of the competition anyway! As attractive as some qualities of other battery types may be, they must also handle issues like availability, cost, reliability, and recyclability.

*T*echtalk
*T*⁸⁸ **EV Pack Sizes**

I recommend the following pack sizes for the listed vehicle (curb) weights (includes battery weight):

Pack Capacity	Final EV Weight (lbs)
20 kWh	above 2,500
17 kWh	2,000
12 kWh	1,500
8 kWh	1,000
6 kWh	750

These values are good where the EV's mission is medium-speed (50 mph) and medium-range (45 miles). High-speed or long-range EVs may need to add 3-5 kWh of capacity, if there is space for the extra capacity.

Lead-acid technology is almost a century old, and its shortcomings are well known. Many experts agree that today's lead-acid battery is not the best it can be. Lack of incentives and funding have prevented its own advancement. Still, lead-acid batteries have an industry behind them, which includes the facilities to recycle the batteries at the end of their service life (2-3 years in an EV). They're inexpensive, too. At this point, they have the best cost per pound or per watt of any battery type.

As the market expands in the next decade, the energy and power densities, along with better packaging, will improve for the lead-acid battery as well as other battery types.

Performance and Range Expectations

I don't envy prospective EV owners in estimating the speed and range of an EV of a given weight, pack voltage and battery capacity. At this point, the technology lacks "standards," so the novice must wade through a slurry of facts, claims, and beliefs. Fortunately, there are rules of thumb that will cut through the tech-talk about speed and range.

For example, for any commercially-produced (or converted) vehicle, it helps to know the answers to two questions. What is the EV's maximum speed? What is the EV's range? Suppose the answers are 60 mph speed and 90 miles range. What does this mean? Given together, these answers *imply* that the EV will have a 90-mile range at 60 mph. No way!

EV designers and owners know to apply the 33 percent rule to these two figures. The rule states that only one-third (33%) of one of these values is available when the other is maxed. So, at 60 mph speed, only 30 miles of range is likely. And 90 miles' range is achieved only if the EV's speed is close to 20 mph. In the early 1990s, the greatest complaint of EV owners who purchased their vehicles from a conversion house were the exaggerated claims about range at top speed.

Knowing this, always ask "What range will the speed give?" Or, quoted a range, ask "Travelling at what speed?" Steer clear of anyone who does not willfully clarify any values of speed and range claimed of an EV.

How Many Batteries?

The mission, weight, and physical size of the vehicle that will become an EV will have much to do with the size of the battery pack.

These factors form a triangle, with a variation in any one of them affecting the other two.

Most conversions will have both the need and the room for a 20 kWh battery pack. Prototypes are harder to pin down. Nevertheless, it is possible to estimate the size of pack based on the EV's curb weight (Techtalk T88).

The BVWR Value

There is another way to relate battery capacity and vehicle weight. EV prototypes have proven conclusively the merit of a high ratio of battery weight to vehicle weight in the finished EV. Thirty percent (30%) is the *minimum* ratio for optimum performance and range in conversions. A BVWR (battery-to-vehicle weight ratio) of 35-40% should be the target in most prototypes or scratchbuilts. A skilled designer can achieve a BVWR as high as 45-50%.

I've evaluated the BVWRs of four EVs—two of them conversions and the other two scratchbuilts (Techtalk T89). Study these examples for a greater appreciation of the importance of low weight. Note the performance of other examples (see Fig. 3-76, Chapter 3) of similar size and weight.

Making Battery Choices

An EV designer, intent on using lead-acid batteries with the best capacity per pound, is stuck with two basic sizes for a 120V pack. Ten 12V, 110Ah batteries or twenty 6V, 220 Ah batteries. Think of it as two sizes of tank. One weighs 600 lbs and the other is 1,200 lbs.

Actually, there *are* other options. However, when analyzed, a rash of factors leap in motion. It can be difficult to maintain perspective. A more systematic approach to these options may help (Techtalk T90). In any case, there is no *single* right answer.

Low-Voltage versus High-Voltage Systems

There are a number of reasons to choose high voltage systems (120-144v) over low-voltage systems (72-108v) in EVs of over 2,000 pounds of final curb weight. Issues like line losses, motor speed, and the nature of electronic controllers favor the high-voltage system (Techtalk T91).

Briefly, the transfer of high rates of power in EVs causes losses (heating) in the wires connecting batteries, controllers, and motors at low voltages. As well, higher motor speeds are assured in high-voltage systems. Finally,

---

Techtalk

T89 Battery-to-Vehicle Weight Ratios

Let's look at the BVWR (battery-to-vehicle weight ratio) of four vehicles: Geometric, EVX, Speedster, and Formula E.

Note: Weights are estimated. BVWR is curb weight. Add driver and passenger weight (i.e., 150 lbs each) to the vehicle's curb weight to represent the actual "run weight."

Geometric. As a 1992 (gas) car, this Geo Metro weighed 1700 lbs. It weighed 1,500 pounds as a glider (gas-related components removed) and 1650 lbs after conversion to an EV (without battery pack), when it was renamed Geometric.

With a 800-lb pack (144v, 12kWh), curb weight is 2450 lbs and BVW = 32.6%.

With a 1,200-lb battery (120V, 20kWh), curb weight is 2,800 lbs and BVW = 42%.

EVX. As a 1992 (gas) car, this Honda Civic VX weighed 1900 lbs. It weighed 1700 lbs as a glider and 1850 lbs after conversion to an EV (without battery pack), when it was renamed EVX.

With a 600-lb pack (120V, 10kWh), curb weight is 2,450 lbs, and BVW = 24.4 %.

With a 1,200-lb pack (120V, 20kWh), curb weight is 3,050 lbs, and BVW = 39.3%.

Speedster Two. An EV prototype, the Speedster Two weighed 400 lbs (without battery pack).

With a 360-lb pack (72V, 6kWh), curb weight is 760 lbs and BVW = 47.4%.

Formula E. A converted Formula 440 racer, the Formula E weighed 700 lbs (without battery pack).

With a 500-lb pack (120V, 7kWh), curb weight is 1,200 lbs and BVW = 41.7%.

Note: See Applications for more detail on the Geometric (A11 and A58), EVX (A10 and A56), Speedster (A44 and A45), and Formula E racer (A28 and A57). Also, review Fig. 3-76.

---

electronic controllers efficiently convert higher battery voltages into current for the motor at the low end while maintaining high-end performance.

Weight

Batteries are heavy. The two most popular sizes of battery are the 6V/220 Ah and 12V/105 Ah units. Depending on the manufacturer, these will weigh approximately 55-70 lbs. This explains their popularity. This weight is just manageable for an adult.

You must carry the battery away from your body (or risk holes in your clothing next day). You may have to position the battery in an awkward place. A carrying strap helps with either situation (Fig. 8-10). Batteries of higher capacity are available in both 6V and 12V packages, but their increased weight will make them more difficult to manage. Beware!

Select lightweight cases for your EV batteries. Rubber cases can add 7-10 lbs per battery to your pack's weight. Multiplied by 10-20 batteries, this is a lot of dead weight. Polypropylene cases are thin and light, yielding higher kWh values per pound of battery. Take

care, though. The lightweight cases are more fragile, are easily punctured by a bolt or a sharp edge of metal, and will need a better overall support structure.

Ask the manufacturer if you can get empty cases for your layout prior to purchase. Four or five cases are enough. Offer a deposit. Believe me, it makes a big difference to "trial fit" your batteries this way. Re-positioning 75 pounds of battery gets old fast.

Techtalk

T90 Options in Sizing the Battery Pack

Several options exist for sizing a battery pack to an EV. Let's look at possible configurations and issues, listing the merits and limits of each.

•*HALF* Pack. Ten (10) 12V, 110 Ah batteries. In a conversion, this 120V pack is for light duty only. The lighter overall weight (600 lbs of battery) gives good acceleration and speed. Hill climbing will quickly load the pack down, dropping the voltage. Don't expect to zoom up many hills very fast. Also, drive the vehicle conservatively if you expect to have a range beyond 25-30 miles.

•*FULL* Pack. Twenty (20) 6V, 220Ah batteries. This is a standard pack size for conversions that have the room. With 1,200 lbs of battery pack, acceleration and hill climbing will be affected somewhat. Yields excellent range and high travel speeds.

• *LOVO* (Low-Voltage) Pack. A battery pack of lower overall voltage can be built with 6V batteries. Eighteen of them yields 108V. Sixteen yields 96V. Fourteen yields 72V. While pack capacity is lowered, voltage is dropping at a faster rate than the vehicle's curb weight.

In scratchbuilts, there is merit in packs of this size when the vehicle is light. For cars that weigh 2,000 lb as an ICE, the performance from a 72V pack would (I believe) be a disappointment. Even 96V is marginal. A pack of 108V is okay for driver-only operation. The jump to 120V is a noticeable improvement, particularly with passengers.

• *HIVO* (High-Voltage) Pack. A pack voltage higher than 120V is

another way to increase the designer's options. Adding even one 12V battery (to 132V) helps, and adding two (to 144V) is even better. Voltage and capacity are rising at a faster rate than the vehicle's curb weight.

With higher voltages, the vehicle's motor controller is the limiting factor. For example, a Curtis PMC 1221 controller (72-120V rating) *might* handle 132v but *not* a 144V pack. (Fortunately, a 144V model is now available.)

• *LOCA* (Low-Capacity) Pack. Drop the capacity of a 6V battery for overall lower weight. Using twenty 6V batteries of lower capacity is a way to reach 120V with a lower pack weight. However, this pack will have difficulty delivering 400A without seriously affecting battery efficiency, vehicle range, and battery service life.

• *HICA* (High-Capacity) Pack. How about a higher aH capacity of 12V batteries, so that 10-12 of them yield a higher overall capacity? While a Trojan 27TMH (at 60 lbs) will deliver 85 Amps for 35 minutes, a Trojan 5SH (87 lbs) will yield 85 Amps for 70 minutes. That's double the capacity for less than a 50% weight gain.

High-capacity 12V batteries jam a lot of plates tightly together, affecting electrolyte circulation and overall efficiency. At 87 lbs, this battery is hard for one person to handle and its bigger case is a tough fit in cramped spaces.

• *TWIN* Pack. Two 120V packs running in parallel is a remaining possibility. This is different than the *FULL* pack, although 20 batteries are involved. This was the arrangement in the EVX (Application A10) for fast charging in the Phoenix races.

Subsequently, the EVX was used solely as a street and highway vehicle. The *TWIN* pack proved to work very well. Although there are twice as many cells in the EVX twin pack (compared with twenty 6V batteries), I reasoned that the good mileage might be attributed to each pack sharing the motor current. In theory, they might labor less and exhibit overall better efficiency than each battery in the pack working at full motor current.

After 20,000 miles on the speedometer, several other advantages have been revealed in the *TWIN* arrangement. First, I can operate the car on one pack. Removing one pack (ten batteries) drops my BVWR (battery-to-weight weight ratio) from 36% to 22%, but the car weight drops, performance is snappy, and my range only drops to 60% of its value with a full pack. Two, the two battery packs can be wired in series for 220V charging. And, three, with all of one pack in a warmer location (rear versus under the hood), cold weather operation is easier (one part of the pack carries the load until the other warms up).

There is no way that I can positively state that twin packs of 12V batteries is a better arrangement than a full pack of 6V batteries (of equal Ah capacity). It's just an unknown.

Each EV design should be evaluated in light of the merits and limitations of the *HALF, FULL, LOVO, HIVO, LOCA, HICA,* and *TWIN* arrangements. Don't forget to include the vehicle curb weight in these evaluations. Comparing the BVWR percentages will reveal the relative performance gain or loss of each choice.

Battery Posts

There are several types of posts available on batteries. They are: tapered-round, side-terminal, L-type, square, and tapered-round-and-stud (Techtalk T92).

The square-post is currently the preferred terminal post for the EV battery. Why? Most posts are lead, a good but not excellent conductor. At high current levels, the resistance of lead generates heat. During extended use of the battery, the heat accumulates and the lead softens. Later, as the posts cool, they shrink. With the tapered-round post, the connector will eventually lose its tight fit. This results in a high-resistance contact, a place for corrosion to set in, and maybe a spark gap. This is a dangerous condition in a gas-filled compartment. The expand-contract effect is less severe in the square post. Tighter connections of the interconnects can be achieved and sustained.

The side-terminal post will become more popular with EV batteries, particularly when they are built into modules. Newer designs, like the Genesis battery, recess these plates into the angled sections of the plastic case, easing interconnection and assuring greater protection against accidental shorts. The side-terminal reduces the overall height of a battery. Every installation of a battery pack I've seen could benefit from a lower battery height. Where the battery module is retained in an under-car receptacle, battery height is critical.

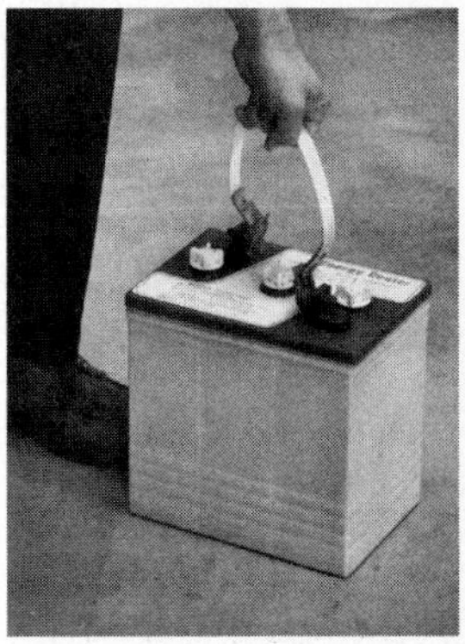

Fig. 8-10: Use a battery strap to move batteries.

T 91 Techtalk
High- vs Low-Voltage Packs

Factors such as line losses, motor speed, and the nature of electronic controllers favor the use of a high-voltage battery pack in EVs.

Line losses

Line losses represent power that is consumed in the wires while transferring electricity to the load. These losses are a function of the amperage that flows through the wire and the wire's resistance. The formula that defines this relationship more precisely is I_2R (pronounced Eye Squared Are).

The power consumed by a load (i.e., a motor) is the product of voltage (E) and current (I), or $P = (E) \times (I)$.

What factor is common to both equations? The answer is current (I). If we decrease current (I), the losses go down. Unfortunately, so does the power transferred to the load. But what happens if we increase the voltage of the system? Power (P) increases but losses do not.

So, if the load (i.e., a motor) is designed to operate at a higher voltage, it doesn't need as much current to do the same job (wattage). Less current results in less power consumed by the wires in transporting the electricity to the load. Conversely, if a motor has a lower voltage rating, it needs more current for the same horsepower rating. Current increases —and so do losses.

The I_2R relationship says it more precisely. If you halve the voltage and double the current (same total power), you get four times the heat losses. If you double the voltage and halve the current, you've cut your losses by four. Since current (I) is a square function, a small change will produce a big effect.

Motor speed

There is a relationship between voltage and DC motor rpm. The higher the voltage, the greater the rpm. In the motor section, it was indicated that a DC motor could produce significantly greater amounts of horsepower than its rating for brief periods of time. This lets you use a DC motor that will power the EV at a specific speed for long periods of time but exceed the horsepower rating for short duration loads like acceleration, higher speeds, and hill climbing, as needed.

The question is: how can the motor be made to deliver more power? The answer is: it must "see" a higher voltage supplied to it. This causes it to draw more current and work harder. If your battery pack has a voltage equal to the motor's rated voltage, it cannot easily supply the higher voltage needed to increase motor horsepower.

Electronic controllers

Electronic controllers employ a bucking-circuit technique. This permits a battery pack to be configured at a much higher voltage than that of the motor itself. At normal speeds, then, the motor receives its rated voltage and power from the controller.

What happens to the difference in voltage? The controller transforms it into current. This may be verified by noting the current delivered to the motor from the controller. When the voltage of the battery pack is higher than the motor voltage, the measured current at the motor turns out to be greater than the current supplied by the batteries to the controller. This anomaly is easily explained: the product of current and voltage on each side of the controller is identical (ignoring the small losses due to controller inefficiency). The controller, then, is effectively stepping down the voltage and stepping up the current.

This arrangement lets you depress the accelerator pedal further and send more voltage to the motor, exceeding its rated voltage for those moments when you need the extra horsepower.

Types of Battery Posts

The **tapered-round** post, or automotive terminal, is used by most SLI-type batteries in ICE cars. The tapered-round post makes for a snappy connect and disconnect. The positive pole of the battery is typically larger in size than the negative pole. This identifies the battery's polarity and helps refit interconnects that have been temporarily removed. It is the most problematic post type in EV applications and is not recommended for use.

The **side-terminal** is becoming more popular in automobiles today, offering a tighter package through a lower profile. Here, the post is a flat plate recessed into the top or side of the battery case, with a threaded hole ready to receive a lug and bolt.

The **L-type** post offers an L-shaped chunk of lead with a square hole in it. The square hole lets you use a carriage bolt, minimizing the number of wrenches needed to affix a lug or interconnect to the terminal. A standard threaded bolt will fit this hole.

The **square** post is conventional on heavy-duty batteries. It has one or more holes drilled in it for a bolt, and the interconnecting straps have a flat-stock lug with a corresponding bolt hole.

The **tapered-round-and-stud** post adds a threaded stud to the top of the standard tapered-round post. This is common on marine batteries, offering several ways to connect the battery into a system. A nut and washer on the stud will maintain pressure on a tapered-round-and-stud connector so that it does not loosen over time. Use a washer large enough to clear the tapered-round post itself. Its performance in EVs is only marginally better than the tapered-round-and-stud post.

There are combinations of these posts on batteries for different applications. For example, some manufacturers solder flat lugs with right-angle bends to the square post for some applications. Newer packaging may introduce other types, too.

The bolts used to secure lugs, connectors, or terminals to battery posts should be plated to resist corrosion.

B. Install Battery

As the installation of the batteries begins, several decisions must be made. Will the batteries be fixed in position or will they be made "exchangeable"? Where will they go? How should their weight be distributed? What about access for maintenance? How are they arranged and interconnected? These are some of the issues of the installation process that you will be called upon to design and execute.

Fixed or Exchangeable?

The traditional battery installation puts batteries where they will fit. This will be in the emptiness of the engine compartment, under the hood or trunk lid, in the back seat space, or in several of these locations. This method usually sticks the batteries in a box, bolts the box to the chassis, and transfers the limitations of the battery pack to the vehicle itself.

In recent years, the quick exchange of an EV's battery pack has been demonstrated in a number of prototypes *and* conversions. For the many advantages it offers, there's little doubt that Battery Exchange Technology will flourish as an infrastructure and easily compete with the "better battery" direction. Individual EV owners need not wait for this to evolve. The battery pack can be arranged as a "module" and fit into a "receptacle." Any exchange system that will today house the lead-acid battery will receive tomorrow's battery technologies with minor packaging adjustments.

General Placement Issues

Carefully consider these placement issues: balance, space, access, venting, and drainage.

Balance

The battery pack is heavy. Depending on vehicle type, it can easily contribute 20%-40% of the vehicle's final weight. Different springs and shocks will handle the weight. The important thing is balance.

Do not upset the original front-to-rear weight ratio of the vehicle. A vehicle that is tail-heavy or nose-heavy relative to its original design could be dangerous under normal or adverse driving conditions, like emergency braking or swerving to avoid an obstacle. Improper weight distribution, then, can contribute to an accident.

Maintaining a good balance of weight in an EV will often prevent you from placing the full battery pack in one spot. In conversions, this usually means splitting the pack into two parts. In a prototype's design, the designer has more options about weight distribution and packaging.

Nevertheless, the laws of physics work in both situations. In four-wheeled vehicles, the front-to-rear weight distribution is usually about 50-50. In three-wheel vehicles of the motorbike layout (two steered wheels up front), the front-to-rear weight distribution is likely to be 75-25 or higher.

There are several ways to honor this balance (Techtalk T93). This effort will preserve the way the vehicle handles and the overall safety of the conversion.

Space

The battery pack is found where it fits. In a standard conversion—under the hood (Fig. 8-11) and in the trunk (Fig. 8-12) are the most likely locations for parts of the battery pack. In compacts, part or all of the back seat area is often used. There is nothing wrong with this method as long as the issue of balance is not violated.

It is handy to have at least one, if not half a dozen, empty battery cases to test fit the number of batteries that a specific location will accommodate. Be conservative. Allow space for the battery support structure, tie-downs, battery swelling (more on this soon), the enclosure (box), lid and insulation.

A battery pack must be supported and secured in the EV. Channel iron or aluminum and a wood or a sheet metal box take up space. Think! Just because a box will fit *inside* the trunk or under the hood does *not* mean it will fit *through* through the trunk and hood openings! By all means, builds it on the table. Just don't be one of those people that builds an airplane in a basement and then discovers—guess what!

Access

Access to the battery pack is essential. At least, this means you must be able to maneuver individual batteries into the pack's support structure (or enclosure). Figure that each one will weigh at least 60 pounds! It is not fun to weasel these through the frame, under an axle, by a steering column, and over some brake-lines.

The primary reason for ensuring easy access to the battery pack is for maintenance. Face it. If it's a major effort just to *expose* the batteries, maintenance will suffer. Proper placement of the pack also makes a visual inspection easy. Ensure that there is room to add water to needy cells without spillage and to take those quarterly hydrometer readings.

Venting

Batteries can emit gases. In a lead-acid battery, it will be hydrogen and oxygen. Since the electrolyte is dilute sulfuric acid, sulphur-smelling fumes may result, too. For safety and olfactory reasons, then, provide a means to vent these gases to the outside of the vehicle. This is particularly true for battery boxes located in the rear seat space, rear area of a fastback, or the trunk. A venting system requires a battery enclosure, plus inlet and outlet vents.

---

*T*echtalk
93 Distributing Battery Weight

The ratio of front-to-rear weight in a vehicle should be closely estimated and maintained.

For example, in the conversion, you'll be removing ICE (internal combustion engine) and the fuel, engine cooling, and exhaust systems. You'll be adding electric motor and batteries. Figuring the weight distribution can be guesswork. It doesn't have to be. The vehicle's manufacturer knows the front-rear weight distribution. If it's not printed in the operator's manual, call and ask.

A smart move is to weigh the vehicle on a scale before the conversion starts. This will give you precise values for the front and rear axle weights. Highway truck-scales are a quick way to find this value. At home, a scale with a maximum reading that is greater than one-fourth the weight of your vehicle can be rotated under each wheel of the vehicle in turn. (A bathroom scale will not work on a 3-wheel vehicle heavier than 700 lbs or a 4-wheel vehicle heavier than 900 lbs.) Use wood blocks (i.e., short 2x4s) under the other wheels while one is weighed. If not at the same height as the scale itself, the readings will be off. This takes a while to do, but maintains accuracy.

Carefully weigh the components you remove—engine, cooling system, fuel system, and exhaust system—and note their distance from the vehicle's center of gravity (cg; review Figure. 2-12 and 2-13)). Weigh the components—electric motor, batteries, boxes, adaptor plates, etc.—that you add, and also note their distance from the cg. Multiply object weights times distance and compare both sides of the equation. Adjust battery positioning and recompute. A re-weigh should confirm the accuracy of this method.

Fig. 8-11: Under the hood is a popular location for part of the battery pack.

Fig. 8-12: The trunk is another popular spot for a portion of the battery pack.

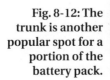

Hydrogen is usually vented from batteries during the charge cycle, particularly during the equalizing charge. Hydrogen is amazingly volatile. It loves to expand and dissipate. It will escape through microscopic holes (even in porous steel). It is odorless and will leave your mouth dry. It is also flammable and explosive over a wide range of mix ratios with oxygen.

Hydrogen gas rises. Where the outside vent is high, hydrogen gas will vent itself from a well-designed battery enclosure. Figure out where air can enter to replace the vented gases and encourage free venting.

Rarely will the engine compartment require any special venting. For other locations, more elaborate vents may need to push or pull the gases free. Install a 12VDC brushless fan (a brush motor could ignite a gaseous mixture) with a minimum rating of 10 cfm (ten cubic feet per minute) of air exchange.

Drainage

No matter how good the enclosure, there will come a time when you want to clean the batteries. Dust *will* accumulate. Electrolyte may spray out of the vent caps during gassing or rough road conditions. You'll make mud of the dust with any spills when watering the batteries during maintenance. Unprotected interconnects may show signs of corrosion that must be wirebrushed.

Consider adding a few drainage holes to your battery enclosure(s). The presence of interconnects and battery tie-downs (steel bars or straps) makes hand cleaning the tops of the batteries a tough job. Design the placement of drainage holes with care. Insulation under the batteries should be waterproof and installed with drainage in mind. Trapped water is extra weight, corrodes metal and rots wood, defeats insulation, and will eventually mildew and stink.

Fitting the Battery Pack

Once the type and number of batteries and their general location are decided for the vehicle, it is time to "fit" the pack layout to the vehicle. Like fitting a suit, this involves precise measurements and allowances. Allowances are adjustments that account for weight (support), movement (battery shifts), material thickness (enclosure material), spread (battery swelling), and an insulating layer (cold weather use).

Structural Support

Irrespective of where the battery pack is located, it must be secured to (and supported by) the vehicle chassis. Batteries are *heavy* Structural support, then, involves more than handling battery weight. What happens in a collision with a wall or another vehicle? Or a roll-over? The battery pack must be adequately supported for all of these conditions. This is a job for a professional. Use one.

Structural support begins with handling the pack's dead weight. Framework uses angle iron, T-beams, I-beams, and box tubing to start (Fig. 8-13). It must be braced and triangulated with flat stock, to make itself rigid and to secure it to hard points on the chassis itself. This is ideal for supporting batteries in the engine compartment and in any cut-away of body metal in the vehicle midsection (Fig. 8-14). The vehicle chassis in the trunk area is able to handle some battery weight if reinforced at anchor points with flat stock.

Aluminum angle may be used in the engine compartment if the firewall is intact and strong.

These materials do not add significantly to the dimensions of a battery pack, adding only 3/8-5/8 of an inch to the length and width of the installed pack.

A steel case (or receptacle) will supply structural support *and* act as an enclosure for a battery pack (Fig. 8-15). More often, the box acts only as an enclosure and usually slides down into (sets on) the framework.

Make certain that the framework would support the pack's weight if the vehicle was sitting on its roof. When velocity is added into the equation, the forces acting to rip the pack away from the chassis are *multiples* of those exerted by the pack's weight. They will work down, up, *and* sideways. (Is this scaring you? Good! This is not the project for a Welding 101 student.)

Battery Tie-Downs

A battery tie-down is a metal strap or bar that keeps the batteries secured in the battery enclosure (Fig. 8-16). It may also be a cloth or synthetic-weave strap, provided that it is rated to handle structural loads *and* is unaffected by electrolyte.

Tie-downs do more than keep the batteries in place during a rollover or collision. They also prevent them from shifting position while traversing rough roads or negotiating tight curves. Loose batteries may strain interconnects, cause electrical shorts, splash electrolyte out of their vent caps, or inflict physical damage on a battery.

The tie-down is secured into a structural component, not just the enclosure. It must be designed so that it (or a section of it) removes to install and remove batteries. It should not block a battery fill cap.

Most tie-downs, particularly metal ones, should not touch the battery cases themselves. Instead, they are spaced a distance above the tops of the batteries, and standoffs (blocks made of wood, plastic, or dense foam) bridge the gap. This setup leaves room for interconnects and avoids corrosion and ground faults between the tie-down materials and the batteries.

Where the enclosure and lid are structural in nature, the standoffs may be secured to the underside of the lid (Fig. 8-17), and the tie-downs affixed once the lid is closed.

Enclosure Materials

Battery enclosures (or boxes) may be steel, aluminum, fiberglass, Lexan, plywood, or (welded) polypropylene. Include the width of the material used for the enclosure in fitting the pack to the chassis. If the box is intended simply to enclose the pack, the material will be from one-sixteenth (1/16) to one-half (1/2) inches thick. Where the pack's enclosure is also structural (partially or wholly), the material's thickness should double or triple these values.

It is not possible to specify a thickness of material without knowing the size and shape of the box, the weight of the batteries within, and the way the box will secure to the vehicle chassis.

Polypropylene and plywood are popular enclosure materials. Polypropylene is unaffected by battery acid and "welds" nicely. Plywood is easy for many people to handle, but must it must be treated with sealant and varnish or it will degrade around batteries.

Battery Swelling

Batteries "swell" in use. The lead plates of lead-acid batteries, like other battery types, will expand over time, adding to the battery's length and width, as much as 0.25 inches on each side. The effect is most pronounced in end cells. A half-inch stretch per battery in a row of five batteries adds up to several inches of "swell". A tight fit, then, gets tighter. Remove

Fig. 8-13: Steel frames provide structural support.

Photo: ElectroAutomotive

Photo: ElectroAutomotive

Fig. 8-14: Framework that extends the battery pack through the floor must be secured to the chassis.

Photo: Schless Engineering

Fig. 8-15: An exchangeable battery module.

Fig. 8-16: Tie-downs to secure the batteries must withstand the forces of an accident.

Photo: ElectroAutomotive

Fig. 8-17: Spacers and straps (around the box) will secure batteries.

a battery, and you may find that it, or a new one, will not fit back in. So, leave room for swelling, using extra insulation to fill the initial gap. Remove it later, when things get tight.

Insulation

All EVs will benefit from insulating the battery pack. This minimizes the effect of hot *and* cold weather on the batteries, helps to maintain an equal SOC (state of charge) between cells and batteries in the pack, and aids the battery-warming system in its job.

Only a few types of insulating material will work. Rigid insulation, like polyurethane foam, works best. Avoid using styrofoam and fiberglass insulation. Both react with spilled electrolyte. Fiberglass insulation requires too much room, and its insulating properties are

Techtalk

Battery Warming Systems

There are many methods of keeping the pack warm in colder climes. Let's look at garaging the EV, heater plates, thermal wire, and ac heating.

Garaging the EV. Where the EV can be stored in a garage, the temperature of the battery pack will stay warmer than outside winter temperatures. If the garage is not attached to the house, it will eventually get cold enough to require an additional battery warming system.

Battery Heater Plates. One way to heat the batteries in an EV is the battery heater plate. Available commercially, they are designed to warm the 12V SLI battery in an ICE car. A battery heater plate is a thin ceramic or metal "hot plate" that is placed under a battery and comes in a variety of sizes (to fit various case sizes) and ratings (larger wattages for colder climes). These will work nicely for an EV's battery pack. You will need as many of the heater plates as the number of batteries in your pack.

Battery heater plates may come as 12VDC or 120vac units. Since they are resistive devices, they will work on ac or DC alike. They will even work at lower voltages, at decreased output, of course.

If your EV uses a 108v or 120v battery pack, the 120vac heater plate is a good option. Wire each heater plate in parallel with other heater plates (Fig. 8-18), or plug them all into a power strip. Plug the power strip directly into the 120vdc pack or into the wall socket when recharging.

The 12VDC variety of heater plate is also useful in the battery pack. When wired in series with other plates in the pack, these may be powered by the charger itself, plugged into the pack or plugged into the wall socket. For example, if the pack consists of ten 12V batteries, ten heater plates wired in series will plug directly into the pack voltage (120VDC) or the wall socket (120V, 60-cycle ac).

If not included, a thermoswitch must be added to this circuit to prevent overheating of the battery.

Thermal Wire. A popular technique among EV hobbyists for heating their batteries is the thermal wire. This is similar to the device sold in garden supply outlets that wraps around a pipe. When plugged into the wall, this gizmo keeps the pipe from freezing in winter. A number of these units will perform the same function in an EV battery pack.

An electric (sleeping) blanket is a crude example of a thermal wire system. However, this technique is fraught with inherent dangers and not recommended for use in EVs.

While it is usually best to install the heat source below the batteries, thermal wiring is often threaded through and around batteries in a pack, heating them from the sides. This is a great retrofit to a battery pack.

Thermal wire has the advantage of heating batteries in the most practical and low-cost way. Various layouts are possible, including ones that avoid putting the heating wire right next to insulation. It does require leaving some space between the batteries, but you'll want to do this anyway to allow for lead plate expansion as the batteries age. Position thermal wires as close as possible to the bottom of the battery (but not under it). This way, convective currents in the electrolyte of each cell distribute the warmth throughout the battery. Seal the space between the batteries directly above the thermal wires. This will help cut down on heat losses.

AC Heating. A problem with heating plates and thermal wire is that the battery case acts like an insulator, resisting the flow of heat from an outside source. Thus, where the heat is generated between battery and insulation, the heat is equally happy to go both ways. Heat lost through insulation is a net loss to the system. Is there a way that the batteries can be heated from within?

A method exists for heating batteries with ac power. For it to work, a zero DC potential must exist.

Applying ac directly to a battery pack will only result in a popped circuit breaker or blown fuse.

To achieve zero DC potential, use a variation of an old backpacker's trick. Want to prevent a dead flashlight if it is accidentally switched on inside the pack? Reverse one cell in the 2-cell flashlight. The opposing voltages cancel out any chance of current flow if the circuit is completed. To use the flashlight, reverse the cell back to its previous orientation.

In my Honda VX, with its two paralleled, 120V battery packs, a zero DC potential is accomplished by turning off the circuit breaker and applying the ac across the two positive pack leads (Fig. 8-19). In other EVs, the pack must be electrically split in two and re-wired to produce the zero DC potential.

Once at zero DC potential, the ac signal sees only the combined internal resistance of the twenty batteries in the pack and discharges its energy in the form of heat. The internal resistance of a pack is highest when it is charged or when cold. Hence, a depleted pack should be fully charged before applying the ac heating technique.

A simple experiment in my Honda VX with a common ac welder (i.e., 25vac, 75-Amp capacity) showed 13 amps of current flow (325 Watts) through the twenty batteries. The test was too short to see what temperatures would be reached or sustained without temperature-sensing or control equipment.

I have seen no report of the efficiency and long-term effect of ac heating on batteries. Still, the equipment is simple: a low-voltage, high-current source of ac power. From the utility grid, it would require only a transformer, like the one used in service station battery chargers or welders. A timer switch or a thermoswitch should control the overall heating effect. Of whatever form, ac heating seems an ideal method of keeping batteries warm in cold climes. Its main disadvantage is that it won't work without an AC source.

defeated when compressed. As little as one-quarter inch (1/4") of polyurethane foam will work for the tropics. Colder climates will demand one-half to three-quarters of an inch (1/2-3/4") of insulation, depending on the battery warming system that's installed. These values are smaller for boxes made of polypropylene or plywood, since these materials contribute some resistance to heat flow.

Insulation may be contained within the battery enclosure or secured to the outside of the box. Inside, it acts somewhat as a padding material and gap-filler. Outside, it won't interfere with battery washdown or cleaning up a spill. That it is applied inside more than outside is simply a convenience to the designer. Glued outside the enclosure, the insulation requires more cut-and-fit, must be protected from the elements, and requires more finishing work to look nice.

Wherever it goes, insulation fits around, below, and above the batteries, adding to the width, length, and height of the pack. Leave room for it.

Battery Warming System

While insulation is important in keeping the batteries warm, it only delays the transfer of heat. A battery warming system offsets the heat losses through insulation, and ensures that the battery pack will stay warm and operational in colder climes.

Review the options for a battery-warming system (Techtalk T94). Select one and allow room for it. Briefly, heater plates install under the batteries, between the battery cases and insulation, adding height to the enclosure. Obtain one to find this dimension. Thermal wire may be installed under a battery, but the standard application puts it between batteries, low down. Overall, this adds little extra dimension.

Fig. 8-18: Thermal plates use very little energy to keep batteries warm.

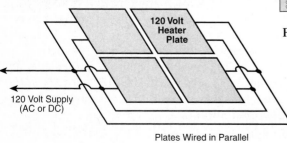

120 Volt Heater Plate

120 Volt Supply (AC or DC)

Plates Wired in Parallel

Install Battery Warming

Battery packs are adversely affected by temperature extremes. For this reason, the battery warming system should operate automatically or semi-automatically.

Automatic operation of battery warming will depend on thermal sensing. Sensors should turn on the battery warming system when outside temperatures fall and shut it off when the batteries are warm. This will involve *two* sensors. Presettable thermoswitches in the correct ranges (say, ON at 50 degrees F and OFF at 65 degrees F) will do the job.

Semi-automatic operation of the battery warming system is possible. This might let the EV owner operate a timer circuit. One setup is to use a timer switch (like the 30-60 minute ones used in storage units or saunas) that will shut off the warming system after a preset time. This is also an excellent way to pre-heat the batteries just before the EV is to be used.

A more sophisticated timer circuit would use a 24-hour timer. The EV owner, then, can estimate the overall battery warming period and set the ON and OFF points. This is more practical for climates with long cold spells.

Timers of either type cannot tell when the battery pack is too warm. These circuits should use a NC (normally-closed) thermoswitch with a presettable value of 75-95 degrees wired in series with the timer switch. Use several, positioning them at different places in the battery pack (Fig 8-20). Only one of them has to work to interrupt power, but all of them have to be cool enough to restart power flow, offering the highest level of safety and reliability for the system. Use silicone sealant or epoxy to adhere thermocouples to the battery cases for best operation.

Design the battery warming system to operate off the pack voltage for use when the vehicle is operated. However, make certain that it will work when plugged into the charging source. Surplus houses stock 24-hour timers that work off 110vac. These can't be used on 120VDC. For on-the-road use, use a relay wired for lock-out to ensure that the battery warming system (turned on by the driver) will shut off when the EV is stopped. The 110vac timer, then, works only when the EV is plugged in and unattended.

The timers used in drip irrigation systems are low-voltage DC units that work on 110vac (with their own converter). They may be "tapped" to work off the 12V AUX system when on the road.

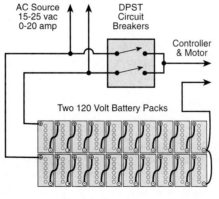

AC Source 15-25 vac 0-20 amp

DPST Circuit Breakers

Controller & Motor

Two 120 Volt Battery Packs

Fig. 8-19: AC warming heats the batteries from within.

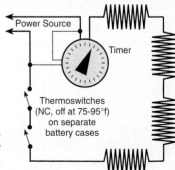

Power Source

Timer

Thermoswitches (NC, off at 75-95°f) on separate battery cases

Fig. 8-20: Sensors can switch battery heaters ON *or* OFF.

Finally, ac heating works internally (in the battery), so choosing this method of battery warming adds nothing to the overall dimensions. Since it is an experimental system, back it up with heater plates or a thermal wire system.

The battery warming system should be designed to work automatically or semi-automatically (Techtalk T95). A simple ON-OFF switch is not recommended. It can result in a depleted battery pack, an overheated pack, or wasted electricity.

T96 Techtalk — How Will the Pack fit?

Here are some thoughts about the process I use to fit the battery pack to the vehicle.

•Be conservative in estimations. You can force-fit anything with a tape measure! Don't forget that you have to build it. Also, if it won't fit, it won't fit! Once you "cut," you may compromise earlier design decisions (i.e., structural) or lose the viability of other options (i.e., an alternate location).

•Obtain and "test fit" empty battery cases. It's easier to see unmoveable interference points with empty cases. Tape them together for best results. Get one "lid" for the battery case. How much does it add to the width or length of the battery? Use it to verify the battery's true height, too.

•Try many layouts. Record them. Paper models lower the risk of mental goofs. Good first discoveries may be replaced with excellent later discoveries. Or an earlier rejection revived after further examination.

•Battery packs can be any shape. Square. Rectangular. Asymmetrical. Odd shapes usually add to the construction cost, but they *can* be made and may be needed to make it work.

•Avoid designs that cut into structural members. Today's fuel-efficient cars expect every bit of "tin" to contribute to the structural whole. Still, "stamped" sheet metal is less structural than I-beam, T-beam, or BoxBeam in the vehicle chassis. Don't let your invisible battery box slice through these, unless you have a professional remedy.

•To your measurements, *add* space for:
- structural support. Angle iron, T-beams, I-beams, and box tubing add slightly (but significantly) to dimensions.
- the material used to make the battery enclosure. This figure may be as little as 0.25 inches to as much as several inches, depending on the material.
- insulation. Insulation fits around, below and above the batteries, adding to the width, length, and height of the pack. Anticipate it.
- battery swelling.
- tie-downs. Usually affect height of the battery box.
- venting battery gases. Air inlet, gas exhaust, vent fan, and ducting—where will they be? A vent hole, blocked by a battery casing, is not going to work.
- the battery heating system of choice.

Measurements

With structural support, battery tie-downs, enclosure materials, battery swelling, insulation, and battery warming in mind, you are ready to fit the design to the reality! It's time to make the critical measurements in fitting the pack to the vehicle.

If you do not have empty battery cases in hand, you should have a copy of the list of batteries a manufacturer builds, with the dimensions (length, width, depth) of each battery type.

A tape measure, a pencil and paper, and an open mind are the only tools useful for this process. The tape measure finds length, width, and depth. The pencil and paper records these measurements. The open mind allows you to see in three dimensions, through metal and aluminum and plastic, and judge if it will work or not. An open mind helps you assess each possibility, balancing options and conditions (Techtalk T96).

Imagine applicable battery types in rows and columns, side-by-side, varying in orientation and numbers. Think asymmetrical. You've got some total (number of batteries) to achieve. If eight fit here, will the other ten fit there? It's a back and forth process. It may take hours. Do as much as you can at one sitting. Review the options a day later. A fresh perspective helps.

Above all , write and draw profusely. Many a good idea is lost when unrecorded the moment it occurs. Images will fade.

Battery Orientation in the Pack

About half of the battery packs in EVs I've seen in two decades could have benefited from a 30-minute exploration of various layout patterns. The battery pack layout that skips this step usually looks like it! Interconnects run every which way, crossing over others, vent caps are blocked, everything looks "added on." It's all like a big experiment in process. The word "amateurish" applies.

A practical layout of the batteries *within* the pack considers many factors (Techtalk T97). Playing with "paper" batteries helps you move past mistakes that will feel tougher once you actually start moving weight.

I suspect that several good layouts are possible for any given "column and row" that available space will permit (Fig. 8-21). Still, when I have explored different layouts, shifting the orientation of even one battery may result in a layout superior to the others in several respects. So, my recommendation is to draw the pack in five (5) distinct configurations. Strive for major differences, but follow any path that looks promising, too. A "natural" arrangement is a great prize!

Interconnects

Batteries in a pack are joined together using an interconnect. This may be wire, flat stock (copper, lead, etc.), copper tubing, or braided strap (Techtalk T98). The interconnect is a conductor, is strong but flexible and is sized to handle the highest current the motor will draw. It must also handle heavy currents for a sustained period of time, i.e., an hour's time. The interconnect may include a lug or fastener added to each end of the conductor to interface with the type of battery post.

Techtalk T98 — Interconnects

Stranded copper wire is better than solid copper wire for use in interconnects. DC current at these voltages and currents likes lots of surface area, present in multi-strand and absent in solid. With large wire size, multi-strand gives flexibility to the cable also, allowing you to work with it.

Welding cable is a popular interconnect. The 00 (pronounced double-ought) gauge has hundreds of strands of copper wires inside a good thick insulator. EV parts houses use a cable for interconnects of the same size, but it has thousands of strands of even smaller wire. Either one works well.

A lug or fastener is crimped, screwed, or soldered to each end of the welding cable. Some commercially-sold interconnects mold the welding wire in lead to the lead fastener. Crimped connectors give a better mechanical connection than ones screwed in place. Do not solder the lug to the wire. It's difficult to do well. For #00 size wire, buy the jig that lets you hammer it together. Or get it done.

Hobbyists often make their own battery connectors out of copper tube or several strips of copper flatstock. This works if the interconnects don't cross each other, or the layout won't be changed. This type of interconnect is not very flexible, and must be custom fashioned.

How are they made? First, measure the distance separating the battery posts to be connected, noting the point of any necessary bends. Cut a section of this length out of 1/2 inch (or larger) copper tubing

Techtalk T97 — Battery Layout in the Pack

Each installation is different. However, I keep the following factors in mind when I experiment with any layout. Think of this as a design puzzle.
- Align batteries so that all positive poles go in one direction. Do this in as many rows and columns as possible. If this will not work, reverse a row rather than one battery.
- Minimize the length of interconnects. It saves material, costs less, and looks neater.
- Standardize the interconnect. One or two standard lengths of interconnect helps with assembly and allows interchange of interconnects in the pack. Again, the pack looks neater.
- Avoid crossovers. Try to keep interconnects from crossing one another. Route interconnects around the perimeter to avoid crossovers.
- Don't block vent caps. Cells with vents caps blocked by interconnects are likely to be skipped in watering or hydrometer checks. Even if the interconnect can be nudged aside to release the vent cap, dust or debris can be dislodged into the cell opening during watering.
- Separate tie-downs and interconnects. Avoid pressing an interconnect into the battery top with a tie-down, unless it is part of an overall scheme to buffer the gap.
- Minimize close proximity of high voltage. Avoid layouts that put battery posts of a high voltage difference adjacent to one another. If this is unavoidable, design layout so that the removal of one interconnect elsewhere will safely disable an offending row.
- Leave room for fuse(s). The main battery fuse is attached directly to the most positive post of the EV's battery pack. Leave room for this fuse and the connection of the battery cable that exits the battery box.
- Allow for interconnect expansion. Straight interconnects may look neat but may fracture or stress battery posts with normal expansion (heat) and contraction (cold) or weight shifts. Stress-relief, in the form of bends or s-turns in the interconnect is recommended.
- Establish the entry/exit points of the positive and negative leads from the battery pack.

or flatstock. If it's tubing, squash the ends first, then drill holes for the bolts. If it must bend, squash the area of the bend. Hollow tubing will facture if bent without a tubing bender.

If it's flatstock, bend the strips together, so they'll fit, then drill the holes for the bolts. Slip thin, flexible plastic tubing over the copper tube or flatstock if it must be insulated. Old bicycle tubing will do and so will heat-shrink tubing. Use the heat of a closely–held match, soldering gun, or heat gun to shrink the tubing for a snug fit. Do not use electrical tape for insulation. It becomes a gooey mess in no time.

Interconnects will heat during heavy discharge currents, so allow for some expansion and contraction in the layout, too.

Fig. 8-21: This layout ensures access to the battery vent caps despite interconnects and tie-down bars.

The Safe Install

Familiarize yourself with safety procedures around batteries (see Battery Maintenance, this chapter). The task of positioning and connecting batteries is repetitious to a degree, but it's important to stay alert (Techtalk T99). Between what two points are you installing that connector? Where are you setting that tool?

C. Operating a Battery Car

There isn't much to the operation of a battery pack. You drive the EV, discharging the battery. You plug it into an energy source, recharging the battery. Periodically, you perform maintenance. If you are faithful about servicing the pack, it will be a long time before you will have to replace the battery pack with a new one.

Relative to the battery pack, let's talk about the final system check, performance, avoiding sulfation, monitoring the pack, shifting gears, and getting stuck out.

Final System Check

The final system check usually precedes the first drive by only minutes, so it starts the operation section relative to the battery pack. Chomping on the bit to "try 'er out," it's difficult to take the time and really look things over before you apply power. It pays big dividends to do so.

Just like a test pilot, a good "walk around" and a strong "visual check" is called for. You might be amazed at what this ritual will find. Dangling wires. Tools left on top of hardware. Missing fuses.

Trip the circuit breaker on and off, ensuring its setting and your ability to reach it. Power the system up slowly. Your ears and nose are good assets when performing the first system checks. Listen for clicks that should be there or absent. At the least bit of sparking or "hot' smell, disconnect what you've just done and re-check everything.

Have wire cutters in hand and a fire extinguisher in reach, pin pulled and ready. If wires start to smoke, trip the breaker or shut off whatever you just turned on. If a short occurs and continues, use the cutters. *Never use your hands to rip anything off.* Burned hands only compound the problem.

The First Drive

After months, maybe a year, of hard work, it's easy to want to "see what it'll do," but that's not the purpose of the first drive. Pilots who build their own planes get a fellow pilot to perform the first test flight. A friend will be cautious but not-overly protective, like an owner will be. You can do your own check, but alter your frame of reference to get the same effect. Use all your senses, be systematic about the checkout (acceleration, cornering, braking, handling, monitoring gauges, etc.), and stop and look at things again. You want to spot a problem where an adjustment fixes it, not a replacement.

Of course, enjoy yourself and smile, too.

Performance

Floorboarding the pedal, or "lead-footing" it, pushes capacity estimations into a twilight zone. As Ah meters improve, they'll be able to keep track of energy consumption in this mode. Until then, lead-footing is something you do only when range is not an issue.

The nice thing about limited range is that you quickly learn how far away certain places are. This is not a statement about one's capacity to make it someplace or not. If I know beforehand that I'm going to "full-range" the vehicle, I'm *very* conservative with the way I accelerate and use energy at every turn of the road. This does *not* mean that I go slow. That's dangerous and, if you're as sensitive as I am about the perceptions people have about EVs right now, it's counter-productive.

Avoid Battery Sulfation

Get in the habit of plugging your car in as soon as you return. I like to charge at night, when utility energy is less expensive *and* I don't contribute to the daily peak (utility) load. However, if my EV has been driven long or hard, I plug in, even if it's only for a while. In winter, I may continue the charge, too. The more depleted the pack is, the more susceptible it is to sulfation and freezing.

Monitoring the Battery

Having gauges and using them are two different things. At first, everyone who has an EV is frightened of getting stuck out, and the gauges are watched obsessively. But what are you looking at?

Instrumentation is a teacher. The ammeter is teaching you how to control the rate of power consumption with your foot, and how much energy it takes to do certain things. Experiment! Going up hills too slowly can use more power than doing it at a medium rate, usually near the high end of a gear.

The voltmeter is teaching you that it really "lugs" the battery when high rates of energy are routed to the motor. Watch the voltmeter dip as you increase the pedal action. The voltmeter will also give you an instantaneous DOD (depth of discharge) reading of the battery pack. Steady the battery current to 75A and note the voltmeter reading. This will verify the Ah meter reading, too.

Once you have mastered the voltmeter and ammeter, you've graduated. Forget them and enjoy driving your EV. Think of them as "training wheels" that you may disregard. Or keep them around. As this point, they're good for troubleshooting, for making it clear that you own an electric, and for describing what's going on to the interested passenger.

Shifting Gears

The biggest mistake to make when shifting gears in an EV's transmission is doing it too soon. A series motor can wind up to 5000 rpm, no sweat. This is not *over*-revving it. So, figure that your shift points are 5-10 mph higher on the speedometer for every gear. The important thing is to start out in the next higher gear with motor rpm not dropping lower than 2,200-2,500 rpm. An EV motor is not harmed by "lugging it" but it does use more power than necessary for the job.

Getting Stuck Out

My best indicator of range is the trip odometer. I find it very reliable. I reset it to zero when I take off. This works without error for a full charge and conservative driving. I "guestimate" (a blend of estimating and guessing) if I'm uncertain of the EV's SOC or the range.

It works. I have never been stuck out. I have come *very* close. Still, I've never had to tow an EV home. Yet!

D. Maintain Battery

A regular checkup of an EV is essential for maintaining performance and range, and a long service life for the battery pack. This checkup is focused entirely on the battery pack. At most, you'll only need to add water to the batteries. This checkup occurs every 6-8 weeks. No big deal to you, perhaps, but very big deal to the EV, though.

You may perform these checks instinctively, or you may need to set up a schedule. Either way, it's unavoidable. Vow to do maintenance.

Is It a Chore?

Maintaining a battery pack at this stage of its development (mid-1990s) is an adventure. Here, you'll don safety goggles, grab a bottle of battery fuel (distilled water), open the inspection hatch (hood or box lid), and expose the power source for the "rotational electromagnetic drive" system. You'll dodge electrons, fuel the batteries with lifegiving water, and polish the brass (interconnects). You may also apply the TCH (temperature-compensating hydrometer) to verify a state of readiness.

It's okay. A little fantasy doesn't hurt when it comes to chores. I've found it to help me keep a maintenance schedule.

This section is concerned with things which will keep your EV strong and your batteries alive as long as possible. Separately, I've included a check list of "do's and don'ts" in the company of batteries. That's the part that keeps *you* strong and alive as long as possible.

Staying Alive

Got your attention, right? Good! I originally entitled this section, Safety First. When I thought about it, I figured that phrase might get me a yawn.

Wrong effect!

Safety around packs is a matter of staying alive and avoiding injury. You would not go blindly sticking your fingers or face just anywhere in the presence of a screaming engine. Or play with matches close to a can of gasoline. Apply the same respect for a battery pack. There are bushels of energy quietly residing inside each one of those heavy plastic boxes. Mistakes here are not habit-forming.

Prepare for Maintenance

As with any adventure, prepare for EV maintenance as you would a campout or a small vacation.

Gather Materials

Gather together the tools and other materials you'll need for maintenance. Distilled water bottles. Battery water dispenser (Fig. 8-22). Gloves. Goggles. Eye wash and baking soda (Fig 8-23). Customized wrenches. Record log. Wire brush. Multimeter (Fig. 8-24).

Keep most of these in a box, crate, sack, or cabinet for the next check.

Fig. 8-22: A battery water dispenser

Fig. 8-23: Have an eye wash kit and baking soda handy.

Fig. 8-24: Learn how to operate a multimeter.

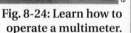

Fig. 8-25: Insulate tools against electrical shorts.

Wear Safety Goggles

Wear safety goggles *every time* you work on or near the battery pack in an EV. The plastic glasses which completely "cup" your eyes—side, top, and bottom as well as front—offer the best protection. Normal prescription glasses that won't shatter are okay.

What are they for? If you should ever short one or more batteries, however temporarily, you'll notice that there are now little hollows in the posts or connectors. That's where current melted the lead or copper to slag and "blew" it out of there. Didn't notice it, huh? Flying molten metal.

Safety glasses also protect against sprayed or splashed electrolyte. Know where the eyewash kit and box of baking soda are *before* working on the battery pack.

Tools

Never use metal tools around batteries without insulating them. Metal is a conductor. If it makes a connection across any two posts in the pack (one battery or several), a "short" will result. Shorting out a battery is the gravest danger anyone can face in working on a pack (Techtalk T100). It is the stuff of nightmares.

Build a small set of tools that you will use exclusively with the battery pack. This includes at least one open-closed end (combo) wrench, probably a one-half inch (1/2") size. A crescent wrench or another fixed wrench (of the right size) may sometimes help with an interconnect's bolt.

The tools must be "prepped" for use. Except for the working part, insulate the metal so that only a bit, maybe an inch (1") or so, remains exposed. Do a good job. Even if these tools are jammed between two posts, the insulation must hold up to avoid a short.

There are three ways to insulate a metal tool: tape wrap, heat-shrink tubing, and rubberizing.

Tape wrap means wrapping friction tape around the tool (Fig. 8-25). Avoid electrical tape. It's pretty, but it becomes sticky goo in hot weather. Wrap the tape to make several layers.

Heat-shrink tubing of the appropriate size can be fitted over the tool. A heat gun (or hair dryer) will shrink this special tubing, reducing its size to conform nicely to the tool's shape.

Rubberizing is done using a commercial product in which you dip the tool (some goo in a can), pull it out, and let it set. The goo hardens into a rubbery covering that insulates the metal.

Remove Jewelry

When working on the battery pack, it's a good idea to remove a ring, necklace, or watch. If they've got metal parts, they're conductors, and you don't want them near batteries. It's a painful jig you'll be dancing, trying to get them off after they've been turned red-hot in a few milliseconds.

No Smoking

"No smoking or open flame" is the rule when working around batteries. Post this message at the charging station. After heavy charge *or* discharge, hydrogen or oxygen

disassociated from the water in the electrolyte may be present. It will dissipate quickly, but a trapped pocket could ignite, and flame sucked into a battery will usually detonate the battery, loudly, violently, perhaps destructively. A strong smell of sulphur? Hydrogen and oxygen will be close by.

Prop the battery box lid open for a few minutes to vent any gas remaining in the area before you begin work.

Avoid Electrical Shock

Electrical shock is possible in an EV, particularly if voltages above 36 Volts are present. Heck, 1-1/2 Volts can kill you under the right conditions! One-third of an amp of current flowing in your body will kill you. Don't leave wiring exposed. If you must get into the innards of your EV, disconnect the ground lead of the batteries. Use a voltmeter, not your hand or finger, to see if voltages exist. Don't forget to open the circuit breaker.

Keep Records

Performing maintenance (hydrometer checks and battery watering, below) without writing down the readings is time wasted. Records are the only way you can tune in quickly to the needs of your battery pack. You don't set the maintenance schedule. Records do. Your job is to interpret the data on the sheet and set a schedule that honors the information.

I dislike many kinds of recordkeeping. However, a little paperwork relative to the battery pack goes a long way (Techtalk T101). Think of it as R&D (research and development). From it stems the clues about the minimum and maximum time until the *next* check.

Perform Visual Check

Do yourself a favor at the start of maintenance, and throughout the process. It's called a "visual check." Open a lid, then stop and look around. Look at everything, one thing at a time, lingering for a moment. Until you close the lid, keep your eyes open for what they can tell you.

A good visual check is the best preventive maintenance there is. It's amazing what you'll see. Maybe a crack in some insulation. A wire is pulling away from its connector. There's a thin layer of dust. A trickle of fluid vents from under one cap. There's a look of corrosion to that battery post. There's a sign of sprayed acid around this other cap. You may take an immediate action or simply jot down a note in the records. Once this works for you, you'll respect what it reveals.

Clean Batteries

Clean the batteries before adding water. This is the only way to ensure that dust, dirt, and debris won't fall into the cells, contaminating them, when the vent caps are removed. With the vent caps on, sprinkle the case tops lightly with baking soda to help neutralize any electrolyte that has sprayed out of the caps. Note the places that it sizzles a lot.

If your pack can be hosed off, add water to the baking soda. Apply a soft, half-inch wide brush, loosening dust and debris, and removing corrosion. Wirebrush any corroded terminals.

Accumulated dust and spilled acid provide a pathway for electrons, and they'll "leak" away into the night, accelerating the self-discharge of a battery or the whole pack that sits idle. Increase the frequency of checks if a dust layer is present.

Position the car for best drainage from the battery box. Use a water hose, no nozzle and small flow, for the final rinse.

If there's no drainage with your pack, a mist of water that is toweled or sponged off will do.

Add Water

Batteries require periodic water addition. During normal operation of the battery, water is dissociated, a process whereby electrical energy separates the water into its two component parts—oxygen and hydrogen. Since these are free gases, they vent from the battery and are lost. (In sealed batteries, the gases are recombined and recovered.) Self-discharge and hot weather will increase evaporation losses of the water in the electrolyte. Low water levels alter the chemistry of the battery and expose the battery plates to air. Neither condition is good. The remedy is to to add water.

How much is dependent on many things. A quick check once in a while will help establish this schedule. It's a little hard to figure the height of the solution in the battery as we peer down the fill-hole (after removing the vent cap, of course) but the aim here is to keep the stuff *above* the lead plates but *below* the "full" line. Once you've worked with a battery for a while, you'll acquire a knack for this. If you can't peer down the hole, use a metered water dispenser (Fig. 8-26).

Fig. 8-26: This dispenser will meter the water into the cell.

Fig. 8-27: Mike Brown demonstrates good hydrometer procedure.

Photo: ElectroAutomotive

Did you know that adding water to batteries is a flagrant violation of the most basic safety rule in a chemistry lab? The rule says: "Never add water to acid." It's true! However, batteries are an exception to this rule. The electrolyte's solution is weak. As well, the water hits the acid down inside the vent holes. Still, wear safety glasses.

It's necessary to have battery gasses—hydrogen and oxygen—vented from the battery cell, but battery acid slopping out of the cells is undesirable. So, we use vent caps. These have an inner chamber which contains both gasses and solution. Theoretically, the gasses should pass through a tiny hole in the top of the cap, dissipating into the environment. Any electrolyte solution (liquid) that makes it that far should run back into the cell.

Use Distilled Water

The battery will only be as good as the water that's added to it. If you take it from the tap, you're adding minerals and other particulates that will contaminate the cells. Use distilled water. Filtered water, drinking water, or rain water aren't as good.

An individual battery will be damaged if the electrolyte level in any one of its cells falls below the top of its plates. If you discover this condition on the road, it is better to add whatever water you can find than to proceed with this condition.

Do Not Add Acid

You should never need to add acid to your battery. The sulfuric acid in solution with the water is very dilute and does not dissociate itself or need replenishment during normal use. If acid has been sprayed out, treat the cause (heavy charge or discharge currents) and not the symptom.

The restoration of the "specific gravity" of the electrolyte in the cells of a battery is a difficult and dangerous job.

Hydrometer Readings

A hydrometer is a simple device which measures the specific gravity of the cells in the batteries. Since acid is driven out of the plates during the charging process, the acid-to-water ratio of the electrolyte is highest following a full charge. When the battery is nearly depleted, it will read its lowest specific gravity. Thus, by comparing the reading taken from a hydrometer with a reference, the approximate SOC of the battery can be measured.

Maintenance Records and Schedules

The only effective way to insure the batteries will not run out of water, or that the batteries are getting a proper charge, is to set up a schedule of maintenance. The frequency of this schedule is determined by the information you glean from the records you keep. Once the schedule is established, your biggest challenge will be to faithfully follow it.

The frequency of the maintenance schedule will become clear after the first or second time you perform maintenance. A hydrometer check of the entire pack *and* "metered" water replacement will write the script. What will you learn? How much water the batteries dissociate per mile, week, or charge/discharge cycle. How long it takes to build up a certain amount of dust on the batteries.

Establish a record sheet. It should have a space for the date, mileage (if you have an odometer), number of charge/discharge cycles—as much or as little as you wish. Number your batteries, on a drawing or on the top of the battery itself. Identify the cells. Don't write on the vent caps (they may move around). Instead, the number one (1) cell is the one closest to the positive terminal of the battery. There are three cells for a 6V battery and six for a 12V battery. The record sheet should have space to write the specific gravity (i.e., 1.125) for every cell in the pack. Run off copies of the blank form for easy use in subsequent maintenance checks. Tailor it to what you will really fill in and use. Keep it simple, or you may gradually stop using it.

What kicks in the maintenance check? Establish a schedule that works for *you*. This may depend on the number of charge/discharge cycles, a specific number of miles of use, or a period of time (i.e., 2 months). Greater use of the EV and hot weather should increase the frequency of the maintenance check.

Once a workable schedule is designed, you can resort to checking the pilot cell with the hydrometer.

The hydrometer is a squeeze-bulb-and-tube affair which is used to suck some of the battery acid from a cell into the tube, where it gives buoyancy to a small float (Fig. 8-27). How much buoyancy is the measure of the specific gravity. A scale on the float translates the degree of flotation into a precise reading. This process is repeated for every cell in the battery, and the readings are written down. Repeat this procedure for the remainder of the batteries in the pack.

With only a slight variance, each of the batteries should read approximately the same ,throughout the pack. If not, there are four possible reasons why it doesn't: low water, new water, temperature, or low SOC (Techtalk T102). Determine which one it is and take the necessary action.

Hydrometer readings are the only inexpensive and accurate way to find the state-of-charge of your batteries and to ensure they are equalized. This information is vital if you want to maximize battery life. Keep records!

Find the Pilot Cell

Long-time EV users have learned how to avoid checking every battery to see the state of water use. Instead, they check one cell of one battery, and know immediately if the pack needs water or has a low SOC. How do they do it? They find the "pilot" cell.

When the battery pack is topped off (watered and equalized), the pilot cell is that cell that reads lower than any other. It applies to both SOC and water level. The *next* time you perform maintenance, test the pilot cell first. When this cell "tests" charged, all the rest must be! And if its water is okay, so are the rest.

Pilot cell monitoring is not a bad technique but, of course, it is just a sample and limited to the information that sampling one cell can give you. This does not replace a full pack checkup. Still, it is intended to give you a spot check in hot weather or after heavy EV use. The pilot cell is established over a period of time. Subsequent pack maintenance may establish another cell as the pilot cell.

Maintain a High SOC

Initiate an equalizing charge to the battery pack after water has been added to it. The bubbling will help mix the newly-added water uniformly with the electrolyte.

Investigate alternate means of performing the equalizing charge. There are three alternatives to the equalizing charge of a series-wired battery pack. Parallel charging (Techtalk T103) is possible with smaller EVs. Applied charging (Techtalk T104) requires owner

---

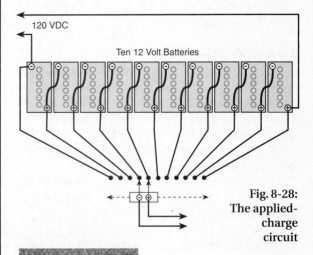

Fig. 8-28: The applied-charge circuit

Fig. 8-29: The dual-pole, multi-position switch for applied-charging

Techtalk
T104 Applied Charging

In its simplest form, applied charging involves opening the lid of the battery box, connecting a charger's leads across the posts of a needy battery, and waiting until it's charged. This is inconvenient, hazardous, and tedious work. A safer and more convenient method is to bring leads out from each battery in the pack to a terminal strip. Voltmeter checks are easy, and a boost charge can be applied without opening up the battery pack.

How many wires are brought out? At first glance, it might appear that a pack containing ten batteries would require twenty wires, two for each battery's positive and negative posts. Think again! Each interconnect in the series-wired pack joins the positive post of one battery with the negative post of the next battery. One wire from this interconnect, then, will serve to read either as the negative pole of one battery *or* as the positive pole of the other. So, only a few wires are really needed to serve the ten batteries. Careful! Keep them in order (Fig. 8-28).

Now, imagine you have the leads of a 12V battery charger in your hands, positive and negative. Do you see how you can hook them up to charge *any* battery? Good. How would you charge the battery next to it? Easy, you'd slide b*oth* leads simultaneously up or down the strip choosing *only* adjacent terminals. Shifting both leads by the same amount avoids polarity reversal and selecting adjacent terminals avoids trying to charge more than one battery (and a higher voltage) at a time. This isn't a hazard. If you miss, it just won't work.

The next step in the evolution of this technique adds a two-pole, multi-position, rotary switch (Fig. 8-29) and a DPDT (center off) toggle switch. The number of positions on the rotary switch must exceed the number of batteries in the pack by one (or more).

While the wiring seems very

Techtalk
T103 Parallel Charging

The series-discharge, parallel-charge method of specific battery charging is demonstrated in the wiring scheme of the NoPed, built by Ely Schless (review Chapter 4). Using wires of equal length, both the positive and negative leads of each of the twelve, 12V batteries are brought out from the battery box and terminated in two 12-pin receptacles.

For vehicle operation, twin plugs are inserted in the pack's receptacles, effectively wiring the batteries in the pack in *series* and routing 144V to the controller. To recharge the pack, both of these plugs are removed from the battery receptacles, isolating the batteries from each other. Two plugs from the charger are inserted into the battery pack's receptacles. These pins connect all positive leads from the batteries to the charger positive lead, and all negative battery leads to the charger's negative lead. A 12V, 30A (30-Amp) Todd charger, then, effectively supplies almost 3 Amps of charge rate to each of the pack's twelve batteries.

As well, a multimeter is able to read the voltage of any battery by applying the test leads to the appropriate pins in the receptacles.

Wiring note: Do not wire all of the positive battery leads into one receptacle and all of the negative battery in the other. Instead, wire each battery to adjacent pins in a receptacle. The pins in these receptacles are numbered. Establish a protocol, i.e., negatives go to odd-numbered pins and positives to even-numbered pins. Stay alert!

complicated, it isn't. Once wired and checked out, this circuit eliminates the possibility *and* consequences of mistakes, and increases the functionality, too.

How does it work? With the toggle switch flipped to the MTR (meter) side, the rotary switch lets you look at the voltage of any (and all) batteries in the pack, in sequence, in a few seconds' time. It wasn't until I saw how each battery was taking the "hill" (under load, climbing a grade) that I *really* got a glimpse of what was happening inside the pack. In this mode, the batteries cannot hide their SOC, particularly as they near depletion. When a battery is resistant to current (low on water), it shows up as a *higher* voltage drop. When it has a low SOC, it shows up as *lower* voltage drop. You will spot the best and worst batteries in the pack through these readings. Where the batteries are numbered and correspond with labels around the faceplate of the rotary switch, you'll have a list of what needs an applied charge.

If the wires you've brought out from the battery interconnects are large enough (18 gauge or larger), a 12V charger connected to the same two wipers of the rotary switch

(maintain polarity!) will supply charge current to the battery selected by the rotary switch position (Fig. 8-30). Select a contact (amp) rating of the rotary switch that will handle the highest charge current you'll to use. Since the battery should be in the "finish charge" region of the charge cycle, this rate should be not more than C/20 or C/30.

How does it work? Select the correct battery with the rotary switch. Flip the toggle to CHG (charge). Turn on (or plug in) the charger. Charge current should now flow. Monitor current until a full SOC is reached.

Are you charging more than one battery this way? Turn the toggle switch back to the center off position. Rotate the switch to select the next battery. Return the toggle to CHG. This minimizes contact arcing in the rotary switch

A voltmeter can be used to monitor the batteries during charge. However, don't confuse the charge voltage with battery voltage. Once off the charge, the battery voltage will drop over a period of time to its unloaded value.

A timer that automatically shuts down the applied charge will save you from having to constantly check things. It will avoid the possibility of overcharging, too. Use one.

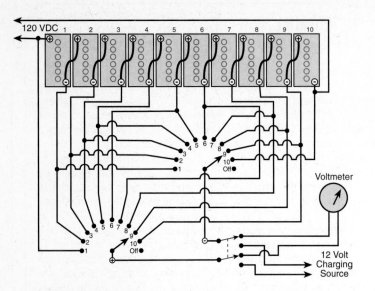

Fig. 8-30: The applied-charge method of maintaining equal SOC

*T*echtalk

*T*105 High-SOC Bypass Charging

Can the process of equalizing the SOC of all batteries in the pack be fully automated? Yes! Alan Cocconi, of AC Propulsion, Inc., has developed (what I refer to as) the "high-SOC-bypass," His system consists of a series of small electronic "modules" glued to the top of each battery in the pack, with wires running to the battery's posts (Fig. 8-32). Each module continuously monitors the battery's voltage and temperature. Circuitry in the module has pre-set (adjustable) voltage threshholds, high and low.

How does it work? As the battery pack finishes the bulk phase and begins the finishing phase of the charge cycle, the modules go into action. Any module that detects the approach of a full SOC for the battery it monitors will begin to "shunt" (route) current through itself. When a full SOC is reached, the module will shunt an amount of current *equal* to the charge current itself. Effectively, then, this battery no longer receives any charge current. As each battery reaches a full SOC, it is "bypassed." When the last battery in the pack has reached a full SOC, the charger shuts down.

The high-SOC bypass is a delicate operation. The circuit of each module uses a MOSFET (or other power device) to supply enough resistance to keep the battery from discharging itself while shunting current. A bypass is the not the same thing as a short. Substituting a relay for the module will short out the battery, wires will glow cherry-red, insulation will burn, etc.

A 4-wire telephone cable exits each of Cocconi's modules, communicating data to a microprocessor and various dash instruments. This system could also relay control instructions back to the modules themselves.

participation. High-SOC bypass (Techtalk T105) is a fully automatic way of maintaining a high state-of-charge without initializing a bulk equalization charge.

Add Anti-Corrosion

When the batteries have been scrubbed and rinsed clean, don't forget to apply a new, thin coat of anti-corrosion gel to the posts and interconnects, as needed. Several products are available commercially, or use Vaseline around the connectors. Wipe off any excess.

Wash Acid from Clothes

Battery acid will eat your clothes. Like the weevil, it likes cotton. It won't do it at first contact, but within 12-18 hours, the cloth disintegrates. Even if only a few drops of the stuff gets on your clothes, you'll have holes. Be careful where you brush your sleeve, or what you wipe your hands on, or where those drops falling from the hydrometer are landing. Wear old clothes around batteries or shove everything into some water in the sink. Baking soda can be used, but enough water will simply dilute the acid.

Fig. 8-31: Ely Schless builds a battery pack for a Cocconi car which uses a high-SOC bypass method of charging.

Fig. 8-32: High-SOC bypass modules installed in a pack

The electrolyte in a lead-acid battery is a very dilute solution of sulfuric acid (H_2SO_4) and water. This is an irritant to skin and eyes. Wear safety goggles and wash your hands after maintenance.

Tow Bar

Many EV owners add a towbar to their EV. It's there to help the EV owner transport the vehicle to shows, conferences, Earth Day events, etc. These are perfect places for people to see, touch, sit in, ride or drive an EV.

Adding the tow bar attachment hardware can be challenging, particularly in late-model vehicles. Rather than cut holes through the "plastic" nose of the vehicle (Fig. 8-33), I installed this hardware behind this covering. Since towing the vehicle is a rare event, I pull the nose (Fig. 8-34), bolt the U-shaped hardware to the frame, and attach the towbar (Fig. 8-35). I prefer towing the EV without the nose to driving the vehicle with towbar hardware protruding out of the front of the vehicle.

Fig. 8-33: The tow bar attachments hide behind the nosecone of the EVX.

Fig. 8-34: Removing the nosecone exposes a massive bumper plate.

Fig. 8-35: Hardware is bolted to the bumper plate. The towbar arms snap right into their own hardware. The nosecone goes inside the vehicle under tow.

Drawing: C. Michael

Chapter 9
Getting Back on Track

" ... and the other 50% of the problem with transportation today is the automobile itself."

Transportation accounts for 70% of America's oil consumption. Automobiles gobble 41% of this amount. More than 60% of every square mile in any city in the USA is devoted to the automobile. Imagine the difficulties we face in "cleaning up our act" in these areas. It's easy to monitor and control the emissions of power plants supplying electricity for EVs. Not so the 150,000,000 tailpipes of cars with internal combustion engines.

Fig. 9-1: Helpful hands position SolTrain on the tracks for its maiden run.

Photo: SunTools

Replacing every gas car on the road with an electric one is *not* the answer. Pursuing alternatives to the car—and diversifying the way people and goods move—will yield better, smarter, more economical, and more acceptable transportation solutions. Oil depletion, pollution, traffic congestion, and social degradation provide the incentive.

This is not a job for the auto manufacturers. They continue to discourage *any* competition. Their R&D efforts rarely focus on reducing vehicle weight or power train losses or improving the aerodynamics of enclosures—key ingredients to integrated transportation systems.

If there are personal vehicles zipping about on roads in our future, they can only be elegant designs that are quiet-running and pollution-free. There is a sense of urgency. The planet is feeling the first effects of the greenhouse phenomenon, an event predicted decades ago. Bottom line: we've got to get off the fossil-fuel fix if we're going to reverse the tide.

Fortunately, there are good alternatives. Buses. Trolleys. Station cars. Neighborhood EVs. All may be powered by electricity.

Trucks and Buses

Trucks today look somewhat different than ones even a decade ago. For example, the addition of a fiberglass, aerodynamic shell above the tractor cab increases fuel efficiency by 5-15%. Newer designs take this process further (Application A63).

A number of manufacturers have evolved electric-powered, zero-emission shuttles, trolleys, and buses (Application A64). Electric buses are proving their mettle along diesel-powered buses—in good performance, high reliability, and low maintenance. After several years of testing an electric bus in its fleet, Santa Barbara (California) has replaced its fleet of city buses with ones using electric propulsion (Application A65).

The Station Car

Several years ago, BART (Bay Area Rapid Transit) commissioned a survey of the vehicles in the Park & Ride lots along their rail corridors. Growing ridership has led to full lots. BART reasoned that it could offer (rent/lease) its rail-using customers a small electric vehicle, or "station car." By offering parking privileges for people using a station car, the usefulness (capacity) of BART's park-&-ride lots would be increased. Funds allocated for pollution-abatement of cold-start and hot-soak of vehicle engines could help finance the project. Engines exhibit poor efficiency when operated "cold" and a parked vehicle will emit petroleum vapors while the engine cools down.

Would people using the station cars be able to charge at home? Through a cooperative effort between BART, the DMV, and various city and state agencies, vehicles using the park&rides were identified and crosschecked against types of residences (i.e., homes and apartments). The study indicated that most of the present ridership did *not* have access to recharging receptacles because their cars were parked on the street or in a parking garage.

Out of this effort came the formation of the National Station Car Consortium (NSCC). Its stated goal is "to test the technical and

A 63 — Application
Aerodynamics and Trucks

A complete re-styling of the tractor (truck) body helps overall fuel economy. For example, a Colani prototype sculpts both plastic and glass. Airflow beneath the canopy is directed back alongside the trailer. Airflow at the canopy level is directed upward, over the top of the trailer. A high cockpit and the 3-blade windshield (rotary) wipers ensure good driver visibility.

Photo: Bruce Severance

Fig. 9-2: A Colani design for an efficient truck

A 64 — Application
Electric Buses and Trolleys

Specialty Vehicle Manufacturing's Model #5122 is a 22-foot electric-powered shuttle with a low floor, air-ride suspension, power steering and brakes. It's windows remove for open air configurations.

A more classic (turn of the century) look is found in the Model #3122 Trolley. This low-maintenance EV seats 21 passengers and reaches speeds of 35mph over its 50-90 mile range. The 216V battery pack recharges overnight. A fiberglass body on the welded steel frame is powered by a 32 HP brushless DC motor. Wheelchair access is provided through a special door & lift at the rear of the vehicle.

Fig. 9-3: An electric shuttle is quiet and zero-emission.

Photos: Specialty Vehicle Manufacturing

Fig. 9-4: Electric trolleys are popular in towns that cater to the tourist trade.

A 65 — Application
Electric Buses in Santa Barbara

Electric Shuttle Vehicle (ESV) is one of a small fleet of high-quality transit buses operated by the Santa Barbara Metropolitan Transit District (SBMTD). It utilizes integral chassis and body construction and is powered through its front steer/drive axle by a DC electric motor and an onboard lead-acid battery. Its low floor, large door opening, and simple wheelchair ramp make boarding of all passengers fast and easy.

The vehicle has proven popular in the heavily congested downtown area, particularly with the owners of sidewalk cafes. Regenerative braking enables the bus to recover electrical energy during stops, even down to zero mph. The separately-excited, shunt-wound DC motor has a 30 kW continuous rating. A transfer case designed to fit the traction motor yields an overall reduction ratio of 13.3 to 1

After a year of continuous operation (8-10 hour days and up to 62 miles of range), SBMTD decided to replace its fleet of city buses with ones using electric propulsion.

economic viability of the concept of EVs for access and egress to and from transit stations at both ends of work, shopping, and other trips." The NSCC wants to evaluate station car ownership and leasing options, develop prototypical specifications for the vehicles and charging stations, determine the nature of the electric load on the utility, and get one or more manufacturers to offer station cars. Preliminary analysis reveals that about $100 of electricity could fuel such a vehicle for a full year!

The "station car" is an exciting concept. Combined with site-specific designs that address gridlock (Techtalk T106), it would introduce EV technology in a relatively controlled way. Where the station cars are built with exchangeable battery modules, they could

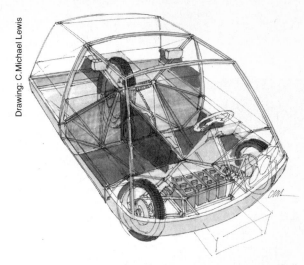

Drawing: C.Michael Lewis

Fig. 9-5: The neighborhood EV (NEV) is designed to meet short-range needs and give access to lightrail or other rail outlets.

Techtalk
T106 Solutions to Gridlock

It is the final presentation by design students in a semester-long project at Art Center College of Design in Pasadena, California. The challenge? Instructor **John Loftus:** "Each 3-person team must select a specific place in L.A. and demonstrate, with photos, graphics, and 3D models, how their solution to gridlock fits." One team's answer?

Rob McCourt: "Los Angeles was raised on the automobile. That creates special problems in designing rapid transit. But — the freeways aren't working."

Sakti Makki: "People need a good option to driving their automobile. Most of the people in the L.A. area have not tried the existing transit system. If they listen to their friends, they hear that it is a hassle to use. How much does it cost? What are the transfer points? It's not user friendly."

Jackson Chan: "Commuters want to make good use of the time they spend traveling to and from work. Rapid transit vehicles could easily include onboard information booths, telephones and fax, banking and shopping capabilities, and a place to put down a laptop computer."

The sponsor? The American Iron and Steel Industry. Project director **George Szostkowski:** "Steel is 100 percent recyclable. We need to develop new systems *and* make our current mode of transportation fully compatible with the environment."

Solutions? The McCourt-Makki-Chan team designed a system that would service the San Bernadino-to-LA route, a 60-mile commuting run to the east of the downtown hub, proposing a twin, dual-purpose monorail on raised tracks above existing freeway medians. On top, a commuter train travels between 5 major points along the route, reaching 50 mph speeds. Underneath, smaller trains are suspended, servicing smaller stations between the big ones. These help a commuter get to a bigger station and transfer to a faster train.

McCourt: "Proximity to the freeways will highlight the system as an option to existing networks. The first day you're stuck in a traffic jam and watch 3 of 4 of these cars whiz by over a 30-minute period, it's going to hit you that you could be at work by now. I think that's the payoff. It will get people to try the system."

Chan: "A single credit card is the key to simplifying ticket payment. (A simulated transit card designed by the team is passed out to the crowd.) You get it when you register your car at the DMV. The card works for everything— ticket purchases, fax machines, telephones, vending machines, even information booths. Retractable work surfaces and business sections in the train add the right touch. As well, each station incorporates park-and-ride areas, taxi and shuttle service, and ground-level mini-malls. Funds derived from the leasing of space for such businesses as convenience stores or child care facilities will help offset the costs of running and maintaining the system." *(This self-funding feature is important in light of a recent IRT Energy Newsbrief finding that only 1 cent out of every 9 cents of Federal gasoline taxes is earmarked for rapid transit.)*

Makki: "The electric-powered trains would run along concrete-reinforced steel tracks and platforms. Platforms would be constructed largely of recyclable plastics. Solar panels mounted on the station rooftops would produce the energy needed to run each station and to help propel the trains."

What about high-speed maglev rail technology? **McCourt:** "This transportation system is designed to be faster than the *current* system, which is rapidly bogging down. It doesn't have to go fast, or use sophisticated technology. Our system design offers reliability and many ways for the commuter to use the commute time constructively. We think that's the winning ticket."

Art Center College of Design is an independent, non-profit, four-year college specializing in professional education in art and design. Projects like this one introduce the students to actual clients and real world design challenges, and expose industry to a refreshing preview of what tomorrow's designers are thinking today.

Application
A 66 SolTrain Saga
Phil & Richard Jergenson

SolTrain was built to demonstrate that at an electric-powered rail vehicle could be refueled from the sun. It was built in less than a month. The one-cylinder engine of the 1940's vintage Speeder was replaced with a GE propulsion system (motor and controller). Six 6V lead-acid, deep-cycle batteries made up the 36V, 220 Ah capacity pack. Six solar panels were added to the custom-built aluminum cab.

Photo: Ted Coombs

Fig. 9-6: SolTrain moves silently between Willits and Ukiah, California.

Fig. 9-7: Richard Jergenson guides SolTrain out of the shop for its first run.

Photo: SunTools

SolTrain made its first scheduled open track run from Fort Bragg to Willits, California during SEER (Solar Energy Exposition & Rally) in August of 1992. The Fort Bragg-Willits railway is used daily by the "Skunk Train." It is relatively short (40 miles) but there's a 1,500 foot difference in altitude between the two sites. Since the solar panels are constantly recharging the batteries (anywhere under the sun!), they assisted the propulsive effort when SolTrain climbed the grade out of Fort Bragg. The propulsive package includes regenerative braking. This ensured a safe descent of SolTrain past Summit by routing this generated power to the batteries. In this way, SolTrain arrived with juice to spare.

Virtually unchanged, SolTrain made the Willits-Ukiah run during SEER 94.

A scratchbuilt SolTrain is in the design stages. It will be lighter, house a more powerful battery pack, and its propulsive effort will be upgraded to include human power. Look for it.

The SolTrain project was originally inspired by Chris Swan in his books on trains and photovoltaic. Additional project help came from Scott Bowers and Wayne Robertson.

Application
A 67 UltraLight Rail

My own vision of a commuter rail system retrofitted to a small town, city, or municipality is Ultra Light Rail (ULR). This design of the ULR system was based on five observations:

•*Expediency*. The system must require only a month to install and test before coming online. It must also be easy to remove or modify.

•*Construction.* The underlying bed of the ULR rail system must work with standard street and road beds.

•*Utility.* The system must serve the community. Where possible, the system should include existing streets dedicated to ULR use, touch (run along or cross) the locations of major services and businesses, and include P&Rs (park and rides) and shipment centers located on key highways at the periphery of the system.

•*Independent Operation*. Each vehicle in the ULR "train" is lightweight and independently powered. Control of each car is transferred to the lead vehicle as it is connected.

•*Zero-emission.* In operation, the system must be reliable, economical, crashworthy, safe, quiet, and produce zero emissions.

Why the ULR Design?

Massive construction is required in most rail projects, often involving years of work, even if a railroad right-of-way exists. This requires major capital investment and a system that cannot adapt to the future because it is literally set-in-concrete.

Where a conventional train requires a heavy locomotive to ensure good traction to pull a big load, a ULR "train" consists of separately-powered railcars. This spreads the tractive effort throughout the length of the train, and traction increases in direct proportion to the weight of occupants (or goods). Also, a ULR train is never longer than that needed to accommodate the ridership.

•Road surfaces that mix trains with automobiles and trucking are accidents waiting to happen. Even with suitable fencing, guardrails, and signals, the drivers of automobiles will turn into the path of quiet-moving trains. Hence, the dedicated streets.

•Towns and cities grow. How much and which way are variables. Even good transportation systems are outdated in 5-15 years. A ULR system can be extended or modified—track modules can be taken up and re-routed, and any anchor holes plugged up in the street.

•Commuter use of the ULR system would have priority during rush hours. At other times, including nighttime, goods move about the city, and to and from peripheral points. NEVs are available to rent for in-town use.

•In many instances, the modular track may be electrified, with sections turned on as a ULR car moves over them. An alternate means of powering the system is exchangeable battery packs. Depleted packs are charged overnight with low-cost utility rates.

ULR lets a community prohibit gas cars from sections of the town.

be rented for daytime use at either end of the transit stations, sidestepping the inconvenience of downtown parking. More importantly, it lets people *experience* electric vehicles. I predict that anyone who leases one of these vehicles will begin using it for other short trips—shopping, transporting children to and from school or other activities, etc.

Neighborhood Electric Vehicle

The station car is similar in concept to that of the neighborhood electric vehicle, or NEV. In the NEV, we have an electric vehicle that is designed for street-only use (no freeway or highway travel). While the NEV's top speed might be limited to 35-45 mph, it would exhibit strong performance due to its lightweight (yet crashworthy) construction.

Rail

Electric propulsion lends itself well to railway use. Even if the track is not electrified, rail offers highly efficient transport of both people and services. Steel wheels on steel track means very low rolling resistance (friction), which explains the ability of trains to haul very heavy loads. Trains rate as high as *ten* times the efficiency of pneumatic tires on vehicles in moving tonnage.

Another reason for the efficiency of transporting goods and people by rail may be found in the difference in grades. Tracks are installed with a maximum 3% grade. Highways and roads may have grades of 12% or more. The difference is a 200-400% savings in fuel to do the same job!

Rail is of benefit to everyone. People and goods that travel by rail relieve the increasing congestion experienced on highways and roads. One rail trolley displaces 25 cars and one small train displaces 125 cars. Since tracks are usually separate from roads, trains are less susceptible to gridlock.

Will existing rail vehicles convert easily to electric propulsion? Larger cars are too heavy. However, a conversion of a standard rail speeder was accomplished in less than three weeks. The result? SolTrain! SolTrain has made two official inter-city runs on standard tracks near Willits, California (Application A66)

LightRail

A growing improvement in railway usage is in commuter applications with the LightRail design. LightRail is similar to standard rail in size, but is designed for the tighter turns (smaller radii of turn) required for city streets. LightRail may be electrified via overhead wires.

It is a challenge to implement LightRail. Imagine the impact on already congested roads while construction is underway! In any case, mixing trains and road traffic on the same streets is not a good idea. Even if additional congestion can be avoided (immediately or long term), the risk of collision is high.

Ultra Light Rail

Wherever LightRail projects will impact small cities in the transitional stages, an Ultra Light Rail system is specifically designed to fast-track this process. The Ultra Light Rail concept originated out of a "blue sky" project which attempted a fresh approach to the design commuter rail in small towns. Rather than fit traditional rail to a city environment, Ultra Light Rail makes use of existing road surfaces because the track is modular and the railcars are lightweight and individually powered (Application A67). Many communities have the necessary talent, materials, and facilities to implement some form of the Ultra Light Rail concept.

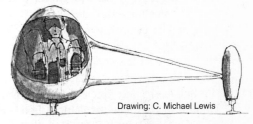

Drawing: C. Michael Lewis

Final Thoughts

Most innovative advances in electric propulsion technology in the past 75 years have come about through the actions of individuals and small groups of people. Even twenty years ago, "electric vehicle" was not the household phrase it is now. I have enjoyed watching it change. The consciousness of humankind *is* increasing, even if we do not always embrace changes that will correct the more adverse influences we bring about. Still, I believe Marilyn McCabe's remark, "When we embrace natural technologies, perhaps we will see ourselves as more natural."

For better than two decades, people have expressed to me their pessimism that drivers will embrace electric drive. I disagree. Sometimes I do not know what's enough until I've had too much. People are ready for some big changes. I believe that EVs offer us a way to do what we want without so many nasty side-effects. Hopefully, I've empowered *some* readers to bring about changes in their own transportation habits and hardware.

Now—it's up to you. Good luck. Have fun!

Sources & References

This section starts with books and papers from my library. These are the ones I *use*. Since portions of my library are several decades old, some of this stuff my be out of print. If that's the case, your best bet may be to check libraries first. If you know of a work that you think should be included here (or something needs updating), contact: Michael Hackleman, POB 327, Willits, CA 95490.Internet email: michael.hackleman@homepower. org

Books & Papers

1996 Buyer's Guide to Electric Vehicles, 36 pages, Spirit Publications, POB 645, Pahoa, HI 96778 Ph/Fax: (808) 965-6074

The Aerodynamics of Human-Powered Land Vehicles, Scientific American, December 1983, 9 pages. Details of aerodynamics employed in many HPV (human-powered vehicle) designs.

Aero Estimation Self-Taught, Del Coates, Road & Track, Aug 1982, p40-44. Good visual aids to estimating drag.

Alternative Cars in the 21st Century: A New Personal Transportation Paradigm, Robert Q. Riley, 1994, 396 pages, Society of Automotive Engineers, Inc. ISBN 1-56091-519-6. Excellent.

Beyond the Automobile: Reshaping the Transportation Environment, Tabor R. Stone, 1971, 148 pages, Prentice-Hall, Inc., Englewood Cliffs, New Jersey

Build Your Own Electric Vehicle, Bob Brant, 1994, 310 pages,Tab Books, ISBN 0-8306-4231-5.

Convert It, Michael P. Brown. Covers several conversions in detail, all hard won experience.ElectroAutomotive, PO Box 1113, Felton, CA 95018 (408) 429-1989

Development of an Organic Rankine-Cycle Power Module for a Small Community SolarThermal Power Experiment, T. Kiceniuk, 1985, 124 pages, JPL (Jet Propulsion Laboratory) publication 85-3,, c/o California Institute of Technology, Pasadena, CA. Project produced an 18.7% efficient solar-thermal turbine. Remarkable!

Direct Use of the Sun's Energy, Farrington Daniels, 1964, 272 pages, Ballantine. One of the finest works on harnessing the sun's energy without combustion or resource depletion. One of my mentors.

Doran Electric Vehicle, Rick Doran, 96-pages. Plans and illustrations for building a Doran Electric. Good detail on roll-resistant physics. (702) 359-7356

The Electric Car Book, Barbara Whitener, 1981, 96 pages, Love Street Books, PO 58163, Louisville, KY 40258. A delightful book on EVs from the 1970's.

EV Engineering Guidebook: Electric Vehicle Conversions for the 1980s, Paul Shipps, 1981, 62 pages. Supplements, 21 pages. VW Beetle & Rabbit, Chevette, Honda Civic, Datsun B210, Pinto, and Fiat 128.

The Forbidden Fuel: Power Alcohol in the 20th Century, Hall Bernton, William Kovarik, and Scott Sklar, 1982, 274 pages, Boyd Griffin, ISBN 0-941726-00-2.

Fuel from Water: Energy Indepedence with Hydrogen, Michael A. Peavey, 1988, 244 pages, Merit Products, Inc. No-nonsense theory, chemistry, and hands-on projects. ISBN: 0-945516-04-5

Future Drive: Electric Vehicles and Sustainable Transportation, Daniel Sperling, 1995, 176 pages, Island Press. Excellent work. ISBN1-55963-328-X

The Golden Thread, Ken Butti and John Perlin, 1980, 291 pages, Van Nostrand Reinhold Co., ISBN 0-442-24005-8

Land Use Strategies for More Livable Places, Steve Weissman & Judy Corbett, 1992, 89 pages, Local Government Commission, 909 12th Street, #205, Sacramento, CA 95814.

Launches & Yachts: The 1902 Elco Catalog, reprinted by William C. Swanson. Shows good EV design in boats 100 years ago. Swanson Marine Enterprises, 829 Copley Ave, Waldorf, MD 20602 (301) 843-1367.

Opportunities for Electric Vehicles, (31 pages) Howard O. Wright, 425 32nd Ave. Eugene, OR 97405. "Bouncing ball" physics for lightweight vehicle builders.

OTEC Heat Transfer Experiments at Keauhole Point, Hawaii, 1982-83, John Larsen-Basse and Thomas H. Daniel, 1983, 5 pages, National Energy Laboratory, Keahole Point, Kailua-Kona, Hawaii 96740.

Renewable are Ready: People Creating Renerable Energy Solutions, Nancy Cole and P.J. Skerrett, 1995, 240 pages, Chelsea Green, ISBN 0-930031-73-3.

Rethinking the Role of the Automobile, Michael Renner, 1988, 70 pages. Worldwatch Institute, 1776 Massachusetts Ave, N.W. Washington, DC, 20036.

Seeking Light at the End of the Tunnel, Bennis Simanaitis, Road & Track, Aug. 1982, p32-35. Aerodynamic material.

Stirling Cycle Engines, Andy Ross, 1977, 121 pages. Solar Engines, 2937 W. Indian School, Phoenix, AZ 85017.

Supercars: The Coming Light-Vehicle Revolution, Amory Lovins, 1993, 32 pages, Rocky Mountain Institute, 1739 Snowmass Creek Road, Snowmass, CO 81654-9199. Phone: (303) 927-3851.

Technical Book Buyer's Guide, Gilbert T. Lopez, Tom Cloney, 1994, 354 pages, United Techbook Company ISBN 1-880072-01-7

Tesla's Engine: A New Dimension for Power, Jeffrey Hayes, 1994, 224 pages, Tesla Engine Builder's Association, ISBN 1-884917-33-X.

Why Wait for Detroit? Drive an Electric Car Today, Steve McCrea and R. Minner, 1992, 161 pages, South Florida Electric Auto Association. ISBN 1-897857-92-02.

Wind Car: Land Sailer for the Highway. Article, *Popular Science*, Nov. 1976, 4 pages. Jim Amick's windmobile.

Vortex (plan car), Dolphin Vehicles, 1270G Lawrence Station Road, Sunnyvale, CA 94089. (408) 734-2052

Manufacturers

AC Propulsion, Inc. (Alan Cocconi) 462 Borrego Ct, Unit B, San Dimas, CA 91773 (909) 592-5399; Fax (909) 394-4598

Burkhardt Turbines (John Takes/Peter Talbert), 1258 N. Main St, #B2B, Fort Bragg, CA 95437 (707) 961-0459, Fax (707) 964-4181

EcoElectric Corporation (Mary Ann Chapman), PO Box 85247, Tucson, AZ 85754 (520) 770-9444, Fax (520) 770-9908 email: ecoelec@primenet.com

Cruising Equipment, 6315 Seaview Ave NW, Seattle, WA 98107 (206) 782-8100, Fax (206)782-4336

Electric Vehicles of America, Inc. (Bob Batson),48 Acton St., Box 59, Maynard, MA 01754 (508) 897-9393, Fax (508) 897-6740 email: evamerica@aol.com

ElectroAutomotive (Michael Brown, Shari Prange.), PO Box 1113, Felton CA 95018 (408) 429-1989

Eyeball Engineering, 5420 Via Ricardo, Riverside, CA 92509-2415 (909) 682-4535, Fax (909) 682-6275

Green Motorworks, Inc. William Meurer, 5228 Vineland Ave, North Hollywood, CA 91601 (818) 766-3800, Fax 766-3969gmwbill@aol.com

Horlacher AG, Faserverstarkte Kunststoffe, Postfach 50, Guterstrasse.9, CH-4313 Mohlin, 061 851 21 18

KTA Services (Ken Koch) 944 West 21st St. Upland, CA 91784 (909) 949-7914, Fax (909) 949-7916

MendoMotive, 110 W. Elm St., Fort Bragg, CA 95437

Schless Engineering, Inc (Ely Schless), 3165 E. Main St., Ashland, OR 91601 (541) 488-8226 email: eschless@aol.com

Solar Car Corporation, 1300 Lake Washington Road, Melbourne, FL 32935 (407) 254-2997, Fax (407) 254-4773

Solectria Corporation, 68 Industrial Way, Wilmington, MA 01887 (508) 658-2231, Fax (508) 658-3224

Specialty Vehicle Manufacturing Co., 9250 Washburn Rd. Downey, CA 90241 (310) 904-3434

Suntera, POB 341, Honokaa, HI 96727, (808) 775-7771, Fax: (808) 775-9363

ZAP Power Systems, (707) 824-4150, Fax (707) 824-4159

Zond Energy Systems (Mary McCann)POB 1910, Tehachapi, CA 93561 (805) 822-6835, Fax (805) 822-7880

People

Amick, Jim, 1464 Cedar Bend Dr., Ann Arbor, MI 48105-2305

Beasley, Clark, Electrathon America, 1251 W. Sepulveda Blvd. #142, Torrance, CA 90502 (310) 539-9223

Bennett, Tom, 13 Crestfield Ct, Lake Oswego, OR 97035

Bittman, Michael, UROWN Power Company, PO Box 796, Pt. Townsend, WA 98368 (206) 385-7341

Carpenter, Tom , Mobile Services International., HCR5201, Keaau, HI 96749 Phone/fax: (808) 982-5768

Dolphin Vehicles, PO Box 110215, Campbell, CA 95011-0215 spombo@aol.com

Doran, Rick, 39.95 624 S. Archer St., Anaheim, CA 92804 (702) 359 7356

Frey, Jon, 14000 Tomki, Redwood Valley, CA 95470 (707) 485-7525 email: frey@pacific.net

Gay, Jerry, 8037 24th Ave NW, Seattle, WA 98117 (206) 789-9989, Fax (206) 789-9974

Hackleman, Brett email: bhackleman@gnn.com

Heckeroth, Stephen, 30151 Navarro Ridge Rd., Albion, CA 95410 Phone/fax: (707)937-0338 email: solarcon@mcn.org

Jergenson, Richard and Phil (BoxBeam) Suntools, POB 1029, Willits, CA 95490 (707) 459-2624

Johnson, Stevi, PO Box 384134, Walkoloa, HI 96738 (808) 883-8923

Kearney, Alan email: alan_kearney@mcoe.k/2.ca.us

King, Richard, U.S. Dept of Energy, Washington, DC 20585

Leeds, Michael, 738 Chestnut St. Santa Cruz, CA 95060 (408) 423-6060

Lewis, C. Michael, 18 South St., Portland, ME 04101 (207) 773-3006

Lucas, Gail, Desert Research Institute, PO Box 19040, Las Vegas, NV 89132 email: gail@snsc.dri.edu

MacCready, Paul,Aerovironment, Inc, 222 E. Huntington Dr., Monrovia, CA 91016. (818) 357-9983, Fax: (818) 359-9628

MacDougall, Ruth, SMUD (Sacramento Municipal Utility District), POB 15830, Mail 601, Sacramento, CA 95852-1830

Murphy, Mark, Blue Sky Design, 1925 W. 25th Place, Eugene, OR 97405

Orawiec, Richard, Good Ship Esther Foundation email: chinax@macatawa.org

Parks, Dann email dann@vvol.com

Pio, Greg, 335 Pennsylvania Ave, Santa Cruz 95062 (408) 426-0842

Pliskin, Daniel pliskin@nexsys.net

Pyle, Walt H-ION Solar Co., 6095 Monterey Ave., Richmond, CA 94805

Rahders, Richard (408) 426-3783, Fax (408)426-2526 email: fmjg65c@prodigy.com

Raymond, Eric, Solar Flight Research, 32655 Flight Way, Winchester, CA 92596 (909) 926-2484, Fax (909) 926-1518

Root, Ben c/o Home Power, POB 520, Ashland, OR 97520. Internet email: ben.root@homepower.org

Seal, Michael, Vehicle Research Institute,Western Washington U., Bellingham, WA 98225-9045

Stevenson Projects, PO Box "K", Del Mar, CA 92014 (619) 481-3111

Stevenson, Joe, 1032 Arthur Ct, Petaluma, CA 94954 email: omni@mcn.org

Sundin, Olof, c/0 Seattle Electric Vehicle Association, 306 S. Michigan, Seattle, WA 98108 (206) 762-4404, Fax (206) 634-0263 email: evsnw@seamac.wa.com

Swanson, William, 829 Copley Ave, Waldorf, MD 20602

Swets, Ben email: am880@lafn.org

Van de Ven, Mary, 747 Amana St, Suite 1720, Honolulu, HI 96814 (808) 941-6133

Worden, Donna (541) 488-8499

Periodicals

Home Power Magazine. Six issues,$22.50/yr. POB 520, Ashland, OR 97520. How to use sustainable energy sources for home, farm, and business. Hands-on. Editorial/Advertising (916) 475-3179; Subs & BkIssues (800) 707-6585 (Visa/MC), email: hp@homepower.org Web: http://www.homepower.com/hp

Transitions: Securing Hawai'i's Future through Energy Diversity, Hawai'i's Energy Extension Service, 99 Aupuni St. #214, Hilo, HI 96720. (808) 933-4558

Recumbent Cyclist News, P.O.Box 58755, Renton, WA 98058. Six issues, $28/yr, 32 pages.

Auto-Free Bay Area Coalition, POB 10141, Berkeley, CA 94709. Six issues, $25/yr, 16 pages.

City Cyclist and Auto-Free Press, Transportation Alternatives, 92 St. Marks Place, New York, NY 10009

HPV News, International Human Powered Vehicle Association, POB 51255, Indianapolis, IN 46251

Human Power: Technical Journal of the IHPVA, 21 Winthrop Street, Winchester, MA 01890-2851 (317) 876-9478

EV Components

Electro Automotive Catalog, 26 pages. (408) 429-1989

KTA Services EV Catalog. (909) 949-7914

Northern Hydraulics Inc., P.O. Box 1499, Burnsville, MN, 55337-0499. Phone (612) 894-8310. Hardware.

Burden's Surplus Center, 1015 W. "O" St., Lincoln, NB 68501.(402) 474-4055, Fax: (402) 474-5198. Hardware.

C & H Sales Co., P.O. Box 5356, Pasadena, CA 91107-0356. Phone (800) 325-9465. Hardware.

Comet Industries, Div. of HOFFCO, Inc., 358 NW "F" St., Richmond, IN 47374. Subassemblies

Prototyping Skills

Box Beam SourceBook, Phil and Richard Jergenson, 1994, 108 pages, Suntools, POB 1029, Willits, CA 95490. Dozens of projects prove utility of BoxBeam in building prototypes. Important if you don't have a welder and shop.

There Are No Secrets, Harry Higley, 83 pages, 1981. Harry Higley & Sons, P.O. Box 532, Glenwood, Ill, 60425. Extremely helpful info on fiberglassing and woodworking.

The Internet for Dummies, John R. Levine and Carol Baroudi, 1993, 355 pages, IDG Books Worldwide, Inc. ISBN 1-56884-024-1. There's a world of information out there. Plug into the people who do it.

Designing with Core, Hal Loken and Martin Hollmann, 1988, 125 pages. Aircraft Designs, Inc., 25380 Boots Rd, Monterey, CA 93940. Phone (408)649-6212. Also **Modern Aircraft Design: Vol 1**and **Vol 2**, Martin Hollman, 1987.

Stephenson Projects. Stephenson Projects, P.O. Box K, Del Mar, CA 92014.Phone (800-786-3121. Plans for building land and water craft (i.e., SolExplorer).

Groups, Clubs, & Events

Cal Poly Pomona Solar Team, College of Engineering, 3801 W. Temple Ave, Pomona, CA 91768 (909) 869-2600

CSLA Solar Team, California State University Los Angeles, School of Engineering & Technology, 5151 State Univ Dr., LA 90032 email: rlandis@oasis.calstatela.edu

California Air Resources Board, 9528 Telstar Ave, El Monte, CA 91731. "On the Move" newsletter at (800) 242-4450. These are the folks behind the 2% ZEV mandate. Good idea!

The Electric Boat Regatta. Andrew Muntz, Snohomish County PUD, P.O. Box 1107, Everett, Washington, 98206. (206) 258-8444. Annual event; write for rulebook.

The International Human Powered Vehicle Association. IHPVA, P.O. Box 51255, Indianapolis, IN 46251 USA.

Electric Auto Association (EAA),1249 Lane Street, Belmont, CA 94002. EAA is national non-profit, multi-chapter group.

Electric Vehicle Association of Southern California (EVA OSC), 12531 Breezy Way, Orange, CA 92669.

LTA (lighter-than-air) *Society*. Contact: William F. Kerka, 1800 Triplett Blvd, Akron, OH 44306. Airship info, library, and history

Midwest Renewable Energy Association, PO Box 249, Amherst, WI 54406 (715)824-5399, Fax (715)824-5399. Annual fair, Workshops in building and RE systems.

Northeast Sustainable Energy Association (NESEA), 50 Miles St., Greenfield, MA 01301 (413) 774-6051, Fax (413) 774-6053. Annual Tour de Sol, annual Energy/Transportation events.

Renewable Energy Development Institute (REDI) and *Solar Energy Expo and Rally* (SEER). REDI/SEER, 733 S. Main st #234, Willits, CA 95490. (707) 459-1256.

Index

T

U-V

W-Z